Abstracts of

Cecil County Maryland

Land Records

1734-1753

June D. Brown

HERITAGE BOOKS
2008

HERITAGE BOOKS
AN IMPRINT OF HERITAGE BOOKS, INC.

Books, CDs, and more—Worldwide

For our listing of thousands of titles see our website at
www.HeritageBooks.com

Published 2008 by
HERITAGE BOOKS, INC.
Publishing Division
100 Railroad Ave. #104
Westminster, Maryland 21157

Copyright © 1999 June D. Brown

Other books by the author:
Abstracts of Bucks County, Pennsylvania, Land Records, 1711-1749
Abstracts of Cecil County, Maryland Land Records, 1673-1751

All rights reserved. No part of this book may be reproduced or transmitted in any form or by any means, electronic or mechanical, including photocopying, recording or by any information storage and retrieval system without written permission from the author, except for the inclusion of brief quotations in a review.

International Standard Book Number: 978-1-58549-038-7

Table of Contents

Introduction .... v.

Deed Book Number 5 (1734—1739) 1

Deed Book Number 6 (1739—1745) 81

Deed Book Number 7 (1745—1753) 145

Index 227

INTRODUCTION

Cecil County was created from Baltimore County and Kent County in 1674. Initially the boundaries extended from the mouth of the Susquehanna and down the eastern side of the Bay to Swan Point and from there to Hell Point, and so up the Chester River, to its head. Subsequently, the southern boundary was changed by an Act of 19 April 1706 which stated that after 1 May 1706 Kent County would be bounded by a line drawn from the south point of Eastern Neck, up the Bay to Sassafras River, up the said river to the south end of Long Horse Bridge, thence by a line drawn by east and by south to the exterior bounds of the Province.

It is believed that the first settlement of the English, within the present limits of Cecil County, was upon Palmer's Island (later called Watson's Island), near the mouth of the Susquehanna. William Clayborne established a trading post on the island as early as 1627.[1]

For a listing of land patents of Cecil County, 1649-1774 see *Inhabitants of Cecil County, Maryland 1649-1774*, compiled by Henry C. Peden, Jr. Also contained in this volume are a list of naturalizations, petitioners, tax lists and sundry other lists.

Other publications of possible interest include the following: *Cecil County Bible Records*, by Gary L. Burns (Cecil County Genealogical Society, 1990); *Land Patents of Cecil County* (Family Line Publications, 1986); *Early Anglican Church Records of Cecil County*, by Henry C. Peden, Jr. (Family Line Publications, 1990); *Births, Deaths and Marriages of the Nottingham Quakers, 1680-1889*, by Alice L. Beard (Family Line Publications, 1989); *Revolutionary Patriots of Cecil County, 1775-1783*, by Henry C. Peden, Jr. (1991); *The 1693 Census of the Swedes of the Delaware*, by Peter S. Craig (SAG Publications, 1993); and *History of Cecil County, Maryland*, by George Johnston (originally published 1881, reprinted by Clearfield Company, Inc., 1998).

F. Edward Wright
Westminster, Maryland
1998

---

[1] See George Johnston, *History of Cecil County, Maryland* (1881), pp. 7-8.

Deed Book No. 5
1734 - 1739

P. 1   Deed.   Richard Hoe of Cecil Co. and Jane his wife, for £65.3s.1p and 4,040½ lbs of tobacco, to Edward Drewry of Philadelphia, PA, gent., 200 acres of land, part of a tract called Knowlwood on Elk River. Said land was bequeathed by Francis Smith in his Last Will and Testament to his sister Sarah Pierce, the wife of Henry Pearce, and to the heirs of her body. Made 12 Mar 1733. Wit: Jno. Ward, G. Wilson, John Ward, Jr. Ackn: 12 Mar 1733/4. JPs: Thos. Colvill, Jno. Copson. Edward Drewry paid to Jas. Paul Heath 8 shillings alienation fine for the land. Rec: 13 Mar 1733. Wm. Knight, Clerk.

P. 3   Deed.   James Bull of Cecil Co., yeoman, to William Rumsey of the same county, gent., 50 acres of land, for 200 lbs of tobacco and to end a dispute concerning a neck of land called Wadmore's Neck which is part of the lands of William Dare, deceased, which William Rumsey purchased from the said William Dare's surviving executor William Dare, Jr., now also deceased. Wadmore's Neck interferes with the southeast end of 300 acres of land, part of a tract called Colletton conveyed by William Dare, Sr. to Thomas Bull, deceased father of the said James Bull. The 50 acres of land being conveyed here is the part of the said 300 acres which is southeast of and bounded by the 70 acres lately sold by James Bull to John Mainley and also by a tract of land called Bailey. Made 14 Mar 1733. Wit: John Jackson, Benja. Pearce, Jr. Ackn: 15 Mar 1733/4. JPs: B. Pearce, Tho. Colvill. Jas. Paul Heath received 1 shilling from Mr. William Rumsey for the alienation fine on 21 Mar 1733/4. Rec: 24 Mar 1733. Wm. Knight, Clerk.

P. 5   Deed of Gift.   Walter Scott, Sr. of Cecil Co., cordwainer, for the love, good will and natural affection he has for two of his sons, Walter Scott, Jr. and Charles Scott, both cordwainers of the same county, gives to them 180 acres of land, part of a tract called Ashmore which Walter Scott, Sr. lately purchased from Peter Attwood of St. Marys Co., gent., to be equally divided between them. Walter Scott, Jr. is to have the western moiety of the land and Charles Scott to have the eastern moiety. Made 25 Mar 1734. Wit: Evert Everdson, Jr. and JPs B. Pearce, Wm. Rumsey. Ackn: same day by Walter Scott, Sr. and his wife Grace. On 27 Mar 1734 Jas. Paul Heath received 7s.2½p from Charles Scott, the alienation fine. Rec: 28 Mar 1734. Wm. Knight, Clerk.

1

P. 6   Deed.   James Paul Heath of Cecil Co., gent., for £70, to Evert Evertson, Jr. of the same county, planter, 140 acres of land by lands called Skelton, Sarah's Joynture, Heath's Second and Fourth Parcels and by the land of _____ Booker which was resurveyed for James Heath, deceased, and called Heath's Middle Parcel. Said land is part of Heath's Second and Fourth Parcels originally granted by patent dated 10 Dec 1714 to James Heath, father of said James Paul Heath, and is also part of the Middle Parcel granted to James Heath by patent dated 6 Jun 1726. Made 27 Mar 1734. Wit: Theos. Grew [Greer?], Alphonso Cosden. Ackn: 27 Sep 1734. JPs: B. Pearce, Wm. Rumsey. On 30 Mar 1734 Evert Evertson paid 5s.8p alienation fine. Rec: 1 Apr 1734. Wm. Knight, Clerk.

P. 9   Deed.   William Boulding of Cecil Co., for £12, to Thomas Beetle of the same county, a tract of 50 acres of land on Elk River. [Boulding is also spelled Boalding, Bouldin.] Made 4 Feb 1733. Wit: Martin Alexander, Paul Alexander, Thomas Bouldin. Ackn: 17 Apr 1734. JPs: R'd. Thompson, Thos. Johnson, Jr. On 26 Apr 1734 James Paul Heath received 2 shillings alienation money from Thomas Beetle. Rec: 26 Apr 1734. Wm. Knight, Clerk.

P. 10   Deed.   William Boulding, Sr. of Cecil Co., for £100, to William Boulding, Jr. of the same county, a plantation and 130 acres of land already in William Boulding, Jr.'s possession on Back Creek by the lands of Gavin Hutcheson, Thomas Beetle and Thomas Boulding. Made 5 Feb 1733. Wit: Thomas Bouldin, Paul Alexander, Martin Alexander. Ackn: 17 Apr 1734. JPs: R'd. Thompson, Thos. Johnson, Jr. The alienation fine of 5s.10p paid by William Boulding, Jr. to Jas. Paul Heath on 26 Apr 1734. Rec: 26 Apr 1734. Wm. Knight, Clerk.

P. 12   Lease.   James Paul Heath of Cecil Co., gent., for rents and services and because the said Heath is moving, to John Jackson of the same county, chirurgeon, his wife Jane and his son William, 300 acres of land, part of 2 tracts, one called Heath's Range, the other called Worsell Manor, by lands called Colletton, Knowledge and Coxes Forest. Lease is for the term of 21 years. Rent of £6 due every 7 June. At the expiration of the lease, Jackson agrees to leave on the premises one dwelling house with two brick chimneys, one barn 25x20 feet framed, a convenient corn house, a Negro quarter and a fenced orchard of 250 apple trees. Made 7 Jun 1733. Wit: Thomas Crouch, Rich'd. McClure. Ackn: 30 Apr 1734. JPs: Thos. Johnson, Jr., A. Barry. Rec: 29 Apr 1734. Wm. Knight, Clerk.

P. 15   Deed.   Abram Penington, late of Cecil Co., now of Virginia, yeoman, for £50, to John Graham of Cecil Co., a tract of 160 acres on the east side of Susquehanna River which William Teage, son and heir of Edward Teage, late of Cecil Co., by deed dated 14 May 1714 conveyed to the said Abraham Penington. Made & Ackn: 29 Jan 1733. Wit: John Blacke, Eliz. Jackson, Jane Manyer. JPs: Edw'd. Jackson, A. Barry. Rec: 2 May 1734. Wm. Knight, Clerk.

P. 17   Deed.   James Foster of Cecil Co., planter, for 5 shillings and 150 acres of land out of a tract called Jones' Green Spring, to Thomas Price of the same county, 60 acres of land, part of a tract called Sparnal's Delight on the south side of Goldsmith's Branch. Also another tract of 24 acres adjoining the first called Beatle's Folley by a tract called Collet. James was bequeathed the land by the Last Will and Testament of his deceased father Richard Foster of the said county. Made & Ackn: 3 Jun 1734. Wit. & JPs: Thos. Colvill, Thos. Johnson, Jr. Alienation received by Jas. Paul Heath from Thomas Price for the lands called Sperman's Delight and Beetle's Folly on the same day. Rec: 11 Jun 1734. Wm. Knight, Clerk.

P. 19   Deed.   William Foster of Cecil Co., planter, for £5 and 250 acres of land out of a tract called Jones' Green Spring, to Thomas Price, Sr. of the same county, 50 acres of land called Wales formerly taken up, resurveyed and patented by William Morgan. Said 50 acres is on the east side of Elk River by land formerly laid out for Thomas Maddocks and Charles Vincent called Two Necks, by land formerly belonging to the orphans of Robert Morgan and by land formerly belonging to Thomas Skelton. Made & Ackn: 3 Jun 1734 by William Foster and his wife Mary. Wit. & JPs: Thos. Colvill, Thos. Johnson, Jr. Alienation of 2 shillings received by Jas. Paul Heath from Thomas Price on the same day.

P. 20   Deed.   John Milward of Kent Co., planter, for 2,000 lbs of tobacco and 100 bushels of winter wheat, to Thomas Ward of Cecil Co., planter, a tract of 218 acres of land called Wheeler's Point on the north side of Sassafras River. Made & Ackn: 11 Jun 1734. Wit: William Mason, Robert Veazey. JPs: Edward Jackson, Thos. Johnson, Jr. Rec: same day. Wm. Knight, Clerk.

P. 23   Deed.   George Martin of Cecil Co., husbandman, for £52.10s, to William McDowell of the said county, a tract of 150 acres called Martin's Delight on the east side of Susquehanna River by a tract of land called Poplar Valley. [McDowell also spelled McDowel, McDowall.] Made 11 Jun 1734. Wit: John Graham, Saml. Young. Ackn: same day by George Martin and his wife Dorothy. JPs: Wm. Rumsey, Thos. Johnson, Jr. On the same day Jas. Paul Heath received from William McDuel [sic] 6 shillings for the alienation fine. Rec: same day. Wm. Knight, Clerk.

P. 25   Deed.   William Boulding of Cecil County, for £50, to Alexander Boulding of the same county, a plantation and 150 acres of land already in the possession of said Alexander Boulding by the lands of ____ Booker and Thos. Boulding. Made 5 Feb 1733. Wit: Martin Alexander, Thomas Bouldin, Paul Alexander. Ackn: 17 Apr 1734. JPs: R'd. Thompson, Thos. Johnson, Jr. Rec: 12 Jun 1734. Wm. Knight, Clerk.

P. 26   Deed.   James Dawson and Mary his wife of Talbot Co., planter, for £35, to John Williams of Cecil Co., feltmaker, 500 acres, already in the possession of the said John Williams, called Anchor and Hope by Susquehanna River and by land called Roycraft's Choice laid out for John Bollen. Said land was surveyed for and granted to Daniel Carroll of St. Marys on 25 Mar 1679. Made & Ackn: 27 Apr 1734. Wit. & JPs: Risd'n. Bozman, P. Benson. On 5 Jun 1734 Risdon Bozman and Pervy Benson certified as JPs by Thos. Bullen, Clerk of Talbot County. On 27 May 1734 Jas. Paul Heath received from John Williams 4 shillings alienation fine. Rec: 12 Jun 1734. Wm. Knight, Clerk.

P. 29   Deed.   Thomas Price of Cecil Co., planter, to James Foster of the same place, planter, 150 acres, the westernmost part of a 400-acre tract called Jones' Green Spring by Long Creek and by Henry Ward's land. Said land was formerly laid out and granted to William Harris of Kent Co., gent., father of James Harris of Kent Co., gent., who sold the land to John Jawert, late of Cecil Co., gent., who sold it to Thomas Price by deed dated 30 Dec 1719. Made 10 May 1734. Wit. & JPs: Thos. Colvill, Thos. Johnson, Jr. Ackn: 3 Jun 1734 by Thomas Price and his wife Mary. On 18 Jun 1734 Jas. Paul Heath received from James Foster 6 shillings alienation fine. Rec: 18 Jun 1734. Wm. Knight, Clerk.

P. 31   Deed.   John Largent of Cecil Co., planter, and Eviess his wife, for £100 (half silver money of Maryland, half paper money of Pennsylvania), to George Gallasbie of Lancaster Co., PA, farmer, a tract of 241 acres called Green's Delight on the east side of Susquehanna River by Wm. Boarn's tract of land called Jamaico. [Largent also spelled Sargent.] Made & Ackn: 4 May 1734. Wit: Alex'r. Ewing, Nath'l. Ewing. JPs: Edward Jackson, A. Barry. Alienation fine of 9½ shillings paid 4 Jun 1734 to Jas. Paul Heath. Rec: 20 Jun 1734. Wm. Knight, Clerk.

P. 33   Deed.   William Boulding, Sr. of Cecil Co., for £100, to Thomas Boulding of the same county, the plantation and 250 acres of land on which the said William Boulding now lives on Back Creek by Thomas Beetle's land

and by land now belonging to William Boulding but formerly surveyed for Edward Booker. Made 3 Feb 1733. Wit: Martin Alexander, Paul Alexander, Thomas Beetle. Ackn: 17 Apr 1734. JPs: R'd. Thompson, Thos. Johnson, Jr. Rec: 20 Jun 1734. Wm. Knight, Clerk.

P. 35   Valuation of Estate.   At the request of Thomas Etherington, guardian of Henry Hendrickson, an orphan of Cecil Co., and being sworn by JP Capt. William Rumsey, James Husband and Robert Marcer entered and viewed the property of the said Henry Hendrickson on 25 May 1734 and found an old frame dwelling house 40x20 feet with 2 rooms on the floor and 2 brick chimneys; a 15-foot shed, clapboard, rough. The rafters of the house are rotten and several of them broken and falling in, the covering rotten also; the false plates and the "cills" at each door are decayed; the brick work needs pointing; the plastering is broken and also some of the underpinning. Also an old log kitchen 20x15 feet with a brick chimney; an old log storehouse, same length and breadth, much decayed; a round log shop same length and breadth with a shed along one side 10 feet wide, clapboard covering; a 20-foot corn house 8 feet wide; a 50-foot tobacco house needs new posts and weather boards; a 30-foot tobacco house needs weather boards and gable ends; about 53 apple trees, 40 of which are young and growing in an orchard, the other 13 stand scattered about the plantation and are old and decayed; the fencing is in bad repair and the rails very old. According to the best of their skill and judgement, they estimate the annual value of the plantation to be 700 lbs of tobacco. The woodlands lying next to Thomas Mercer's land useful for timber to raise the yearly rent. Rec: 20 Jun 1734. Wm. Knight, Clerk.

P. 36   Valuation of Estate.   John Ward and Robert Marcer, duly sworn by JP Col. Benja. Pearce, enter the lands of John Kimber, a minor under the guardianship of John Cox, to determine the yearly rent of the property, and after viewing the land certify that the value is 800 lbs of tobacco a year. They found on the land a new log house with a brick chimney measuring 20x19 feet; an old tobacco house with new posts and covers 30x20 feet; a log barn 20 feet square with a plank floor and a shed; a corn house 15 feet long; a kitchen 17 feet long; an old shop 20x15 feet; a log house 20x15 feet; another log house 20x15 feet; and 78 old apple trees. The fencing on the plantation is in good repair and the guardian is not allowed to clear any land but what is within the fencing but may have timber for keeping the place in good repair. Made 23 Mar 1733/4. Rec: 20 Jun 1734. Wm. Knight, Clerk.

P. 36   Lease.   Ephraim Augustine Herman of Cecil Co., gent., for yearly rents and services, to John Hamm, Jr. of the same place, planter, 53 acres of land called Hamm's Necessity, part of Bohemia Manor, on Herring Creek by Charles Dearmott's land. Lease is for the term of the natural lives of the said John Hamm, Jr., his son Thomas Hamm and his daughter Mary Hamm. Rent of 16s.4p and 2 fat ducks due every 10 Dec. [Dearmott is also spelled Dermott.] Made 20 May 1734. Wit: Rich. Whitton, Theophilus Grew. Ackn: 14 Aug 1734. JPs: Edward Jackson, Jno. Copson. Rec: same day. Wm. Knight, Clerk.

P. 38   Deed.   George Martin of Cecil Co., husbandman, for £52.10s, to Hugh Boyde of Philadelphia Co., PA, 150 acres called Martin's Enlargement, part of a tract called Martin's Delight on the east side of Susquehanna River. Made 26 Jul 1734. Wit: Francis Sumorfield, John Graham, Wm. Beezley, Edwd. Jackson, John Jones. Ackn: 14 Aug 1734 by George Martin and his wife Dorothy. JPs: Edward Jackson, A. Barry. Rec: same day. Wm. Knight, Clerk.

P. 40   Deed.   William Boulding of Cecil Co., for £12, to Richard Boulding, 50 acres of land, part of a tract formerly belonging to ____ Rawson. Made 4 Feb 1733. Wit. & JPs: R'd. Thompson, Thos. Johnson, Jr. Ackn: 17 Apr 1734. Rec: 8 Aug 1734. Wm. Knight, Clerk.

P. 42   Deed.   George Martin of Cecil Co., husbandman, for £15, to Emmanuel Grub of Newcastle Co., PA, yeoman, a tract of 150 acres of land called Reponsation by land called Poplar Valley originally surveyed for Nicholas Hyland, by land called Slate Hill surveyed for Thomas Johnson, Jr., and by land called the Barrons. Made 26 Jul 1734. Wit: Edward Jackson, John Jones. Ackn: same day by George Martin and his wife Dorothy. JPs: Edward Jackson, Jno. Copson. Rec: 14 Aug 1734. Wm. Knight, Clerk.

P. 44   Lease.   Ephraim Augustine Herman of Cecil Co., gent., for £2.5s, to Elizabeth Alcock of the same county, widow and executrix of the Last Will and Testament of Humphrey Alcock, late of said county, deceased, 108 acres of land in Bohemia Manor formerly leased to Charles Bowen, the same land previously leased to the said Humphrey Alcock. The lease is for the term of 3 natural lives: that of Henry Makey, John Alcock and Mary Alcock, the son and daughter of Humphrey and Elizabeth Alcock. Rent of £2.5s and one fat capon or 2 dunghill fowls due every 10 Dec.

By deed dated 4 Mar 1722, Ephraim Augustine Herman leased to Humphrey Alcock land in Bohemia Manor called John Crow's Delight and another tenement of land formerly leased by Charles Bowen. The lease was for the term of 3 natural lives, paying £4.10s annually. By deed of release dated 16 Nov 1727, Humphrey Alcock released to Ephraim Augustine Herman the land called Crow's Delight and thus reduced the rent and the cost of adding another life to the lease. One of the lives counted in the said lease was that of James Makey, who is now also deceased. Made 15 Aug 1734. Wit. & JPs: Tho. Colvill, Wm. Rumsey. Ackn: same day by Col. Ephr. Aug. Herman. Rec: 15 Aug 1734. Wm. Knight, Clerk.

P. 47   Deed.   John McManus of Cecil Co., attorney, for £40, to Henry Rippen, mariner, a 250 acre tract of land called Plain Dealing in Kent Co. on the north side of Chester River by land taken up by Thomas Grunvin called Horn Hill. Made 16 Aug 1734. Wit: Jas. Calder, Wm. Knight. Ackn: 16 Aug 1734. JPs: Tho. Colvill, R'd. Thompson. Rec: same day. Wm. Knight, Clerk.

P. 48   Deed.   Thomas Stratton of Cecil Co. (and his wife Hannah), for £65, to Robert Patton of Cecil Co., yeoman, 150 acres of land bounded by the division line of the said Thomas Stratton and the heir of John Macknet, late of the said county. Said land is part of 2 tracts, one called Hispaniola and the other Bulin's Range, which are part of 300 acres which Thomas Stratton bought from Samuel Alexander, late of the said county, by deed dated 20 Mar 1729. Made 28 Aug 1734. Wit: R'd. Thompson, Hance Patten, Margarett Little. Ackn: same day. JPs: Richard Thompson, Tho. Colvill. Rec: 2 Sep 1734. Wm. Knight, Clerk.

P. 50   Commission.   Charles Lord Baltimore appoints as Justices of the Peace for Cecil County: John Hall, Richard Tilghman, Mathew Tilghman Ward, John Rousby, Benjamin Tasker, Philip Lee, John Rider, Michael Howard, George Plater, Edmond Jennings, Thos. Colvill, Edward Jackson, Richard Thompson, John Baldwin, William Rumsey, John Copson, Andrew Barry, Thomas Johnson and John Veazey. Made 17 Oct 1734. Signed by Saml. Ogle. Rec: 12 Nov 1734. Wm. Knight, Clerk.

P. 54   Deed.   Thomas Price of Cecil Co., planter, to William Foster of the same place, planter, 250 acres of a 400 acre tract called Jones' Green Spring on Long Creek by Henry Ward's land. Said land formerly laid out for and granted to William Harris of Kent Co., father of James Harris of Kent Co. who sold the land to John Jawert, late of Cecil Co., gent., who sold the land to Thomas Price by deed dated 30 Dec 1719. Made 10 May 1734. Wit. & JPs: Tho. Colvill, Thos. Johnson, Jr. Ackn: 3 Jun 1734 by Thomas Price and his wife Mary. James Paul Heath received 10 shillings alienation fine from William Foster on 10 Jun 1734. Rec: 13 Jun 1734. Wm. Knight, Clerk.

P. 56   Deed.   Grace Hollingsworth, widow of Thomas Hollingsworth of Christiana Hundred, Newcastle Co., Territories of PA, deceased, and his son

Thomas Hollingsworth of the same place, both executors of his Last Will and Testament, and Abraham Hollingsworth, eldest son and heir of the said deceased Thomas Hollingsworth, for £100, to John Passmore of Kennett Township, PA, yeoman, 2 tracts of land in Cecil Co. on Elk River totaling 300 acres. By a warrant for 500 acres of land dated 10 Sep 1719 granted to the said Abraham Hollingsworth and Stephen Hollingsworth, both of Cecil Co., a tract of land called Partner's Parcell was laid out for them in Cecil County containing 400 acres. The certificate of survey is dated 25 Nov 1719. By deed dated 13 Mar 1721/2 and recorded in Lib. J. D. No. 3, folios 268-269, Abraham and Stephen Hollingsworth conveyed to the said Thomas Hollingsworth the father 250 acres of the land. Since then Abraham and Stephen Hollingsworth obtained a patent for the 400 acres from Richard Tilghman, Esq., Keeper of the Seal, dated 1 May 1724 (including the 250 acres sold to Thomas) and recorded at Annapolis in Lib. No. 5, folio 571. By warrant dated 13 Apr 1720 granted to Thomas Hollingsworth the father, a 50 acre tract called Jacob's Adventure was laid out and surveyed for him in Cecil County on 7 Sep 1720. The patent for the 50 acres is recorded at Annapolis.

In his Last Will and Testament dated 13 Apr 1727, Thomas Hollingsworth appointed his wife Grace and his son Thomas executors. He bequeathed to his son Abraham Hollingsworth the said 2 tracts of land on the condition that Abraham pay to his mother Grace £20, at which time she would convey the said 300 acres to Abraham. Made 30 Oct 1734. Wit: Christopher Wilson, William Passmore, Jacob Hollingsworth. Grace Hollingsworth appoints Abraham Hollingsworth her attorney to acknowledge the deed on 2nd da 9th mo 1734. Wit: William Passmore, Christopher Wilson. Ackn: 4 Nov 1734 by William Passmore and Abraham Hollingsworth. JPs: A. Barry, Thos. Johnson, Jr. Alienation fine of 12 shillings received from Mr. Andrew Barry by Jas. Paul Heath on 4 Nov 1734. Rec: 14 Nov 1734. Wm. Knight, Clerk.

P. 62   Deed.   John Penington of Cecil Co., planter, for £21.6s, to Isaac Bowers of the same county, planter, 71 acres of land called Penyworth which was formerly granted to Henry Pennington and lies on the north side of Sassafras River by land granted to Gartis Morgin and by land formerly surveyed for William Glover. Made 16 Sep 1734. Wit: Wm. Rumsey, Wm. Knight. Ackn: 14 Nov 1734. JPs: Wm. Rumsey, John Veazey. Rec: 15 Nov 1734. Wm. Knight, Clerk.

P. 63   Deed of Gift.   Thomas Mercer, Sr. of Cecil Co., planter, and his wife Elizabeth, for the love, good will and affection they have for their loving son Thomas Mercer, Jr. of the same county, planter, give to the said Thomas

Mercer, Jr. and his wife Jane a parcel of land lying between Harman's Branch and the plantation that used to belong to Henry Hendrickson, deceased, called Mount Hermon. After the death of Thomas, Jr. and his wife Jane, the land should go to Thomas' and Elizabeth's son Robert Mercer. Made 7 Nov 1734. Wit: Benjamin Childs, Rich'd. Bentham. Ackn: 15 Nov 1734. Rec: 16 Nov 1734. Wm. Knight, Clerk.

P. 64   Deed.   John Jones of Cecil Co., farmer, and his wife Mary, for £30, to Samuel Wilds of Newcastle Co. upon Delaware, farmer, 50 acres of land, part of a tract of 200 acres called Dolevan laid out for Thomas Wilds by 2 warrants for 100 acres each dated 28 May and 2 Oct 1713 which were surveyed 4 Jan 1713/4 on the east branch of Elk River. Fifty acres of this land was sold by Thomas Wilds to Isaac Miller who sold it to Griffith Nicholas. Griffith Nicholas, executor for Samuel Wilds, sold it to the said John Jones. Also another tract of land which Samuel Wilds sold to Jones containing 49 acres. Made 11 Nov 1734. Wit: G. Lawson, Joshua Wilds. Ackn: 18 Nov 1734. JPs: A. Barry, Thos. Johnson, Jr. Alienation fine of 3 shillings paid by Samuel Wilds to Jas. Paul Heath on 12 Nov 1734. Rec: 19 Nov 1734. Wm. Knight, Clerk.

P. 67   Deed.   Martin Alexander of Cecil Co., for £4, to James Wallace of the said county, part of a tract called Sligo formerly taken up by Samuel Alexander, late of said county, and sold by said Samuel to the said Martin Alexander. Said land is bounded by John Brevard's land and contains 15½ acres. Made 2 Sep 1734. Wit: Jos. Wood, Jr., Robert Patton. Ackn: same day by Martin Alexander and his wife Susannah. JPs: Wm. Rumsey, R'd. Thompson. Rec: 20 Nov 1734. Wm. Knight, Clerk.

P. 68   Deposition.   Margaret Miner, late widow of Adam Wallace of Cecil Co., deceased, states that about 2 years past, in her husband Adam Wallace's lifetime, his son-in-law Andrew Thompson said to his father-in-law Adam Wallace that he (Andrew) thought that there was but 100 acres of land put in his patent. Adam Wallace answered so there is, but James Wallace's land is put in the same patent with his the said Adam Wallace, which makes 200 acres. The deponent says not. Made 29 Jul 1734. JP: R'd. Thompson. Rec: 20 Nov 1734. Wm. Knight, Clerk.

P. 68   Deed.   Nathaniel Dougherty of Cecil Co., planter, for £24, to Thomas Lindsey of the said county, shoemaker, a 75 acre tract of land called Dougherty's Endeavor located a little below Abraham Penington's plantation on Susquehanna River. Made 1 Oct 1734. Wit: Wm. Teague, Moses

Ruth. Ackn: 2 Oct 1734. JPs: Jno. Copson, Edward Jackson. Rec: 21 Nov 1734. Wm. Knight, Clerk.

P. 71   Deed.   Nathaniel Dougherty of Cecil Co., planter, for £15, to William Teague of the said county, planter, a 50 acre tract of land called Dougherty's Desert on the east side of Susquehanna River on the northeast side of a tract of land sold by William Teague to Abram Penington. Made 1 Oct 1734. Wit: Thomas Lindsey, Moses Ruth. Ackn: 2 Oct 1734. JPs: Jno. Copson, Edward Jackson. Rec: 21 Nov 1734. Wm. Knight, Clerk.

P. 73   Assignment of Lease.   John Campbell assigns to Richard Price all his right and title to a lease [details of lease not given.] Made & Ackn: 9 Dec 1734. Wit: John Baldwin, John Veazey. Rec: 6 Jan 1734. Wm. Knight, Clerk.

P. 73   Release.   Christian Tute of Cecil Co., discharges John McManus of said county, gent., and Richard Dowdall of Kent Co., gent., executor of the Last Will and Testament of Major John Dowdall, late of Cecil Co., gent., deceased, for £23 in full satisfaction for the said Tute's maintenance during his life and of all legacies left him by the said Maj. John Dowdall by his Last Will and Testament. [Tute also spelled Touite.] Made 23 Dec 1734. Wit: Aug. Thompson, Dom Carroll. Rec: 8 Jan 1734. Wm. Knight, Clerk.

P. 74   Assignment of Lease.   Daniel Hukill assigns to Thomas Ebthrop all his right and title to the part of the land which his son Daniel Hukill now lives on. Made 13 Apr 1731. Wit: R'd. Thompson, Mary Wilson.
Daniel Hukill assigns to his grandson Daniel Hukill, son of Richard Hukill, all his right and title to the part of the land where Samuel Hughs now lives. Made 18 Apr 1734. Wit: R'd. Thompson, Mary Wilson. Ackn: both assignments on 19 Apr 1731. JPs: R'd. Thompson, Thos. Colvill. Rec: 15 Jan 1734. Wm. Knight, Clerk. Memo: these assignments were endorsed on a lease from Col. Herman to Daniel Hukill recorded in Lib. J. D. No. 3, folio 258-259. [See June D. Brown, *Abstracts of Cecil County Maryland Land Records 1673-1751*, (Westminster, MD: Family Line Publications, 1998) pg 147, entry P. 420.]

P. 75   Mortgage.   Samuel White of Cecil Co., farmer, for £15, to Henry Baker of the same county, farmer, his (White's) plantation called Connecticut in New Connought Manor and one black and white cow about 9 years old. This writing void if White repays Baker on or by 10 Oct next. Made 8 Jan 1734. Wit: Jethro Browne, Mary Baker. Ackn: 17 Jan 1734. JP: Jno. Copson. Rec: 25 Jan 1734. Wm. Knight, Clerk.

P. 75   Mortgage.   Isaac Bowers of Cecil Co., planter, for £15.10s, to William Rumsey of the same county, gent., a tract of 71 acres called Pennyworth on the north side of Sassafras River originally granted to Henry Pennington by patent dated 13 Aug 1684. Void if Bowers repays Rumsey on or by 25 Mar next. Made 4 Dec 1734. Wit: Charles Brown, Thos. Colvill. Ackn: 5 Dec 1734. JP: Thos. Colvill. Rec: 30 Jan 1734. Wm. Knight, Clerk.

P. 77   Deed.   Augustine Bowyer of Kent Co., and Rebecca his wife (eldest daughter of Thomas Christian and Sarah his wife) and Thomas Baker and Ann his wife (another daughter of Thomas and Sarah Christian), for £10 to each of the two couples, to William Rumsey of Cecil Co., gent., part of a tract of land called Round Stone by Northeast River. Land was originally granted to John Wheeler by patent dated 15 Feb 1659 for 300 acres which descended to Sarah Christian, eldest daughter of the said John Wheeler. [Name also spelled Boyer.] Made 31 Oct 1734. Wit: Thos. Colvill, Rich'd. Thompson, Jno. Yorkson. Ackn: 1 Nov 1734. JPs: Thos. Colvill, Rich'd. Thompson. Alienation fine of 1s.4p rec'd by Jas. Paul Heath from William Rumsey on 29 Nov 1734 for sixty and two-thirds acres of land, part of a tract called Round Stone. Rec: 30 Jan 1734. Wm. Knight, Clerk.

P. 79   Deed.   Mary Sealey, widow and executrix of the Last Will and Testament of Joseph Sealey, late of Cecil Co., deceased, for £35 to pay her deceased husbands debts, to Abraham Alman of the same county, 140 acres of land in Bohemia Manor now in the possession of said Mary leased by Ephraim Aug't. Herman 1 Apr 1727 to Joseph Sealey and recorded in Lib. S. K. No. 5, folios 70-71. Lease is for the term of the three natural lives cited in the lease which are yet in being. [Sealey also spelled Seelye.] Made 7 Sep 1734. Wit: Sabina Rumsey, Wm. Rumsey. Ackn: 28 Sep 1734. JPs: Wm. Rumsey, Rich'd. Thompson. Rec: 12 Mar 1734. Wm. Knight, Clerk.

P. 80   Release.   Francis Land, for £52.2s.6p, releases to Hugh Walker, assignee of Abraham Hollingsworth, [unspecified] tracts of land. Made 4 Nov 1734. Wit: Thomas Tomson, Christian Land. The deed this assignment refers to was recorded 9 May 1732 in Lib. S. R. [J. R.?] No. 5, folios 429-430. Rec: 12 Mar 1734. Wm. Knight, Clerk.

P. 81   Deed.   Mary Kemp, relict, and Gerard McKenney, son and heir of Alexander McKenney, deceased, all of Cecil Co., for £25, to Jonathan Stilley of Newcastle Co. on Delaware, 100 acres of land called Fedard on the west side of Elk River by land called Hopewell. Henry Johnson of Cecil Co. conveyed the tract to Alexander McKenney of the same place by deed dated 17 Dec 1718. [Gerard McKenney is also called Garrat McKenney.] Made &

Ackn: 9 Jan 1734. Wit: Rachell Kelly, Jno. Copson. JPs: Jno. Copson, A. Barry. Rec: 12 Mar 1734. Wm. Knight, Clerk.

P. 82 Deed. William Rumsey of Cecil Co., gent., for £35, to John McFarland, late of Cecil Co. but now of Newcastle Co. upon Delaware, planter, 100 acres of land, part of Rumsey's Ramble, formerly in the tenure of George Cathey, by a tract called Batchelor's Fund and by Samuel Bond's field. By patent dated 30 Oct 1731 recorded in Lib. P. No. 8, folio 105, Edward Rumsey of Cecil Co. was granted a 300 acre tract of land called Rumsey's Ramble in the fork of the Northeast River in Cecil Co. adjoining the tracts called Coxes Park and Batchellor's Fund. Edward Rumsey, by deed dated 3 Aug 1733 conveyed the land to the said William Rumsey, ackn. 4 Aug 1733 before Benjamin Pearce and Richard Thompson and recorded 27 Aug 1733 in Lib. S. K. No. 6, folio 122-123. Made 17 Feb 1734. Wit: Thos. Moxon, Mathew Stasy. Ackn: 12 Mar 1734 by Wm. Rumsey and his wife Sabina. JPs: John Baldwin, John Veazey. Rec: 14 Mar 1734. Wm. Knight, Clerk.

P. 85 Lease. Ann Margarett Vanderheyden of Cecil Co., for yearly rents and services, to John Gullick, Jr. of the same place, planter, 100 acres of land, part of a tract called Three Bohemia Sisters, by Broad Creek between the lands of Hans Patten and said Gullick, by a small branch which is the division between the lands of John Edwards and the said John Gullick and by the old mill path. Lease is for the term of the natural lives of the said John Gullick, Jr., his sister Ann Gullick and his brother Daniel Gullick. Rent of 500 lbs of tobacco in cask and 2 dunghill fowls to be paid on or by 10 Mar yearly. [Ann Margarett is also called Ann Margretta.] Made & Ackn: 10 Mar 1734. Wit: R'd. Thompson, James Bouldin. JPs: R'd. Thompson, John Veazey. Rec: 14 Mar 1734. Wm. Knight, Clerk.

P. 87 Deed. Robert Holy of Cecil Co., planter, and Ann his wife, for £5 and 800 lbs of tobacco, to Thomas Sharp of the same place, 75 acres of land, part of a tract called Confusion by a tract called the Society. Charles Lord Baltimore granted the tract called Confusion to the said Thomas Holy [sic] by patent dated 26 Jul 1723. Made 10 Mar 1735. Wit: John Kanky, Samuel Young. Ackn: 11 Mar 1734/5. JPs: Edw'd. Jackson, Thos. Johnson, Jr. Rec: 14 Mar 1734. Wm. Knight, Clerk.

P. 89 Deed. Robert Holy of Cecil Co., planter, and Ann his wife, for £5 and 800 lbs of tobacco, to Joseph Steel, 70 acres of land, part of a tract called Confusion by the land of Thomas Sharp. Charles Lord Baltimore granted the tract called Confusion to the said Robert Holy by patent dated 26 Jul 1723.

Made 10 Mar 1735. Wit: John Kanky, Samuel Young. Ackn: 11 Mar 1734/5. JPs: Edw'd. Jackson, Thos. Johnson, Jr. Rec: 14 Mar 1734. Wm. Knight, Clerk.

P. 90   Deed.   Robert Pennington, Jr. of Cecil Co., planter, and Rachel his wife, for £4.10s, to Richard Freeman of the said county, planter, lot # 24 in Amelea Ann Town on Sassafras River in Cecil Co. containing ½ acre of land. Made & Ackn: 14 Mar 1734. Wit: Wm. Pearce, Benja. Pearce. Rec: 16 Mar 1734. Wm. Knight, Clerk.

P. 92   Deed.   Dominick Carroll of Cecil Co., gent., for £35, to Hugh Terry of said county, planter, 50 acres of land, part of a tract called Addition by the southern branch of Omaly's Creek. Also a parcel of land south of the main road from Sutton's Mill to Chamberlin's Bridge adjoining the tract called Addition. Made 15 Mar 1734/5. Wit: Robert Penington, Sr., John Winterbery. Ackn. before JPs John Baldwin, A. Barry. Rec: 16 Mar 1734. Wm. Knight, Clerk.

P. 93   Deed of Gift.   Thomas Mercer, Sr. of Cecil Co., planter, for the natural love and affection he has for his son John Mercer, gives to John Mercer and his wife Elizabeth, after the death of said Thomas Mercer, Sr., one half of the plantation that he (Thomas Mercer) now lives on. If John Mercer should die then to his daughter-in-law Elizabeth during her widowhood. If she should marry or die, then he gives all his right and interest of the plantation to his well beloved son Robert Mercer. Made 11 Mar 1734. Wit: Dom Carroll, James Tuite. Ackn. before JPs John Baldwin, John Veazey. Rec: 20 Mar 1734. Wm. Knight, Clerk.

P. 93   Deed.   Hugh Terry of Cecil Co., planter, to Dominick Carroll of said county, gent., all his interests in any part of the tract of land called Addition on the southwest side of Omaly Creek northward of the main road from Sutton's Mill to Chamberlin's Bridge in exchange for said Dominick Carroll's interests in a parcel of land on the southward side of the said road on the east side of and adjoining the Addition tract. Made & Ackn: 15 Mar 1734/5. Wit: Robert Pennington, Sr., John Winterbery. JPs: John Baldwin, A. Barry. Rec: 20 Mar 1734/5. Wm. Knight, Clerk.

P. 94   Receipt.   Written on the back of a deed from William Boulding to Richard Boulding recorded in Lib. W. K. No. 2, folio 40 is a receipt from Jas. Paul Heath who received from Richard Boulding the alienation fine for 50 acres of land. Made 10 Feb 1733. Rec: 20 Mar 1734. Wm. Knight, Clerk.

P. 94   Receipt.   Written on the back of a deed from William Boulding to Thomas Boulding recorded in Lib. W. K. No. 2, folios 33-34 is a receipt from Jas. Paul Heath who received from Thomas Boulding the alienation fine for 250 acres of land. Made 10 Feb 1733. Rec: 20 Mar 1734. Wm. Knight, Clerk.

P. 94   Receipt.   Written on the back of a deed from William Boulding, Sr. to William Boulding, Jr. recorded in Lib. W. K. No. 2, folios 10-11 is a receipt from Jas. Paul Heath who received from William Boulding, Jr. the alienation fine for 130 acres of land. Made 10 Feb 1733. Rec: 20 Mar 1734. Wm. Knight, Clerk.

P. 95   Deed.   Robert Turnbull of Cecil Co., weaver, and Margaret his wife, for £17.10s, to James Armstrong of the same place, farmer, 100 acres of land, half of a tract called Clements' Venture. Charles Lord Baltimore granted a warrant dated 8 Jun 1717 to Peregrine Frisby of Cecil Co., gent., for 200 acres of land. The warrant was renewed 13 Feb 1717/8 and was assigned by Peregrine Frisby to Michael Clements of said county, farmer. A tract of land was surveyed and laid out for Michael Clements called Clement's Venture in Cecil Co. near the head of Elk River containing 200 acres. The patent of confirmation is dated 10 Aug 1727. Michael Clements sold the land to Robert Turnbull by deed dated 5 Mar 1725/6. Made & Ackn: 18 Apr 1735. Wit: John Nelson, John Jones, John Thomas. JPs: Wm. Rumsey, A. Barry. Rec: 29 Apr 1735. Wm. Knight, Clerk.

P. 97   Deed.   James Alexander of Cecil Co., weaver, and his son Moses Alexander and Mary his wife, for £23, to William Sample of Chester Co., PA, weaver, 40 acres of land by a tract called Newmunster by James Alexander's land. Said land part of 92¾ acres purchased from Thomas Stevenson of Bucks Co., PA which was part of 903 acres purchased from Robert Roberts of Queen Anns Co. by deed dated 15 Aug 1718. Made 8 Apr 1735. Wit: David Alexander, John McCallmont. Ackn: 11 Apr 1735 by Capt. James Alexander, Moses Alexander and Mary, wife of Moses Alexander. JPs: A. Barry, Edward Jackson. Rec: 29 Apr 1735. Wm. Knight, Clerk.

P. 98   Deed.   Theophilus Ivary of New England, mariner, for £100, to John Kankey of Cecil Co., 164 acres of land on Elk River and Pate's Creek, part of a tract called St. John's Manor. Made & Ackn: 28 Apr 1735. Wit: G. Lawson, James Foster. JPs: Edward Jackson, A. Barry. Rec: 30 Apr 1735. Wm. Knight, Clerk.

P. 101   Deed.   Henry Reynolds and Bartholomew Johnson of Cecil Co., planters, for £10, to Anthony Dushene of the same place, yeoman, a marsh on the west side and near the head of Elk River by a tract called Price's Venture. Reynolds and Johnson will defend the land against any claims of John Campbell and John Prichcot. [Anthony Dushene's name is also spelled Antoney Dushene.] Made 28 Mar 1735. Wit: Wm. Smith, Edw'd. Taylor, John Nelson, Simon Johnson. Ackn: 31 Mar 1735 by Henry Reynolds, Bartholomew Johnson and their wives Elizabeth Reynolds and Sarah Johnson. JPs: Jno. Copson, Edward Jackson. Rec: 9 May 1735. Wm. Knight, Clerk.

P. 103   Deed.   Nathaniel Wilds of Newcastle Co. upon Delaware, PA, sadler, son and heir of John Wilds, for £50, to Joshua Wilds of Cecil Co., farmer, a tract of land called Black Mash. Charles Lord Baltimore granted a warrant dated 2 Dec 1713 for 200 acres of land to John Wilds of Cecil Co., surveyed 4 Jan 1713/4 and laid out a tract called Black Mash in Cecil Co. patented 2 Dec 1714 and recorded in Lib S, folio 88. [Joshua Wilds also called Josiah Wilds.] Made & Ackn: 17 May 1735. Wit: John Gilesland, J. Kirkpatrick, John Lawson. JPs: A. Barry, Edward Jackson. Alienation fine of 8 shillings rec'd from Joshua Wilds by Jas. Paul Heath on 18 May 1735. Rec: 3 Jun 1735. Wm. Knight, Clerk.

P. 105   Deed.   Nathaniel Wilds of Newcastle Co. upon Delaware, PA, sadler, son and heir of John Wilds, for £20, to Joshua Wilds of Cecil Co., farmer, 64 acres of land called Cefen Kure. Charles Lord Baltimore granted a warrant to John Wilds of Cecil Co. dated 3 Jun 1714 for 64 acres of land. The land called Cefen Kure was surveyed and laid out in Cecil Co. 15 Aug 1714 by Wilds' other tract called Black Marsh. Patent of confirmation dated 10 Sep 1716. [Joshua also spelled Joshuah.] Made & Ackn: 17 May 1735. Wit: John Gilesland, J. Kirkpatrick, John Lawson. JPs: A. Barry, Edward Jackson. Alienation fine of 2s.7p rec'd from Joshua Wilds by Jas. Paul Heath on 18 May 1735. Rec: 3 Jun 1735. Wm. Knight, Clerk.

P. 108   Deed.   Richard Price of Cecil Co., planter, for £120, to John Campbell of the same county, gent., 100 acres of land on the east side of Elk River already in Campbell's possession, part of a tract called the Dividing originally surveyed 27 May 1661 for Gasper Guieren for 600 acres. Made & Ackn: 9 Dec 1734. Wit: John Veazey, Robert Pennington. JPs: John Baldwin, John Veazey. Receipt of consideration money witnessed by Thos. Redford, James Robb. Ackn: 30 May 1735 by Sarah Price, wife of Richard Price. Jas. Paul Heath received 2 shillings alienation fine from John Campbell on 8 Jan 1734. Rec: 2 Jun 1735. Wm. Knight, Clerk.

P. 110   Lease.   William Bristow, Jr., of Cecil Co., yeoman, for yearly rents and services, to Samuel Jackson of the same place, blacksmith, 190 acres of land, part of a tract called Hopewell on the west side of little Elk River. Term of the lease is 8 years with rent of £5 due 1 Apr yearly. Jackson agrees to clear the meadow which is adjacent to James McKey's place and will keep up half of the partition fence between Jackson and McKey and between Jackson and Andrew Barry. He will not clear more than 30 acres of upland. Jackson may cut down what wood he needs to make coal for his blacksmith trade. [Bristow is also spelled Bristoll.] Made & Ackn: 15 Mar 1735. Wit: Jno. Kanky, George Lawson. JPs: Edward Jackson, A. Barry. Rec: 3 Jun 1735. Wm. Knight, Clerk.

P. 111   Receipt.   Written on the back of a deed from John Milward to Thomas Ward recorded in Lib. W. K. No. 2, folios 20-22 is a receipt from Jas. Paul Heath for 4s.4½p received from Thomas Ward for the alienation fine for 218 acres, part of Wheeler's Point. Made 10 Jul 1734. Rec: 9 Jun 1735. Wm. Knight, Clerk. [See pg 3, Entry P. 20.]

P. 111   Deed.   Robert Pennington, Jr. of Cecil Co., planter, for £8, to Thomas Spencer of Bideford, Great Britain, lot #6 and lot #13 which are part of a tract in Cecil Co. on Sassafras River called Buntington of which part of it has lately been surveyed and laid out into several lots and streets and called Amelia Ann Town. Rachel Pennington, wife of said Robert, releases her right of dower for which Rachel is paid 5 shillings by Thomas Spencer. Made 2 May 1735. Wit: JPs John Baldwin, John Veazey. Ackn: same day. Rec: 25 Jun 1735. Wm. Knight, Clerk.

P. 114   Deed.   Robert Pennington, Jr. of Cecil Co., planter, for £8, to John Buck, merchant in Biddeford, Great Britain, several lots which are part of 2 tracts of land on Sassafras River called Buntington and Happy Harbor, lately surveyed and laid out into lots and streets called Amelia Ann Town: lot #14 (part of Buntington), lot #2 and a moiety of lot #3 laid out by the same survey and part of Happy Harbor. For 5 shillings paid by Buck, Rachel Pennington, wife of said Robert, releases her right of dower. Made 2 May 1735. Wit. & JPs: John Baldwin, John Veazey. Ackn: same day. Rec: 26 Jun 1735. Wm. Knight, Clerk.

P. 117   Lease.   Araminta Herman of Cecil Co., widow of Col. Ephraim Augustine Herman, late of said county, deceased, and natural guardian of Ephraim Herman, now an infant and the only son of the said Ephraim Augustine and Araminta Herman, for yearly rents and services, to James Taylor of said county, land in Bohemia Manor formerly leased by the said Ephraim Augustine Herman to Charles Dorment by the road that leads from Bohemia Ferry to Elk Ferry, by land formerly leased to John Dye and by

Robert Veazey's pasture. Also 40 acres adjoining this land on Caterpillar Hill. Lease is until Ephraim Herman reaches the full age of 21 years. Rent of 40 shillings due every 10 Dec. Taylor will plant and fence 100 apple trees. Made & Ackn: 12 Jun 1735. Wit: Joshua George, John Beetel. JPs: Tho. Colvill, Jno. Copson. Rec: 26 Jun 1735. Wm. Knight, Clerk.

P. 119   Deed of Release.   John Read of Cecil Co., merchant, for £30, releases to Mary Noeland of the same county, widow, 100 acres of land, part of a tract called Hopewell which the said Mary purchased from Stephen Hollingsworth, Robert Holy and Robert McCay by deed dated 5 May 1732. By deed dated 6 Aug 1733 recorded in Lib. S. K. No. 6, folios 162-163 Mary conveyed the land to the said John Read. Made & Ackn: 26 May 1735. Wit: David Alexander, James Aikin. JPs: A. Barry, Thos. Johnson, Jr. Rec: 26 Jun 1735. Wm. Knight, Clerk.

P. 121   Deed.   Robert Pennington, Jr., of Cecil Co., planter, and Rachel his wife, for £4, to William Hogg of the same county, tailor, lot #16, half an acre on Sassafras River in Amelia Ann Town. Made & Ackn: 11 Jun 1735. Wit: Alexander Lang, James Cummine. JPs: Edward Jackson, R'd. Thompson. Rec: 27 Jun 1735. Wm. Knight, Clerk.

P. 122   Deed of Release.   Thomas Stratton of Kent Co. in the Territories of PA, for £50 and because he is moving, quit claims to Richard Nash of Cecil Co., 125 acres of land already in the possession of said Richard Nash, part of 2 tracts of land, one called Hispaniole formerly released by William Richardson to Samuel Alexander and the other tract called Bullin's Range adjacent to the first tract was acquired by said Samuel Alexander by patent from Lord Baltimore. Samuel Alexander sold 125 acres of the land to the said Thomas Stratton by deed of release dated 20 Mar 1729. Said land is bounded by a tract sold by Thomas Stratton to Robert Patton. Made 15 Apr 1725 [sic.] Wit: R'd. Thompson, Martin Alexander. Ackn: 16 Apr 1735 by Thomas Stratton and his wife Hannah. JPs: R'd. Thompson, A. Barry. Alienation fine of 5 shillings rec'd by Jas. Paul Heath from Richard Nash 12 May 1735. Rec: 27 Jun 1735. Wm. Knight, Clerk.

P. 124   Deed.   John Copson of Cecil Co., merchant, for £30, to Robert Whitaker of the same place, weaver, 100 acres of land, part of a tract called Coxes Park. By warrant dated 27 Feb 1719 and another warrant dated Aug 1720 a tract of 469 acres of land called Coxes Park was surveyed and laid out for William Cox of Cecil Co. who by deed dated 9 Jan 1722 conveyed the land to John Copson. Charles Lord Baltimore, by the hand of Governor Benedict Leonard Calvert, granted to John Copson by patent dated 23 Nov

1728 the above mentioned tract of land. Patent recorded in Lib. P. M., folio 25. Made 13 Jun 1735. Wit: Wm. Knight, John Williams. Ackn: 12 Jun 1735. Alienation fine of 4 shillings rec'd by Jas. Paul Heath from Robert Whitaker same day. Rec: 3 Jul 1735. Wm. Knight, Clerk.

P. 127   Valuation of Estate.   Thomas Pearce and Henry Pennington, Jr., at the request of Charles Scott, guardian of John Terry, an orphan of Cecil Co., sworn by JP William Rumsey, viewed the lands and plantation of the said orphan and found a dwelling house 25x16 feet, all clapboard, with earthen floor, needing new covering; one old milk house 10-foot square, clapboard; a small rough log house 15x12; a rough round log corn house 20x8, clapboard covering; one old tobacco house; 2 barracks; a kitchen and log house so decayed they are not worth repairing; 12 apple and 3 cherry trees, the fencing needs new rails. They estimate the annual value to be 600 lbs of tobacco. They allow the dower of the orphan's mother, now the wife of Charles Scott and the other two-thirds toward the orphan's maintenance. The guardian may clear all the land on the east side of the plantation but not any further south. The orphan's rights are for 69 acres and they think that the timber on the whole woodland will scarcely be sufficient to keep the place in good repair. Made 5 Apr 1735. Rec: 3 Jul 1735. Wm. Knight, Clerk.

P. 128   Valuation of Estate.   John Price and James Wroth viewed the land of the orphan of Henry Henrexon now in the possession of Wm. Ward. They found that the plantation is small with 2 small old log houses and one tobacco house not finished and much out of repair. They allow him to clear from the northwest end of the plantation eastward up a valley until it joins Capt. Frisby's land to get rails and timber to repair the place. They value the place at 400 lbs of tobacco yearly. Made 29 Mar 1735. JP: John Veazey.

On the same day they viewed another piece of land of the orphan of Henry Henrexon now in the possession of Thomas Davis called Mary's Park and found the land uncleared and of no use. They allow him to settle the land on the lower end of the tract near the head of Sassafras Road where "the caterpillars has hilled" a quantity of timber and he may clear across the tract 40 acres and use the timber for the plantation. After the year 1740, if the land is settled, they will value it to 500 lbs of tobacco a year. Made 29 Mar 1735. JP: John Veazey. Rec: 3 Jul 1735. Wm. Knight, Clerk.

John Price and James Wroth viewed another piece of land of the orphan of Henry Hendrexon now in the possession of Thomas Davis called the Levell. They found the plantation very much out of repair and only one small tobacco house on it. The land well worn but little to clear. They allow him 3,000 or 4,000 tobacco hills to clear every year between the plantation and the road and to haul 400 rails for repairing the fencing. They value the place at 390 lbs of tobacco a year. Made 29 Mar 1735. JP: John Veazey. Rec: 3 Jul 1735. Wm. Knight, Clerk.

P. 129   Deed.   Edward Reynolds of Cecil Co., planter, for £20 and because he is moving, to James Paul Heath of the same county, gent., 40 acres of land, part of a tract called Sarah's Joynture. Made 7 Jul 1735. Wit: Wm. Knight, M. Rainey. Ackn: same day by Edward Reynolds and his wife Mary. JPs: John Baldwin, Wm. Rumsey. Rec: 10 Jul 1735. Wm. Knight, Clerk.

P. 131   Deed.   William Reynolds and John Reynolds, Sr., both of Cecil Co., planters, for £32.10s, to Joshua George, attorney of Cecil Co., 65 acres of land, part of a tract called Sarah's Joynture by a tract called Ashmore and a tract called the Dividend. Made 4 Aug 1735. Wit: Thos. Yorkson. Ackn: 13 Aug 1735 by William Rannals alias Reynolds. JPs: Edward Jackson, Wm. Rumsey. Alienation fine of 2s.7p rec'd by Jas. Paul Heath from Joshua George on same day. Rec: 18 Aug 1735. Wm. Knight, Clerk.

P. 133   Assignment of Lease.   Thomas Breeding of Bohemia Manor in Cecil Co., for 5 shillings and certain agreements, to David Waddle of the same county during his natural life, the whole use and occupation of the land which the said Thomas Breading holds from Col. Ephraim Augustine Herman in Bohemia Manor and all the household goods, wearing apparel and stock (except for his working tools.) It is well known that Thomas Breeding is much given and addicted to strong drink and when drunk is very liable to be imposed on in bargains. The agreement is made in order to secure for himself and his wife support and maintenance during their natural lives. In the event that Jane Breeding, the wife of said Thomas Breeding, should survive him, then the land and goods will revert back to her. If the said Thomas should survive his wife, then this agreement is void. [Thomas' name is also spelled Briding.] Made & Ackn: 15 Mar 1734. Wit: Saml. Young, Law. Gueycett. JPs: R'd. Thompson, A. Barry. Rec: 15 Sep 1735. Wm. Knight, Clerk.

P. 135   Lease.   Anna Margaretta Vanderheyden of Cecil Co., for yearly rents and services, to William Price of the same county, planter, 200 acres of land, part of a tract called Three Bohemia Sisters on Back Creek and Long Creek. Lease is for the term of the natural lives of the said William Price, his wife Sarah and his brother Ephraim Price. Rent of £3 due 15 Jan yearly. Made & Ackn: 19 May 1735. Wit. & JPs: John Baldwin, John Veazey. Rec: 18 Sep 1735. Wm. Knight, Clerk.

P. 137   Deed.   Jonathan Stilley of Newcastle Co. on Delaware, for £25, to Garret McKenney of Cecil Co., a tract of land called Fedard on the west side of Elk River bounded according to a deed made by Garret McKenney and his mother Mary Kemp to the said Jonathan Stilley dated 9 Jan 1734 recorded in Lib. W. K. No. 2, folios 73-74. [Garret's name also spelled Gerratt and McKenne, McKinne.] Made 4 Oct 1735. Wit: Rachell Kelly, Willm. Deoran. Ackn: same day. JP: Jno. Copson. Alienation fine of 4 shillings rec'd by Jas. Paul Heath 17 Oct 1735. Rec: 14 Oct 1735. Wm. Knight, Clerk.

P. 138   Deed.   Samuel Gilpin and Edward Taylor, both of Cecil Co., yeomen, for £400, to John Copson of the same county, a 700 acre tract of land called Kinsby. Charles Lord Baltimore, by the hands of his governor Charles Calvert, granted to Joseph Carter a tract of 700 acres of land called Kinsby in Cecil Co. by patent dated 9 Nov 1726 recorded at Annapolis in Book P. L. No. 6, pg 352. Joseph Carter and his wife Sarah conveyed the land to the said Samuel Gilpin and Edward Taylor by deed dated 2 Mar 1732, ackn. the 14th day of the said month and year and recorded in Lib. S. K. No. 6, folios 44-48. Made 23 Sep 1735. Wit: Thos. Colvill, Thos. Johnson, Jr. Ackn: same day by said Gilpin and Taylor and their wives Jane Gilpin and Mary Taylor. JPs: Thos. Colvill, Thos. Johnson, Jr. John Copson paid the £400 consideration money to Gilpin and Taylor on 18 Sep 1735. Wit: Jethro Browne, Wm. Rumsey. Rec: 12 Nov 1735. Wm. Knight, Clerk.

P. 141   Valuation of Estate.   At the request of Araminta Herman, widow and guardian of Augustine Larramore, an orphan of Cecil Co., and sworn in by JP William Rumsey, George Veazey and John Roberts entered the property of the said orphan and found an old rotten grist water mill on another tract of land adjacent to the plantation and on the plantation a reasonably good framed dwelling house 30x18 feet with plank floors and petitions plastered and ceiled with a brick chimney and cellar, the glass windows and plastering somewhat broken; a log kitchen joining one end of the dwelling house somewhat out of repair with a brick chimney; a milk house and log cellar very rotten and old; 2 small old log houses and a small log house built for a smith's shop; 2 pretty good tobacco houses, one 50-foot, the other 40-foot, rough clapboard work; an old tobacco house not worth repairing; an old corn house and a hen house; a good large orchard and 2 small orchards, the fencing in indifferent repair and the rails old. They estimate the annual value of the 300 acre plantation at 1,000 lbs of tobacco. They allow 100 acres to be cleared of timber to use for repairs. They say the grist mill is so rotten and decayed that it cannot be repaired and would be of considerable expense to rebuild it. Made 9 Sep 1735. Rec: 12 Nov 1735. Wm. Knight, Clerk.

P. 142   Deed.   John Copson of Cecil Co., merchant, for £200, to Samuel Gilpin of the same place, yeoman, a tract of land called Coxes Park (excluding 100 acres sold to Robert Whitaker) the remainder being 369 acres. By patent dated 23 Nov 1728 recorded in Lib. P. L. folio 25, John Copson was granted a tract of 469 acres of land called Coxes Park in the fork of Northeast River. By deed dated 13 Jun 1735, John Copson sold 100 acres of the land to Robert Whitaker. Made 18 Sep 1735. Wit: Wm. Rumsey, Wm. Deoran. Ackn: 23 Sep 1735. JPs: Thos. Colvill, Thos. Johnson, Jr. Rec: 21 Nov 1735. Wm. Knight, Clerk.

P. 144   Deed.   John Loftus and Susanah his wife of Cecil Co., joiner, for £40, release to Robert Crocker, mariner, and his wife Rachel, all their rights to a tract of land called None So Good in Finland on Back Creek on Sassafras River and one-third of all the personal estate left to them by their father Thomas Crocker, late of said county, by his Last Will and Testament. Made 11 Nov 1735. Wit: John Hussey, John Baldwin, Wm. Rumsey. Ackn: same day. JPs: John Baldwin, Wm. Rumsey. Rec: 24 Nov 1735. Wm. Knight, Clerk.

P. 145   Deed.   Thomas Phillips of Cecil Co., yeoman, and Eliner his wife, for £5, to Samuel Houston of Chester Co., PA, 30 acres of land called Phillips' Bottom in Milford Hundred, Cecil Co., on the eastern branch of Northeast Creek by George Robinson's land called Doe Hill. Thomas and Eliner Phillips have a patent on the land. Eliner Phillips made her mark with a "T". Made & Ackn: 2 Dec 1735. Wit: Francs. Hurd, A. Barry. JP: Jno. Copson. Alienation fine of 1 shilling paid by Samuel Houston to Jas. Paul Heath on 16 Dec 1735. Rec: 17 Dec 1735. Wm. Knight, Clerk.

P. 147   Deed.   William Rumsey of Cecil Co., gent., for £140, to Samuel Gilpin of the same place, yeoman, a tract of land called Rumsey's Ramble and part of a tract called Stoney Chase by a tract called Coxes Park, the acreage from the both totaling 350 acres. By patent dated 30 Oct 1731 recorded in Lib. P. S. No. 3, folio 105, Edward Rumsey of Cecil Co. was granted a tract of 300 acres of land called Rumsey's Ramble in the fork of Northeast River adjoining a tract called Coxes Park and another tract called Batchellor's Fund. Edward Rumsey conveyed the tract to William Rumsey by deed dated 3 Aug 1733, ackn. 4 Aug before JPs Benjamin Pearce and Richard Thompson and recorded 27 Aug 1733 in Lib. S. K. No. 6, folios 122-123. William Rumsey conveyed to John McFarland of Newcastle Co. upon Delaware 100 acres of the tract called Rumsey's Ramble by deed dated 17 Feb 1734 recorded 14 Mar 1734 in Lib. W. K. No. 2, folios 74-76. William Rumsey also holds another tract of land called Stoney Chase in the same fork of the river, the original patent of 400 acres dated 26 Oct 1732 and granted to John Baldwin of Cecil Co., gent., who conveyed it to William Rumsey by deed dated 10 Sep 1733 recorded in Lib. S. K. No. 6, folios 151-153. Made 18 Sep 1735. Wit: Jno. Copson, Willm. Deoran. Ackn: 23 Dec 1735 by William Rumsey and his wife Sabina. JPs: John Baldwin, John Veazey. Rec: 30 Dec 1735. Wm. Knight, Clerk.

P. 150   Deed.   Samuel Gilpin of Cecil Co., yeoman, for £112, to Edward Taylor of the same place, yeoman, 200 acres of land, part of 2 tracts called Rumsey's Ramble and Coxes Park by a tract called Batchellor's Fund, by John McFarland's land and by Robert Whitaker's land.

By patent dating 30 Oct 1731 recorded in Lib. P. L. No. 3, folio 105, Edward Rumsey of Cecil Co. was granted a tract of 300 acres of land called Rumsey's Ramble in the forks of the Northeast River by a tract called Coxes Park and by a tract called Batchellor's Fund. Edward Rumsey sold Rumsey's Ramble to William Rumsey of the same county, gent., by deed dated 3 Aug 1733. William Rumsey sold 100 acres of Rumsey's Ramble to John McFarland of Newcastle Co. by deed dated 17 Feb 1734. By another deed even dated with this present deed, William Rumsey sold to Samuel Gilpin all the remainder of Rumsey's Ramble (excluding what was sold to John McFarland.) By patent dated 23 Nov 1728 recorded in Lib. P. L. [No. 5?] folio 25, John Copson of Cecil Co., gent., was granted a tract of 469 acres called Coxes Park in the fork of Northeast River. John Copson conveyed 100 acres of Coxes Park to Robert Whitaker by deed dated 13 Jun 1735 and on the same day conveyed the remainder of Coxes Park to Samuel Gilpin. Made 18 Sep 1735. Wit: Jno. Copson, Wm. Rumsey. Ackn: 23 Sep 1735 by Samuel Gilpin and his wife Jane. JP: Jno. Copson. Rec: 31 Dec 1735. Wm. Knight, Clerk.

P. 154   Deed.   Robert Thompson of Cecil Co., gent., for £100, to John Baldwin of the same place, gent., a tract of 200 acres called Saven's Rest on the south side of Bohemia River and St. Augustine's Branch. Said land was conveyed by William Savin and his wife Elizabeth to Rowland Williams who conveyed it to John Tyliard who bequeathed the land to his daughters Ephesus (wife of George English) and Hester (wife of Richard Green.) They conveyed the land to Hugh McGregory and his wife Elizabeth who then conveyed it to John Thompson, who by his Last Will and Testament, devised the land to his son the said Robert Thompson. Made 12 Jan 1735. Wit: Wm. Rumsey, John Veazey, John Thompson. Ackn: 13 Jan 1735. JPs: Wm. Rumsey, John Veazey. Rec: 20 Jan 1735. Wm. Knight, Clerk.

P. 157   Deed.   William Hatcher of Bucks Co., PA, wheelwright, and his wife Ann, for £43, to James McClure of Cecil Co., farmer, 166½ acres of land in Cecil Co. by the place where James McClure's old house stood on Elk River. Said land is a one-third part of a tract called Newmunster which is part of 500 acres sold by Thomas Stevenson of Bensalem Township, Bucks Co., PA, to Johannas Vansandt of the same township by deed dated 17 May 1714. Johannas Vansandt, by his Last Will and Testament dated 13 Oct 1714, left the 500 acres to be equally divided between his 5 children John, Elizabeth, Jacobus, Ann and Rachel, of whom John and Rachel died without issue and the land was divided between the 3 survivors. William Hatcher married Ann Vansandt. Made 19 Nov 1735. Wit: Samuel Gelfton [Gilpin?], Rich'd. McClure. Ackn: same day in Philadelphia before JP Thomas Lawrence. Ackn: in Cecil Co. 24 Jan 1735/6 by James Alexander, attorney for William and Ann Hatcher. JP: Jno. Copson.

Power of Attorney: William Hatcher and Ann his wife of Bucks Co., PA, wheelwright and spinster, because they are moving, appoint as their attorney their well beloved friend James Alexander of Milford Hundred, Cecil Co., to acknowledge a deed to James McClure. Made 19 Nov 1735. Wit: Rich'd. McClure, Samuel Gelfton. Ackn: in Cecil Co. 24 Jan 1735 by Richard McClure. JP: Jno. Copson. Rec: 26 Jan 1735. Wm. Knight, Clerk.

P. 160   Deed.   Richard Bennett of Queen Annes Co., gent., for a sum of money paid by Phillip Stoops to George Woodhead of Cecil Co. and for £50 paid by Richard Bennett by order of George Woodhead, to Phillip Stoops of Cecil Co., planter, a tract of land called Bonnington in Cecil Co. on the north side of Sassafras River originally surveyed for George Goldsmith for 200 acres. Made 6 Nov 1735. Wit: Jno. Stevens, John Beck. Ackn: 12 Nov 1735. JP: Robert Gordon. Alienation fine of 4 shillings collected from Phillip Stoops by Jas. Paul Heath on 1 Dec 1735. Rec: 5 Feb 1735. Wm. Knight, Clerk.

P. 161   Deed.   John Jobson of Cecil Co., planter, for £22 (£10 of silver and gold), to Thomas Jones of the same place, planter, all his rights to a tract of 87½ acres of land called Happy Harbor on the north side of Sassafras River by Drake's old mill. Made & Ackn: 12 Feb 1735. Wit: Wm. Knight, Charles Coatts. JPs: John Baldwin, Wm. Rumsey. Rec: 12 Feb 1735. Wm. Knight, Clerk.

P. 163   Deed.   John Carr of Long Island, for 4,000 lbs of tobacco, to William Bristow, Jr. of Cecil Co., 100 acres by land formerly belonging to John Numbers and by land formerly belonging to Harman Kinkey on Elk River which Cecilius Lord Baltimore granted to Capt. John Carr in a tract of land called Capt. John's Manor by patent dated 1675. The said John Carr is the heir of Capt. John Carr. William Bristow will honor a bond made by Capt. John Carr to Simon Dawkins in 1674 for making over the said 100 acres of land. [John Numbers is also called John Numberson.] Made 24 Jan 1735. Wit: Walter Kerr, Robert Gibson, Robt. Holy. Ackn: same day. JPs: Andw. Barry, Thos. Johnson, Jr. Rec: 9 Mar 1735. Wm. Knight, Clerk.

P. 165   Release.   Richard Bennett of Queen Annes Co., gent., for a competent sum of money and because he is moving, to Bartholomew Jacobs of Cecil Co., farmer, a tract of 500 acres called Stockton on the branches of Bohemia River, formerly purchased by Richard Bennett from John Toas (by his attorney William Comegies) and Peter Massey and his wife Sarah. Made 6 Nov 1735. Wit: John Ofment [Osment? Olment?], James Steawart. Ackn: 12 Nov 1735. JP: Robert Gordon. Alienation fine of 20 shillings rec'd from Jacobs by Jas. Paul Heath on 20 Nov 1735. Rec: 9 Mar 1735. Wm. Knight, Clerk.

P. 166   Lease.   Araminta Herman of Cecil Co., gent. [sic], for yearly rents and services, to Benjamin Lancaster of the same place, planter, land in Bohemia Manor by Charles Dirmot's land, lately deceased, on the south side of Herring Creek by Robert Veazey's line. Lease is for the term of 19 years paying yearly to Araminta Herman at her dwelling house every 10th of Dec 30 shillings and 2 dunghill fowls. Made & Ackn: 9 Mar 1735. Wit. & JPs: John Baldwin, John Veazey. Rec: 10 Mar 1735. Wm. Knight, Clerk.

P. 168   Deed.   John Penington of Cecil Co., and Elizabeth his wife, Susanah Justice, Esther Lewis and Anne Worley, daughters of the said John Penington, for £11.8s, to Robert Cummings of said county, 3 acres, 3 roods, 11 perches of land on Northeast River, part of a tract called Arrundell which the said Penington purchased from _____ Sequences. The Peningtons and their daughters agree that Cummings has free liberty of a road from the gum tree to the main road. [Esther Lewis' name is also given as Heaster Lewis. Cummings also spelled Cumings, Cummins.] Made 4 Sep 1735. Wit: John Lloyd, Luke Stanly. Ackn: 16 Oct 1735. JP: Jno. Copson. Rec: 10 Mar 1735. Wm. Knight, Clerk.

P. 170   Deed.   Samuel Wild of Newcastle Co. on Delaware, farmer, for £15, to John Copson of Cecil Co., gent., a tract of 244 acres called Landive by Joseph Carter's land called Kinsly now in possession of said John Copson. Excepting out of the tract 100 acres which Griffith Nicholas bequeathed to Mary and Margaret Nicholas when they come to their full age.

Charles Lord Baltimore by the hands of Richard Tilghman, Chancellor, granted to Griffith Nicholas, then of Cecil Co. (but now deceased) a tract of 224 acres of land called Landive in Cecil Co. by patent dated 18 May 1722 recorded at Annapolis in Lib. C. E. No. 1, folios 415-417. By his Last Will and Testament dated 5 Dec 1726 and proved before Stephen Knight, gent., Griffith Nicholas appointed the said Samuel Wild his sole executor with power to raise money to pay his debts. Made & Ackn: 9 Mar 1735/6. Wit: Robert Whitker, William Deoran. JPs: Edward Jackson, A. Barry. Samuel Wild rec'd 9 Mar 1735/6 from Maj. John Copson £15. Wit: Rachel Kelley, Will. Deoran. Rec: 10 Mar 1735. Wm. Knight, Clerk.

P. 173   Deed.   Thomas Sharp of Cecil Co., farmer, because he is moving and for £9.15s, to Alexander Logan of the same county, 14 acres of land called Guiel Glass, part of Thomas Sharp's plantation in Millford Hundred. Made 12 Dec 1735. Wit: John Smith, Thomas Sharp, Jr. Isabella Sharp, wife of Thomas Sharp, relinquishes her right to the land. Ackn: 6 Mar 1735 by Thomas and Isabella Sharp. JPs: A. Barry, Edward Jackson. On 30 Dec 1735 Jas. Paul Heath rec'd 7d sterling alienation fine from Alexander Logan. Rec: 10 Mar 1735. Wm. Knight, Clerk.

P. 175   Valuation of Estate.   At the request of Araminta Herman, widow and guardian of her son Ephraim Herman, an orphan of Cecil Co., and duly sworn by JP John Baldwin, Thos. Johnson, Jr. and James Veazey entered the land of Bohemia Manor now occupied by the said Araminta Herman and her son, and found a brick 2 story dwelling house, 2 rooms on a floor and a brick shed joined to it but not finished, and the dwelling house much out of repair with the sleepers over the cellar being entirely rotten and decayed and in danger of falling, the garrets of no use without immediate repair having never been finished, the fireplaces in the chambers much decayed and sunk; a brick kitchen of one story adjoining the dwelling house, very old, the rafters, laths and shingles quite decayed; a small one story storehouse of brick, much decayed; an old decayed log hen house; an old log Negroes quarters, the covering very bad; a framed barn 30 or 40 feet long in good repair but needs doors; 3 very old decayed tobacco houses of little or no use and not worth repairing; the orchard has about 100 old apple trees, much decayed, the fencing old. They estimate the plantation has 350 acres all of which, except 20 or 30 acres, are cleared and fenced within 4 fields and the woodland they think necessary for the orphan to clear for firewood and repairs. They value the yearly income of the plantation to be £10. Made 15 Dec 1735. Rec: 11 Mar 1735. Wm. Knight, Clerk.

P. 176   Deed.   Samuel Wild of Newcastle Co., province of PA, farmer, and his wife Mary, for £90, to Fargus Smith of Cecil Co., blacksmith, land which Charles Lord Baltimore granted to Samuel Wild by a warrant dated 2 Dec 1713 for 200 acres of land surveyed and laid out in Cecil Co. called Springs Head by land called Newmunster and patented 10 Dec 1714. [Wild is also spelled Wilde. Fargus is also spelled Forgus.] Made 26 Jan 1735/6. Wit: Thomas White, James Stewart, Jno. Thomas. Ackn: 27 Jan 1735. JP: Jno. Copson. Alienation fine of 8 shillings rec'd by Jas. Paul Heath 7 Feb 1735. Rec: 17 Apr 1736. Wm. Knight, Clerk.

P. 178   Release.   William Rumsey of Cecil Co., gent., rec'd from Isaac Bowers £16.8s in full discharge of a mortgage on the land called Pennyworth and releases the land to said Bowers. Made 7 Nov 1735. Wit: Sabina Rumsey, George Scott. This release is on the mortgage recorded in this book, folios 75-76. [See pg 11, entry P. 75.] Rec: 10 May 1736. Wm. Knight, Clerk.

P. 179   Deed.   John Campbell of Cecil Co., gent., for £50, to Zebulon Hollingsworth of the same place, gent., one moiety of a tract of land called Price's Venture on the north side of Elk River containing 75 acres of land. Price's Venture (250 acres) was granted to William Price by patent 20 Jul 1623 [sic.] Made 21 Nov 1735. Wit: Wm. Rumsey, Antho. Carroll. Ackn: 7 Apr 1736. JPs: Wm. Rumsey, John Baldwin. Rec: 10 May 1736. Wm. Knight, Clerk.

P. 180   Release.   Christopher Hendrickson of Cecil Co., planter, for 15 shillings, to John Winterbury of the said county, planter, 192 acres of land called Hendrickson's Choice on Elk River opposite a tract formerly taken up by Mounce Anderson. Said land was sold by Christopher Hendrickson, deceased (father of the said Christopher Hendrickson), to Thomas Kimber by deed dated 20 Mar 1718. Made & Ackn: 15 Apr 1736. Wit. & JPs: John Baldwin, John Veazey. John Winterbury paid 2 shillings alienation fine to Jas. Paul Heath 20 Apr 1736. Rec: 10 May 1736. Wm. Knight, Clerk.

P. 183   Deed.   Walter Shewell of New Brittain, Bucks Co., PA, executor and devisee of the Last Will and Testament of Thomas Kimber of Sassafras Neck, Cecil Co., yeoman, for £120, to John Winterbury of Cecil Co., planter, one moiety of a tract of land called Hendrickson's Choice and the marsh by Roger Larramore's land containing 100 acres.

Christopher Hendrickson of Cecil Co., planter, by deed dated 20 Mar 1718/9, conveyed to Thomas Kimber, father of the said Thomas Kimber, a tract of 192 acres of land called Hendrickson's Choice on Elk River formerly taken up by Mounce Anderson and also a parcel of 8 acres adjoining Hendrickson's Choice. Thomas Kimber the Elder, by his Last Will and Testament dated 20 Dec 1722 bequeathed to his sons James Kimber and Thomas Kimber all the said 200 acres of land to be divided equally between them by a direct line from the land late of Roger Larramore. His son James should have the part of the land which adjoins Garret Otterson's land and his son Thomas should have the other part and also to divide the marsh with James taking the lower part and Thomas the upper part. William Rumsey made the survey which divided the land on 9 May 1729.

Thomas Kimber the Younger, deceased, by his Last Will and Testament dated 10 Dec 1734 bequeathed, among other legacies and bequests, to his brother-in-law Walter Shewell the remainder of his estate, in which manner Shewell became seized of a moiety of Hendrickson's Choice. Made 22 Mar 1735. Wit: John Pickering, Wm. Rumsey. Ackn: same day. JPs: John Baldwin, Wm. Rumsey. Alienation fine of 2 shillings rec'd 20 Apr 1736 by Jas. Paul Heath from John Winterbury. Rec: 10 May 1736. Wm. Knight, Clerk.

P. 187   Deed.   John Edwards of Cecil Co., planter, for £26.10s to Dennis Nowland of the same county, planter, a moiety of 115 acres of land, part of a tract called Dayley's Desire, the estate rights of his brother Phillip excepted. Phillip Edwards, late of Cecil Co., deceased, father of said John Edwards, purchased 115 acres of land from Thomas Smith by deed dated 9 Nov 1715. Said land was part of a tract called Dayley's Desire. By his Last Will and Testament dated 4 and 5 Jun 1721, Phillip Edwards devised the land thus: "I give and bequeath to my two sons John and Philip all my Real Estate to be divided Equally between them both the plantation I now live on to my Eldest Son John that whereon John Watson lived to my Youngest Son Philip." [Nowland also spelled Nooland.] Made 26 Mar 1736. Wit: Henry McCay, Wm. Rumsey. Ackn: 5 Apr 1736 by John Edwards and his wife Mary. JPs: Thos. Colvill, John Baldwin. Alienation fine of 2s.3¾p rec'd 20 Apr 1736 by Jas. Paul Heath. Rec: 2 Jun 1736. Wm. Knight, Clerk.

P. 189   Deed.   Robert Penington, Jr. of Cecil Co., planter, for £4.5s, to John Morton of the said county, tailor, lot #11 (½ acre) in Amelia Ann Town on the north side of Sassafras River. Made 1 May 1736. Wit: John McManus, William Ellis. Ackn: 1 May 1736 by Robert Penington and Rachel his wife. JPs: Wm. Rumsey, John Veazey. Rec: 8 Jun 1736. Wm. Knight, Clerk.

P. 191   Commission of the Peace.   Charles Lord Baltimore appoints as Justices of the Peace for Cecil Co. John Hall, Richard Tilghman, Matthew

Tilghman Ward, John Rusby, Benja. Tasker, Philip Lee, John Rider, Michael Howard, George Plater, Edmund Jennings, Charles Hammond, Thomas Colvill, Edward Jackson, Richard Thompson, John Baldwin, William Rumsey, Thomas Johnson, Andrew Barry, John Veazey and Robert Story, all of Cecil Co., gents. Made 10 Mar 1735. Signed in the margin by Samuel Ogle, Gov. Rec: 8 Jun 1736. Wm. Knight, Clerk.

P. 195 Deed. Zebulon Hollingsworth, because of the money paid by Matthias Johnson to his father Henry Hollingsworth for a tract of land called Batchellor's Content and for 5 shillings, a tract of 100 acres called Hollingsworth's Fourth Parcel (formerly called Batchellor's Content.)

Henry Hollingsworth, late of Cecil Co., deceased, by deed dated 21 Mar 1717 recorded 8 Jul 1718 in Lib. J. D. No. 3, folio 72, conveyed to Matthias Johnson of said county a tract of 100 acres called Batchellor's Content. Because Hollingsworth was moving, Charles Lord Baltimore granted the land by patent dated 10 Jun 1734 recorded in Annapolis in Lib. E. I. No. 1, folio 433, to Zebulon Hollingsworth of the said county, son of the deceased Henry (the land not having previously been patented) and called it Hollingsworth's Fourth Parcel. Made 7 Jun 1736. Wit: Jno. Copson, Willm. Deoran. Ackn: same day. Rec: 8 Jun 1736. Wm. Knight, Clerk.

P. 197 Deed. David Wallace of Milford Hundred, Cecil Co., and his wife Barbara, for £130, to Peter Geerison of the same place, a tract of 200 acres called Snow Hill which David Wallace bought from Thomas Johnson, and part of a tract called Snow Hill Addition, and 50 acres called Haile Hill. The exception is the 2 acres which David Wallace granted for the use of the Presbyterian congregation. Quit rents are due to the chief lord or William Penn or other proprietor of Pennsylvania. The Snow Hill tract was granted to Thomas Johnson by warrant dated 3 Aug 1713, surveyed 20 Jan 1713, patented 4 Jul 1719 and recorded in Lib. P. L. No. 4, folios 137-138 and by the same records the tract called Snow Hill Addition. The tract called Hailes Hill was bought by Wallace from Edward Ellis, now deceased but then of said county, and granted to Ellis by warrant dated 12 May 1720, surveyed and patented 8 May 1720 and recorded in Lib. P. K. No. 5, folio 33. [Geerison also spelled Geirison.] Made 8 Apr 1736. Wit: John Copson, Rachel Kelly. Ackn: 13 Apr 1736. JP: Jno. Copson. Rec: 11 Jun 1736. Wm. Knight, Clerk.

P. 200 Mortgage. Peter Geirison of Milford Hundred, Cecil Co., and Sarah his wife, for £55, to David Wallace of the same place, 200 acres of land called Snow Hill and part of Snow Hill Addition [see previous entry P. 197 for details of land.] Peter Geirison is to repay David Wallace £7 in

May 1737, thereafter £12 every May through 1741. Upon completion of the repayment, this deed is void. Made 13 Apr 1736. Wit: Jno. Copson, Will. Deoran. Ackn: 13 Apr 1736. JP: Jno. Copson. Rec: 11 Jun 1736. Wm. Knight, Clerk.

P. 203   Deed.   William Pollock of Cecil Co., cordwainer, and Margaret his wife, for £37.10s and because they are moving, to Walter Betty, late of Ireland, blacksmith, 80 acres of land, part of a tract called Moyn (where David Alexander now lives) on Christiana Creek by the land of James and Moses Alexander. Made 2 Apr 1736. Wit: James Alexander, Isaac Breeding, J. Lawson. Ackn: 5 Apr 1736. JP: A. Barry, R'd. Thompson. Rec: 11 Jun 1736. Wm. Knight, Clerk.

P. 205   Deed.   John Winterberry of Cecil Co., planter, for £30, and Susanna Ward of the said county, spinster, a fenced field and half of an orchard which was bequeathed to John Winterberry by the Last Will and Testament of William Veazey, late of Cecil Co., deceased. Said field adjoins the land where Michael Reiley now lives and is part of Veazey's dwelling plantation called Sparnon's Delight. Made 15 Apr 1736. Wit: Jno. Campbell, John Baldwin. Ackn: 16 Apr 1736. JPs: John Baldwin, John Veazey. Rec: 13 Jul 1736. Wm. Knight, Clerk. John Winterberry rec'd the £30 from Susanna Ward on 15 Apr 1736.

P. 206   Deed of Gift.   Col. John Ward of Cecil Co., gent., for the natural love and affection he has for his son John Ward, Jr. and for 5 shillings, to John Ward, Jr., of the same county, 200 acres, part of a tract called Cox Forest on the south side of Bohemia River at the head of Smith's Creek. Made & Ackn: 14 Jul 1736. Wit: John Baldwin, J. Pennington. JPs: John Baldwin, Wm. Rumsey. Rec: 21 Jul 1736. Wm. Knight, Clerk.

P. 207   Lease.   Col. Ephraim Augustine Herman of Cecil Co., for rent and services, to William Hood of Dorset Co., gent., 125 acres of land lately in the possession of Capt. James Moody, deceased, in Bohemia Manor by Hogg Creek, by the land that was leased to Soloman Bowen and by Herring Creek. Also another tract of land lately occupied by Bennet Jump by land lately occupied by Humphrey Alcock and belonging to James Bayard, gent., and by Nicholas Vandegrift's and _____ Maccoy's land, the whole contained between the lands aforesaid. Lease is for the term of the natural lives of the said William Hood, his wife Alice Hood and Sidney George, son of Joshua George and Alice his wife. Rent of £3.50s due 10 Dec yearly. Made 28 Jan 1734. Wit: Thos. Colvill, Ch. Browne. Herman empowers William Alexander or Joshua George to deliver the land to Wm. Hood. Made same day. On

1 Feb 1734 Joshua George delivered the land to Mr. Wm. Hood. Rec: 22 Jul 1736. Wm. Knight, Clerk.

P. 209   Lease.   Anna Margreta Vanderheyden of Cecil Co., for 5 shillings and for rents and services, to James Boulding, Elizabeth Boulding and William Boulding, the son of William Boulding, Jr., 130 acres of land, part of a tract called Three Bohemia Sisters by the land of William Price, the old King's Road and by Long Creek. Rent of 40 shillings due every 25 Mar from 1738 onward. Made 9 Aug 1736. Wit: John Baldwin, William Price. Ackn: 6 Aug 1736 [sic.] JPs: John Baldwin, John Veazey. Rec: 10 Aug 1736. Wm. Knight, Clerk.

P. 211   Mortgage.   Daniel Benson of Cecil Co., planter, for £25 and 950 lbs of tobacco in cask, to William Rumsey of the same county, gent., 100 acres of land where the said Daniel now lives which descended to him from his father who purchased it from Robert Rumsey of Salem, NJ. Said land part of a 500 acre tract called King's Aim in Cecil Co. at the head of a branch of Bohemia River. Benson to pay the tobacco to Rumsey on or by 10 Dec next and the £25 on or by 7 Sep 1738. Made 7 Sep 1736. Wit: Henry Flale, Wm. Knight. Ackn: 8 Sep 1736. JPs: John Baldwin, Rich'd. Thompson. Rec: 10 Sep 1736. Wm. Knight, Clerk.

P. 215   Deed.   Robert Pennington, Jr. of Cecil Co., planter, and Rachel his wife, for £5.10s, to Julian Annis of said county, widow, lot #12 (½ acre) in Amelia Ann Town on the north side of Sassafras River. Made 10 Aug 1736. Wit: Robert Pennington, John Baldwin. Money rec'd and deed ackn. next day. JPs: Thos. Colvill, John Baldwin. Rec: 18 Sep 1736. Wm. Knight, Clerk.

P. 217   Deed.   Robert Pennington, Jr. of Cecil Co., planter, and Rachel his wife, for £3, to Julian Annis of said county, widow, lot #23 (½ acre) in Amelia Ann Town on the north side of Sassafras River. Made 10 Aug 1736. Wit: Robert Pennington, John Baldwin. Money rec'd and deed ackn. next day. JPs: Thos. Colvill, John Baldwin. Rec: 18 Sep 1736. Wm. Knight, Clerk.

P. 219   Deed.   Richard Dowdall of Kent Co., gent., for £450, to Augustine Thompson of Queen Annes Co., a tract of 400 acres called Ward Oake, once in Talbot Co., but now Kent Co., on the north side of Chester River. Also 2 other tracts on the north side of Chester River adjoining the first tract, one of the tracts called Addition to Ward Oake, the other Dowdall's Fancy. Also a moiety of a tract of land called None So Good in Finland in Cecil Co. (75 acres) on the north side of Sassafras River and Back Creek which was where

Maj. John Dowdall lived in his lifetime. Made 1 Jul 1736. Wit: Arthr. Miller, J. Bird. Ackn: 2 Jul 1736. JP: S. Knight. Alienation fine of 1s.6d rec'd by Jas. Paul Heath on 2 Jul 1736. Rec: 1 Oct 1736. Wm. Knight, Clerk.

P. 221 Release. Richard Dowdall of Kent Co., gent., for 10s, releases to Augustine Thompson of Queen Annes Co., a tract of land in Cecil Co. called Sheffield. Richard Dowdall and John McManus by deed of mortgage dated 26 Nov 1733 conveyed to Augustine Thompson a tract of 500 acres of land called Sheffield on Sassafras River at Back Creek by John Wheeler's land at Axell Creek. Dowdall and McManus were to repay Thompson £88.2s.10p and 2,028 lbs of tobacco on or by 16 Oct 1735. Made 1 Jul 1736. Wit: Arthr. Miller, J. Bird. Ackn: next day. JP: S. Knight. Rec: 1 Oct 1736. Wm. Knight, Clerk.

P. 223 Deed. Isaac Bowers of Cecil Co., planter, and Esther his wife, for £45, to Richard Houghton of the same county, carpenter, 71 acres of land called Pennyworth, formerly granted to Henry Penington, on the north side of Sassafras River by land granted to Gartis Morgan and by land formerly surveyed for Wm. Glover. Isaak Bowers made his mark with the traditional "X", Easter Bowers made her mark with an "I". Made 6 Aug 1736. Wit: J. McManus, Robert Penington. Ackn: same day. JPs: John Baldwin, Wm. Rumsey. Rec: 25 Oct 1736. Wm. Knight, Clerk.

P. 226 Deed. William Teague of Cecil Co., and Isabella his wife, for £35, to Joseph Frezar of Lancaster Co., PA, yeoman, a tract of land called Teague's Forest by land called Teague's Endeavors. William Teague was granted a special warrant dated 5 Oct 1728 for 200 acres of vacant land in Cecil Co. near Susquehanna River (recorded at Annapolis.) William Rumsey, Surveyor for Cecil Co. working under the Surveyor General Michael Howard, on 3 Apr 1729 certified that he had surveyed and laid out the land in 3 separate tracts called Teague's Chance (50 acres), Teague's Forest (100 acres) and Hopewell (50 acres.) Charles Lord Baltimore patented the land to him. William Teague made his mark with a "T" and Izabla Teague made her mark with an "E". Made 1 Sep 1736. Wit: Isaac Sanders, Sam. Calwell. Ackn: same day. JP: Jno. Copson. Alienation fine of 4 shillings rec'd from Joseph Frazier 10 Sep 1736 by Jas. Paul Heath. Rec: 10 Nov 1736. Wm. Knight, Clerk.

P. 228 Deed. Adam Sherrill [Sherwill] of Cecil Co., yeoman, and his wife Elizabeth, for £50, to Samuel Caldwell, late of Lancaster Co., PA, yeoman, 100 acres of land, part of a tract called Three Partners. Charles Lord Baltimore conveyed by patent dated 16 Sep 1720 recorded at Annapolis in

Lib. C, folios 321-322, a tract of land in Cecil County. By deed dated 13 Dec 1725 and recorded in Lib. S. K. No. 5, folios 9-10 Thomas Jacobs conveyed to William Sherwill, father of the said Adam Sherwill, 200 acres, part of a tract called Three Partners. William Sherwill conveyed to his son Adam 100 acres of the land. [Name is also spelled Sherwell.] Made & Ackn: 1 Sep 1736. Wit: Isaac Sander [Lander?], Benjam. Brittain. JP: Jno. Copson. Alienation fine of 4 shillings rec'd by Jas. Paul Heath 10 Sep 1736. Rec: 10 Nov 1736. Wm. Knight, Clerk.

P. 231 Deed. Samuel Gillpen of Cecil Co., yeoman, and Jane his wife, for £100, to William Bristow, cooper, of Cecil Co., a moiety of land, including half the corn mill and half the saw mill, on the east side of the northwest branch of Elk River below the county road. Said land Zebulon Hollingsworth bought from Elias Everson and his wife Mary by deed dated 22 Jun 1728. Made 21 Sep 1736. Wit: Jno. Copson, Willm. Deoran. Ackn: 14 Oct 1736. JP: Jno. Copson. Rec: 11 Nov 1736. Wm. Knight, Clerk.

P. 232 Deed. Thomas Loftain of Cecil Co., planter, for £30 paper currency and £20 gold or silver, to William Husbands of said county, planter, a tract of 65 acres called Mount Pisga by Lord Baltimore's land called Mount Pleasant and by Connawango Creek. Made 5 Aug 1736. Wit: Nath. Ewing, William Mitchell. Ackn: next day by Loftain and his wife Eleanor. JPs: Wm. Rumsey, Edward Jackson. Rec: 11 Nov 1736. Wm. Knight, Clerk.

P. 235 Deed. James Alexander of Milford Hundred, Cecil Co., gent., for £30, quit claims to Moses Alexander, a tract of land which James & Moses Alexander jointly bought from Thomas Stevenson of Bucks Co., PA, gent. Made 20 Oct 1736. Wit: James Alexander, John Cowen, Robert Pepper. Ackn: 8 Nov 1736. JPs: A. Barry, Edward Jackson. Rec: 12 Nov 1736. Wm. Knight, Clerk.

P. 236 Deed. Thomas Beard [Baird] of Cecil Co., planter, and Mary his wife, for £40, to William Rumsey of the same county, gent., 100 acres of land, the third part of a tract called the Round Stone at the mouth of North East River granted by patent dated 15 Feb 1659 to John Wheeler for 300 acres. Said 100 acres of land descended to Mary Beard as co-heir of John Wheeler. Made & Ackn: 18 Oct 1736. Wit: Thos. Colvill, John Veazey, Robert Pennington, Jr. JPs: Tho. Colvill, John Veazey. Alienation fine of 2 shillings rec'd by Jas. Paul Heath from Wm. Rumsey 12 Nov 1736. Rec: 14 Nov 1736. Wm. Knight, Clerk.

P. 239   Deed.   James Paul Heath of Cecil Co., gent., for £100, to Hugh Matthews of the same place, chirurgeon, 200 acres of land, part of 2 tracts, one called Heath's Third Parcel, the other Heath's Third Parcel Addition by the eastern line of a tract called Manwaring Hall (now in the possession of the said Hugh Matthews) where that line crosses the southern line of a tract called Dividend. Also the tract called Manwaring Hall beginning at Bohemia Landing and containing 400 acres except for the part that is called Booker's Uppermost on the south side of the Landing. James Paul Heath's father James Heath, deceased, was granted the tract called Manwaring Hall. Made 16 Nov 1736. Wit: Wm. Rumsey, R'd. Thompson, Wm. Pearce. Ackn: same day by Heath and his wife Rebecca. JPs: R'd. Thompson, Wm. Rumsey. Alienation fine of 8 shillings paid 25 Nov 1736. Rec: 29 Nov 1736. Wm. Knight, Clerk.

P. 242   Deed.   Robert Pennington, Jr. of Cecil Co., planter, and Rachel his wife, for £7.10s, to Robert Croker of the same county, mariner, lot #17 and lot #3 in Amelia Ann Town on the north side of Sassafras River. Made & Ackn: 18 Oct 1736. Wit. & JPs: Wm. Rumsey, John Veazey. Rec: 11 Dec 1736. Wm. Knight, Clerk.

P. 243   Deed.   Emanuel Grubb of Newcastle Co. upon Delaware, farmer, and Ann his wife, for £120, to Robert Story of Cecil Co., gent., a tract of 165 acres called the Swamp on the east side of Shannon River (now called North East River) by land called Whitton's Forest. Said land is part of the land that belonged to George Talbot and was sold by him to Thomas Hitchcock by deed dated 11 Aug 1684 recorded in Lib. C., folios 159-160. Also a parcel of land called Paradise on the south side of Shannon River adjoining the other tract and containing 150 acres. This was also part of George Talbot's land and sold by his wife Sarah Talbot to Edward Johnson by deed dated 27 Aug 1686 recorded in Lib. C., folio 434. By the Last Will and Testaments of the said Edward Johnson and the said Thomas Hitchcock the lands became the property of Ann Grubb, one of the daughters of Thomas Hitchcock. Made & Ackn: 19 Oct 1736. Wit. & JPs: Wm. Rumsey, Thos. Johnson, Jr. Rec: 11 Dec 1736. Wm. Knight, Clerk.

P. 247   Deed.   Richard Bennett of Queen Annes Co., merchant, for £40, to John Baxter of Cecil Co., planter, a tract of land called Sargent's Neck [or Largent's Neck?] formerly surveyed for John Sargent [Largent?] for 100 acres. The land was sold to Abraham Pennington who mortgaged the land to Richard Bennett. Made 22 Oct 1736. Wit: James Stewart, J. Beck. Ackn: 25 Oct 1736. JP: Robert Gordon. Alienation fine of 4 shillings paid to Jas. Paul Heath 30 Oct 1736. Rec: 11 Dec 1736. Wm. Knight, Clerk.

P. 249   Deed.   Nicholas Reynolds of Cecil Co., planter, for £80, to Jacob Everdson of the same county, carpenter, the tract of land where he the said Nicholas Reynolds now lives which is part of a larger tract called Sarah's Joynture originally surveyed and laid out 13 Sep 1681 for Richard Peacock for 600 acres and by various transferences became the property of John Reynolds who, by deed of gift dated 2 Mar 1730 recorded in Lib. S. K. No. [?], folio 271, conveyed to his son the said Nicholas 125 acres of the tract by the land of William Reynolds. Made 6 Dec 1736. Wit: Wm. Rumsey, John Penington. Ackn: 11 Dec 1736 by Nicholas Reynolds and his wife Eleanor. JPs: Wm. Rumsey, R'd. Thompson. Alienation fine of 5 shillings rec'd by Jas. Paul Heath. Rec: 21 Dec 1736. Wm. Knight, Clerk.

P. 251   Deed.   Spry Godfrey Gundry of Baltimore Co., planter, for £20, to William Rumsey of Cecil Co., gent., a tract of 485 acres called New Hall at the head of Elk River. The survey was made in the name of John Larkin of Ann Arundel Co. in Mar 1681. By deed dated 19 Mar 1685 it was sold to Benjamin Gundry and Gideon Gundry. Benjamin and Gideon Gundry have since both died intestate, Gideon without issue, and the land descended to Spry Godfrey Gundry, the only son of Benjamin Gundry and heir as well to the said Gideon Gundry, his uncle. Made & Ackn: in Baltimore Co. 7 Aug 1736 by Spry and his wife Mary. Wit: Gilbert Crockett, Aga. Massey, Wm. Dallam. JPs: Aguila Paca, Richard Caswell. Paca and Caswell certified as JPs by J. Wells Stokes, County Clerk. Rec: 4 Jan 1736. Wm. Knight, Clerk.

P. 254   Deed.   Henry Snicker of Baltimore Co., planter, and Catherine his wife, for £100, to Caleb Pennell of Cecil Co., yeoman, 114 acres of land, part of a tract called Slate Hill on the east side of Susquehanna River by land called Poplar Valley. Made 15 Oct 1736. Wit: Isaac Sanders, James Bradley. Ackn: 1 Dec 1736. JP: Jno. Copson.

   Power of Attorney.   Henry Snicker, by obligation dated 18 Oct 1734 is bound to Caleb Pennell for £100 conditioned for a legal conveyance of a tract of land which the said Snickers bought from Thomas Johnson adjoining a tract of land called Poplar Valley. Snickers and his wife Catherine have conveyed the land to Caleb Pennell and Snickers appoints Catherine to be his attorney to acknowledge the deed. Made 15 Oct 1736. Wit: Isaac Sanders, James Bradley. Ackn: 1 Dec 1736 by Isaac Sanders, a Quaker. JP: Jno. Copson. Rec: 24 Jan 1736. Wm. Knight, Clerk.

P. 257   Deed.   Augustine Boyer and his wife Rebecca and Thomas Baker and his wife Ann, all of Kent Co., for £20, to Thomas Beard of Cecil Co., all their right and each of their part of a tract of land called Norland containing

44 acres being 2 one-third parts of a total of 66 acres on the north side of Sassafras River and in the dwelling plantation of the said Thomas Beard. Said land came to the said Augustine Boyer and Thomas Baker by their marriages to Rebecca and Ann, daughters of Thomas and Sarah Christian who were the co-heirs of John Wheeler. Made & Ackn: 18 Oct 1736. Wit. & JPs: Thos. Colvill, John Veazey. Rec: 16 Feb 1736. Wm. Knight, Clerk.

P. 259 Deed. William Runnalds of Cecil Co., planter, for £2.6s.8p, to Joshua George of the same county, attorney at law, 4¾ acres of Sarah's Joynture adjoining the 65 acres for a total of 69¾ acres by tracts of land called Askmore and the Dividend. By deed dated 4 Aug 1735, for £32.10s, Joshua George purchased from the said William Runnalds 65 acres of land, part of Sarah's Joynture. Runnalds agreed to sell George an additional 4¾ acres of Sarah's Joynture adjoining the 65 acres. [Runnalds also spelled Rennals.] Made 23 Feb 1736. Wit: Ben. Bradford, Tho. Yorkson. Ackn: 9 Mar 1736. JPs: John Veazey, Robert Story. Alienation fine of 2½p paid to Jas. Paul Heath 24 Feb 1736/7. Rec: 9 Mar 1736. Wm. Knight, Clerk.

P. 261 Release. William Rumsey of Cecil Co., gent., for £36 instead of a previously agreed sum of 950 lbs of tobacco, releases the mortgage on 100 acres of land to Daniel Benson of said county, planter. By deed dated 7 Sep 1736, for £25 and 950 lbs of tobacco, Daniel Benson mortgaged 100 acres of land, part of King's Aime, to William Rumsey. Daniel was to pay the £25 by or on 10 Dec and the tobacco by or on 17 Sep 1738. Made 7 Mar 1736. Wit: A. Barry, Hugh Lawson. Ackn: 11 Mar 1736. JPs: Edward Jackson, A. Barry. Rec: 11 Mar 1736. Wm. Knight, Clerk.

P. 263 Deed. John Macmanus [McManus] of Cecil Co., gent., because he is moving and for £50, to John Campbell and Joshua George of said county, gent., a tract of land on the north side of Sassafras River called None So Good in Finland, the same tract of land which Maj. John Dowdall lived on in his lifetime and where John Macmanus now lives. It is agreed that John Macmanus may continue to live on the premises during the rest of his natural life and that afterwards it shall descend to his eldest son that shall be living by his present wife, saving her one third of the estate. In case she shall survive the said John Macmanus or in case he should die without heirs of the body of his wife the daughter of the said John Campbell, then the land descends to his right heirs or to whomever he names in his Last Will and Testament. Made & Ackn: 30 Mar 1737. Wit: Benjamin Bradford, Thomas Forster. JPs: Thos. Johnson, Jr., A. Barry. Rec: 31 Mar 1737. Wm. Knight, Clerk.

P. 265   Deed.   William Renalds of Cecil Co., planter, for £5, to William Rumsey of the same county, gent., 10 acres of land by a tract called the Dividend. Said land is part of a tract called Sarah's Joynture which was originally surveyed on 13 Sep 1681 for 600 acres for Richard Peacock and on 13 Sep 1725 resurveyed and patented to John Reynolds, the father of the said William Reynolds for 660 acres. [Reynolds is also spelled Rennals.] Made 5 Mar 1736. Wit: Mary Samson, Catherine Wood. Ackn: 9 Mar 1736. JPs: Tho. Colvill, John Veazey. Alienation fine of 5p rec'd from William Rumsey 25 Mar 1737 by Jas. Paul Heath. Rec: 2 Apr 1737. Wm. Knight, Clerk.

P. 266   Mortgage.   William Beasting of Cecil Co., planter, for £50, to William Rumsey of the same county, gent., 120 acres of land, part of a tract called Swan Harbor where the said Beasting now lives on Bohemia River at Omealy's Creek. Part of the tract of Swan Harbor descended to William Beasting from his deceased father William Beasting who was the devisee of James Holloway, the surviving partner and joint purchaser of 350 acres, part of the original tract, from John Poole of Baltimore Co. William Beasting is to repay William Rumsey on or by 6 Dec next. [Beasting also spelled Beastin, Beaston.] Made 6 Dec 1736. Wit: John Baldwin, John Thompson. Ackn: 30 Mar 1737. JPs: Edward Jackson, A. Barry. Rec: 2 Apr 1737. Wm. Knight, Clerk.

P. 269   Deed of Gift.   Henry Penington of Frederick Town on Sassafras River, yeoman, to settle a dispute and for the natural love and affection he has for his brother Robert and for 5 shillings, to Robert Penington of the same place, innholder, 50 acres, part of a tract of land called Happy Harbor by a tract called Buntington and by land formerly belonging to Jarvis Morgan called Middle Neck. This land was devised to him by the Last Will and Testament dated 4 Mar 1708 of his deceased father Robert Penington which was devised to him by the Last Will and Testament of his brother John Penington, deceased, about 1696. Also 70 acres of land, part of the tract called Buntington, bounded according to a deed of release from John Copson to the said Henry Penington. Buntington was given to the said Robert Penington [the father?] by deed of gift dated 5 Oct 1711 from Ann Penington, his mother. A dispute between Henry and Robert Penington arose about the bounds and the title of the tract called Buntington which was originally granted by patent dated 7 Oct 1667 to Abraham Strand, as well as a part of the tract called Happy Harbor originally granted by patent dated 10 Apr 1671 to Richard Leak for 400 acres. Made 25 Mar 1737. Wit. & JPs: Wm. Rumsey, Thos. Johnson, Jr. Ackn: 1 Apr 1737 by Henry Penington and his wife Mary. Alienation fine of 2s.5p rec'd 18 Apr 1737 by Jas. Paul Heath. Rec: 19 Apr 1737. Wm. Knight, Clerk.

P. 273   Deed.   Robert Penington of Fredericks Town on Sassafras River, for £100, to William Rumsey of Cecil Co., gent., 120 acres, part of 2 tracts of land, one called Buntington, the other Happy Harbor which was deeded to him by his brother Henry Penington, except lot #45 in said town which Robert has taken up and entered in his name where he now lives. Made 1 Apr 1737. Wit: Wm. Hutchison, Robert Story. Ackn: same day by Robert Penington and his wife Rachel. JPs: Thos. Johnson, Jr., Robert Story. On 18 Apr 1737 Jas. Paul Heath rec'd 2s5p alienation fine. Rec: 19 Apr 1737. Wm. Knight, Clerk.

P. 275   Lease.   James Craig, executor of Humphrey Alcock, late of Cecil Co., deceased, carpenter, for rents and services, to William Hamilton and Matthew Steel, both of Cecil Co., planters, 130 acres (the dwelling plantation lately belonging to Humphrey Alcock) on Col. Harman's manor [Bohemia Manor.] Lease is from 1 Nov last to a full 9 years for rent of £8.5s. Made 23 Feb 1736/7. Wit: Wm. Knaresborough, Wm. Ellis. Ackn: 25 Apr 1737. JPs: Wm. Rumsey, R'd. Thompson. Rec: 25 Apr 1737. Wm. Knight, Clerk.

P. 277   Deed.   Thomas Penington of Cecil Co., planter, for £2, to John Buck of Bithford, Great Britain, esq., lot #27 in Fredericks Town. Made 30 Apr 1737. Wit: John Baldwin, Thos. Spencer. Ackn: same day by Thomas Penington and his wife Rosamond. JPs: Wm. Rumsey, John Veazey. Alienation fine of 1 penny rec'd 3 May 1737 by Jas. Paul Heath. Rec: 6 May 1737. Wm. Knight, Clerk.

P. 279   Deed.   Abraham Cox of Cecil Co., to Robert Croker of the same county, and his wife Rachel, lot #41 in Frederick Town on the north side of Sassafras River. [Abraham also called Abram.] Made & Ackn: 2 May 1737. Wit: Wm. Rumsey, John Loftus. JPs: Wm. Rumsey, John Veazey. Rec: 6 May 1737. Wm. Knight, Clerk.

P. 279   Deed of Gift.   John Ward of Cecil Co., gent., and his wife Mary, for the natural love and affection they have for their son Peregrine Ward, a tract of land called Greenfield by Hen Island Creek containing 750 acres. Made 5 Apr 1737. Wit. & JPs: Wm. Rumsey, John Veazey. Ackn: same day by Col. John Ward and his wife Mary. Rec: 11 May 1737. Wm. Knight, Clerk.

P. 281   Receipt.   Written on the back of a deed from James Hall to Robert Cory dated 1 May 1731 and recorded in Lib. S. K. No. 5, folio 336: Jas. Paul Heath rec'd 5 Apr 1737 from Alex. Logan 2 shillings alienation fine for the within 50 acres of land which was left by Robert Curry to his wife Tenent Curry. Rec: 14 Jun 1737. Wm. Knight, Clerk.

P. 281   Release.   James Harris of Kent Co., and Augustina his wife, release to John Sutton of Cecil Co., eldest son of Josias Sutton, late of said county, deceased, all his interests in 100 acres of land plus a water mill and a dam. By deed dated 20 Aug 1719 recorded in Cecil Co. Lib. D., No. 3, folios 183-185, James and Augustina Harris conveyed to Josias Sutton 100 acres of land, part of a tract called Elsecks Lodge [sic; should be Essex Lodge] on the south side of Bohemia River west of Omelly or Scotchman's Creek, with the water mill on its 10 acres. The use of the mill was valued by a jury at 500 lbs of tobacco and Thomas Browning was paid for the same before the mill was condemned. Also 10 acres of land on the other side of the dam, which is part of Swan Harbor belonging to William Beaston. The dam and its land was valued at 500 lbs of tobacco by the jury which was paid to William Beaston. This deed appears not to have been acknowledged or recorded in the time limits set by an Act of Assembly. By this omission disputes may arise, as is the case with Mary Overstock, late wife of the said Josias Sutton (who died intestate) and mother of his eldest son John Sutton. Made 14 Apr 1737. Wit: Hercules Coutts, _____ McCarris [or is it Mas. Harris?] Ackn: in Kent Co. 14 Apr 1737. JPs: Charles Hynson, Henry Evans; certified by James Smith, County Clerk. Rec: 16 Jun 1737. Wm. Knight, Clerk.

P. 284   Deed.   Daniel Benson of Cecil Co., planter, and his wife Mary, for £100, to Philip Stoops of the said county, yeoman, 100 acres of land, part of a tract called King's Aim originally laid out for 500 acres. Mary Benson made her mark with a "W" [unless the clerk recopying the deed mistook an "M" for a "W".] Made 12 Mar 1736. Wit: Wm. Rumsey, Wm. Knight. Ackn: same day. JPs: Wm. Rumsey, R'd. Thompson. Jas. Paul Heath collected 4 shillings alienation fine on Lady Day 1736. Rec: 7 May 1737. Wm. Knight, Clerk

P. 286   Deed.   Robert Weldon of Cecil Co., planter, £1.18s, to John McDermot of the said county, planter, lot #33 in Frederick Town on the north side of Sassafras River. Made 30 May 1737. Wit: Vall'tin Sillcock, Patt. Keran. Ackn: 30 May 1737. JPs: Wm. Rumsey, John Veazey. Rec: 31 May 1737. Wm. Knight, Clerk.

P. 287   Deed.   Peter Garrison of Milford Hundred in Cecil Co., and Sarah his wife, for £25, to Alexander Logan of the same place, 50 acres of land, part of 2 tracts called Snowhill and Snowhill's Addition (15 acres of Snowhill and 35 acres of Snowhill's Addition.) The Garrison's hold the lands called

Snowhill, Snowhill's Addition and Hail Hill by deed dated 8 Apr 1736 from David Wallace of said county. The tract called Snowhill was taken up by Thomas Johnson of said county by warrant dated 3 Aug 1713, surveyed 20 Jan 1713 and patented 4 Jul 1719. Made 30 Mar 1737. Wit: Robert Moor, A. Barry, Mary Barry. Ackn: 4 Apr 1737. JPs: A. Barry, R'd. Thompson. Alienation fine of 2 shillings rec'd by Jas. Paul Heath on 5 Apr 1737. Rec: 14 Jun 1737. Wm. Knight, Clerk.

P. 290   Deed.   Samuel Jones of Cecil Co., farmer, for £50, to William Alexander of the same county, gent., a tract of 400 acres called Ballyconnell on the east side of the east branch of Elk River. The said land is that part of Ballyconnell which was formerly granted and sold by Thomas and Rebecca John to the father of the said Samuel Jones. Made 31 Mar 1737. Wit: George Elleer, Mich'l. Coulter, Will McKnight. Ackn. & Rec: 15 Jun 1737. JP: Jno. Copson. Wm. Knight, Clerk.

P. 292   Lease.   William Alexander of Cecil Co., gent., for rents and services, to Samuel Jones of the same county, farmer, 400 acres called Ballyconnell [see previous entry.] The half part where Samuel Jones now lives is leased for the term of 11 years. Samuel Jones will pay every year during the lifetime of his mother 1 bushel of wheat and every year after her death 7 bushels of wheat, 6 bushels of rye and 6 bushels of Indian corn. To be paid on 1 Jan yearly. The other half of the land, where Samuel's brother John Jones now lives is leased for the term of 4 years, paying 1 Jan every year 1 bushel of wheat. 31 Mar 1737. Wit: Geo. Elleer, Mich'l. Coulter, Will McKnight. Ackn. & Rec: 15 Jun 1737. JP: Jno. Copson. Wm. Knight, Clerk.

P. 294   Deed.   Hugh Boyd of Cecil Co., husbandman, for £112, to Nathan Boys of Chester Co., PA, a tract of land called Martin's Enlargement and part of a tract called Martin's Delight on the east side of Susquehanna River, together containing 150 acres of land. Made 29 Mar 1737. Wit: William Deoran, Rachell Kelly. Ackn: same day by Hugh Boyd and his wife Mary. JP: Jno. Copson. Alienation fine paid 1 Apr 1737 to Jas. Paul Heath. Rec: 15 Jun 1737. Wm. Knight, Clerk.

P. 296   Deed.   Paul Poulson, Randall Death and his wife Honour Death, all of Cecil Co., planters, for £30, to Thomas Coulson of West Nottingham, Chester Co., PA, joiner, 200 acres of land on the east side of Susquehanna River, part of a 500 acre tract called Glass House originally taken up by Richard Gray on 11 Apr 1678. On 1 Feb 1684 Richard Gray and his wife Rachel sold the land to Cornelius Comegys. Made 22 Mar 1736/7. Wit: Mich'a. Coulter, John Largent. Ackn: 25 Mar 1737. JPs: Edward Jackson,

Robert Story. Jas. Paul Heath rec'd the alienation fine on Lady Day, 1737. Rec: 15 Jun 1737. Wm. Knight, Clerk.

P. 299   Deed.   William Hugg of Cecil Co., tailor, and his wife Mary, for £4, to James Wallis, innkeeper of the same county, lot #16 (½ acre) in Frederick Town (formerly known as Amelia Ann Town) on Sassafras River bought from Robert Penington, Jr. and his wife Rachel by deed dated 1735. Made, Ackn. & Rec: 15 Jun 1737. Wit: Edward Johnson, Edward Jackson. JPs: Edward Jackson, A. Barry. Wm. Knight, Clerk.

P. 301   Deed of Gift.   Abraham Watson and Susanah Watson of Cecil Co., for the great love and affection they have for their son William Watson and for 5 shillings, 50 acres of land, part of a tract called Sinklair's Purchase by Octarara Road leading to the lower ferry on Susquehanna River. [Abraham is also called Abram.] Made & Ackn: 15 Jun 1737. Wit. & JPs: Edward Jackson, A. Barry. Alienation fine paid to Jas. Paul Heath 16 Jun 1737. Rec: 16 Jun 1737. Wm. Knight, Clerk.

P. 302   Valuation of Estate.   Andrew Wallace of Cecil Co., guardian to the children of Adam Wallace of the said county, deceased, by the consent of the Justices of Cecil Co., made application to JP Richard Thompson to nominate 2 freeholders to view the lands and buildings of the orphans of Adam Wallace. In compliance with this, Thompson appointed Richard Boulding and Thomas Craig, who viewed the plantation of 327 acres on 21 Mar 1736 and found 1 very old log house 20x18 feet, another 20x16 feet old log out house, an old 14x10 feet out house, an old log barn, a field with about 10 acres of it cleared land with good fence, 6 acres with good fencing and 16 acres of scrubby apple trees and ordinary fence, 20 acres in good fence on one side, the rest bad fencing, a piece of old field of 8 acres without a fence. The viewers value the yearly rent about £3. The guardian may have liberty to clear the uncleared land within the fenced area and about 4 acres between the house and field. Also about 10 acres of another tract of 100 acres with a very old log house on it can be cleared. Timber may be cut for rails and repairs. Rec: 15 Jun 1737. Wm. Knight, Clerk.

P. 303   Release.   William Knight of Cecil Co., gent., at the special request of Robert Penington, to Stephen Penington of the same county, a minor son and heir of the said Robert Penington, late of said county, deceased, lot #44 in Frederick Town. By an act of assembly Robert Penington erected a town on the north side of Sassafras River at Penington Point from his tracts of land called Buntington and Happy Harbor. Robert Penington took up lot #44 and entered it in the name of William Knight. Rachel Penington,

Robert's widow, insinuated to William Knight that Stephen Penington is the true heir and legal representative of Robert who died intestate. Made 15 Jun 1737. Wit: Thos. Colvill, John Veazey. Ackn: next day. Rec: 16 Jun 1737. Wm. Knight, Clerk.

P. 305   Assignment of Lease.   Samuel Newman and Jonathan Newman, for £70, to Enoch Jenkins, all their claim to a lease of land. Written on the back of a lease from Ephraim Augustine Herman to Walter Newman recorded 15 Nov 1722 in Lib. J. D. No. 3, folios 336-337. Made 15 Jun 1737. Wit: Tho. Jacob, Howell James. Ackn: same day. JPs: R'd. Thompson, Thos. Johnson, Jr. Rec: 16 Jun 1737. Wm. Knight, Clerk.

P. 306   Deed.   Cornelius Tobit of Cecil Co., gent., for £12, to William Hutchinson of the same county, merchant, lot #49 in Frederick Town on Sassafras River. Made & Ackn: 17 Jun 1737. Wit: Peter Bayard, Will'm. Douglas, Alphonso Cosden. [Tobit also spelled Tobitt.] Rec: 17 Jun 1737. Wm. Knight, Clerk.

P. 307   Deed.   John Chamberlin of Cecil Co., for £1.17s.6p, to Mrs. Angelica Coppen of the same county, lot #29 in Frederick Town on Sassafras River. Made & Ackn: 17 Jun 1737. Wit: Robert Veazey, Alphonso Cosden, Robert Veazey. Rec: 17 Jun 1737. Wm. Knight, Clerk.

P. 308   Mortgage.   John Sutton of Cecil Co., eldest son and heir of Josias Sutton, late of said county, deceased, for £80, to William Rumsey of said county, gent., 100 acres of land on the east side of Bohemia River west of Omealy alias Scotchman's Creek, part of a tract called Essex Lodge originally conveyed to William Brokus alias Brockers by patent dated 20 Jul 1673 for 700 acres. Also a water mill (which has been condemned) on 10 acres and another 10 acres on the other side of the dam which is part of a tract called Swan Harbor. Sutton is to repay Rumsey on or by 26 Apr next. Made 26 Apr 1737. Wit: Jacob Ozier, Charles Coatts. Ackn: 17 Jun 1737. Rec: 18 Jun 1737. Wm. Knight, Clerk.

P. 311   Deed.   William Chamberlin of Cecil Co., planter, for £2, to Thomas Spencer of Bideford, Great Britain, lot #43 in Frederick Town. Made & Ackn: 15 Jun 1737. Wit. & JPs: R'd. Thompson, Thos. Johnson, Jr. Alienation of 1 penny rec'd from Thomas Spencer by Jas. Paul Heath on 15 Jun 1737. Rec: 25 Jun 1737. Wm. Knight, Clerk.

P. 313   Deed.   Benjamin Blaidenburgh of Cecil Co., cordwainer, for 20 shillings, to John Buck of Bitheford, Great Britain, esq., a moiety of lot #28 in Frederick Town lying on the west side of lot #27 and measuring 87 feet wide. John Buck will build before 18 Dec 1738 a house which shall cover 400 square feet with a brick chimney. Made 9 Jul 1737. Wit: John Bubenheim, James Bayard. Ackn: same day. JPs: R'd. Thompson, Wm. Rumsey. Alienation fine of 1 penny rec'd by Jas. Paul Heath same day. Rec: 13 Jul 1737. Wm. Knight, Clerk.

P. 314   Deed.   John McManus of Cecil Co., gent., for £88.2s.8p and 2,028 lbs of tobacco plus interest from 20 Nov 1733 paid by James Paul Heath of the same county, gent., to Augustine Thompson of Queen Annes Co., gent., to release a tract of land called Sheffield containing 500 acres (which was mortgaged by the said John McManus to Augustine Thompson) and also for £80 paid to said John McManus, to James Paul Heath the said tract called Sheffield which was lately the estate and inheritance of John Dowdall, late of Cecil Co., deceased, and devised by him the said John Dowdall to the said John McManus and Richard Dowdall, who released his moiety to the said John McManus. Made 21 Feb 1736. Wit: Rob't. Jackson, Jos. George. Ackn; 24 Feb 1736. JPs: Thos. Colvill, Wm. Rumsey. Jas. Paul Heath rec'd the alienation fine on 24 Feb 1736/7. On 13 Jul 1737, Elizabeth McManus, wife of John McManus, acknowledged the deed. Same JPs. Rec: 15 Jul 1737. Wm. Knight, Clerk.

P. 316   Deed.   Hugh Matthews of Cecil Co., doctor, for £50 and because he is moving, to James Paul Heath of the same county, gent., a tract of land called Manwaring Hall at the head of Bohemia River except 400 acres of the tract at Bohemia Landing Point reserved for Hugh Matthews. Also a tract called Booker's Uppermost which is contained within the lines of Manwaring Hall. Also 60 acres out of Manwaring Hall and also the land conveyed by the said Heath to Matthews lying between the 60 acres and Manwaring Hall. Made & Ackn: 13 Jul 1737. Wit. & JPs: R'd. Thompson, Wm. Rumsey. The alienation fine rec'd by Jas. Paul Heath 14 Jul 1737. Rec: 15 Jul 1737. Wm. Knight, Clerk.

P. 318   Deed.   Terrance O'Bryan of Cecil Co., tailor, and his wife Sarah, in compliance with a previous agreement with John Atkey, deceased, to his widow Ann Atkey, the widow Angelico Copen, and Mary Penington, wife of William Penington, all of Cecil Co., the devisees and heirs of John Atkey of said county, deceased, 80 acres of land.
  By deed dated 9 Dec 1715, John Atkey conveyed to Sarah Avelman [Auelman?] the 80 acres of land where the said John Atkey was then living with goods and effects, and John Atkey was to be able to continue to live there for the rest of his natural life. If Sarah Avelman was to leave the ser-

vices of John Atkey before his death, in her capacity as his housekeeper, then their agreement would be broken and void. Long before his death, Sarah Avelman married Terrance O'Bryan and left the service of John Atkey, and Sarah was paid for her services. By writing dated 23 Feb 1724/5, Terrance and Sarah O'Bryan became bound to John Atkey for £200 on condition that they convey the 80 acres of land back to John Atkey.

By his Last Will and Testament dated 1 Jul 1723, John Atkey devised part of his land to Thomas and John Smithson and "I likewise leave the remainder of my tract of land I now live upon to my beloved wife Ann Atkey during her natural life and after her decease to my daughters Angellica Coppen and Mary Penington to them and their heirs forever to be equally divided." Made 16 May 1737. Wit: Wm. Rumsey, Rich'd. Penington. Ackn: 30 May 1737. JPs: Wm. Rumsey, John Veazey. Rec: 18 Jul 1737. Wm. Knight, Clerk.

P. 321   Deed.   Augustine Thompson of Queen Annes Co., for £106.9s.3p money of Great Britain and £105.12s.8p money of Maryland and 2,634 lbs of tobacco, to James Paul Heath of Cecil Co., a tract of land called Sheffield. The consideration money was due to Augustine Thompson from John McManus, who had mortgaged his 500 acre tract called Sheffield to said Thompson. McManus has since sold Sheffield to James Paul Heath with the agreement that Heath would pay off the mortgage. Made 25 Jun 1737. Wit: Charles Hynson, Ebenezer Blakiston. Ackn: in Kent Co. before JPs Charles Hynson, Ebenezer Blackiston. James Smith, Clerk of Kent Co., certifies the JPs on 27 July 1737. Rec: 30 Jul 1737 in Cecil Co., Wm. Knight, Clerk.

P. 323   Deed.   John Morton of Frederick Town, Cecil Co., tailor, for £15, to Thomas Williams, late of Philadelphia, PA, but now of Georgetown, Kent Co., MD, merchant, lot #36 in Frederick Town. Made & Ackn: 9 Aug 1737. Wit: Thos. Stewart, Alphonso Cosden, Richard Thompson. Rec: same day. Wm. Knight, Clerk.

P. 324   Deed.   William Teague of Cecil Co., yeoman, for £25, to John Graham of the same county, yeoman, 20 acres, part of a tract called Teague's Endeavor. Also a 50 acre tract called Hopewell on the east side of Susquehanna River adjoining Teague's Endeavor. Lord Baltimore granted to William Teague by patent dated 10 Sep 1716 the 100 acre tract of land called Teague's Endeavor. Said patent recorded in Annapolis in Lib. P. L. No. 4, folio 142. Made & Ackn: 18 Jun 1737. Wit: Rich'd. Thompson, Robert Patterson, William Mitchell. JPs: Wm. Rumsey, Robert Story. Alienation fine of 2s.10p and quit rents of 2s.10 were rec'd by Jas. Paul heath on 1 Jul 1737. Rec: 10 Aug 1737. Wm. Knight, Clerk.

P. 327   Deed.   William Teague of Cecil Co., yeoman, for £120, to John Graham of the same county, yeoman, a tract of land called Teague's Delight on the east side of Susquehanna River on the north side of Connawingo Creek and by a new oak determined to be the boundary by a court held in June 1736. Charles Lord Baltimore granted to Edward Teague of Cecil Co. by patent dated 10 Nov 1695 recorded at Annapolis in Lib. C. No. 3, folios 542-543 the tract of 130 acres called Teague's Delight. Edward Teague died intestate. His only child is the said William Teague. Made & Ackn: 18 Jun 1737. Wit: R'd. Thompson, Robert Patterson, William Mitchell. JPs: Wm. Rumsey, Robert Story. Alienation fine of 5 shillings rec'd by Jas. Paul Heath 1 Jul 1737. Rec: 10 Aug 1737. Wm. Knight, Clerk.

P. 330   Bond.   By deed dated last April 1st, for £100, Robert Penington mortgaged to William Rumsey part of 2 tracts of land called Buntington and Happy Harbor containing 120 acres. Penington was to repay Rumsey on or by 25 Mar next. By another bond Robert Penington obligated himself to William Rumsey and _____ Baldwin. Made 1 Apr 1737. Wit: Wm. Hutchison, Robert Story. Rec: 13 Aug 1737. Wm. Knight, Clerk.

P. 331   Deed of Gift.   Robert Penington of Frederick Town, Cecil Co., innholder, for 5 shillings, for the natural love and affection he has for his brother Henry and to settle a dispute between them concerning the bounds and title of a tract of land called Buntington and another tract called Happy Harbor, releases to Henry Penington of the same place, yeoman, all his interests in the said 2 tracts of land, except for 120 acres which the said Henry previously released to Robert. Made 25 Mar 1737. Wit: Wm. Hutchison, Wm. Rumsey. Ackn: same day by Robert and his wife Rachel. JPs: Wm. Rumsey, Thomas Johnson, Jr. Rec: 13 Aug 1737. Wm. Knight, Clerk.

P. 333   Release.   Capt. John Colvill releases to Joshua George of Cecil Co., all his claim to his mortgaged land. On 2 Nov 1730 Joshua George mortgaged to the said John Colvill and Benjamin Tasker, esq., 1,000 acres, part of Middle Neck, and 500 acres called Chesterfield with several Negroes for £400. £100 was advanced to Joshua George by John Colvill. On 30 Oct 1731 Joshua George paid the £128.11s.9p in gold to John Colvill. Made & Ackn: 30 Aug 1737. Wit: Thomas Colvill, Wm. Rumsey. Rec: 31 Aug 1737. Wm. Knight, Clerk.

P. 334   Deed.   Philip Cazier of Cecil Co., gent., for £275, to John Poilloun of the same county, yeoman, 200 acres of land, part of a tract called Coxes Forest. Made 7 Jun 1737. Wit. & JPs: Thos. Colvill, Wm. Rumsey. Ackn:

same day by Philip and his wife Catherine. Alienation fine of 8 shillings collected by Jas. Paul Heath same day. Rec: 30 Sep 1737. Wm. Knight, Clerk.

P. 337   Power of Attorney.   Walter and Robert Scott of the Island of Madeira, merchants, appoint as their attorneys Frances Bartlet, widow of the deceased Benjamin Bartlet, late of this Island, merchant, and Sarah Moody her sister, widow of the deceased Capt. James Moody, late of Bohemia River, Maryland, to recover debts due them the said Walter and Robert Scott, particularly from Joshua George of Bohemia River and the estate of the said Capt. James Moody. Also to recover papers and clearances which may be in the hands of Dr. Rich'd. Hill of London Town, South River, MD, (to whom they formerly granted a power of attorney to the same effect with this, which they hereby revoke.) Made 25 Apr 1737. Wit: Willm. Mount, John Sheirvine. Ackn: in Cecil Co. 4 Jun 1737 by William Mount. JP: Thomas Colvill.

Walter and Robert Scott rec'd from Sarah Moody, administratrix with Joshua George of the estate of Capt. James Moody, £85, part of what is due them by the estate, it being the value set on the plantation on Bohemia Manor where Capt. James Moody dwelt in his lifetime and where he died. Received in Madeira 18 Apr 1737. Rec: 6 Oct 1737. Wm. Knight, Clerk.

P. 338   Deed.   John Jones of Cecil Co., farmer, and his wife Anne, for £40, to Samuel Jones of the same place, farmer, 200 acres of land where the said John Jones dwells on the east side of the main branch of Elk River and on Elk River itself. Made & Ackn: 9 May 1737. Wit: Rachell Kelly, Will. Deoran. JP: Jno. Copson. Rec: 3 Oct 1737. Wm. Knight, Clerk.

P. 340   Deed.   Robert Holy of Cecil Co., and Ann his wife, for £27, to Joseph Thompson of the said county, 40 acres of land, part of a tract called Hopewell on the south line of the tract by Mary Nowland's corner and by the Thompson land formerly in the possession of Isaac Perkins. Charles Lord Baltimore granted to Matthias Vanbebber of the said county a tract of land called Hopewell by patent dated 10 Sep 1716 recorded in Lib. P. L. No. 4, folio 155. By his deed dated 15 Feb 1725, Matthias Vanbebber granted 420 acres, the remainder of the tract, to Robert Holy. Made & Ackn: 20 Sep 1737. Wit: Samuel Hill, A. Barry. JPs: A. Barry, Edward Jackson. Alienation fine of 20p rec'd by Jas. Paul Heath from Joseph Thomson 30 Sep 1737. Rec: 5 Oct 1737. Wm. Knight, Clerk.

P. 342   Assignment of Lease.   Enoch Jenkins of Cecil Co., farmer, for £41, to Abraham Alman of the same county, innholder, 280 acres of land in Bohemia Manor by the main road to Newcastle near Alman's house, by Back Creek and by Robert Withers' plantation. For the same terms and the remaining lives in the original lease. Rent of 7 bushels of winter wheat and 2 dunghill fowls to be paid every 23 March at the manor house. By lease dated 15 Nov 1722, Ephraim Augustine Herman of Cecil Co., gent., leased to Walter Newman of the same county, planter, 280 acres of land, part of Bohemia Manor, being 2 tenements of land, for the term of 6 natural lives (3 lives for each tenement.) Walter Newman assigned part of his lease to his son Richard Newman by lease dated 21 Oct 1725. Richard, William and Jonathan Newman, sons of Walter Newman, were three of the lives in the original lease. By lease dated 16 Mar 1729 Richard Newman assigned the lease to Enoch Jenkins for £35 for the same term and times as in the original lease. Walter Newman, by his Last Will and Testament, devised the remainder of the land to his two sons Samuel Newman and Jonathan Newman, and to avoid any controversies, Walter Newman's eldest son Walter endorsed the back of the original deed on 14 Oct 1736, assigning any of his interests in the lease over to his brothers. Samuel and Jonathan Newman, for £70, on 19 Oct 1736, assigned the lease to Enoch Jenkins. Made 1 Oct 1737. Wit: Thomas Harper, Wm. Rumsey. Ackn: 6 Oct 1737. JPs: Wm. Rumsey, Pereg'n. Ward. Rec: 7 Oct 1737. Wm. Knight, Clerk.

P. 345 Deed. William Ward of Cecil Co., carpenter, for £100, to James Paul Heath of the same county, merchant, land on Sassafras River, part of a tract called Herman's Mount originally patented to Godfrey Herman who assigned it to Cornelius Uringson on 22 Apr 1659. Cornelius Uringson and his wife Eleanor, by deed dated 13 Mar 1675 conveyed the land to William Ward, father of the said William Ward, who left it to his son John Ward. By deed dated 20 Apr 1721 John Ward conveyed the land to his brother William Ward. Made 7 Oct 1737. Wit: John Veazey, Pereg'n. Ward, John Ward, Jr. Ackn: same day by William and his wife Ann. Rec: 11 Oct 1737. Wm. Knight, Clerk.

P. 348 Deed of Gift. Sarah Moody and Joshua George, administrators of the estate of Capt. James Moody, for the affection they have for Benjamin Moody, only son of the said James Moody, give to Benjamin Moody all the plantation on Bohemia River that the said James Moody bought from the said Joshua George. The plantation will be the right of Sarah Moody during her natural life. If Benjamin Moody survives his mother Sarah Moody then the whole will be his for the term of his natural life. The debts of the said James Moody were more than he had estate to pay, particularly to Walter and Robert Scott. The plantation has been valued at £85 which Sarah Moody will pay to Walter and Robert Scott. In case Sarah cannot negotiate the matter with the Scott's, then this deed is void. Made 30 Feb 1735. Wit: Jno. Copson, Thos. Colvill. Rec: 29 Oct 1737. Wm. Knight, Clerk.

P. 349   Deed.   Robert Penington of Cecil Co., planter, for £65, to William Beastin of the same county, innholder, the southernmost part of lot #20 of 84 square perches in Cecil Town on the south side of Bohemia River next to Cecil Street. Made 30 Sep 1737. Wit: Hugh Terry, John Ryland, Jr. Ackn: same day by Robert and his wife Mary Penington. JPs: A. Barry, Robert Story. Rec: 1 Nov 1737. Wm. Knight, Clerk.

P. 350   Lease.   Rachel Green, widow of Thomas Green, deceased, late of Cecil Co., to Samuel Crawford of Lancaster Co., PA, weaver, for yearly rents and services, the western 125 acres of a tract of 250 acres called Coxes Fancy on the Susquehanna River. Lease is for 14 years. Rent of £2.10s yearly paid 10 Nov except for the last 2 years. Samuel Crawford will clear and fence 40 acres of the land, particularly that place where the dead trees are between the south side of the tract and the graves of the said Thomas Green and his daughter. Samuel Crawford will also build a good dwelling house convenient to a spring and will cover and shingle the old dwelling house, and build a clay chimney on it. He will also plant 50 apple trees by the last day of March next. If Rachel Green shall clear within one year of this date from the "interruption" of John Smith, then Crawford will pay rent for the last year. [Crawford is also spelled Craford.] Made 13 Aug 1737. Wit: Jed'ah. Alexander, Isaac Sanders [Landers?] Ackn: 5 Nov 1737 by William McDowell, attorney for Rachel Green. JPs: Edward Jackson, Robert Story.

P. 354   Power of Attorney.   Rachell Green, widow of Thomas Green, late of Cecil Co., deceased, appoints her trusty friend William McDowell of Cecil Co., yeoman, to be her attorney to acknowledge a lease made to Samuel Crawford. Made 13 Aug 1737. Wit: Jedidiah Alexander, Isaac Sanders [Landers?] Ackn: 5 Nov 1737 by Jedidiah Alexander, JP: Robert Story. Rec: 8 Nov 1737. Wm. Knight, Clerk.

P. 355   Deed.   Anthony Dushene of St. Georges Hundred, Newcastle Co. upon Delaware, yeoman, for 66 acres of land and marsh (which John Anderson agreed to convey to him before his death in an agreement dated 9 Mar 1736/7 in exchange for 100 acres called Successor lying opposite on the shore), to Jacob Anderson, John Anderson, and James Anderson of the same place, sons and heirs of John Anderson of the same place, deceased, all that marsh on the west side and near the head of Elk River contained within the west line of a tract called Price's Venture now in the possession of Anthony Dushene. Land to be divided amongst them as their father directed. Made 26 Aug 1737. Wit: Willm. Deoran, Rachell Kelly. Ackn: 3 Oct 1737 by Anthony and his wife Jemima. JP: Jno. Copson. Rec: 10 Nov 1737. Wm. Knight, Clerk.

P. 356   Deed.   Anthony Dushene of St. Georges Hundred, Newcastle Co. upon Delaware, yeoman, and Jemima his wife, for 66 acres of land and marsh adjoining said Anthony's now dwelling plantation in exchange for 100 acres [see previous entry]except for 6 acres which was sold to Hollingsworth where John Kinkey's mill now stands), to Jacob Anderson, John Anderson, and James Anderson of the same place, sons and heirs of John Anderson of the same place, deceased, 100 acres of land in Cecil Co. in the fork of Elk River, part of a tract called Successor. John Anderson made his Last Will and Testament some time before he agreed to exchange lands with Dushene, and did not alter the Will because his sudden death prevented it. Made 26 Aug 1737. Wit: Willm. Deoran, Rachell Kelly. Ackn: 3 Oct 1737 by Anthony and his wife Jemima JP: Jno. Copson. Rec: 10 Nov 1737. Wm. Knight, Clerk.

P. 359   Deed.   John Ryland, Jr. of Cecil Co., innholder, for 40 shillings, to John Bennet of Georgetown, Kent Co., innholder, lot #55 in Frederick Town on the north side of Sassafras River at the intersection of Frederick Street and Prince Williams Street. Made 11 Nov 1737. Wit: Michael Wallace, Wm. Rumsey. Ackn: same day by John and his wife Rebecca. JPs: Wm. Rumsey, R'd. Thompson. Rec: 11 Nov 1737. Wm. Knight, Clerk.

P. 360   Deed.   James Husbands of Cecil Co., planter, for £122, to James Paul Heath of the same county, merchant, 2 tracts of land, one called Chance of 65 acres which was granted to John Cox on 10 Sep 1683 and the other called Stillington, adjacent to the first, on Sassafras River. Also 122 acres, part of the 2 tracts, which lies westward of the division line of the 2 tracts between William Husbands and Thomas Husbands lands and was sold by Thomas Husbands to the said James Husbands on 24 Nov 1726. Made 7 Oct 1737. Wit: John Veazey, John Ward, Jr., Pereg'n. Ward. Ackn: same day by James and his wife Alice Husbands. JPs: John Veazey, Pereg'n. Ward. Rec: 11 Nov 1737. Wm. Knight, Clerk.

P. 363   Deed.   William Husbands of Cecil Co., planter, for £80, to James Paul Heath of the same county, merchant, land which is part of 2 tracts, one called Chance of 65 acres originally granted to John Cox 10 Sep 1683, the other called Stillington originally granted to Exill Still for 160 acres which lies east of the division line between the said William Husbands land and his brother Thomas Husbands land. Made 14 Oct 1737. Wit: Edward Jackson, Thos. Johnson, Jr., John Ward, Jr. Ackn: 11 Nov 1737 by William Husbands and his wife Mary. JPs: Edward Jackson, Thos. Johnson, Jr. Also on 11 Nov

1737 James Husbands rec'd £80 from James Paul Heath. Wit: George Simco, William Ward. Rec: 11 Nov 1737. Wm. Knight, Clerk.

P. 365   Deed.   William Teague of Cecil Co., yeoman, for £61.10s, to Robert Patterson of the same county, yeoman, a tract of 50 acres of land called Dougherty's Desire on the east side of Susquehanna River by a tract sold by William Teague to Abraham Pennington. Also another 50 acre tract called Teague's Chance on the west side of Connowingo Creek by a small plantation formerly seated by Abraham Penington. By patent dated 9 Oct 1733 recorded at Annapolis in Lib. P. L. No. 8, folio 654, Lord Baltimore granted to Nathaniel Dougherty of Baltimore Co. the 50 acre tract called Dougherty's Desire. Nathaniel Dougherty sold the land to William Teague. Made & Ackn: 18 Jun 1737. Wit: R'd. Thompson, William Mitchell, John Graham. JPs: Wm. Rumsey, Robert Story. Alienation fine of 4 shillings for each tract rec'd by Jas. Paul Heath on 29 Jun 1737. Rec: 12 Nov 1737. Wm. Knight, Clerk.

P. 367   Assignment of Lease.   Thomas Beedle of Cecil Co., planter, for £2, to Abraham Alman of the same county, innholder, a lease of 100 acres of land in Bohemia Manor for the same terms and conditions as stated in the lease. By lease dated 25 Jan 1723 recorded in Lib. D. K. No. 1, folio 75, Ephraim Augustine Herman of Cecil Co., gent., leased to the said Thomas Beedle 100 acres of land in Bohemia Manor for a term of 3 lives: Thomas Beedle, his wife Elizabeth and his son William for yearly rent due every 10 Dec of £1.10s and 2 dunghill fowls. Thomas Beedle assigned the lease to Job Evertson on 18 Jun 1726 and Job Evertson assigned the lease to John Cheek on 9 Nov 1728. John Cheek assigned the lease to John Crow on 12 Mar 1728/9, recorded in Lib. S. K. No. 5, folio 195. John Crow has since died intestate and his widow and administratrix married William Brown. Then, on 23 Mar 1735/6, for £28, William and Martha Brown conveyed the lease to Abraham Alman. Because most of these assignments of the lease were not duly acknowledged and recorded, some doubts as to the title to the premises arose. Made & Ackn: 12 Nov 1737. Wit: Wm. Rumsey, R'd. Thompson. JPs: R'd. Thompson, Wm. Knight. Rec: 14 Nov 1737. Wm. Knight, Clerk.

P. 369   Commission of the Peace.   Charles Lord Baltimore appoints as Justices of the Peace for Cecil County Richard Tilghman, Matthew Tilghman Ward, John Rousby, Benjamin Tasker, Philip Lee, John Rider, Michael Howard, George Plater, Edmund Jenings, James Holyday, Charles Hammond, Thomas Colvill, Edward Jackson, Richard Thompson, William Rumsey, Thomas Johnson, Andrew Barry, John Veazey, Robert Story and

Peregrine Ward. Made 15 Aug 1737. Signed in the margin by Samuel Ogle, Lt. General and Chief Governor. Rec: 14 Nov 1737. Wm. Knight, Clerk.

P. 373   Deed.   Richard Bennett of Queen Annes Co., merchant, to George Hall of Kent Co., planter and guardian of his son John, a minor, for the benefit of the son John, 304 acres of land, part of a tract called Cox's Purchase in Cecil Co. on the north side of Sassafras River, lately purchased by Richard Bennett from Benjamin Cox, being all the remainder part of the tract not already sold by Benjamin Cox to Philip Barrett. The remainder of Cox's Purchase is in exchange for a tract called Terson's Neglect in Kent Co. on the south side of Sassafras River given by the Last Will and Testament of John Hall, father of the said George Hall, to his grandson John Hall, son of George, under the name of Terson's Neck for 160 acres. Made 24 Nov 1737. Wit: John Lockerman [Sockerman?], J. Beck. Ackn: 1 Dec 1737. JPs: Aug. Thompson, F.H. Wright. R'd. Tilghman, Jr., Clerk of Queen Annes Co. On 30 Nov 1737 alienation fine of 12 shillings rec'd by Jas. Paul Heath. Rec: 15 Dec 1737. Wm. Knight, Clerk.

P. 375   Deed.   Edward Drewry of Philadelphia, PA, gent., for £120, to William Boulding of Cecil Co., planter, 200 acres of land, part of a tract called Knowlwood on Elk River at Shallop Cove. This is part of the land devised by Francis Smith in his Last Will and Testament to his sister Sarah Pierce, the wife of Henry Pierce. [Name also spelled Drury.] Made 2 Dec 1737. Wit: John Veazey, Henry Ward. Ackn: same day by William Boulding, Jr. JPs: John Veazey, Pereg'n. Ward. Alienation fine of 8 shillings rec'd by Jas. Paul Heath on 26 Dec 1737. Rec: same day. Wm. Knight, Clerk.

P. 377   Deed.   James Lattemore of Cecil Co., planter, for £4 to William Hutchinson of the same county, merchant, lot #50 in Frederick Town [Lattemore is also called Lattomus.] Made 11 Jan 1737. Wit. & JPs: John Veazey, Pereg'n. Ward. Ackn: 11 Jan 1737/8 by James Lattemore and his wife Diana. Rec: 16 Jan 1737. Wm. Knight, Clerk.

P. 378   Release.   Richard Lewis of Cecil Co., planter, to Peter Bowyer and Esther his wife of the same county, to settle a dispute between Lewis and Bowyer as to the title and dividing line of a tract of 230 acres called John's Delight. Said land is part of St. John's Manor and by the Last Will and Testament of Richard Lewis, Sr., deceased, was devised to his sons the said Richard Lewis, Jr. and John Lewis, now deceased, to be equally divided between them after the death of their mother (who has since died.) Richard Lewis and Peter Bowyer made a bonded agreement dated 18 Feb 1736 for £100 arbitrated by Thomas Johnson, Nicholas Hyland and William Rumsey of Cecil Co., gents., who made their determination on 23 Feb 1736. They said that Richard Lewis will, within 4 months, make a deed of partition releasing to Esther Bowyer his estate right to the northernmost moiety of the land by Thomas Hitchcock's land and by Elk River containing 110 acres, which by a survey now made is found to be half of the tract. This is to be Esther Bowyer's land for the rest of her natural life and after her death to John Lewis, son of John Lewis, deceased, according to the intent of the Last Will and Testament dated 13 Nov 1735 [of John Lewis.] Peter Bowyer and Esther will, within 4 months, make a deed of partition releasing to Richard Lewis the southernmost moiety of the tract by the lands that belonged to Christopher Mounts and up Elk River and containing 110 acres. Since the buildings which belonged to John Lewis, deceased, are on the southern moiety of the land, the arbitrators have judged that on or by 1 Apr 1738 the said Richard Lewis shall pay to Peter Bowyer and Esther the sum of £25 to enable them to build and improve the northern moiety of the land. Now the 4 months time period for executing the deed of partitions has elapsed, and by mutual agreement, Richard Lewis releases to Peter and Esther Bower the northern moiety of the land and after her death to John Lewis, son of the deceased John Lewis. Made 4 Oct 1737. Wit: Sam'l. Young, Jno. Copson. Ackn: same day. JP: Jno. Copson. Rec: 19 Jan 1737. Wm. Knight, Clerk.

P. 381   Release.   Peter Bowyer and his wife Esther, executrix and devisee of the Last Will and Testament of John Lewis, late of Cecil Co., deceased, to Richard Lewis of Cecil Co., planter, to settle a dispute [see previous entry for details.] Now Peter Bowyer and his wife Esther release to Richard Lewis the southernmost moiety of the tract of land called John's Delight, part of St. John's Manor, containing 110 acres. [Bowyer is also spelled Boyer.] Made 4 Oct 1737. Wit: Sam'l. Young, Jno. Copson. Ackn: same day. JP: Jno. Copson. Rec: 19 Jan 1737. Wm. Knight, Clerk.

P. 385   Deed.   Philip Jobson of Kent Co., planter, for £70, to Philip Stoops of Cecil Co., planter, 87 acres, the north part of a tract of land called Happy Harbor. John Jobson, late of Cecil Co., chirurgeon, deceased, owned 174 acres of the Happy Harbor tract which was originally patented on 10 Apr 1671 to Richard Leak for 400 acres. By his Last Will and Testament proved before Matthias Vanderheyden of Cecil Co. on 30 Dec 1713 he devised in these words "I give unto my son Philip Jobson all that part or parcel of land which I bought of Quinton Crafford being the north part of land for to have and to hold for him and his heirs forever." Made 29 Oct 1737. Wit. & JPs: John Veazey, Pereg'n. Ward. Ackn: same day by Philip and his wife Ann Jobson. Alienation fine rec'd by Jas. Paul Heath 10 Nov 1737 from Philip Stoopes. Rec: 1 Feb 1737. Wm. Knight, Clerk.

P. 387   Deed.   John McManus of Cecil Co., attorney, for £10 and 722 lbs of tobacco, to Valentine Sillcock of the said county, glasiour [glazier?], 2 lots on the north side of Sassafras River in James Town also called Oald Town. Said lots adjoin the lot formerly owned by Miles Godment and now in the possession of James Wallace. John McManus acquired these lots by the Last Will and Testament of Maj. John Dowdall, deceased. Made 21 Jan 1737. Wit: John Coppin, Wm. Davis, Bryan Eagleson. Ackn: 24 Jan 1737 by John and his wife Elizabeth McManus. JPs: R'd. Thompson, John Veazey. Rec: 2 Feb 1737. Wm. Knight, Clerk.

P. 388   Release.   Christopher Hendrickson of Cecil Co., planter, to William Rumsey of the same county, gent., 92½ acres of land, part of a tract of land called Jamaica except for the part of the land mentioned in a deed made between Alexander Maver of Cecil Co., surgeon, and his wife Esther to Henry Hendrickson of the said county, planter, dated 25 Aug 1721 [see June D. Brown, *Abstracts of Cecil County, Maryland Land Records 1673-1751* (Westminster, MD: Family Line Publications, 1998) pg 142, entry P. 376.] By mortgage dated 25 Feb 1731 Christopher Hendrickson, for £15 and 5,000 lbs of tobacco, mortgaged to William Rumsey the tract of land called Jamaica in Sassafras Neck. The repayment of the mortgage is past due and Hendrickson is not able to pay Rumsey. Made 2 Jan 1737. Wit: John Johnson, Judith Blidenburgh. Ackn: 5 Jan 1737. JPs: John Veazey, Pereg'n. Ward. Alienation fine of 3s.8½p rec'd from Mr. Rumsey by Jas. Paul Heath 30 Jan 1737. Rec: 2 Feb 1737. Wm. Knight, Clerk.

P. 390   Deed.   Fouch Davis of Cecil Co., planter, for £50, to Thomas Davis of the same county, planter, a tract of 57 acres called Mary's Joynture south of a tract called King's Delight on a branch of Back Creek, during the natural life of the said Fouch Davis. Made & Ackn: 28 Jan 1737. Wit: John Clark, Mary Penington, John Ward, Jr. JPs: Wm. Rumsey, Pereg'n. Ward. Alienation fine of 2s.3½p rec'd same day from Thomas Davis by Jas. Paul Heath. Rec: 9 Feb 1737. Wm. Knight, Clerk.

P. 392   Deed.   William Rye of Cecil Co., planter, for £18, to Thomas Davis of the same county, planter, land on Sassafras River near the head of Back Creek being the middle 100 acres of a tract called the Levell by land formerly belonging to Thomas Linsey but now owned by the said Thomas Davis. Made & Ackn: 5 Jan 1737. Wit: Wm. Rumsey, John Veazey, John Ward, Jr. JPs: Wm. Rumsey, John Veazey. Alienation fine of 2 shillings rec'd from Thomas Davis by Jas. Paul Heath 28 Jan 1737. Rec: 9 Feb 1737. Wm. Knight, Clerk.

P. 394 Deed. John Winterberry of Cecil Co., planter, for £55, to John Beedle of the said county, planter, 50 acres of land which was devised to him by the Last Will and Testament of William Veazey, late of Cecil Co., deceased, dated 14 Apr 1733 in these words: "I give and bequeath to John Winterbeary all that parcel of land belonging to me being part of a tract of land called True Game lying on the south side of the head of Capt. John's Creek to be held by the said John Winterbury his heirs and assigns forever." Made 7 Oct 1737. Wit. & JPs: John Veazey, Pereg'n. Ward. Ackn: same day by John and his wife Mary Winterbury. Alienation fine of 1 shilling rec'd from John Beedle by Jas. Paul Heath on 31 Oct 1737. Rec: 17 Feb 1737. Wm. Knight, Clerk.

P. 395 Deed. John Baldwin, lately sheriff of Cecil Co., to William Alexander of said county, gent., a tract of land called the Inspection. The estate of John Smith, formerly sheriff of Cecil Co., was exposed to sale for the benefit of his creditors by the then sheriff John Baldwin. One of the sale items was a 100 acre tract of land called the Inspection for which the certificate was returned in John Smith's name, but no patent was issued. The land was sold at auction to Richard Dowdall for which Dowdall was to pay £22.10s. Dowdall never paid the money. Robert Alexander was a large creditor of the said John Smith and his debt has not yet been satisfied. Robert Alexander, now deceased, made his cousin William Alexander his executor of his Last Will and Testament. Made & Ackn: 23 Feb 1737. Wit: John Ward, Jr., Moses Andrews. JPs: A. Barry, Robert Story. Rec: 27 Feb 1737. Wm. Knight, Clerk.

P. 397 Assignment of Lease. Written on the back of a lease from Col. Ephraim Augustine Herman to James Maccay: Thomas Cowan and his wife Rosanah, for £52, assigns the lease to Robert Withers. Made 14 Jan 1737. Rosanah Cowan made her mark with an "A." Wit: John Harper (Smith), James Read. Ackn: 21 Jan 1737. JPs: R'd. Thompson, Wm. Rumsey. Rec: 11 Mar 1737. Wm. Knight, Clerk.

P. 397 Release. Christopher Hendrickson of Cecil Co., planter, son of Mary, the eldest daughter of Thomas Kilton, late of said county, deceased, and John Jobson, son of Esther, the other daughter of Thomas Kilton, to William Rumsey of the same county, gent., for sums of money and tobacco already paid and expended by William Rumsey, for services he has performed and for £5, 2 tracts of land already in Rumsey's possession: the 200 acre tract called Withers and the 300 acre tract called Bayley.

By deed dated 26 Apr 1701, Thomas Whitton and his wife Ruth, for 6,769 lbs of tobacco, mortgaged to the said Thomas Kilton, a tract of 200 acres called Withers near land formerly belonging to John Wheeler and a tract of 300 acres called Bayley adjoining Withers. Whitton was to repay Kilton on the next 25 Nov, but it does not appear the said sum of tobacco was ever repaid. Regardless of the unpaid mortgage, Thomas Whitton sold the 200 acres called Withers to Isaac Hargrave by deed dated 3 Jul 1703, and as the said Hargrave has since died, the land became escheat to the Lord Proprietary of Maryland. William Rumsey, at considerable charge, has obtained a special warrant of escheat and resurvey of the land. Richard Whitton, son and heir of Thomas Whitton, for £75, sold the 300 acres called Bayley to William Rumsey by deed dated 27 Jun 1728. Christopher Hendrickson and Thomas Kilton are the true and legal heirs of Thomas Kilton. Made 5 Jan 1737. Wit. & JPs: John Veazey, Pereg'n. Ward. Ackn: 5 Jan by Hendrickson and 17 Feb by John Jobson. Rec: 28 Feb 1737. Wm. Knight, Clerk.

P. 399 Deed. Charles Carroll of Annapolis, esq., for £90, to James Armstrong and Archibald Armstrong of Cecil Co., farmers, land in Cecil Co. called Addition said by the grant recorded in Lib. E. I. No. 1, folio 160, to contain 300 acres. Made 22 Dec 1737. Wit: Geo. Stewart, La. Maynard. Ackn: 23 Dec 1737. JP: Robert Gordon. Rec: 14 Mar 1737. Wm. Knight, Clerk. Jas. Paul Heath rec'd 12 shilling alienation fine from James Armstrong on 31 Dec 1737.

P. 401 Lease. Robert Holy of Cecil Co., to John Williams of said county, laborer, and his wife Mary, for yearly rents and agreements, 30 acres of land, part of a tract called Hopewell on the west side of Little Elk River. Lease is for the term of the natural lives of the said John and Mary Williams. Yearly rent of 20 shillings due every 1 March. John Williams will clear no more than 20 acres. Made & Ackn: 14 Mar 1738. Wit: Sarah McElroy, Mary Barry, A. Barry. JPs: A. Barry, Edward Jackson. Rec: same day. Wm. Knight, Clerk.

P. 402 Assignment of Lease. On the back of a lease from Col. Ephraim Augustine Herman to Obadiah Holt recorded 10 Jun 1731 in Lib. S. K. No. 5, folios 349-350, the said Obadiah Holt assigns the lease to Peter Polson for 5 shillings. Made & Ackn: 2 Feb 1737. Wit: Tho. Colvill. JPs: Tho. Colvill, Robert Story. Rec: 17 Mar 1737. Wm. Knight, Clerk.

P. 402 Assignment of Lease. On the back of a lease from William Sinclars execs. to Obadiah Holt recorded 10 Jun 1731 in Lib. S. K. No. 5, folios 348-349, Obadiah Holt assigns all his interest in the lease to Peter Polson for

5 shillings. Made & Ackn: 2 Feb 1737. Wit: Tho. Colvill. JPs: Tho. Colvill, Robert Story. Rec: 17 Mar 1737. Wm. Knight, Clerk.

P. 403   Valuation of Estate.   At the request of Thomas Boulding, guardian of Joseph Lowman, an orphan of Cecil Co., Zebulon Hollingsworth and William Currier, sworn in by JP Andrew Barry, viewed the land and plantation of the late Samuel Lowman, deceased, and found a house of squared logs 20x15 feet with fireplaces above and below and brick oven but much out of repair; another log house 22x15 feet and an entry between this and another adjoining 11-foot wide frame house and a stack of chimneys with 3 fireplaces. All the said houses have middling good joists and floors but very bad roofs with 3 closets and doors to all and a cellar 16x15 feet, stoned wall, some of it fallen down, not worth repairing. Another log house 10x8 feet with a good clapboard roof; a corn house of square logs 19x6 feet; a small barn with square logs 14x11 feet with a good roof; a house office; a straggling orchard of 20 odd apple trees and 8 English cherry trees; about 36 acres cleared land, badly fenced. They estimate the yearly income of the plantation to be 1,000 lbs of tobacco. The little plantation, which has one squared log house 15x12 feet, a cellar 11x9 feet, they estimate its yearly value as 300 lbs of tobacco. Made 19 Nov 1737. Wit: A. Barry. Rec: 17 Mar 1737. Wm. Knight, Clerk.

P. 404   Deed.   Peter Bouchell of Cecil Co., gent., for £10 and because he is moving, to James Bayard of said county, merchant, 100 acres of land, part of Bohemia Manor, the easternmost part of the neck of land formerly conveyed by Samuel Bayard and Henry Sluyter to Peter Sluyter alias Vorsman and bounded on the south by Bohemia River, on the east by land which belonged to John Moll but now belongs to James Vanbebber and on the north and west by land that belonged to Vorsman. Made & Ackn: 17 Mar 1737. Wit: Jos. George, John Baldwin. JPs: Wm. Rumsey, A. Barry. Rec: same day. Wm. Knight, Clerk.

P. 405   Lease.   James Bayard of Cecil Co., merchant, for £10 and because he is moving, to Peter Bouchell of the same county, gent., 100 acres of land, part of Bohemia Manor, the easternmost part of a neck of land formerly conveyed by Samuel Bayard and Henry Sluyter to Peter Sluyter alias Vorsman [same description as in previous entry P. 404.] Rent of 10 shillings to be paid 23 Mar yearly at the dwelling house of James Bayard. Made & Ackn: 18 Mar 1737. Wit: Hugh Matthews, Jos. George. JPs: Wm. Rumsey, Pereg'n. Ward. Rec: same day. Wm. Knight, Clerk.

P. 406   Deed.   Thomas Colvill of Cecil Co., gent., to James Hughes of the same county, planter, for £1.17s.6p and an agreement that James Hughes will build a house on lot #21 which Thomas Colvill has taken up in Frederick Town on the north side of Sassafras River. The house will cover 400 sq ft and have a brick chimney. In return, Thomas Colvill gives to James Hughes the western moiety of the lot, across from George's Alley, with the buildings already made by James Hughes. Made 17 Mar 1737. Wit: Wm. Rumsey, Wm. Knight. Ackn: 18 Mar 1737. JPs: Wm. Rumsey, John Veazey. Rec: same day. Wm. Knight, Clerk.

P. 408   Assignment of Lease.   John Segar of Cecil Co., to John Holland and John Lusby of Cecil Co., in return for Holland and Lusby having made bail for Segar in 2 actions of debt in Cecil County Court between John McCullough, administrator of Tole McCullough, plaintiff, and the said Segar, defendant, for £20 and for £8.14s.6p, assigns to Holland and Lusby a lease of land for the terms and lives stated in the said lease. Made & Ackn: 18 Mar 1737. Wit. & JPs: Wm. Rumsey, A. Barry. Rec: 18 Mar 1737. Wm. Knight, Clerk.

P. 408   Assignment of Lease.   Written on the back of a lease dated 1 May 1728 recorded in Lib. S. K. No. 5, folios 138-139 from Ephraim Augustine Herman to Rene Julien: Rene Julien, for £40, to Henry McCay, the within lease of land for the terms and lives stated in the lease. Made & Ackn: 15 Mar 1737. Wit: Hugh Walker, Thos. Yorkson. JPs: Edward Jackson, A. Barry. Rec: 24 Mar 1737. Wm. Knight, Clerk.

P. 409   Deed.   Nicholas Dorrell of Cecil Co., planter, and Elizabeth his wife, for £45, to Benjamin Wimsley of the same place, farmer, 166 acres and 120 perches of land, part of a tract called New Munster by the main branch of Elk River. Made & Ackn: 24 Mar 1738. Wit. & JPs: John Veazey, Pereg'n. Ward. Ben. Wimsley paid the alienation fine on 23 Apr 1738 to Jas. Paul Heath. Rec: 25 Mar 1738. Wm. Knight, Clerk.

P. 412   Deed.   Nicholas Dorrell of Cecil Co., planter, and Elizabeth his wife, for £45, to Hugh Ross of the same place, farmer, 166 acres and 106 perches of land [later in the deed it says 120 perches], part of a tract called New Munster on Elk River on the west side of its main branch. Nicholas Dorrell will defend the land against any claims of the heirs of John Vansant. Made & Ackn: 24 Mar 1738. Wit. & JPs: John Veazey, Pereg'n. Ward. Rec: 25 Mar 1738. Wm. Knight, Clerk.

P. 415   Assignment of Lease.   John Seagar of Cecil Co., planter, for £100, to John Holland of the same county, merchant, 2 leases of land in Bohemia Manor for the terms and conditions stated within the 2 leases. By lease dated

21 Jan 1726, Ephraim Augustine Herman of Cecil Co., gent., leased to James Calder of the same county, merchant, ½ an acre of land in Bohemia Manor on Bohemia River at Ferry Point where Bohemia Ferry is now kept and by _____ Mason's lot. Lease was for the term of 3 natural lives and 5 shillings rent due every 10 May. By another lease dated 12 Apr 1727, Ephraim Augustine Herman leased to John Seagar 100 acres of land in Bohemia Manor on Bohemia River by _____ Mason's lot. Lease was for the term of 3 natural lives and rent of £3 and 2 dunghill fowls due every 23 Nov. John Seagar endorsed this lease claiming that the point of land leased to James Calder and the fenced wheat field belonging to Herman should be forever disclaimed. James Calder had assigned his lease to John Seagar on 14 Aug 1736. Made 24 Mar 1737. Wit. & JPs: Tho. Colvill, Wm. Rumsey. Ackn: 1 Apr 1738. Rec: 1 Apr 1738. Wm. Knight, Clerk.

P. 418 Release. Col. John Ward of Cecil Co., gent., made a deed of gift to his son Thomas Ward for 200 acres of land, part of a tract called Colleton in Cecil County. Since Thomas Ward has since died, his son Peregrine Ward became heir of the said land. Peregrine Ward and his wife Mary oblige themselves and their heirs to Col. John Ward and his wife Mary to occupy the plantation during their natural lives. Made 5 Apr 1737. Wit: Wm. Rumsey, John Veazey. Rec: 7 Apr 1738. Wm. Knight, Clerk.

P. 418 Assignment of Lease. Henry McCay of Cecil Co., planter, to Robert Withers of said county, blacksmith, a lease of land which was formerly occupied by John Dehoof and then leased to James McCay (except 15 acres) according to the terms and conditions of the said lease. By lease dated 10 Aug 1731, Ephraim Augustine Herman leased to James McCay 140 acres of land (this land formerly belonged to John Dehoof) for the term of the natural lives of the said James, his sister Rosannah and James McCay, son of the said Henry McCay for 40 shillings and 2 dunghill fowls due every 10 Dec. James McCay the leasee, has since died and by his Last Will and Testament dated 9 Feb 1733 he bequeathed the leased land to Rosannah McCay during her lifetime and at her decease to Henry McCay if Henry's son James should survive and live longer than Rosannah. Rosannah and her husband Thomas Cowan, for £52, assigned their right and interest in the land to Robert Withers, who is now in possession of the land. Henry McCay has recently purchased from Rene Julien another tenement of land in Bohemia Manor which is adjacent to the land leased to James McCay and is very inconvenient for want of water. Robert Withers, for £50, has agreed and assigned 15 acres of his land to Henry McCay, which land includes a small branch of water. Made & Ackn: 30 Mar 1738. Wit: Hugh Matthews, Wm.

Rumsey. JPs: Wm. Rumsey, R'd. Thompson. Rec: 10 Apr 1738. Wm. Knight, Clerk.

P. 421   Deed of Gift.   Peregrine Frisby of Cecil Co., gent., for 5 shillings and for the brotherly love and affection he has for James Frisby, to James Frisby of the same county, the northernmost moiety of a tract of land called Frisby's Meadows on the north side of Sassafras River (where the said Peregrine now lives.) Made & Ackn: 12 Apr 1738. Wit. & JPs: John Veazey, Pereg'n. Ward. Rec: 12 Apr 1738. Wm. Knight, Clerk.

P. 422   Deed.   John Williams of Cecil Co., feltmaker, and his wife Mary, for £100, to Thomas Shepherd of Cecil Co., planter, 284 acres of land called Roycraft's Choice. A tract of 300 acres called Roycraft's Choice on the northeast side of Susquehanna River originally granted to John Roycraft of Cecil Co. was claimed by 2 of his granddaughters as co-partners and with their then husbands Francis January and Josias Ward, by separate deeds, conveyed the tract to the said John Williams who obtained a warrant for a resurvey of the land and a patent dated 24 Aug 1736. Made 14 Mar 1737. Wit. & JPs: R'd. Thompson, A. Barry. Ackn: 15 Mar 1737. Alienation fine of 11s.4½p collected from Thomas Shepherd by Jas. Paul Heath on 5 Apr 1738. Rec: 14 Apr 1738. Wm. Knight, Clerk.

P. 424   Deed.   John Williams of Cecil Co., feltmaker, and his wife Mary, for £200, to Thomas Shepherd of Cecil Co., planter, a 500 acre tract called Anchor & Hope. The tract of 500 of acres called Anchor & Hope on the northeast side of Susquehanna River was granted by patent to Daniel Carnall of St. Marys Co. and by his Last Will and Testament devised the land to his wife Deborah Carnall who also died and left the land to her 3 daughters Mary (now the wife of James Dawson), Ann (the late relic of James Lloyd) and Deborah (the now wife of John Hawkins.) By separate deeds, they all conveyed the land to the said John Williams. Made 14 Mar 1737. Wit. & JPs: R'd. Thompson, A. Barry. Ackn: 15 Mar 1737. Thos. Shepperd paid the alienation fine of 20 shillings to Jas. Paul Heath on 5 Apr 1738. Rec: 14 Apr 1738. Wm. Knight, Clerk.

P. 426   Release.   John Jobson of Cecil Co., planter, for the respect he has for his cousin Christopher Hendrickson and in justice to William Rumsey and for 20 shillings, releases to William Rumsey of the same county, gent., a tract of land called Jamaica (except that part of the land conveyed in a deed made by Alexander Maver and Esther his wife, the mother of the said John Jobson, to Henry Hendrickson of Cecil Co., planter, dated 25 Aug 1721.) By deed dated 2 Jan 1737 Christopher Hendrickson, the son of Mary, the eldest daughter of Thomas Kilton, deceased, for £20.9s.6p and 7,467 lbs of tobacco, for a mortgage dated 25 Feb 1731 he made to William Rumsey and was unable to pay, conveyed to William Rumsey a tract of land called Jamaica. This land of 185 acres was originally granted to Thomas Kilton. The said John Jobson is the son of Esther, the other daughter of Thomas Kilton (who is also deceased but was joint heir with her eldest sister Mary, since deceased.) John Jobson is satisfied that the money due on the said mortgage is the full value of the tract of land. Made 17 Feb 1737. Wit. & JPs: John Veazey, Pereg'n. Ward. Ackn: same day by John Jobson, eldest son of Esther Jobson, deceased. The alienation fine for 92½ acres, the moiety of Jamaica, was 3s.8½p paid by William Rumsey 20 Feb 1737 to Jas. Paul Heath. Rec: 24 Apr 1738. Wm. Knight, Clerk.

P. 428 Deed. Thomas Rickets of Cecil Co., blacksmith, and Mary his wife, for £120, to Richard Lewis of the same county, farmer, a tract of land called Tryall in Cecil Co. Charles Lord Baltimore granted to Robert Hodgson of Cecil Co. by patent signed by Richard Tilghman, Keeper of the Seal, dated 10 Jul 1725 recorded at Annapolis in Lib. P. L. No. 6, folio 220, one acre [sic] of land called Tryall by a tract laid out for John Browning and Richard Marsh called Successor. Robert Hodgson sold the tract called Tryall to said Thomas Rickets by deed dated 26 Apr 1728 and recorded 30 Apr 1728 in Lib. S. K. No. 5, folios 132-133. Made & Ackn: 7 Jan 1737/8. Wit: Rachell Kelly and JP Jno. Copson. Alienation fine for the within 100 acres of land was rec'd by Jas. Paul Heath from Richard Lewis on 20 Jan 1737. Rec: 28 Apr 1738. Wm. Knight, Clerk.

P. 430 Deed. Alexander Boulding of Cecil Co., for £35, to Thomas Beetle of the same county, a plantation of 50 acres, part of a tract called Uppermost. Part of the tract was sold to Thomas Price, Jr. and the remainder of the tract which belonged to Alexander Boulding was sold to the said Thomas Beetle. Made 15 Feb 1737. Wit: Jno. Copson, Thomas Price. Ackn: 16 Feb 1737/8. JP: Jno. Copson. The alienation fine of 2 shillings was paid on 20 Feb 1737 to Jas. Paul Heath. Rec: 28 Apr 1738. Wm. Knight, Clerk.

P. 431 Deed. Richard Nash of Cecil Co., for £55 and because he is moving, to Andrew Alexander of the same county, 125 acres of land already in said Alexander's possession, by land formerly sold to Robert Patton by Thomas Stratton, part of 2 tracts, one called Hispaniola formerly released by William Richardson to Samuel Alexander and the other tract called Bullen's Range, adjacent to Hispaniola, purchased by the said Samuel from the Lord Proprietary and recorded at Annapolis. The said 125 acres is part of a parcel formerly sold and released to Thomas Stratton by Samuel Alexander by deed of release dated 20 Mar 1729 and conveyed to Richard Nash by Thomas Stratton by deed of release dated 15 Apr 1735. Made 20 Apr 1738. Wit: Jno. Copson, Rachell Kelly. Ackn: same day by Richard and his wife Elizabeth Nash. JP: Jno. Copson. On 21 Apr 1738 Andrew Alexander paid the alienation fine of 5 shillings to Jas. Paul Heath. Rec: 28 Apr 1738. Wm. Knight, Clerk.

P. 433   Assignment of Lease.   George Scott of Kent Co., cordwainer, for £50, to William Knight of Cecil Co., gent., a lease of 126 acres of land called Scott's Tanyard, except what is set aside for the use of Walter Scott, for the terms and conditions in the lease. By a lease dated 26 Mar 1722, Ephraim Augustine Herman of Cecil Co., gent., leased to Walter Scott of the same county, cordwainer, 126 acres of land called Scott's Tanyard, part of Middle Neck or Little Bohemia Manor, on St. Augustine's Creek and by tracts called Clifton, Arsmore and Heath's Fifth Parcel. Lease was for the term of 3 natural lives and yearly rent of 18 shillings and 2 dunghill fowls due every 23 Nov. Walter Scott assigned the lease 10 Mar 1731 to his son George Scott, reserving to himself for his natural life the free use of the back house, the mill and half the tanyard. Made & Ackn: 1 May 1738. Wit: S. Knight, Pereg'n. Frisby. JP: Stephen Knight. Rec: 2 May 1738. Wm. Knight, Clerk.

P. 436   Deed.   Michael Jobson of Kent Co., cordwainer, for £80, to Phillip Stoops of Cecil Co., planter, 100 acres of land, part of a tract called Civility. By deed dated 10 Mar 1714, Henry Penington of Cecil Co., planter, and his wife Elizabeth, for 6,000 lbs of tobacco, sold to John Jobson of said county, chirurgeon, a tract of 100 acres, part of a tract called Civility on the north side of Sassafras River by Back Creek and by a tract of land called Happy Harbor formerly belonging to Henry Penington, deceased. By his Last Will and Testament proved 30 Dec 1713 [sic] by Matthias Vanderheyden, John Jobson bequeathed the tract to his son Michael Jobson. Made & Ackn: 24 Apr 1738. Wit. & JPs: John Veazey, Pereg'n. Ward. On 26 Apr 1738 Philip Stoops paid to Jas. Paul Heath 4 shillings alienation fine for the within 100 acres, part of a tract called Happy Harbor [sic.] Rec: 2 May 1738. Wm. Knight, Clerk.

P. 438   Deed.   Alexander Boulding of Cecil Co., and Mary his wife, for £35, to Thomas Price, Jr. of the same county, the plantation and 100 acres of land already in the possession of the said Thomas Price, Jr. by Richard Boulding's land and by the southeast corner of a tract called Uppermost. Made 14 Nov 1737. Wit: Jno. Copson, John Hatham. Ackn: 16 Feb 1737/8. JP: Jno. Copson. Alienation fine of 2 shillings rec'd by Jas. Paul Heath on 20 Nov 1737. Rec: 3 May 1738. Wm. Knight, Clerk.

P. 440   Deed.   William Rennalds and Edward Rennalds of Cecil Co., planters, for £140, to Joshua George of the same county, gent., 195 acres of land, part of a tract called Sarah's Joynture lying southward of Herman's Branch or Mill Branch. Made 28 Apr 1738. Wit: Will Alexander, Robert Story. JP: S. Knight. Alienation fine of 7 shillings rec'd by Jas. Paul Heath 1 May 1738. Rec: 5 May 1738. Wm. Knight, Clerk.

P. 441   Deed.   Richard Lewis of Cecil Co., planter, eldest son of Richard Lewis of the said county, deceased, for £120, to Thomas Rickets of the same county, blacksmith, 110 acres of land now in the possession of the said Thomas Rickets, part of St. John's Manor on the west side of Elk River near the mouth of Cockerell's Creek. Richard Lewis will warrant the land against any claims of the heirs of his brother John Lewis, deceased. Made & Ackn: 7 Jan 1737/8. Wit: Rachell Kelly, John Copson. JP: Jno. Copson. Alienation fine of 4s.5p rec'd by Jas. Paul Heath 20 Jan 1737 and 2½ shillings quit rents will be due next Lady Day 1738. Rec: 13 May 1738. Wm. Knight, Clerk.

P. 443   Assignment of Lease.   Enoch Jenkins, for £60, assigns his rights to a lease to Robert Withers on 20 May 1738. This lease for land in Bohemia Manor was originally made by Ephraim Augustine Herman to George Steil and recorded in Lib. J. D. No. 3, folios 343-344. George Steil assigned the lease to Enoch Jenkins 16 Mar 1726. Wit: ___win [not clear], John Jenkins. Ackn: 14 Jun 1738. JPs: Robert Story, Pereg'n. Ward. Rec: 23 May 1738. Wm. Knight, Clerk. [Two leases to George Stile which appear to be for the same land are recorded 2 years apart in earlier deed books. For abstracts, see June D. Brown, *Abstracts of Cecil County Maryland Land Records 1673-1751* (Westminster, MD: Family Line Publications, 1998) pg 135, entry P. 286 and pg 160, entry P. 524.]

P. 444   Deed.   Philip Edwards of Cecil Co., planter, for £25, to Dennis Nowland of the same county, planter, a moiety of a 115 acres, part of a tract called Dayley's Desire devised to him by the Last Will and Testament of his deceased father. Made & Ackn: 12 Apr 1738. Wit: John Bubenheim, James Bayard. JPs: Thos. Colvill, Wm. Rumsey. Jas. Paul Heath collected the alienation fine of 2s.3½p on 15 Apr 1738. Rec: 1 Jun 1738. Wm. Knight, Clerk.

P. 445   Deed of Gift.   Thomas Harper of Cecil Co., farmer, for the natural love and affection he has for his son Jacob and for rents and services, to Jacob Harper of said county, 100 acres of land next to John Carnan's land and part of a larger tract which the said Thomas Harper holds by a lease from Col. Ephraim Augustine Herman as part of Bohemia Manor. Term is for the natural lives of John Harper and William Harper, two sons of Thomas Harper, paying 10 shillings every 10 Oct to Thomas Harper. And Jacob agrees he will not sell or transfer the lease to any one except his father or one of his brothers without their consent. Made & Ackn: 14 Jun 1738. Wit. & JPs: Wm. Rumsey, Pereg'n. Ward. Rec: same day. Wm. Knight, Clerk.

P. 447   Deed.   Henry Penington, Sr. of Cecil Co., planter, and his wife Rebecca, for £10, to John Bennet of George Town, Kent Co., innholder, lot #55 in Frederick Town on the north side of Sassafras River on Frederick Street. Made & Ackn: 20 Jun 1738. Wit. & JPs: Wm. Rumsey, Per. Ward. On 24 Jun 1738 Jas. Paul Heath collected 1 penny alienation fine for the lot. Rec: 24 Jun 1738. Wm. Knight, Clerk.

P. 448   Deed.   John Veazey of Cecil Co., gent., and Rebecca his wife, for £100, to Col. John Ward of the same county, 100 acres of land on the west side of Harbor Creek being the easternmost boundary of a 500 acre tract called Pain's Lot formerly belonging to John Atkey. Made & Ackn: 11 May 1738. Wit. & JPs: R'd. Thompson, Thos. Johnson, Jr. Rec: 5 Jul 1738. Wm. Knight, Clerk.

P. 450   Deed.   John Baldwin of Cecil Co., gent., to Mary Thompson of said county, spinster, 100 acres of land. By deed dated 25 Apr 1729, John Baldwin bought from Matthias Matthiason alias Freeman 100 acres of land, part of 3 tracts called Corneluison, Matthiason's Point and Mattson's Range. By deed dated 12 Jan 1735, for £50 discount as part of the consideration for a tract of land called Savin's Rest, John Baldwin sold the 100 acres to Robert Thompson, who by deed of gift dated 14 Jan 1735 conveyed the land to the said Mary Thompson, saving for himself the use of the place during his natural life. It was neglected to record these last 2 deeds within the time limited by law. So the said Robert Thompson, by his Last Will and Testament dated 7 Jan 1737/8, devised the land "to my niece Mrs. Mary Thompson & her heirs that Tract of Land called Matthiason's Range some time since given her by my deed tho' not recorded, which I had in Exchange from Mr. John Baldwin for a tract called Savin's Rest both lying in Sassafras Neck in the County aforesaid." John Baldwin has agreed to transfer the title to Mary Thompson. Made & Ackn: 15 May 1738. Wit. & JPs: R'd. Thomp-son, John Veazey. Alienation fine paid 3 Jun 1738 to Jas. Paul Heath. Rec: 21 Jul 1738. Wm. Knight, Clerk.

P. 452   Deed.   Fouch Davis of Cecil Co., planter, for £5, to Henry Penington of Frederick in the same county, planter, lot #35 in Frederick Town on Sassafras River. Made & Ackn: 28 Jan 1737. Wit: John Price, Mary Price. JPs: Wm. Rumsey, Pereg'n. Ward. Rec: 24 Jul 1738. Wm. Knight, Clerk.

P. 453 Deed. John Price of Cecil Co., planter, for £5, to Henry Penington of Frederick in the same county, planter, lot #10 in Frederick Town on Sassafras River. Made 27 Jan 1737. Wit: Wm. Rumsey, Jas. Paul Heath. Ackn: next day by John and his wife Mary Price. JPs: Wm. Rumsey, Pereg'n. Ward. Rec: 24 Jul 1738. Wm. Knight, Clerk.

P. 455 Receipt. Written on the back of a defeasance from William Rumsey to Robert Penington recorded in this book folio 330, William Rumsey says on 21 Mar 1737 he received from Rachel Penington for her son Stephen Penington, son and heir at law to Robert Penington, deceased, £106, the consideration money and interest for one year. Also 6 shillings alienation fine paid to James Paul Heath and 33 shillings satisfaction for 132 lbs of tobacco charges for recording two deeds relating to the same land. Rec: 23 Aug 1738. Wm. Knight, Clerk.

P. 455 Deed. Samuel Swift of Bucks Co., PA, executor and legatee of John Swift, late of said place, deceased, for £15 and because he is moving, to Benjamin Pearce of Cecil Co., planter, 159 acres of land in Cecil Co. Charles Lord Baltimore, by patent dated 1 Jul 1701, granted to Matthew Smith a tract of 159 acres called New Intersection on Browning's branch of Bohemia River in Cecil Co. By his Last Will and Testament dated 29 May 1705 and recorded in Philadelphia, Matthew Smith devised the land to Katherine Blany of the said city. By her deed dated 18 Dec 1706, she conveyed the 159 acres to John Swift of Bucks Co., PA, and it was recorded in Cecil Co. Lib. W. H. No. 1, folios 73-74 by John Dowdall, Clerk. By his Last Will and Testament dated 17 Feb 1732/3 and recorded in Philadelphia, John Swift bequeathed all his lands and real estate to his grandson the said Samuel Swift. Samuel Swift appoints James Bayard and William Hutchinson of Cecil Co. to be his attorneys. Made 1 Jun 1738. Wit: Thos. Noxon, James Steel, Jr., James Sanders. Ackn: in Cecil Co. on 31 Jul 1738 by Thomas Noxon of Newcastle Co., gent., James Bayard and William Hutchison. JPs: Wm. Rumsey, R'd. Thompson. Received on 7 Jun 1738 by Jas. Paul Heath from Benjamin Pearce 6s4½p alienation fine. Rec: 25 Aug 1738. Wm. Knight, Clerk.

P. 458 Deed. John Severson of Cecil Co., planter, for £22, to Francis Bonner of the same county, cordwainer, 22 acres of land out of a tract formerly called Hendrickson, now called Severson's Delight, on the south side of Elk River by the easternmost corner of a tract belonging to the said Bonner called Clementson (excepting only 30 sq ft at the old graveyard for a burying ground.) Made 24 Mar 1737. Wit. & JPs: Wm. Rumsey, John Veazey. Ackn: 14 Apr 1738 by John and his wife Sarah Severson. Jas. Paul Heath rec'd the alienation fine of 11p on 14 Apr 1738. Rec: 2 Aug 1738. Wm. Knight, Clerk.

P. 459   Deed.   John Campbell of Cecil Co., gent., for £5, to John Lovering of Biddeford, County Devon, Great Britain, mariner, lot #1 in Frederick Town on the north side of Sassafras River. Made & Ackn: 7 Jul 1738. Wit: Jas. Paul Heath, Wm. Rumsey. JPs: Wm. Rumsey, Thos. Johnson, Jr. Rec: 9 Aug 1730. Wm. Knight, Clerk.

P. 461   Deed.   James Husbands of Cecil Co., planter, for £15.10s, to James Paul Heath of the same county, merchant, 16 acres of land, part of a tract of land called Hogpen Neck on the east side of a channel of Axill's Creek (sometimes called Wheeler's Creek.) Made 8 Jul 1738. Wit. & JPs: Wm. Rumsey, Thos. Johnson, Jr. Ackn: same day by James and his wife Alice Husbands. Rec: 9 Aug 1738. Wm. Knight, Clerk.

P. 462   Deed.   William Reynolds of Cecil Co., planter and eldest son and heir of John Reynolds, late of said county, deceased, for £5 and to settle a dispute, to Jacob Everdson of said county, carpenter, 125 acres, part of a tract called Sarah's Joynture. By deed of gift John Reynolds gave to his son Nicholas Reynolds part of a tract called Sarah's Joynture. He also mentioned this gift in his Will. Nicholas Reynolds sold the 125 acres of land to Jacob Everdson. Some dispute has arisen concerning the title and bounds. Made 26 Jul 1738. Wit: Ben Pearce, James Bayard. Ackn: 31 Jul 1738. JP: Wm. Rumsey. Alienation fine of 5 shillings paid same day to Jas. Paul Heath. Rec: 11 Sep 1738. Wm. Knight, Clerk.

P. 464   Mortgage.   Christian Peters of Cecil Co., gent., for £37.6s.5p sterling money of Great Britain and £23 money of MD, to James Bayard of said county, gent., a tract of 850 acres called Vanbebber's Forest in North Elk Parish. Christian Peters is to repay James Bayard within 5 years. Made & Ackn: 11 Aug 1738. Wit. & JPs: Wm. Rumsey, R'd. Thompson. John Bubenheim witnessed the exchange of money. Rec: 19 Sep 1738. Wm. Knight, Clerk.

P. 465   Assignment of Lease.   Thomas Brideing of Cecil Co., cordwainer, for £40, to Thomas Stewart of said county, planter, a lease for 150 acres in Bohemia Manor. By a lease dated 10 Mar 1732, Ephraim Augustine Herman leased to the said Thomas Brideing 150 acres in Bohemia Manor. The lease was for the terms of the natural lives of the said Thomas Brideing, his wife

Jane, and Jane's son, Alexander Waddle. Made & Ackn: 26 Jun 1738. Wit: Judith Bledenburgh, Wm. Rumsey. JPs: Wm. Rumsey, R'd. Thompson. Then on 20 Jul 1738 Thomas Stewart assigned the lease to Alexander Waddall. Wit: John McIheney, William Wilson. Ackn: 13 Nov 1738. JPs: John Veazey, Pereg'n. Ward. Rec: 15 Nov 1738. Wm. Knight, Clerk.

P. 467 Lease. William Alexander of Cecil Co., gent., leases to Robert Lucas of the same county, brass founder, 1 acre of land on Glover's Hill near the head of Elk River, part of a tract called Friendship, including the dwelling house lately built at the cost and charge of the said Robert Lucas on the north side of the main road. Lease is for the term of the natural lives of Mary Lucas (daughter of said Robert Lucas), Thomas Jacobs (son of Thomas Jacobs) and Stephen Hollingsworth (son of Zebulon Hollingsworth.) Rent of 20 shillings due ever 11 July. Made 15 Sep 1738. Wit: Jo. Wallace, Tho. Colvill. Ackn: 13 Nov 1738. JPs: Tho. Colvill, Wm. Rumsey. Rec: 16 Nov 1738. Wm. Knight, Clerk.

P. 469 Deed. William Rumsey of Cecil Co., gent., for £5, to John Thompson of the same county, yeoman, 27 perches of land, part of a tract called the Middle Parcel. Made 29 Sep 1738. Wit: Wm. Knight, John Baldwin. Ackn: 2 Nov 1738. JPs: Thos. Johnson, John Veazey. Rec: 20 Nov 1738. Wm. Knight, Clerk.

P. 469 Deed of Gift. Thomas Davis of Cecil Co., planter, and Rebecca his wife, for the natural love and affection they have for Henry Penington the Younger and also for 5 shillings, to Henry Penington, a minor and younger son of Henry Penington, Jr., and godson to the said Thomas Davis, lot #23 in Frederick Town on the north side of Sassafras River. If Henry Penington the Younger dies without heirs, then the land goes to his father and mother Henry and Mary Penington, Jr. during their natural lives and after their death the land is to return to the said Thomas Davis or his heirs. Made 24 Jun 1738. Wit: John Ward, Jr., James Hughes, Alice Hughes. Ackn: 13 Aug 1738. JPs: John Veazey, Pereg'n. Ward. Rec: 29 Nov 1738. Wm. Knight, Clerk.

P. 471 Deed. Edward Rumsey of Cecil Co., millwright, for £5, to John Watson of London, Great Britain, mariner, lot #31 in Frederick Town on the north side of Sassafras River. Made 27 Sep 1738. Wit: Ann E. Nichols, Wm. Rumsey. Ackn: 14 Oct 1738 by Edward and his wife Margaret Rumsey. JPs: Wm. Rumsey, R'd. Thompson. Rec: 30 Nov 1738. Wm. Knight, Clerk.

P. 472   Deed.   William Rumsey and John Baldwin of Cecil Co., gents., for £25, to John Watson of London, Great Britain, mariner, lot #31 in Frederick Town on the north side of Sassafras River. Said lot is part of a tract called Baldwin's Lot originally 10 acres patented to William Rumsey and John Baldwin. Made 29 Sep 1738. Wit: Ben. Bradford, James VBebber. Ackn: 2 Nov 1738. JPs: Thos. Johnson, John Veazey. Rec: 30 Nov 1738. Wm. Knight, Clerk.

P. 473   Deed of Gift.   Araminta Young of Cecil Co., widow, for the natural love and affection she has for her son Ephraim Augustine Herman, an infant, to secure for him part of her present estate and for his maintenance and livelihood when he arrives at the age of 21 years or be married, 5 Negroes named Little Harry, Luck, Jeny, Davy and Sam. Araminta Young intends to soon marry William Alexander. The said Negroes are to be said Herman's from the day of his 21st birthday or his marriage. Until that time they shall remain in the employ of the said Araminta. If Ephraim Augustine Herman should die without issue, then the Negroes are to go to the heirs of the said William Alexander by him of the body of Araminta Young. Made 25 Jul 1738. Wit: Mary Coursey, Augusteen Larramore, Will Alexander, Alex. Cumming. Rec: 6 Jan 1738. Wm. Knight, Clerk.

P. 474   Deed.   Edward Taylor of Cecil Co., yeoman, for £90, to James Smith of the same county, yeoman, 200 acres of land, by land called Batchelor's Fund and the corner of John McFarland's land and by Robert Whitaker's land. By deed dated 18 Sep 1735 recorded in Lib. W. K. folios 127-130, Samuel Gilpin of Cecil Co. conveyed to Edward Taylor the said tract of 200 acres in Cecil Co., part of 2 tracts belonging to said Gilpin, one called Rumsey's Ramble, the other called Coxe's Park. Made 13 Dec 1738. Wit: Jno. Copson, Sam'l. Thompson. Ackn: 30 Dec 1738 by Edward and his wife Mary. JP: Jno. Copson. Alienation fine of 8 shillings rec'd 20 Jan 1738 by Jas. Paul Heath. Also the quit rents of 4 shillings. Rec: 24 Jan 1738. Wm. Knight, Clerk.

P. 476   Deed.   Martin Cartmill of Cecil Co. and his wife Esther, to John Edmondson of the same county, for £35 and because he is moving, 100 acres of land on the north side of the plantation on which Cartmill now lives bounded on the north by John McCullough's land and on the west by Joseph Thompson's land, part of 2 adjoining tracts of land, one called Lidia's Joynture, sold to Cartmill by deed dated 20 May 1727 and the other called Goodwill, patented to Cartmill in 1716. Of the 100 acres, 69 acres and 36 perches are out of Lydia's Joynture and 30 acres and 21 perches are part of Goodwill. Made & Ackn: 16 Nov 1738. Wit: John Cage, Robert Williams,

William Taylor. JPs: William Rumsey, A. Barry. Alienation fine of 4 shillings rec'd by Jas. Paul Heath on 4 Dec 1738. Rec: 31 Jan 1738. Wm. Knight, Clerk.

P. 478 Deed. David Wallace of Kent Co. on Delaware, farmer, and his wife Barbara, for £55 to pay off Peter Garrison's mortgage, to William Donnell of Cecil Co., farmer, part of 2 tracts of land called Snowhill (86 acres) and Snowhill Addition (64 acres) and also a whole tract called Haill Hill (50 acres) the 3 tracts adjoin each other and contain a total of 200 acres. Two of these tracts were granted to Thomas Johnson — Snowhill by warrant dated 3 Aug 1713, patented 4 Jul 1719 and Snowhill Addition will appear in the same records. Haill Hill was granted to Edward Ellis by warrant dated 12 May 1720 and patented 8 May 1723. Thomas Johnson granted Snowhill and Snowhill Addition to David Wallace by deed dated 16 Nov 1722. Edward Ellis granted Haill Hill to David Wallace by deed [date not given.] David Wallace granted all three tracts of land to Peter Garrison and to secure £55 Peter Garrison mortgaged them to David Wallace. The exception is 2 acres granted by David Wallace for the use of the Presbyterian congregation for their meeting house and graveyard and a road to the spring. The quit rents come due to the fee of William Penn. [Barbara Wallace's name is also spelled Barbra.] Made & Ackn: 25 Aug 1738. Wit: Adam Short, William Houston. JP: Jno. Copson. Alienation fine of 8 shillings paid to Jas. Paul Heath 2 Sep 1738. Rec: 31 Jan 1738. Wm. Knight, Clerk.

P. 480 Lease. John Copin of Cecil Co., planter, to John Penington, Jr. of Cecil Co., planter, for yearly rents and services, 107 acres of land which formerly belonged to John Atkey. Lease is for a term of 14 years. After the first 3 years, rent of £4.10s due every year. Penington will build a dwelling house 20x18 feet and a 40-foot tobacco house. Penington will allow Copin to fell 4 walnut trees. [Copin's name also spelled Copen, Coppen.] Made 13 Jan 1736. Wit: Rob't. Thompson, Henry Penington, Sr. Ackn: 8 Mar 1736. JPs: R'd. Thompson, A. Barry. Rec: 10 Mar 1736. Wm. Knight, Clerk.

P. 481 Deed. Henry Penington, Jr. of Cecil Co., carpenter, and Ann his wife, late widow of Cornelius Clements of the said county, deceased, for £20, to Isaac Clements of Kent Co., planter, 82 acres of land which the said Cornelius Clements purchased from Thomas Severson, part of 2 tracts called Homely and Smoking Point on Elk River near Larramore's Branch. Made & Ackn: 9 Mar 1736/7. Wit: Thos. Stewart, Arnold Bassett. JPs: R'd. Thompson, A. Barry. Rec: 10 Mar 1736. Wm. Knight, Clerk.

P. 483   Deed.   William Rumsey of Cecil Co., gent., for £107.13s and 6 shillings paid by Rachel Penington, mother and guardian of Stephen Penington of the same county, son and heir of Robert Penington, late of said county, deceased, to the said Stephen Penington 120 acres, part of 2 tracts of land, one called Buntington and the other called Happy Harbor. Before his death, Robert Penington conveyed this land to the said William Rumsey by deed dated 1 Apr 1737. Ten acres, part of Baldwin's Lot within the bounds of Happy Harbor, is excepted and is that which Robert obliged himself by bond to convey to the said William Rumsey and to John Baldwin and was originally granted to said Rumsey and Baldwin. Also excepted is the land lying between Buntington and Sassafras River and southeast of Happy Harbor. Rumsey gained right to this land from an act of assembly made at a session held at Annapolis 19 Mar 1735 to erect a town in Cecil Co., later called Frederick Town, on the north side of Sassafras River at Penington Point on the tracts of land called Buntington and Happy Harbor. Made 23 Nov 1738. Wit: John Baldwin, Wm. Knight. Ackn: 24 Nov 1738. JPs: Thos. Colvill, A. Barry. Rec: 19 Feb 1738. Wm. Knight, Clerk.

P. 485   Deed.   James Vanbebber of Cecil Co., gent., for £150, to James Bayard of the same county, merchant, the easternmost half of the southernmost part of a tract called Rich Neck on Bohemia River. Said land is part of the land granted to Augustine Herman and conveyed by him to Petrus Sluyter alias Vorsman who conveyed it to Nicholas Delamontange. Jesse Delamontange conveyed it to James Vanbebber. Made 23 Jan 1738. Wit: Benja. Sluyter, Robert Withers. Ackn: same day by James and his wife Ann Vanbebber. JPs: Wm. Rumsey, R'd. Thompson. Rec: 26 Feb 1738. Wm. Knight, Clerk.

P. 486   Deed.   Peter Garrison of Cecil Co., planter, because he is moving and for £109, to William Donnel of the same place, 200 acres of land, part of 2 tracts of land called Snowhill (86 acres) and Snowhill Addition (64 acres.) Except 2 acres which David Wallace set aside for the use of the Presbyterians for their meeting house and graveyard. Snowhill was granted by warrant dated 3 Aug 1713 and patented 4 Jul 1719 to Thomas Johnson. Also another tract called Hail Hill warranted to Edward Ellis dated 12 May 1720 and patented 1821. Snowhill and Snowhill Addition were conveyed by Thomas Johnson to David Wallace on 17 Nov 1722 and by deed dated 8 Apr 1736 David Wallace conveyed the land to Peter Garrison. Hail Hill was sold by Edward Ellis to David Wallace 28 Jun 1721 and David Wallace sold it to Peter Garrison by deed dated 8 Apr 1736. Made & Ackn: 20 Feb 1738/9. Wit: William Calwall, Rachell Kelly. Alienation fine of 8 shillings paid 26 Feb 1738/9 to Jas. Paul Heath. Rec: 13 Mar 1738. Wm. Knight, Clerk.

P. 488   Mortgage.   Enoch Jenkins of Cecil Co., farmer, to secure the payment of several sums of money, to James Bayard of the same county, gent., a lease of 280 acres of land in Bohemia Manor which was originally made 15 Nov 1722 by Ephraim Augustine Herman to Walter Newman. The lease was for the term of 6 natural lives, that of the said Walter Newman and his sons Walter Newman, Jr., William Newman, Richard Newman, Samuel Newman and Jonathan Newman. Yearly rent of 16 bushels of wheat and 4 dunghill fowls due every 23 March. Walter Newman, Jr., eldest of the surviving sons, assigned his rights to the lease to Samuel Newman on 14 Oct 1736. Samuel Newman and Jonathan Newman the devisees and surviving sons and heirs of Walter Newman, Sr., for £70, on 15 Jun 1737, assigned the lease to Enoch Jenkins. Enoch Jenkins owes £31.11s.3p to John McCool of Newcastle Co. and £27.9s.10p to John Welch. Enoch Jenkins will repay James Bayard within 2 years time. Enoch Jenkins will continue to occupy the land. Made & Ackn: 20 Nov 1738. Wit: John Bubenheim, William Deoran. JPs: R'd. Thompson, Wm. Rumsey. Rec: 16 Mar 1738. Wm. Knight, Clerk.

P. 490   Lease.   William Parsons of Cecil Co., gent., to James Robb of the same place, shoemaker, a piece of land that is part of the Town Point tract by Susanah Walker's land on Bohemia River. For the term of 17 years for rent of 25 shillings and a day's reaping every year. Made 8 Mar 1738/9. Wit: John Milbourn, James Taylor. Ackn: 14 Mar 1738. JPs: Rich'd. Thompson, A. Barry. Rec: 16 Mar 1738. Wm. Knight, Clerk.

P. 492   Deed.   Martin Cartmell of Cecil Co., and his wife Esther, because he is moving and for £3.15s, to John McCullock of the same county, 10 acres of land, part of a tract called Goodwill patented to Martin Cartmill in 1716, on the north side of the said John McCullock's plantation where he now dwells. Made 23 Nov 1738. Wit: William Houston, George Lawson, William Taylor. Ackn: 26 Nov 1738. JPs: Edward Jackson, A. Barry. Rec: 16 Mar 1738. Wm. Knight, Clerk.

P. 493   Valuation of Estate.   George Veazey and James Wroth were appointed by JP Peregrine Ward to view 2 plantations and land called Middle Grounds and Benjamin's Levell belonging to Rebecca Davis, daughter of Fouch Davis, late of Cecil Co., deceased, and under the guardianship of Mr. Thomas Davis. They found a dwelling house 30x20 feet framed and planked with a brick chimney, much out of repair; 3 small old log houses of little worth; an old 40-foot tobacco house, a 30-foot tobacco house, 1 small __?__ open to the field, fencing bad and very old. They allow one third of the land on the southeast side of the plantation [to be cleared?] for the repairs of the houses and fences. They value the plantation at 60 lbs of tobacco a year. On Benjamin's Levell they found a dwelling house 45 feet long, rough work, 1 small house 15 feet, a small cornfield and good fencing. They allow one third of the land adjoining the plantation for the necessary use and to raise the rents for the benefit of the orphan. They value this plantation at 500 lbs of tobacco a year. Made 12 Dec 1738. Rec: 14 Mar 1738. Wm. Knight, Clerk.

P. 494   Deed.   Peter Meekins of Cecil Co., for £5 and 1,500 lbs of tobacco, to Thomas Price, Sr. of the said county, planter, 30 acres of land on Capt. John's Creek between a tract called the Horns and a tract called Spermon's Delight by Mr. Pearce's road. Said land part of a tract called Meekin's Adventure. Made & Ackn: 13 Jan 1738. Wit. & JPs: John Veazey, Pereg'n. Ward. Rec: 15 Mar 1738. Wm. Knight, Clerk.

P. 495   Assignment of Lease.   William Hood of Cecil Co., gent., for yearly rent, to Thomas Roose of the same place, weaver, land in Bohemia Manor where the said Roose now lives, by Herring Creek, by Patrick Burksfield's land and by Bennet's old field. Hood reserves the liberty of fishing at the creek for himself or his people. Lease is for the term of 3 natural lives, that of the said William Hood and Alice his wife and during the natural life of Sidney George, son of Joshua George, attorney. Paying, after the first 2 years, every 10 Dec 600 lbs of tobacco for the first 7 years then thereafter 35 bushels of wheat. This land was originally leased to William Hood by Col. Ephraim Augustine Herman. [Thomas Roose is also called Thomas Rose.] Made 31 Jan 173[7?] Wit: Jere Larkins, Margaret Hamilton [made her mark with an "O."] Ackn: 15 Mar 1738/9. JPs: Wm. Rumsey, A. Barry. Rec: 15 Mar 1738. Wm. Knight, Clerk.

P. 496   Lease.   Robert Commins of Cecil Co., because he is moving, to John Penington, cordwainer, of the same place, a tract of land called Arrundell. Said land formerly belonged to the said John Penington. Lease is for the term of the natural lives of the said John Penington and his wife Elizabeth, except if Elizabeth survives her husband and remarries. Made & Ackn: 28 Feb 1738. Wit: James Baxter, Adam Short. JP: Jno. Copson. Rec: 17 Mar 1738. Wm. Knight, Clerk.

P. 497   Deed.   Hugh Watson of Cecil Co., planter, for £14, to John Lusby of said county, yeoman, 10 acres, part of a tract called Banks on Bohemia River by the 200 acres (part of the same tract) sold to the "Visitors of Cecil County School" and by John Ryland's land called Mulberry Mold. Banks was originally conveyed to Thomas Bostick 25 Jul 1664. Made & Ackn: 8 Mar 1738. Wit: John Ryland, Jr., Aaron Latham. JP: Thos. Colvill. Jas. Paul

Heath collected the alienation fine on 20 Mar 1738. Rec: 19 Mar 1738. Wm. Knight, Clerk.

P. 498   Deed.   William Ward of Cecil Co., planter, for 10,000 lbs of tobacco and £12, to Thomas Savin of the same county, planter, 200 acres of land, all the remaining part of the tract called Indian Range which the said Savin now lives on. The said 300 acre tract was originally taken up by John Hagley and 100 acres was sold out of the tract. William Ward will warrant the land from any claims except any part that should be taken away by an elder survey taken up by Thomas Rumsey and now belonging to the heirs of William Penington, deceased. Made & Ackn: 30 Oct 1738. Wit. & JPs: John Veazey, Pereg'n. Ward. Rec: 21 Mar 1738. Wm. Knight, Clerk.

P. 499   Deed.   Zebulon Hollingsworth of Cecil Co., planter, for 10 shillings and for £60 formerly paid to Zebulon's Uncle Joseph Hollingsworth, to Andrew Hall of the same county, wheelwright, a tract of 100 acres called Hollingsworth's Second Parcel by land which was Abra. Hollingsworth's and by another belonging to Martin Cartmill. This land was granted by Charles Lord Baltimore to Zebulon Hollingsworth by patent dated 10 Jun 1734 signed by Gov. Sam'l. Ogle and recorded in the land office in Lib. E. J. No. 1, folio 437. Made 20 Mar 1738/9. Wit: William Maffitt, Rachell Kelly. Ackn: 21 Mar 1738/9 by Capt. Zebulon Hollingsworth and his wife Ann. JP: Jno. Copson. Jas. Paul Heath rec'd the alienation fine on 18 Apr 1739. Rec: 19 Apr 1739. Wm. Knight, Clerk.

P. 501   Deed.   Escoll Johnson of Salem Co., NJ, for £20, to Simon Denny of Newcastle Co. on Delaware, farmer, 100 acres of land on the west side of Elk River in Cecil Co., part of a tract called Feddart which was formerly the estate of Henry Johnson of said county, who by his Last Will and Testament dated 15 Apr 1721 bequeathed to the said Escoll Johnson the 100 acres of the tract. [Escoll Johnson is also called Ezekiel Johnson.] Made & Ackn: 3 Mar 1738/9. Wit: Garret McKinne, Suluph Stedham, Rachel Kelly. JP: Jno. Copson. Rec: 28 Apr 1739. Wm. Knight, Clerk.

P. 502   Deed.   Isaac Freeman of Kent Co., planter, and Susannah his wife, for 5 shillings, to William Freeman of Cecil Co., 100 acres of land, part of a greater tract called Daniel's Denn on Back Creek in Sassafras River in Cecil Co. by Richard Rumsey's plantation. Made & Ackn: 10 Apr 1739. Wit: John Veazey, Jas. Paul Heath. [Susannah Freeman is called Hannah Freeman in the acknowledgement.] JPs: John Veazey, Robert Story. Alienation fine of 2 shillings paid by William Freeman to Jas. Paul Heath on 12 Apr 1739. Rec: 21 May 1739. Wm. Knight, Clerk.

P. 503   Deed.   John Poillown of Cecil Co., yeoman, for £275, to William Ellis of the same county, planter, 200 acres of land, part of a larger tract called Coxe's Forest. Made 25 May 1739. Wit. & JPs: R'd. Thompson, John Veazey. Ackn: same day by John Poillown and his wife Hannah. Alienation fine of 8 shillings paid 24 May 1739. Rec: 25 May 1739. Wm. Knight, Clerk.

P. 504   Deed.   William Knight of Cecil Co., gent., for £5, to Thomas Spencer of Biddeford, Great Britain, mariner, lot #43 in Frederick Town. Made & Ackn: 25 May 1739. Wit: R'd. Thompson. JPs: R'd. Thompson, John Veazey. Rec: 25 May 1739. Wm. Knight, Clerk.

P. 505   Deed.   William Davis of Cecil Co., house carpenter, and his wife Rachel, for 1,500 lbs of tobacco, to George Hall of Kent Co., gent., a 1 acre lot in James Town called Huse's Lot on the north side of Sassafras River in the possession of James Wallace and formerly taken up by Robert Huse, late of Cecil Co. Made & Ackn: 5 May 1739. Wit. & JPs: Pereg'n. Ward, John Veazey. Alienation fine of 1 penny rec'd by Jas. Paul Heath from George Hall on 16 May 1739. Rec: 1 Jun 1739. Wm. Knight, Clerk.

P. 506   Deed.   William Foster of Cecil Co., planter, for £18, to John Bravard, Jr., blacksmith, of the same place, 55 acres of a 400 acre tract called Jones' Green Spring formerly granted to William Harris of Kent Co., gent, father of James Harris of Kent Co., gent., and sold by the said James Harris to John Jewart, late of Cecil Co., gent., who sold it to Thomas Price by deed dated 30 Dec 1719 who sold it to the said William Foster by deed dated 3 Jun 1734. The 55 acres is the easternmost end of the tract on Long Creek by land belonging to Henry Ward, by the road that leads from Andrew Alexander's to the fording place in Broad Creek and by a tract called Charles' Camp. Made 8 Feb 1738. Wit: Jno. Copson, William Wallace. Ackn: 26 Mar 1739. JP: Jno. Copson. Alienation fine of 2 shillings rec'd 1 Mar 1738/9 by Jas. Paul Heath. Rec: 11 Jun 1739. Wm. Knight, Clerk.

P. 507   Deed.   John Penington of northeast Cecil Co., planter, for £100, to Robert Cumming of the same county, carpenter, 250 acres on the eastern side of the place where the late John Sequence's dwelling house was and on Arundel Creek, part of a tract called Arrundel on the south side of Shannon or Northeast River. Said tract was conveyed by John Sequence to the said John Penington by deed dated 15 Feb 1699 recorded in Lib. D, folio 152. Made 28 Feb 1738. Wit: Ben. Bradford, James Baxter. Ackn: same day by John and his wife Elizabeth Penington. JP: Jno. Copson. Alienation fine of 9 shillings for 225 acres [sic] rec'd by Jas. Paul Heath from Robert Cummings 10 Mar 1738/9. Rec: 11 Jun 1739. Wm. Knight, Clerk.

P. 508   Lease.   Christian Peters of Cecil Co., for rents and services for 10 years, to John Mills and Anna his wife of the same county, 100 acres of land, part of a tract called VanBebber's Forest. Rent of £3 to be paid after the first 2 years every 29 Jan. Mills will plant 100 apple trees and 100 peach trees and will build a house 20x16 feet and fence the place. Wit: William Currer, Susanah Blakey. Ackn: 11 Jun 1739. JP: Jno. Copson. Rec: 12 Jun 1739. Wm. Knight, Clerk.

P. 509   Deed.   William Stoops of Kent Co., for 11,500 lbs of tobacco, to Philip Stoops of Cecil Co., 50 acres of land, part of a tract called Ruke and Pill on Sassafras River originally laid out for 250 acres. Made 21 May 1739. Wit: John Veazey, Pereg'n. Ward. Ackn: same day by William Stoops and his wife Sippry. Alienation fine of 1 shilling paid 7 Jun 1739 to Jas. Paul Heath by Philip Stoops. Rec: 12 Jun 1739. Wm. Knight, Clerk.

P. 510   Deed of Gift.   David Lawson of Cecil Co., because he is moving and for the natural affection and fatherly love he has for his well beloved son Peter Lawson of the same county, to the said Peter Lawson the tract of 100 acres where he now dwells and half of his moveable estate. David Lawson bought this land from Nicholas Harper and his wife Susanah. Made & Ackn: 27 Jun 1739. Wit: Jas. Scott, James Harbuson, A. Barry. JPs: R'd. Thompson, A. Barry. Rec: 3 Jul 1739. Wm. Knight, Clerk.

P. 511   Release.   Jno. Holland and John Lusby release to John Seagar a lease of land which the said John Seagar had used to secure the settlement of a suit of John McCullough, administrator of Tole McCullough. The sums of money have been paid. Made & Ackn: 1 Aug 1739. Evert Evertson. JPs: Edward Jackson, A. Barry. Rec: 1 Aug 1739. Wm. Knight, Clerk.

P. 511   Deed.   Richard Hind of the Parish of St. Mary Magdaline Bermodsey, Co. Surry, mariner, and Elizabeth his wife, and Robert Coulson of Shad Thames, waterman, and Sarah his wife (Elizabeth and Sarah were the only daughters of Samuel Richardson, late of London, mariner, deceased) for £50, to Colonel John Ward of Cecil Co., gent., all their rights and interests in land and personal estate in Kent and Cecil Counties. Made 18 Apr 1739. Wit: John Watson, John Lesly. Ackn: in Cecil Co. 4 Aug 1739 by Capt. John Watson and John Lesly, JPs: John Veazey, Pereg'n. Ward. Richard and Elizabeth Hind and Robert and Sarah Coulson appointed Capt. John Veazey and Thomas Davis of Cecil Co. to be their attorneys. Rec: 14 Aug 1739. Wm. Knight, Clerk.

P. 514   Deed.   John Wiley of Cecil Co., planter, and Mary Wiley, relict of John Wiley, late of said county, for £40, to Samuel McDowell of Newcastle Co. in the territories of Pennsylvania, weaver, 102 acres of land in Cecil Co. now occupied by the said John Wiley, by the part of the tract that belongs to John Smith, late of said county and by Bartholomew Johnson's land. Said land is part of a tract called Newcastle Back Landing formerly condemned [sic] by an Act of Assembly from _____ Groom, merchant of London to Col. Sevin Gale and his wife Betty of Somerset Co. who sold the tract to the said John Wiley, late of Cecil Co., by deed dated 12 Sep 1730. [McDowell is also spelled Macdowell, MackDowell.] Made 16 Jul 1739. Wit: R'd. Thompson, Jno. Bravard, Jr., John Miller, David Miller. Ackn: 31 Jul 1739. JPs: R'd. Thompson, John Veazey. Rec: 31 Jul 1739. Wm. Knight, Clerk.

P. 515   Deed.   Francis Bonner of Cecil Co., planter, and his wife Mary, for £70, to James Paul Heath of the same county, merchant, 2 parcels of land, one of 50 acres, the other 25 acres, both part of a tract called Clemenson at the mouth of Elk River. The said 50 acres of land was conveyed by Michael Clements by deed dated 12 Feb 1717 to Thomas Rogers, now deceased, who was the husband of the said Mary Bonner. The parcel of 25 acres was conveyed by Jacob Clements by deed dated 12 Mar 1717 to the said Thomas Rogers. By his Last Will and Testament, Thomas Rogers bequeathed both parcels of land to the said Mary. Made 25 Mar 1739. Wit: John Veazey, John Wilcocks. Ackn: 10 Apr 1739. JPs: John Veazey, Robert Story. Alienation fine of 18p paid 1 Apr 1739 to Jas. Paul Heath. Rec: 31 Jul 1739. Wm. Knight, Clerk.

P. 516   Deed.   James Paul Heath of Cecil Co., merchant, for £75, to Francis Bonner of the same county, planter, 75 acres of land, part of a tract called Clemenson [see previous entry P. 515.] Made 2 Apr 1739. Wit: John Veazey, John Wilcocks. Ackn: 10 Apr 1739. JPs: John Veazey, Rob't. Story. Alienation fine of 18p collected by Jas. Paul Heath 10 Apr 1739. Rec: 31 Jul 1739.

P. 517   Deed.   Jesse Holton of Cecil Co., planter, and his wife Sarah, for £40, to Francis Bonner of Cecil Co., planter, 75 acres by the lands of Abraham Clements and Garret Othoson, part of a greater tract called Clementson. Made & Ackn: 25 May 1739. Wit: R'd. Thompson, Pereg'n. Ward, JPs. Wm. Mill witnessed the exchange of money. Jas. Paul Heath rec'd 18p alienation fine on 28 May 1739. Rec: 31 Jul 1739. Wm. Knight, Clerk.

P. 518   Deed of Gift.   Paul Polston of Cecil Co., farmer, for the love and affection he has for his daughter Williamincher Davis, gives to her all his right and title to 55 acres of land bounded on the east side by a tract of land called Glass House and Susquehanna River. Made & Ackn: 12 Jun 1739. Wit: Edward Jackson, Elihu Hall. JPs: R'd. Thompson, A. Barry. On 20 Jun 1739 Jas. Paul Heath rec'd 2½ shillings alienation fine. Rec: 1 Aug 1739. Wm. Knight, Clerk.

P. 518   Assignment of Lease.   Written on the back of a lease from Wm. Hood to Thomas Rose for land in Bohemia Manor "recorded in this book folios 495-496" was an endorsement made by Thomas Rose transferring the lease to Thomas Castevens dated 7 Apr 1739. Wit: Jere. Larkins. Ackn: 31 Jul 1739. JPs: Edward Jackson, R'd. Thompson. Rec: 31 Jul 1739. Wm. Knight, Clerk. [For lease, see pg 70, entry P. 495.]

P. 519   Deed.   William Knight of Cecil Co., gent., for £5, to William Hutchinson of the same county, gent., lot #50 in Frederick Town on Sassafras River. Made & Ackn: 13 Aug 1739. Wit. & JPs: Edward Jackson, R'd. Thompson. Rec: 14 Aug 1739. Wm. Knight, Clerk.

P. 519   Deed.   James Armstrong and Archibald Armstrong of Milford Hundred, Cecil Co., farmers, for £15, to Thomas Moore of the same county, farmer, a tract of 50 acres called Addition. Made 1 Aug 1739. Wit: Joseph Ritchy, Joseph Wallace. Ackn: same day. JPs: Edward Jackson, A. Barry. Alienation fine of 2 shillings paid 14 Aug 1739 to Jas. Paul Heath. Rec: 15 Aug 1739. Wm. Knight, Clerk.

P. 520   Assignment of Lease.   Written on the back of a lease from Col. Ephraim Augustine Herman to Martin Nicholson (which was assigned by said Nicholson to John Condon) recorded in Lib. J. D. No. 3, folios 266-267 was an endorsement made by Edward Condon transferring the lease to John Haltham. Made & Ackn: 3 Oct 1739. JPs: A. Barry, Pereg'n. Ward. Rec: 4 Oct 1739. Wm. Knight, Clerk. [For an abstract of this lease, see June D. Brown, *Abstracts of Cecil County Maryland Land Records 1673-1751*, (Westminster, MD: Family Line Publications, 1998) pg 148, entry P. 432.]

P. 520   Assignment of Lease.   John Seegar, Sr. of Cecil Co., for £42.17s.6p and £39 paid to William Alexander, gent., on account of the said John Seegar, Sr. (part of it being arrears of rent due on the land), to John Seegar, Jr. of the same county, a lease of land and all the stock, hogs (except one sow and 2 cows), Indian corn and tobacco now growing on the land. On 31 May

1729 Ephr. Augt. Herman, gent., leased to John Seegar, Sr. 140 acres of land in Bohemia Manor. Rent was for 40 shillings and two dunghill fowls a year for the term of 3 natural lives. Made 22 Aug 1739. Wit: Robert Withers, John Ryland, Jr., Wm. Rumsey. Ackn: same day. JPs: R'd. Thompson, Wm. Rumsey. Rec: 25 Aug 1739. Wm. Knight, Clerk.

P. 522 Release. Matthias VanBebber of Cecil Co., gent., to settle a dispute, gives to Joshua George of the said county, attorney, all of a tract of land called Clifton except the 550 acres which Joshua George just released to Matthias VanBebber on Bohemia River by the part of Clifton held by Stephen Knight or his son William Knight and the part of the land that is Walter Scott's. The dispute between Matthias VanBebber and Joshua George concerns the bounds and title of a tract called Middle Neck claimed by Joshua George and a tract called Clifton, the major part of which is claimed by Matthias VanBebber. Made 23 Apr 1737. Wit: Hugh Matthews, John Slidell. Ackn: 8 Sep 1739 by Dr. Hugh Matthews. JP: Wm. Rumsey. Rec: 15 Sep 1739. Wm. Knight, Clerk.

P. 523 Deed. Col. Thomas Colvill of Cecil Co., for £300, to Peter Lawson of the same place, planter, Back Creek Mill which was formerly Howell James' and all that part of the plantation which said Howell James leased from Joseph Wood, deceased, which lies by the main road from the mill to Elk River. Also the small parcel of land behind the mill. Also the liberty of the landing just above the salt house. Also the parcel of land lying west of the mill where the said Howell James lately lived. Thomas Colvill will be hopper free at the said mill during the term of his lifetime. Made 15 Sep 1739. Wit: Jos. George, Peter Bayard. Ackn: 2 Oct 1739. JPs: Wm. Rumsey, R'd. Thompson. Rec: 3 Oct 1739. Wm. Knight, Clerk.

P. 524 Mortgage. Peter Lawson of Cecil Co., planter, to secure a bond, to Capt. Peter Bayard of the same place, his mill called the Back Creek Mill and it's lands [see previous entry P. 523.] By deed of this same date Peter Lawson has purchased from Col. Thomas Colvill his mill on Back Creek. Also on this same date, Peter Bayard, at the request of and jointly with Peter Lawson has become bound to the said Thomas Colvill in 2 bonds, each for £100, one due 1 Sep next, the other the following September. Made 15 Sep 1739. Wit: Thos. Colvill, Jos. George. Ackn: 3 Oct 1739. JPs: Wm. Rumsey, R'd. Thompson. Rec: 4 Oct 1739. Wm. Knight, Clerk.

P. 525 Deed. Benjamin Pearce of Cecil Co., and Margarett his wife, for £50 and yearly rent of 700 lbs of tobacco in cask and 4 shillings, to Joshua Meekins of the same county for the term of his natural life, 150 acres of land on Capt. John's Creek. If Joshua Meekins should not live for the term of 21 years, then the land goes to his wife Elizabeth Meekins for the full term of 21 years. Rent and 2 capons to be paid every 10 Nov. Made & Ackn: 24 Oct 1739. Wit. & JPs: John Veazey, Pereg'n. Ward. Rec: 25 Oct 1739. Wm. Knight, Clerk.

P. 526   Deed of Gift.   Robert Money, Sr. of Cecil Co., planter, for the natural love and affection he has for his son John Money and for 5 shillings, 80 acres of land, part of 300 acres sold to Robert Money 1 May 1714 by Roger Larramore of the same county and his wife Margaret out of a tract called Larramore's Neck and by the part of the land which Robert Money and his wife Margaret sold to Thomas and Catherine Walmsley on 27 Dec 1714. Made 12 Oct 1739. Wit. & JPs: John Veazey, Wm. Rumsey. Ackn: 5 Nov 1739. Rec: 13 Nov 1739. Wm. Knight, Clerk.

P. 527   Release.   Joshua George of Cecil Co., attorney, to settle a dispute, to Matthias Vanbebber of the same county, gent., 550 acres of land, part of a tract of land called Middle Neck on Bohemia River by the tract called Clifton, by Stephen Knight's or his son William's part of the tract [see entry P. 522 above.] Made 23 Apr 1737. Wit: Susana Cherry, Wm. Rumsey, Hugh Matthews, John Sliddell. Ackn: 29 Oct 1739 by Dr. Hugh Matthews and John Sliddell. JP: Wm. Rumsey. Rec: 30 Oct 1739. Wm. Knight, Clerk.

P. 528   Lease.   John Chambers of Cecil Co., planter, and Rachel his wife, guardian of Stephen Penington of the same county, an infant and heir of Robert Penington, deceased, for rents and services, to William Hutchinson of the same county, innholder, 120 acres of land. Lease is in effect until the said Stephen Penington reaches the age of 21 or the day of his death (if that occurs before he reaches the age of 21.) The yearly interest on the loan will be discounted as the rent until the loan is repaid. By deed dated 1 Apr 1737, Robert Penington, in his lifetime, for £100, mortgaged to William Rumsey of the same county, gent., 120 acres of land, part of 2 tracts of land called Buntington and Happy Harbor to be repaid the following 25 March. Robert Penington died without leaving assets to discharge the debt. The said Rachel borrowed £107.13s from William Hutchinson and has repaid William Rumsey. William Rumsey has released the land to Stephen Penington. Made 13 Nov 1739. Wit. & JPs: Wm. Rumsey, A. Barry. Ackn: 14 Nov 1739. Rec: 14 Nov 1739. Wm. Knight, Clerk.

P. 530   Deed.   Peter Lawson of Cecil Co., planter, £115 and because he is moving, to Sluyter Bouchell of said county, doctor, 100 acres of land in Bohemia Manor which Nicholas Harper sold to David Lawson of said county, who by deed of gift conveyed the land to his son the said Peter Lawson. Made & Ackn: 15 Nov 1739. Wit. & JPs: Tho. Colvill, A. Barry. Wm. Knight and Charles Coatts witnessed the exchange of money on the same day. Rec: 15 Nov 1739. Wm. Knight, Clerk.

P. 531   Deed.   William Jones, Jr. and Mary his wife, for £30, to Rebecca Johnson, all their right and interest in a tract of 1,000 acres called Triumph in Cecil Co. on the north side of Elk River by land formerly belonging to Richard and John Collet and purchased by Mr. Hawkins. Made 12 Jun 1739. Wit. & JPs: R'd. Thompson, John Veazey. Ackn: 31 Jul 1739. Rec: 23 Nov 1739. Wm. Knight, Clerk.

P. 532   Deed.   Joshua George of Cecil Co., to Benjamin Bradford of the same county, physician, 100 acres of land that runs into Middle Neck and is part of the Dividend. Made 1 Nov 1739. Wit: John Davidge. Ackn: 13 Nov 1739. JPs: Edward Jackson, R'd. Thompson. Rec: 5 Dec 1739. Wm. Knight, Clerk.

P. 533   Deed.   Henry Penington, Jr. of Cecil Co., planter, and Mary his wife, for £60 money of Great Britain and £30 money of Maryland and 600 lbs of tobacco, to James Bayard of Cecil Co., merchant, lot #26 in Frederick Town on the north side of Sassafras River on Frederick and Water Streets except for a corner of the lot next to post #26 which was sold to James Paul Heath but not conveyed. Made & Ackn: 20 Nov 1739. Wit: Wm. Rumsey, Wm. Pearce. JPs: R'd. Thompson, Wm. Rumsey. Rec: 14 Jan 1739. Wm. Knight, Clerk.

P. 534   Assignment of Lease.   Written on the back of a lease from Col. Ephraim Augustine Herman to George Steele recorded 18 Dec 1722 in Lib. J. D. No. 3, folios 343-344 is an endorsement by Robert Withers dated 24 Dec 1739 assigning all his interests in the lease to Enoch Jenkins for £60. Wit: Joseph Cochran, Moses Cochran. Ackn: 2 Feb 1739. The lease was previously assigned to Robert Withers by Enoch Jenkins. JPs: R'd. Thompson, Wm. Rumsey. On 24 Dec 1739 Enoch Jenkins of Cecil Co. assigned the lease to John Cochran for £33 and 580 bushels of wheat which was witnessed by Robert Withers and James Craig. Ackn: 2 Feb 1739. JPs: R'd. Thompson, Wm. Rumsey. Rec: 3 Feb 1739. Wm. Knight, Clerk.

P. 535   Deed.   Robert Holy of Cecil Co., yeoman, and Ann his wife, for £136, to Moses Leatham of the same place, yeoman, 256 acres of land by Minian Young's plantation, the northwest part of a tract of 456 acres called Mount Hope which the said Holy bought from Samuel Dorson by deed dated

27 Oct 1724 and recorded in Lib. D.K. No. 1, folios 113-114. [See June D. Brown, *Abstracts of Cecil County Maryland Land Records 1673-1751*, (Westminster, MD: Family Line Publications, 1998) pg 180, entry P. 120.] Made 1 Feb 1739. Wit: Michael Wallace, A. Barry. Ackn: 14 Mar 1739. JPs: A. Barry, R'd. Thompson. Jas. Paul Heath rec'd 10 shillings alienation fine on 20 Feb 1739. Rec: 14 Mar 1739. Wm. Knight, Clerk.

P. 536 Valuation of Estate. John Penington and George Veazey, both of Cecil Co., are appointed by JP Mr. John Veazey to enter and value the estate of the orphan Alphonso Cosden, son of Alphonso Cosden, late of Cecil Co., deceased, and now under the guardianship of Mr. Benjamin Pearce. Penington and Veazey found one large dwelling house framed 45x25 feet with a brick chimney, part planked above and below and a good large kitchen 35x20 feet adjoining the back of the house; 3 old log houses 15 feet square; one old log house 20x15 feet; a 15 feet square dwelling house; 2 milk houses 10 feet square; 2 tobacco houses, one 50x25 and one 60x25; 2 small orchards with little or no fencing. They allow 100 acres of woodland around the plantation for the repairs. They give the plantation's yearly worth as 900 lbs of tobacco. Made 25 Dec 1739. Rec: 14 Mar 1739. Wm. Knight, Clerk.

P. 536 Lease. Anna Margaretta Vanderheyden of Cecil Co., for rents and services, to Hanse Patton of the same county, planter, 100 acres of land on which he now dwells near Broad Creek by the lands of John Gullicks, Hugh Gutheries, Susanah Cleghorn and William Price. Lease is for the term of 3 natural lives, that of the natural life of the said Hanse Patton, his wife Phebe and his son Francis. Rent of £3.2s and 2 dunghill fowls due every 10 Dec. Made & Ackn: 11 Dec 1739. Wit: John Veazey, Francis Alexander. JPs: John Veazey, Pereg'n. Ward. Rec: 14 Mar 1739. Wm. Knight, Clerk.

P. 537 Release. Roger Merrick of Cecil Co., farmer, to Alexander Hutcheson of said county, gent., 250 acres of land on the east side of Elk River at the former line between Roger Myrick's and Evan and Isaac James' corner post. Said land is part of 1,000 acres called Griffin formerly laid out for Griffith Jones of Maryland, gent., and by virtue of an assignment of that quantity from Vincent Lowe, esq., part of a warrant for 5,000 acres granted the said Lowe on 18 Apr 1683. But before the grant was issued, the said Jones, by deed dated 25 Jul 1702, sold the land to Thomas Wolaston (recorded in Lib. J. D. No. 2, folio 160.) Afterwards (after various transactions) David Merrick and his brother Roger conveyed the 250 acres to James and Robert Glens and from them became vested in the right of Alexander Hutcheson who found that no patent for the 1,000 acres had ever been issued. He and other possessors of the tract called Griffin agreed to sue for and obtained a patent of the whole 1,000 acres in the name of David Myrick. The said Roger Myrick is heir to his deceased brother David. Made & Ackn: 31 Mar 1740. Wit. & JPs: R'd. Thompson, A. Barry. Rec: 1 Apr 1740. Wm. Knight, Clerk.

P. 539   *Cecil County to Wit: I hereby certify that the aforegoing pages from folio 1 to folio 539 (inclusive) are truly transcribed from Liber W. K. No. 2. Test: Jo. Baxter, County Clerk.*

[The preceding was abstracted from *Cecil County Court Land Records 1734-1745* microfilm #MSA WK 944-45 photographed by the Genealogical Society, Salt Lake City, Utah, 1948.]

Deed Book No. 6
1739 - 1745

P. 1   Deed.   Abigail Thatcher, widow of Richard Thatcher of Cecil Co., deceased, and Jacob and Amos Thatcher, his only sons, for £67 and because they are moving, to Matthew Arthur of the same province, 200 acres of land on the west side of the main branch of Elk River, part of 1,200 acres which is part of a tract called Newmunster. The tract of 6,000 acres called Newmunster was laid out in Cecil Co. and certified for Edmond Odwyer and other Irishmen on 29 Aug 1683. Edmond Odwyer later conveyed the land to Daniel Toes, Sr., late of said province, mariner, who by his Last Will and Testament bequeathed Newmunster to his children Daniel, John and Sarah Toes. Sarah Toes later married Peter Massey and together they conveyed 1,200 acres of the south end of the tract to Richard Thatcher. There was an Act of Assembly made 26 Feb 1721 signed by Governor Charles Calvert to make a clear title to the 1,200 acres for Richard Thatcher. Jacob Thatcher made his mark with an "E". [Amos Thatcher's name appears only once in the body of the deed, on the second page about halfway down, and his name does not appear at the end of the deed for signatures or marks.] Made 31 Dec 1739. Wit: John Currer, John Ritchy, William Ramsey. Ackn: 16 Feb 1739/40. JP: Jno. Copson. Rec: 2 Apr 1740. Wm. Knight, Clerk.

P. 3   Release.   Charles Sewall of St. Marys Co., gent., for 5 shillings, to Joshua George of Cecil Co., 100 acres of land, part of a tract called the Dividend. Maj. Nicholas Sewall, late of St. Marys Co., father of the said Charles Sewall, by deed of gift gave to his daughter Susannah Douglass and her husband George Douglass a tract of land in Cecil Co. called the Dividend at the head of Bohemia River. Joshua George bought from George and Susannah Douglas the part of the tract that lies south of Herman's Neck Branch where Walter Scott lives containing 100 acres. Made 8 May 1740. Wit: Philip Lee, Wm. Wilkins. Ackn: 9 May 1740. JP: Robert Gordon. Rec: 8 Jun 1740. Wm. Knight, Clerk.

P. 4   Release.   Charles Sewall of St. Marys Co., gent., to William Rumsey of Cecil Co., gent., 230 acres, part of a tract called Divident. Maj. Nicholas Sewall, late of St. Marys Co., father of the said Charles Sewall, by deed of gift gave to his daughter Susannah Douglas and her husband George Douglas a tract of land in Cecil Co. called the Divident at the head of Bohemia River. William Rumsey bought 230 acres of the tract from George and

Susannah Douglas. Made 1 May 1740. Wit: Philip Lee, Wm. Wilkins. Ackn: 9 May 1740. JP: Robert Gordon. Rec: 9 Jun 1740. Wm. Knight, Clerk.

P. 5 Deed. Bartlett Smith of Cecil Co., planter, and Elizabeth his wife, for £50 and 3,000 lbs of tobacco, to William Savin, Jr. of the same county, planter, 93½ acres of land, part of a tract called Dayley's Desire, on the north east side of Sassafras River by land formerly taken up by John Collet. Made 9 Jun 1740. Wit: S. Wilmer, Thos. Savin. Also, Richard Smith of Cecil Co., planter, releases all his right and interest in the 93½ acres to William Savin. Ackn: same day. JP: Levin Gale. Robert Smith rec'd the consideration money from William Savin, Jr. on the same day. Rec: 10 Jun 1740. Wm. Knight, Clerk.

P. 8 Deed of Gift. Joseph McGregory of Salem, NJ, gent., for natural love and affection and for 5 shillings, to his daughter Rebecca and her husband Thomas Davis of Cecil Co. all his lands in Cecil Co. Made & Ackn: 20 May 1740. Wit. & JPs: John Veazey, Pereg'n. Ward. Rec: 11 Jun 1740. Wm. Knight, Clerk.

P. 9 Deed. James Chambers and Rachel his wife, for £1.5s to Frances Farra, widow, lot #48 in Frederick Town on Sassafras River. Said lot was taken up by the said Rachel in her name of Rachel Penington. [Mr. Chambers is called James at the beginning of the deed only; thereafter he is called John. At the end of the deed, they are called John, Jr. and Rachel Chamberlin.] John Chamberlin, Jr. made his mark. Made & Ackn: 12 Jun 1740. Wit: John Veazey, Bartlet Smith. JPs: R'd. Thompson, John Veazey. Rec: 12 Jun 1740. Wm. Knight, Clerk.

P. 10 Deed. Thomas Marsh of Queen Annes Co., gent., and Mary his wife, daughter of Augustin Thompson, late of Queen Annes Co., deceased, gent., for £120, to John Campbell of the same county, gent., a moiety of land in Cecil Co. on the north side of Sassafras River at Back Creek, part of a tract called None So Good in Finland. Said land was formerly possessed by Major John Dowdall, late of Cecil Co., deceased, and devised by him in his Last Will and Testament to Richard Dowdall and John McManus. This moiety of land was conveyed by the said Richard Dowdall to Augustin Thompson who, by his Last Will and Testament, left it to his daughter Mary. Made 1 Mar 1739. Wit: John Thompson, John Knight. Ackn: same day. JPs: John Veazey, Pereg'n. Ward. Alienation fine of 18p paid 20 Mar 1739 to Jas. Paul Heath. Rec: 28 Jun 1740. Wm. Knight, Clerk.

P. 12   Deed.   William Hill and Mary his wife, for £62.10s, to William Rumsey of Cecil Co., gent., 100 acres of land by the road leading from Andrew Peterson's to the head of Sassafras River. Said land is part of a larger tract called Sarah's Joynture surveyed 13 Sep 1681 for Richard Peacock for 600 acres. It was surveyed again on 13 Sep 1725 for John Reynolds, Mary's father, and confirmed to him by patent. John Rennalds gave this land to his daughter Mary Hill by deed of gift dated 6 Jun 1730 recorded in Lib. S. K. No. 5, folios 272-273. Made 14 Feb 1739. Wit: Ben Bradford, R'd. Thompson. Jas. Paul Heath rec'd 4 shillings alienation fine on 10 Mar 1739/40. Rec: 5 Jul 1740. Wm. Knight, Clerk.

P. 14   Deed.   John Bennett of Kent Co., and Elizabeth his wife, for £6, to Thaddy McDermott of Cecil Co., cooper, lot #54 in Frederick Town on the east side corner of Frederick Street and the north side of Prince William Street. Made & Ackn: 14 Aug 1740. Wit: Wm. Knight, Jam. Holliday, Jr. JPs: R'd. Thompson, Pereg'n. Ward. Rec: same day. Wm. Knight, Clerk.

P. 16   Deed.   Andrew Alexander of Cecil Co. and Jean his wife, to Robert Patton of said county, yeoman, 70½ acres of land by a tract of land which the said Alexander purchased from Richard Nash. Said land is part of a tract called Bullin's Range granted to Alexander by patent dated 24 Jun 1740. Made & Ackn: 14 Aug 1740. Wit: John Tree, John Haltham. JPs: John Baldwin, John Veazey. Alienation fine of 2s.10p paid by Robert Patton 20 Aug 1740 to Jas. Paul Heath. Rec: 20 Aug 1740. Wm. Knight, Clerk.

P. 17   Deed.   Joseph MacGregory formerly of Cecil Co. and now of East Jersey, son and heir of Hugh MacGregory, late of Cecil Co., deceased, for £10, to John Baldwin of Cecil Co., a tract of 240 acres called MacGregory's Delight in Cecil Co. on the south sides of Bohemia River and St. Augustine's Branch. The certificate of survey for this land is dated 25 Jul 1689 and on 10 Nov 1695 was patented to Hugh McGregory, who with his wife Elizabeth on 17 Jan 1690 conveyed the land to Jacob Archer of Cecil Co. who died and the land descended to his son Jacob Archer who granted it to John Baldwin by deed recorded in Lib. S. K. No. 5, folios 53-54. Made & Ackn: 19 May 1740. Wit: John Veazey, John Knight, John Thompson. JPs: John Veazey, Pereg'n. Ward. Alienation of 9s.8p paid by Baldwin to Ja. Paul Heath 20 May 1740. Rec: 27 Aug 1740. Wm. Knight, Clerk.

P. 19   Deed.   James Alexander of Cecil Co., farmer, for £85 and because he is moving, to John McCoy of Cecil Co., cooper, 184 acres of land by the land of David Alexander. Said land is part of a tract called Newmunster which James Alexander bought from Thomas Stevenson of Bucks Co., PA by deed dated 18 May 1714. Thomas Stevenson bought the land from Robert Roberts of Queen Annes Co., glover, by deed dated 1 Apr 1714. Made 22 Aug 1740. Wit. & JPs: Robert Story, Nicholas Hyland. Ackn: 25 Aug 1740 by James Alexander and his wife Sophia. Alienation of 3s.8p collected 19 Sep 1740 by Ja. Paul Heath. Rec: same day. Wm. Knight, Clerk.

P. 21   Deed.   Rebecca Johnson of Cecil Co., widow, for £300 and because she is moving, to Simon Wilmer of Kent Co., a tract of land called Triumph in Cecil Co. on the north side of Elk River. This land was formerly purchased by her husband Thomas Johnson on 12 May 1730 from Thomas Crouch, Jr. and his wife Margaret. Made & Ackn: 11 Jun 1740. Wit: R'd. Thompson, John Hyland. JPs: R'd. Thompson, Wm. Rumsey. Alienation of 10 shillings paid 20 Jun 1740 to Ja. Paul Heath. Rec: 24 Sep 1740. Wm. Knight, Clerk.

P. 22   Assignment of Lease.   Henry McCoy (assignee of Rene' Julien by an endorsement on the back of a lease from Ephraim Augustine Herman dated 1 May 1728 to Rene' Julien recorded in Lib. S. K. No. 5, folios 138-139) for £70, assigns to Abraham Allman of Cecil Co., innholder, a lease for land called Nobles Town for the same terms as stated in the original lease. Made & Ackn: 17 Apr 1740. Wit: Wm. Rumsey, Jr., Wm. Rumsey. JPs: Wm. Rumsey, R'd. Thompson. Rec: 15 Oct 1740. Wm. Knight, Clerk.

P. 23   Release.   Bartlet Smith of Cecil Co., planter, quit claims to Richard Smith of the same county, planter, all his right and interest in 93½ acres on the east side of the dividing line, part of a tract of land called Dailey's Desire which was legally divided, surveyed and laid out between Richard and Bartlet Smith. Made 9 Jun 1740. Wit: S. Wilmer, Thos. Savin. Rec: 15 Oct 1740. Wm. Knight, Clerk.

P. 23   Deed.   John Lusby of Cecil Co., and Margaret his wife, for £150, to Robert Porter of the said county, planter, 110 acres of land, part of a tract called Hassell Branch on St. Albin's Creek adjoining a tract called Fryers Hills. John and Margaret Lusby will warrant the land against any claims under Roger Larramore, deceased father of the said Margaret Lusby. Made & Ackn: 20 Aug 1740. Wit. & JPs: John Baldwin, Wm. Rumsey. Alienation fine of 4s.5p paid by Robert Porter 30 Aug 1740 to Ja. Paul Heath. Rec: 6 Nov 1740. Wm. Knight, Clerk.

P. 25   Release.   Richard Thompson of Cecil Co., gent., for 10 shillings, quit claims to Jane Frisby of Kent Co., widow, all his right and interest in an undivided third part of a tract of land called Smith's Hill in New York near

New York City. Made 5 Oct 1738. Wit: John Baldwin, Aug. Thompson, John Thompson. Ackn: 12 Nov 1740 by Richard Thompson. JPs: Thos. Colvill, John Baldwin. Rec: 12 Nov 1740. Wm. Knight, Clerk.

P. 26   Deed.   William Beaston of Cecil Co., planter, for £150 (and also for £50 paid by Hugh Terry to William Rumsey of Cecil Co., gent., to discharge a mortgage dated 6 Dec 1736), to Hugh Terry of the same place, yeoman, 120 acres on Bohemia River and Omealys Creek, part of a tract called Swan Harbor lately in the possession of the said William Beaston but now in the actual possession of Hugh Terry. Made 26 Jun 1740. Wit: Wm. Rumsey, John Veazey. Ackn: same day by William Beaston and Elizabeth his wife. JPs: John Veazey, Pereg'n. Ward. Alienation fine of 3 shillings paid by Terry on 30 Jun 1740 to Jas. Paul Heath, as well as 6 shillings for 2 years quit rents. Rec: 12 Nov 1740. Wm. Knight, Clerk.

P. 27   Deed.   John Baldwin of Cecil Co., gent., for £200, to Philip Stoope of the said county, planter, 100 acres by land taken up by George Goldsmith, by Hen Island Creek and by a tract called Greenfield originally surveyed 6 Aug 1669. Said land is part of a tract called Mapleton originally surveyed and laid out for John Collet 6 Oct 1671 for 200 acres. Made 24 Oct 1740. Wit: John Lusby, John Thompson. Ackn: same day by John Baldwin and his wife Mary. JPs: John Veazey, Pereg'n. Ward. Alienation of 2 shillings paid by Philip Stoopes 20 Oct 1740 to Jas. Paul Heath. Rec: 17 Nov 1740. Wm. Knight, Clerk.

P. 29   Deed.   William Abbott of Cecil Co., bricklayer, for £10, to Philip Stoope of said county, planter, 31 acres called Corengem, part of a tract called Freeman's Park. Philip Stoope has recently purchased a tract of land called Corengem from John Hazlehurst which was granted to said Hazlehurst by patent dated 5 May 1738 for 31 acres. This land was originally surveyed on 22 Jun 1722 for Benjamin Hazlehurst, father of said John Hazlehurst. This tract called Corengem was found to lie within a tract called Freeman's Park originally surveyed 5 Jun 1702 for William Freeman for 300 acres. William Freeman assigned the land to William Abbott who resurveyed the tract to clear it of older surveys but did not consider the tract called Corengem which had a younger survey. Abbott obtained a patent dated 14 Nov 1739 for 190 acres called Freeman's Park which is the part of the original tract which was found clear of other surveys. Made 5 Nov 1740. Wit. & JPs: John Baldwin, Pereg'n. Ward. Ackn: same day by William Abbott and his wife Mary. Alienation fine of 15p collected 11 Nov 1740 by Ja. Paul Heath. Rec: 17 Nov 1740. Wm. Knight, Clerk.

P. 31   Deed.   John Hazlehurst of Kent Co., planter, for £30, to Philip Stoope of Cecil Co., planter, 31 acres called Corengem in Cecil Co. adjacent to and part of a tract called Happy Harbor by the land late of Dr. John Jobson, late of Cecil Co., deceased. [See previous entry P. 29.] This land was surveyed 22 Jun 1722 for Benjamin Hazlehurst, father of the said John Hazlehurst, who died before he could apply for the patent. Made 5 Nov 1740. Wit: John Baldwin, Pereg'n. Ward. Ackn: same day by John Hazlehurst and his wife Mary. Alienation fine of 1s.12p collected 11 Nov 1740 by Ja. Paul Heath. Rec: 17 Nov 1740. Wm. Knight, Clerk.

P. 32   Lease.   William Hood of Cecil Co., farmer, for rent and services, to Joshua Latham of the same county, planter, a field called Bennett Jump's Old Field with all the land between the lands of James Bayard, _____ Burk and Thomas Rose. Lease is for 13 years (if Hoods lease stands so long) and rent of 700 lbs of tobacco due every 10 Dec. Made 13 Jun 1740. Wit: William Lancaster, John Cole. Ackn: 25 Nov 1740. JPs: R'd. Thompson, John Veazey. Rec: 25 Nov 1740. Wm. Knight, Clerk.

P. 33   Deed.   John Price of Cecil Co., planter, for £47.5s to James Paul Heath of the same county, gent., a tract of 340 acres called Mesopotamia on the north side of Sassafras River by land formerly laid out for Andrew Woodbury called the Middle Plantation, by a tract called Woodbury formerly laid out for Edward Jones, by land formerly laid out for Mounce Andrews, by a tract called Henderson's Choice formerly laid out for Hendrick Hendrickson and by land called Lattemore's Neck Enlarged formerly laid out for Roger Lattemore. The patent for this land was granted 10 Aug 1684 to Edward Jones. These parts of Mesopotamia were previously sold by John Price: 80 acres to James Wroth and 112 acres to John Roberts. Made 5 Nov 1740. Wit: John Baldwin, Pereg'n. Ward. John Ward, Jr. witnessed the exchange of money. Ackn: same day by John Price and his wife Mary. Rec: 12 Dec 1740. Wm. Knight, Clerk.

P. 35   Release.   William Rumsey of Cecil Co., gent., for £50 to discharge a mortgage, releases to Hugh Terry of said county, yeoman, the tract of land called Swan Harbor. Hugh Terry bought from William Beastin the tract of land called Swan Harbor on Bohemia River at Omealys Creek and on 6 Dec 1736 mortgaged it to William Rumsey. Made & Ackn: 26 Jun 1740. Wit: William Beastin, John Ryland, Jr. JPs: John Veazey, Pereg'n. Ward. Rec: 20 Dec 1740. Wm. Knight, Clerk.

P. 36   Release.   John Sutton of Cecil Co., planter, for £120 and to discharge a mortgage of £80, to William Rumsey of said county, gent., all the land he previously mortgaged to him. By deed dated 26 Apr 1737 and for £80, John Sutton mortgaged to William Rumsey 100 acres and a water mill with its 10 acres, part of a tract of land called Essex Lodge originally granted by patent dated 20 Jul 1673 to William Browkus alias Brokers for 700 acres on the south side of Bohemia River at Omealys alias Scotchmans Creek. Also 10 acres on the other side of the dam which is part of Swan Harbor. Sutton has not repaid Rumsey. Made 30 Oct 1740. Wit: John Baldwin, John Thompson. Ackn: 27 Jan 1740 by John Sutton and his wife Mary. JPs: John Baldwin, John Veazey. Alienation fine of 4 shillings paid 13 Jan 1740 to Jas. Paul Heath. Rec: 7 Feb 1740. Wm. Knight, Clerk.

P. 39   Deed.   John Thompson of Cecil Co., for £5, to William Rumsey of the same county, gent., 27 perches of land and the grist mill on it, part of a tract called the Middle Parcel. Said mill was built by Rumsey at his cost. Made 27 Jan 1740. Wit. & JPs: John Baldwin, John Veazey. Ackn: same day by John Thompson and his wife Mary. On 30 Jan 1740 Jas. Paul Heath rec'd the alienation fine for the land. Rec: 7 Feb 1740. Wm. Knight, Clerk.

P. 40   Deed.   William Bateman of Cecil Co., planter, in accordance with his father's Will and in consideration that his brother John pay half the costs incurred and for 5 shillings, to his brother John Bateman of the same place, planter, 133 acres, part of the lands called King's Aim and Bateman's Tryal. William Bateman, deceased, father of the said William and John Bateman, made his Last Will and Testament dated 23 Feb 1708 and devised his land to William and John to be divided equally between them. This land was 200 acres, part of a tract called King's Aim. William Bateman the son has lately surveyed the land and taken up 66 acres called Bateman's Tryal adjoining it. Made 24 Sep 1740. Wit: Wm. Rumsey, Benjamin Childs. 5 shillings alienation fine paid 30 Sep by John Bateman to Ja. Paul Heath. Rec: 7 Mar 1740. Wm. Knight, Clerk.

P. 42   Release.   Joshua George of Cecil Co., for 5 shillings, quit claims to John Campbell of said county, all his right and interest in a tract of land called None So Good in Finland. Made & Ackn: 12 Mar 1740. Wit. & JPs: John Baldwin, John Veazey. Rec: 12 Mar 1740. Wm. Knight, Clerk.

P. 42   Deed.   Henry Rippon of Chester Town, Kent Co., mariner, for £18, to Thomas Severson of Cecil Co., planter, a tract of 12½ acres called Price's Intelligence in Cecil Co. adjoining a tract called Larramore's Neck. Made & Ackn: 4 Dec 1740. Wit. & JP: Stephen Knight. Alienation fine of 4 shillings paid on 20 Dec to Jas. Paul Heath. Rec: 10 Mar 1740. Wm. Knight, Clerk.

P. 43 Deed. John Lusby of Cecil Co., yeoman, and his wife Margaret, for £17, to William Beastin of said county, yeoman, 10 acres of land, part of a tract of land called Banks bounded on the north by Bohemia River, on the east and south by the 200 acres of the said tract which was sold to the Visitors of Cecil Co. School and on the west by John Ryland's land called Mulberry Mould. The tract called Banks was originally patented 25 Jul 1664 to Thomas Bostick. Made & Ackn: 29 Aug 1740. Wit: Ben Pearce, John Veazey. JPs: John Baldwin, John Veazey. Rec: 26 Feb 1740. Wm. Knight, Clerk.

P. 44 Assignment of Lease. John Seagar, Jr., of Cecil Co., planter, for £45 and 4,500 lbs of tobacco and because he is moving, assigns to Laurance Lauranson of the same county, planter, a lease for 140 acres of land. Terms are the same as in original lease. Ephraim Augustine Herman, on 1 May 1729, leased to John Seagar, father of the said John Seagar, Jr., 140 acres in Bohemia Manor. The terms of the lease was for 3 natural lifetimes; that of John Seagar the Elder, John Seagar the Younger and Samuel Seagar. John Seagar the Elder assigned the lease to his son John Seagar the Younger. Made & Ackn: 11 Oct 1740. Wit: William Beastin, Thos. Colvill. JPs: Thos. Colvill, John Baldwin. Rec: 11 Mar 1740. Wm. Knight, Clerk.

P. 46 Deed. Benjamin Winslow of Cecil Co., farmer, and his wife Mary, for £170, to John Steel, late of Ireland, gent., 166 acres and 120 perches of land, part of a tract called New Munster on the main branch of Elk River. Winslow bought this land from Nicholas Dorrell of the said county by deed dated 25 Mar 1738. Winslow will warrant this land against any claims of the heirs of Nicholas Dorrell and the heirs of John Vansandt. Made 11 Nov 1740. Wit: Thos. Colvill, Wm. Knight. Signed and sealed by Benj. Winsley and Mary Winsley made her mark. Ackn: 12 Nov 1740 by Benjamin Winslow and his wife Mary. JPs: Thos. Colvill, Nich. Hyland. On 13 Nov Ja. Paul Heath rec'd 3s6p alienation fine. Rec: 12 Mar 1740. Wm. Knight, Clerk.

P. 48 Deed. John Steel, late of Ireland, gent., for £170, to Archibald Steel of Dromore, Lancaster Co., PA, cordwainer, 166 acres and 120 perches of land, part of a tract called Newmunster [see previous Entry P. 46.] Made 20 Feb 1740/41. Wit: John Vanel, A. Barry. Ackn: 21 Feb 1740/41. JPs: A. Barry, Robert Story. Alienation fine of 3s4p paid 12 Mar 1740 to Ja. Paul Heath. Rec: 12 Mar 1740. Wm. Knight, Clerk.

P. 50 Valuation of Estate. John Thompson and John Bateman were requested by Henry Hendrickson, guardian of Matthias Hendrickson, orphan of Cecil Co., to view said orphans estate and was sworn in by JP John Baldwin, gent. They found there was no cleared ground nor any improvements on the land. They allow the guardian 48 acres at the northwest end and 3 years rent free. They estimate the annual value of the estate after the said 3 years to be 500 lbs of tobacco. Made 3 Dec 1740. Rec: 14 Mar 1740. Wm. Knight, Clerk.

P. 51 Commission of the Peace. Charles Lord Baltimore appoints as Justices of the Peace for the County of Cecil Matthew Tilghman Ward, John Rousby, Benjamin Tasker, Philip Lee, George Plater, Edmund Jennings, James Holliday, Charles Hammond, Levin Gale, James Harris, Samuel Chamberlin, Thomas Colvill, Richard Thompson, John Baldwin, William Rumsey, Joseph Huse, Andrew Berry, John Veazey, Robert Story, Peregrine Ward, Samuel Gilpin and Nicholas Hyland. Made by Samuel Ogle, Lt. Gov., 14 Jul 1740. Rec: 23 Mar 1740. Wm. Knight, Clerk.

P. 54 Deed. Thady McDermot of Cecil Co., cooper, for £5, to James Hughes of the same place, innholder, the eastern most moiety of lot #54 on the north side of Sassafras River in Frederick Town on the north side of Prince William Street. Made & Ackn: 6 Feb 1740. Wit. & JPs: John Baldwin, Wm. Rumsey.

P. 55 Deed. Henry Rippon of Kent Co., mariner, for £170, to John Hayes of the same place, carpenter, 200 acres of land in Cecil Co. called Sewall's Pasture, part of a tract called Essex Lodge. Made 23 Dec 1740. Wit: Pereg. Frisby, S. Knight. On 15 Jan 1740 Ja. Paul Heath receive from John Hays 4 shillings alienation fine and 8 shillings rents due. Rec: 28 Mar 1741. Wm. Knight, Clerk.

P. 57 Deed. John Campbell of Cecil Co., planter, for £290, to Peter Jones of Kent Co., planter, the 150 acres which, in his lifetime, John Dowdall, late of Cecil Co., gent., owned, part of a tract of land called None So Good In Finland on Back Creek on the north side of Sassafras River. In his Last Will and Testament, John Dowdall bequeathed the land to Richard Dowdall and John McManus. The said Richard Dowdall sold his moiety of the land to Augustin Thompson. In his Last Will and Testament, Augustin Thompson devised the moiety of the land to his daughter Mary, wife of Thomas Marsh. Then Thomas and Mary Marsh sold the moiety of land to the said John Campbell. John McManus made his Last Will and Testament, devising his moiety of the land to the said John Campbell and Joshua George who released his rights to the land to the said John Campbell. Made 24 Mar 1740. Wit: Wm. Rumsey, Thomas Jones. Ackn: 25 Mar 1741. JPs: Wm. Rumsey, John Veazey. Rec: 4 Apr 1741. Wm. Knight, Clerk.

P. 61 Deed. Thomas Price of Cecil Co., and Elinor his wife, for £42, to Robert Patton of the same county, a plantation and 100 acres of land on the north side of Bohemia Back Creek by Richard Boulding's land and by land called Uppermost. Made 16 Feb 1740. Wit: James Foster, James Redus. Ackn: same day by Thomas Price, Jr. and his wife Elinor. JPs: Wm. Rumsey, R'd. Thompson. Ja. Paul Heath rec'd from Robert Patton on 10 Mar 1740 the alienation fine of 2 shillings and 4 shillings for 2 years rent. Rec: 6 Apr 1741. Wm. Knight, Clerk.

P. 62 Deed. Paul Poulson, late of Cecil Co., planter, to Simon Johnson, Jr., of Cecil Co., planter, 100 acres of land on the north side of Little Elk River, part of a tract called Successor. Made & Ackn: 12 Jan 1740/41. Wit: John Hyland, William Currier. JP: A. Barry. Rec: 15 Apr 1741. Wm. Knight, Clerk.

P. 63 Deed. Richard Bennett of Queen Annes Co., merchant, for £180, to James Heath of Cecil Co., merchant, a tract of land called Stockton Addition (surveyed for Richard Bennett for 225 acres) which lies between the branches of Bohemia and Sassafras Rivers. Made & Ackn: 10 Apr 1741. Wit: R. Porter, J. Lockerman. JP: Sam. Chamberlaine. John Lusby accounts for the alienation fine of 9 shillings on 14 Mar 1741. Rec: 15 Apr 1741. Wm. Knight, Clerk.

P. 64 Deed. Ann Elizabeth Rosentwist, spinster, for £100, to Robert Mercer of Cecil Co., planter, a 150 acre tract of land called Mounsfield. Said land was originally granted to Mounce Anderson (great grandfather to the said Ann Elizabeth Rosentwist) on 1 Jul 1663 and called Mounsfield lying on the south side and near the mouth of Elk River on the south side of the Pond. Made & Ackn: 14 Apr 1741. Wit. & JPs: John Baldwin, John Veazey. John Lusby collected the alienation fine 2 May 1741. Rec: 18 Apr 1741. Wm. Knight, Clerk.

P. 66 Deed. Joseph Alexander of Cecil Co., carpenter, and Margaret his wife, for £60 and because they are moving, to Adam Wilson of Newcastle upon Delaware Co., cooper, 105 acres of land east of the great road from Emmitt's Mill, part of a tract called Newmunster on the east side of the main branch of Elk River. Said land was left to Joseph Alexander by the Last Will and Testament of James Alexander, carpenter, who bought the land from Thomas Stevenson by deed dated 15 Aug 1718. Thomas Stevenson had bought the land from Robert Roberts by deed dated 1 Apr 1714. Made 12 Dec 1740. Wit: Geo. Lawson, Rob't. Gardner, A. Barry. Ackn: 15 Dec 1740.

JPs: A. Barry, Robert Story. Alienation fine of 2 shillings rec'd by John Lusby 10 Jan 1740. Rec: 29 May 1741. Wm. Knight, Clerk, and Francis Key, Clerk.

P. 67 Deed. Colonel John Ward of Cecil Co., gent., for £50, to James Paul Heath of the same county, gent., 2 tracts of land on the north side of Sassafras River, one called Forlorn Hope (126 acres originally granted by patent to Henry Eldersly 1 Oct 1697) and the other called Leake's Addition (100 acres originally granted to Richard Leake 16 Nov 1670.) Both tracts of land were the estate of Elizabeth and Sarah, daughters of Samuel Richardson, late of London, mariner, and his wife Elizabeth who was the only daughter and heiress of Henry Eldersly and his wife Parnell, the widow and devisee of Eldersly's Last Will and Testament. Elizabeth and Sarah, and their husbands Richard Hind and Robert Coulson, by deed dated 18 Apr 1739 sold all their lands in Cecil and Kent counties to the said John Ward. Made: 29 Apr 1741. Wit: Wm. Rumsey, Ben Pearce. Ackn: same day by Col. John Ward and his wife Mary. JPs: Wm. Rumsey, Pereg. Ward. Alienation fine rec'd 10 May 1741 by John Lusby. Rec: 9 May 1741. Wm. Knight, Clerk.

P. 70 Deed. John Bennett of Kent Co., innholder, and Elizabeth his wife, for £12, to Thomas Davis of Cecil Co., planter, lot #55 in Frederick Town in Cecil Co. on the north side of Sassafras River. Made & Ackn: 12 May 1741. Wit. & JPs: John Veazey, Pereg. Ward. Alienation fine paid to John Lusby 12 May 1741. Rec: 6 Jun 1741. Wm. Knight, Clerk.

P. 71 Deed. Samuel Duvall, son of John Duvall of Cecil Co., planter, for 11,200 lbs of tobacco, to Jacob Giles of Baltimore Co., 150 acres, a moiety of a tract of land called Larkin's Desire in Cecil Co. on the east side of Susquehanna River by the land of Samuel Smith's called Heath's, and by the division line of Thomas Sheperd (who bought the other moiety of this land from said Duvall.) [Duvall is also spelled Devall.] Made & Ackn: 11 May 1741. Wit: Nich. Hyland, Wm. Jempson. JPs: Nich. Hyland, Robert Story. John Lusby rec'd the alienation fine of 6 shillings from Jacob Giles 18 May 1741. Rec: 9 Jun 1741. Wm. Knight, Clerk.

P. 73 Deed. William Beastin of Cecil Co., late innholder, for £66, to James Bayard of said county, merchant, the southernmost part of lot #20 at the southwest corner of Cecil Street on the south side of Bohemia River in Cecil Town. Also 10 acres, part of a tract called Banks by Bohemia River by the 200 acres (part of the same tract) sold by Hugh Watson to the Visitors of Cecil Co. School and by John Ryland's land called Mulberry Mould. The tract called Banks was originally granted 25 Jul 1664 to Thomas Bostick. Made 18 Mar 1740. Wit: John Baldwin, Jno. Holland. Ackn: same day by William Beastin and his wife Elizabeth. JPs: Thos. Colvill, John Baldwin. Rec: 22 Jun 1741. Wm. Knight, Clerk.

P. 75   Deed.   John Holtham of Cecil Co., (and his wife Ann) in pursuance of an award dated 14 Mar 1740 and for £20 and 500 lbs of tobacco, quit claims to Andrew Alexander 2 tracts of land called Warwick and Triangle adjacent to each other. Said land formerly owned by John Holtham, late of said county, deceased. [Holtham is also spelled Haltham.] Made & Ackn: 14 Apr 1741. Wit: John Veazey, Ben Pearce. JPs: John Baldwin, John Veazey. Alienation fine rec'd by John Lusby 9 Jun 1741. Rec: 24 Jun 1741. Wm. Knight, Clerk.

P. 76   Deed.   James Paul Heath of Cecil Co., merchant, for £202, to Michael Manycozens of the said county, planter, 202 acres of land on the NW side of the main road leading from Sassafras to the plantation late of Andrew Peterson, esq., deceased, and by tracts of land called Skelton, Sarah's Jointure and Indian Range. Said land is part of several tracts called Stockton's Addition, Heath's Middle Parcel and Heath's Second & Fourth Parcel. [Manycozens also spelled Manycosens.] Made 5 Jun 1741. Wit. & JPs: John Baldwin, Pereg. Ward. Ackn: same day by James Paul Heath and his wife Rebecca. Alienation fine rec'd by John Lusby 6 Jun 1741. Rec: 16 Jul 1741. Wm. Knight, Clerk.

P. 79   Deed.   Michael Manycousins of Cecil Co., planter, for £170, to William Beedle of the same county, a tract of 194 acres called Colleton on the east side of Elk River near the head of St. Albins Creek. [Manycousins is also spelled Manycozens.] Made & Ackn: 5 Jun 1741. Wit. & JPs: John Baldwin, Peregn. Ward. William Beedle paid 3 shillings alienation fine to John Lusby on 16 Jun 1741. Rec: 19 Jul 1741. Wm. Knight, Clerk.

P. 80   Deed.   Benjamin Childs of Cecil Co., planter, for £130, to William Walmsley of the said county, planter, 100 acres of land, part of a tract called Shrewsbury on the north side of Sassafras River south of Pond Creek by land lately belonging to Mounce Andrews. Made 27 Apr 1741. Wit: John Veazey, John Ryland, Jr. Ackn: same day by Benjamin Childs and his wife Martha. JPs: John Baldwin, John Veazey. Alienation fine of 4 shillings paid to John Lusby 14 May 1741. Rec: 27 Jul 1741. Wm. Knight, Clerk.

P. 83   Deed of Gift.   Stephen Knight of Kent Co., gent., for love, good will and natural affection, gives to his son William Knight of Cecil Co., gent.,

300 acres, part of a tract of 1,500 acres of land called Clifton at the head of Bohemia River in Cecil Co. by the land of Walter Scott. Stephen Knight purchased the land from Thomas Larkins of Ann Arundel Co., gent. Made 3 Aug 1741. Wit: Cordelia Knight, Charles Coatts. Ackn: 4 Aug 1741. JPs: Thomas Colvill, Wm. Rumsey. Alienation fine of 12 shillings paid to Pereg. Frisby 5 Aug 1741. Rec: 4 Aug 1741. Wm. Knight, Clerk.

P. 84   Lease.   Elizabeth Jackson of Cecil Co., seamstress, to Henry Jackson of the same county, farmer, all her rights of dowry of a third part of 2 tracts of land called Hart's Delight and Rich Hill with the dwellings and orchards. Lease is for the term of the said Elizabeth Jackson's life. Henry Jackson to pay £8 and 200 gallons of cider yearly. Elizabeth Jackson shall have the use of the old house (which they formerly lived in) for the time that she remains unmarried. Made 10 Apr 1741. Wit: Benja. Chew, Edward Jackson. Memo: the said £8 to be paid in 2 payments yearly: on 10 Mar and 10 Sep. Also Henry Jackson will repair the house at his own cost. Ackn: 11 Aug 1741. JPs: Rich'd. Thompson, Pereg. Ward. Rec: 11 Aug 1741. Wm. Knight, Clerk.

P. 85   Deed.   James Young of PA, for £62.10s and because he is moving, to Augustine Passmore of Millford Hundred, Cecil Co., farmer, 106 acres in Millford Hundred called Bare Point by land surveyed for George Robinson called Doe Hill. Lord Baltimore, by patent dated 2 May 1723, granted to Alexander White a tract of 106 acres of land in Cecil Co. called Bare Point which is recorded in the land office in Lib. PL No. 5, folio 450. Alexander White and his wife, by deed dated 26 Feb 1729/30 recorded in Lib. L. K. No. 5, folios 222-223, sold the land to James Young. Made & Ackn: 6 Jun 1741. Wit: Robert Story, Matts. Seal. JPs: Robert Story, Nichs. Hyland. Alienation fine of 4s.3p paid by Passmore to John Lusby 23 Jun 1741. Rec: 12 Aug 1741. Wm. Knight, Clerk.

P. 88   Deed.   Peter Lawson of Cecil Co., innholder, for £250, to Capt. Peter Bayard and James Bayard of said county, gents., a mill and land on Back Creek where the said Peter Lawson now dwells. Lawson recently bought the premises from Col. Thomas Colvill of said county. Made & Ackn: 15 Aug 1741. Wit. & JPs: Thos. Colvill, R'd. Thompson. Rec: 15 Aug 1741. Wm. Knight, Clerk.

P. 90   Deed.   Charles Carroll of Annapolis, for £20, to Robert Holy of Cecil Co., planter, 122 acres, part of a tract of land called the Society in Cecil Co. (already in the actual possession of said Robert Holy) by the land of Joseph Street. Made & Ackn: 3 Jun 1741. Wit: Robert Gordon, Joshua George. JP: Robert Gordon. Rec: 15 Aug 1741. Wm. Knight, Clerk.

P. 91   Deed.   Henry Penington of Frederick Town on Sassafras River, Cecil Co., innholder, for £100, to William Rumsey of the same county, gent., 100 acres, part of a tract on the north side of Sassafras River called Happy Harbor by land called Buntington. Said land originally granted by patent dated 10 Apr 1671 to Richard Leak for 400 acres. Made 7 Jul 1741. Wit. & JPs: John Baldwin, Pereg. Ward. Ackn: same day by Henry Penington and his wife Mary. Alienation fine paid to John Lusby 1 Aug 1741. Rec: 5 Sep 1741. Wm. Knight, Clerk.

P. 93   Lease.   Thomas Hargrave of Minsworth, Curdworth Parish, Warwick Co., yeoman, only son and heir of Abraham Hargrave, late of the same place, yeoman, deceased, who was the eldest brother and heir of Isaac Hargrave, late of Turkey Point, Cecil Co., MD, planter, deceased, for 5 shillings and because he is moving, leases to Thomas Webb of Hattonfield, West New Jersey, blacksmith, 160 acres and plantation near Turkey Point. Made 2 Aug 1736. Wit: John Gibbons, Samuel Lane. Ackn: in Gloucester Co., NJ 14 Dec 1736 by Samuel Lane. JPs: John Kay, James Hinchman. Ackn: in Cecil Co. 21 Oct 1737 by Samuel Lane. JP: Thos. Colvill. Rec: 5 Sep 1741. Wm. Knight, Clerk.

P. 95   Release.   Thomas Hargrave, for £10, to Thomas Webb [see entry above] 160 acres. Said land was the inheritance of Isaac Hargrave, and at his death, the land descended to Abraham Hargrave who then died and left the land to the said Thomas Hargrave. Made 3 Aug 1736. Wit: John Gibbons, Samuel Lane. Ackn: in Gloucester Co., NJ 14 Dec 1736 by Samuel Lane. JPs: John Kay, James Hinchman. Ackn: in Cecil Co. 21 Oct 1737 by Samuel Lane. JP: Thos. Colvill. John Lusby rec'd the alienation fine of 4 shillings from William Rumsey on 4 Sep 1741 for 200 acres called Withers, supposed to be the land in this deed. Rec: 5 Sep 1741. Wm. Knight, Clerk.

P. 99   Deed.   Thomas Webb of Haddonfield, in the township of Newton in Gloucester Co., NJ, blacksmith, for £50, to William Rumsey of Cecil Co., gent., 160 acres near Turkey Point in Cecil Co. [see above 2 entries.] Thomas Webb appoints James Paul Heath and Dr. Benjamin Bradford, both gents. of Cecil Co., to be his attorneys. Made 25 May 1741. Wit: James Hinchman, John Kaighin, Gervas Hall. Ackn: 24 Aug 1741 by James Hinchman and Dr. Benjamin Bradford, attorney for Webb. JPs: Thos. Colvill, John Baldwin. Rec: 5 Sep 1741. Wm. Knight, Clerk.

P. 103   Deed.   Gavin Hutchinson, late of Cecil Co. but now of Newcastle on Delaware, schoolmaster, and his wife Martha, for £20, to Adam Peterson of Appoq Hundred, Newcastle Co., cooper, a tract of 100 acres called Fatigue in Cecil Co. on Back Creek by the deceased Wm. Bouldin's plantation. Made & Ackn: 9 Jun 1741. Wit. & JPs: John Baldwin, Robert Story. Adam Peterson paid the alienation fine of 4 shillings to John Lusby 1 Jul 1741. Rec: 11 Sep 1741. Wm. Knight, Clerk.

P. 105   Deed.   John Hyland of Cecil Co., farmer, and his wife Martha, for £100 and because they are moving, to Caleb Pennal of Lancaster Co., PA, farmer, 100 acres, part of a tract of land called Poplar Valley on the northeast side of Susquehanna River. The acreage stated is according to a survey made 3 Nov 1715. [Pennal also spelled Pennall, Penniel, Pannel.] Made 28 Oct 1741. Wit: Nich's. Hyland, Will'm. Wye, Adam Lodge. Ackn: next day. JPs: John Veazey, Nich's. Hyland. Rec: 29 Oct 1741. Wm. Knight, Clerk.

P. 108   Deed of Gift.   Thomas Harper to his 3 sons John, William and James Harper, to be equally divided between them, all the land devised to him the said Thomas Harper except 100 acres which the said Thomas leased to his son Jacob Harper. They are not to sell the land during their father's lifetime unless it be from one to the other among themselves. Nor are they to disturb their father in the possession of the lands he has enclosed in his dwelling plantation. Made 30 Mar 1741. Wit: Wm. Knight, Wm. Rumsey. Ackn: 10 Nov 1741 by Thomas Harper. JPs: Thos. Colvill, R'd. Thompson. Rec: 10 Nov 1741. Wm. Knight, Clerk.

P. 109   Lease.   William Alexander of Cecil Co., gent., to Robert Lucas of the same county, brass founder, 9 acres of woodland, part of a tract called Friendship, at the parting of the road leading to Samuel Jones' place from the road leading to George Lawson's store. Lease is for the term of the natural lives of Robert Lucas, Henry VanBebber (son of James VanBebber) and Ann Jacobs (dau. of Thomas Jacobs, miller.) Rent of one ear of Indian corn due 11 Jul yearly. Tenants are to leave a good fence around the said 9 acres. Made 7 Apr 1741. Wit: Anry Borom [sic], Benj. Pilose. Ackn: 1 Jun 1741. JPs: Robert Story, Nich's. Hyland. Rec: 10 Nov 1741. Wm. Knight, Clerk.

P. 110   Deed of Gift.   William Alexander of Cecil Co., gent., and Araminta his wife, to Robert Lucas, founder, Zebulon Hollingsworth, innholder, Thomas Ricketts, blacksmith, Robert Evans, farmer, all of Cecil Co., and David Barr of Newcastle Co., weaver, 1 acre of land, part of a tract called Friendship, at the head of Elk River. A Protestant meeting house is to be built on the land. Land is returned to William Alexander by default of the land going unused for a period of 3 years. Made & Ackn: 1 Jun 1741. JPs: Robert Story, Nich's. Hyland. Rec: 10 Nov 1741. Wm. Knight, Clerk.

P. 112 Deed. George Robinson and Valentine Robinson, sons and heirs of George Robinson, deceased, all of Brandywine Hundred, Newcastle Co., with Joseph Robinson, executor, for £190, to John Passmore of Millford Hundred, Cecil Co., farmer, 400 acres of a tract called Consent. By patent dated 10 Dec 1713, Lord Baltimore granted to George Robinson a tract of 800 acres in Cecil Co. on Elk River called Consent. In his lifetime, George Robinson agreed to convey 400 acres of the land to the said John Passmore. By his Last Will and Testament dated 2 Nov 1738, Robinson appointed his brother Joseph Robinson his executor to convey the land to Passmore. Made & Ackn: 20 Jun 1741. Wit: Robert Story, Mary Story. JPs: Robert Story, A. Barry. Alienation fine of 16 shillings paid to John Lusby by John Passmore 2 Jul 1741. Rec: 10 Nov 1741. Wm. Knight, Clerk.

P. 115 Deed. Robert Wilson of Orange Co., Va, farmer, and his wife Garrate, for £70, to William Irwin of Nottingham, Chester Co., PA, farmer, 122 acres of land in Cecil Co., part of a tract called Providence, by William Hog's line. Charles Lord Baltimore granted a warrant dated 16 May 1716 to Samuel Robinet of Nottingham, Chester Co., PA, farmer, to take 350 acres in any part of Maryland. On 19 Jun 1716 the surveyor laid out for the said Robinet a tract of land called Providence. Samuel Robinet sold 100 acres of the land to Robert Wilson for £52 by deed dated 23 Jun 1733. A patent was obtained for the land dated 8 Jun 1732. The 100 acres sold to Wilson was later resurveyed to amount to 122 acres. Made 3 Aug 1741. Wit: James Allen, John Ruddell. Ackn: 14 Aug 1741 in Cecil Co. by Robert and Garrata Wilson. JPs: Robert Story, A. Barry. Alienation fine of 4s.11p rec'd 18 Aug 1741 by John Lusby. Rec: 10 Nov 1741. Wm. Knight, Clerk.

P. 118 Deed. James Foster and John Foster, executors of William Foster, lately deceased, of Cecil Co., planters, to John Bravard of the same place, blacksmith, 100 acres of land on the north side of Long Creek by the lands of James Foster and John Bravard, Sr. and by the land formerly conveyed by William Foster to John Bravard, Jr. The Last Will and Testament of William Foster authorized his executors James and John Foster to convey a parcel of land to Thomas Price, Jr., for his assignees for which Price has already paid William Foster. John Bravard is the assignee of Thomas Price, Jr. Made 14 Aug 1741. Wit. & JPs: R'd. Thompson, Nicholas Hyland. Ackn: Aug 1741 by James and John Foster and Thomas Price, Jr. John Bravard, Jr. paid 4s alienation fine on 100 acres of land, part of Jones' Green Spring, on 30 Aug 1741 to John Lusby. Rec: 10 Nov 1741. Wm. Knight, Clerk.

P. 120   Deed.   Seth Ruley of Cecil Co., for £80, to Edward Oldham of Chester Co., PA, farmer, 200 acres of land (part of a tract called Siniqua Point in the Manor of Susquehanna alias New Connaught) on the west side of Shannon River adjoining that part of the tract surveyed by Mr. Will'm. Rumsey, then Deputy Surveyor of Cecil Co., 20 Aug 1728 and laid out for Robert Johnson. Land is free of any claim by Seth Ruley or his sister Ann Gater, wife of John Gater. [Seth is also spelled Sieth.] Made 13 Nov 1741 [sic.] Wit. & JPs: Andrew Barry, Nicholas Hyland. Ackn: 10 Nov 1741. Rec: 11 Nov 1741. Wm. Knight, Clerk. John Lusby rec'd alienation fine of 8s on 16 Jan 1741.

P. 122   Deed.   George Johnson of Annapolis, barber, for £65 to Edward Oldham of Pennsylvania, 200 acres of land in Cecil Co., part of a tract called Sinequa Point, by Mr. Currier's plantation and running up the North East River. Made 22 Oct 1741. Wit: Jno. Brice, Henry Baker. Ackn: 23 Oct 1741 by George Johnson and his wife Mary. JP: J. Brice. John Lusby rec'd the alienation fine of 8s on 16 Jan 1741. Rec: 11 Nov 1741. Wm. Knight, Clerk.

P. 123   Deed.   Thomas Coulson and his wife Martha of West Nottingham, Chester Co., PA, for £15, to Joseph Brown of the same place, 100 acres of land in Cecil Co. on the east side of Susquehanna River. Said land is part of a tract of 500 acres called the Glass House originally taken up by Richard Gray 11 Apr 1678 and on 1 Feb 1684 was sold by Richard Gray and his wife Rachel to Cornelius Comegys. The land was conveyed to Paul Poulson and Randall Death who on 2 Mar 1736/7 sold 200 acres of the tract to Thomas Coulson. Made & Ackn: 6 Oct 1741. Wit. & JPs: John Baldwin, Nichs. Hyland. Alienation fine of 4s rec'd from Joseph Brown 29 Oct 1741 by John Lusby. Rec: 11 Nov 1741. Wm. Knight, Clerk.

P. 126   Deed.   Providence Williams of Orange Co., VA, farmer, to William Mitchell of Cecil Co., yeoman, a tract of 222 acres called High Park on the east side of Susquehanna River in Cecil Co. by land taken up by Edward Teague called Teague's Delight. Also a tract of 60 acres called Emery's Choice on the east side of Susquehanna River by Moulton's Marsh and a tract called Penbroke taken up by Edward Teague. Joseph Williams and his wife Lidia, Sarah Williams, the wife of Providence Williams, and Ann Poulson, all of Orange Co., VA, by letter of attorney dated 2 Mar 1736/7 appointed Providence Williams to be their attorney to acknowledge this deed. [Emery's Choice is also called Amorous Choice.] Deed made 8 Mar 1736/7. Wit: Nathaniel Ewing, Isaac Saunders, Hugh Lawson, John Graham, David Patterson, David Denny. Ackn: 10 Mar 1736/7 in Cecil Co. by Providence

Williams. JPs: Edward Jackson, A. Barry. Power of Attorney made in Orange Co., VA 2 Mar 1736/7. Wit. & JPs: M. Morgan, George Hobson. Ackn: in Orange Co., VA by Capt. Morgan Morgan on Tuesday 27 Aug 1741. Test: Jonathan Gibson, Clerk. Rec: in Cecil Co. 11 Nov 1741. Wm. Knight, Clerk.

P. 129 Deed. William Mitchell of Cecil Co., yeoman, for £110, to Samuel Davison of the same place, yeoman, a tract of 222 acres called High Park where the said William Mitchell now lives near Caniwagoe Fall and by a tract called Teague's Delight taken up by Edward Teague. Made 11 Nov 1741. Wit. & JPs: A. Barry, Nichs. Hyland. Ackn: same day by William Mitchell and his wife Mary. Alienation fine of 9 shillings rec'd by John Lusby 12 Nov 1741. Rec: 12 Nov 1741. Wm. Knight, Clerk.

P. 131 Power of Attorney. Christian Land and Samuel Land, executors of Francis Land, late of Newcastle Co., deceased, appoint Joseph Thomas of Newcastle Co., farmer, to be their attorney to acknowledge a quit claim to Roger Merrick, executor of David Merrick of Maryland, lately deceased, all their interest in land "herein mentioned," for £30 and because they are moving, already in his [Merrick's] possession. Made 19 May 1741. Wit: Thomas James, William Moore, John Ricketts, Benjamin Thomas. Ackn: 12 Nov 1741 by John Ricketts, Benjamin Thomas and Joseph Thomas. JPs: Wm. Rumsey, A. Barry. Rec: 12 Nov 1741. Wm. Knight, Clerk.

P. 132 Deed. Suloff Steadham of Cecil Co., planter, for £50, to William Stubey of Newcastle on Delaware Co., weaver, 100 acres, part of a tract of land called Feddart (already in Stubey's possession) on the west side of Elk River in Cecil Co. Said land is warranted from any claim of Michael Johnson, devisee of Henry Johnson, deceased, who purchased the land from Margaret Lindsay. Made & Ackn: 3 Sep 1741. Wit: Job Everson, Wm. Rumsey. JPs: Wm. Rumsey, R'd. Thompson. Rec: 12 Nov 1741. Wm. Knight, Clerk.

P. 133 Assignment of Lease. John Hamm of Cecil Co., for £25, assigns to Peter Lawson a lease of land for the term of the three natural lives stated in said lease. Said lease is from Col. Ephr. Augt'n. Herman to John Hamm for 53 acres of land, part of Bohemia Manor, recorded in Lib. W. K. No. 2, folios 36-37 dated 14 Aug 1734. Made 25 Jun 1741. Wit: Isaac Hamm, John Latham. Rec: 24 Nov 1741. Wm. Knight, Clerk.

P. 134 Lease. Richard Thompson, Sr., of Cecil Co., gent., for rents and covenants, to Richard Thompson, Jr., of the same county, yeoman, part of a tract of land called Three Bohemia Sisters (more commonly called Judith's

Neck) on the north side of Back Creek at Broad Creek and by Jacob Young's cart road and Elk River road. Richard Thompson, Sr. reserves for himself during his natural life the free use and occupation of the plantation houses and buildings where he now lives. Lease is for the term of the natural lives of Richard Thompson, Jr. and his wife Mary and for the natural life of Samuel, the son of Mary the daughter of Rene' Julian, late of Cecil Co. Rent of £1 to be paid yearly during the lifetime of Richard Thompson, Sr. and after his decease £5 yearly to his heirs and legal representatives. Made & Ackn: 23 Nov 1741. Wit. & JPs: John Baldwin, Wm. Rumsey. Rec: 21 Dec 1741. Wm. Knight, Clerk.

P. 136 Deed. Evert Evertson, Jr. of Cecil Co., planter, for £7, to James Paul Heath of said county, gent., 7 acres, part of a tract called Middle Parcel on the south side of the main road that leads from Sassafras to the plantation where Andrew Peterson, deceased, did live. Made 14 Dec 1741. Wit. & JPs: Wm. Rumsey, R'd. Thompson, Jr. Ackn: same day by Evert Evertson and his wife Elizabeth. John Lusby rec'd the alienation fine of 3½p on 23 Dec 1741. Rec: 1 Jan 1741. Wm. Knight, Clerk.

P. 137 Deed. James Paul Heath of Cecil Co., gent., for £17, to Evert Evertson, Jr. of the same place, planter, 17 acres of land by several tracts called Skelton, Sarah's Jointure, Heath's Second & Fourth Parcel and by a tract formerly called Booker's Uppermost (now called Middle Parcel) and is part of Stockton's Addition which was granted 30 Nov 1714 by patent to Richard Bennett for 225 acres. Richard Bennett sold the land to James Paul Heath. Made & Ackn: 18 Dec 1741. Wit: Wm. Rumsey, Robert Mercer. Heath's wife Rebecca released her dower in the land. JPs: Wm. Rumsey, John Veazey. Evert Evertson paid 3½p alienation fine to John Lusby 22 Dec 1741. Rec: 9 Jan 1741. Wm. Knight, Clerk.

P. 138 Deed. William Rumsey of Cecil Co., gent., for £12.10s, to James Paul Heath of said county, gent., a parcel of land called the Scraps east of the south branch of Bohemia River which was granted by patent 10 Nov 1735 to William Rumsey for 12½ acres. Made 14 Dec 1741. Wit: Edward Jno. Wight, R'd. Thompson, Jr. Ackn: 21 Dec 1741 by William Rumsey and his wife Sabina. JPs: R'd. Thompson, Pereg. Ward. Alienation of 6p paid 22 Dec 1741 to John Lusby. Rec: 1 Jan 1741. Wm. Knight, Clerk.

P. 139 Deed. William Rumsey of Cecil Co., gent., for £40, to Robert Mercer of the same county, planter, 24 acres, part of a tract called Barbados west of a tract called Mounsfield and by land called Frisby's Wild Chase. The tract called Barbados was granted by patent 20 Dec 1739 for 180 acres.

Made 14 Dec 1741. Wit: Edward Jno. Wight, R'd. Thompson, Jr. Ackn: 23 Dec 1741 by William Rumsey and his wife Sabina. JPs: R'd. Thompson, Pereg. Ward. Alienation of 11½p paid 23 Dec 1741 to John Lusby. Rec: 1 Jan 1741. Wm. Knight, Clerk.

P. 141   Release.   James Paul Heath of Cecil Co., merchant, for 10 shillings, releases to Michael Manycozens of the said county, planter, 10 acres of land, part of a tract called the Scraps conveyed to Heath by William Rumsey, on the north side of a tract called Skelton. Also 7 acres, part of a tract called the Middle Parcel conveyed to Heath by Evert Evertson, Jr. Both parcels (10 and 7 acres) are contained within the lines of 202 acres lately conveyed by James Paul Heath to Michael Manycosens. Made 18 Dec 1741. Wit: Wm. Rumsey, Robert Mercer. Ackn: same day by Heath and his wife Rebecca. JPs: Wm. Rumsey, John Veazey. Alienation fine of 8p paid to John Lusby 23 Dec 1741. Rec: 1 Jan 1741. Wm. Knight, Clerk.

P. 142   Deed.   William Freeman of Cecil Co., planter, for £25, to James Paul Heath of the said county, merchant, 103 acres of land called Good Luck by a tract called Woodbury (or Middle Plantation) now in the possession of Thomas Marsh, gent. Made 18 Dec 1741. Wit: Wm. Rumsey, Robert Mercer. Ackn: same day. JPs: Wm. Rumsey, John Veazey. Alienation fine of 4⅛s rec'd by John Lusby 23 Dec 1741. Rec: 1 Jan 1741. Wm. Knight, Clerk.

P. 143   Deed.   Thomas Coulson of West Nottingham, Chester Co., PA, joiner, and Martha his wife, for £40, to James Donnell of Cecil Co., miller, 100 acres of land on the east side of Susquehanna River in Cecil Co., part of a tract called the Glass House originally taken up by Richard Gray 11 Apr 1678 and sold by Gray and his wife Rachel 1 Feb 1684 to Cornelius Comegys. The land was since conveyed to Paul Poulson and Randell Death. On 22 Mar 1736/7, 200 acres of the tract was conveyed to Thomas Coulson. Made & Ackn: 1 Mar 1741/2. Wit. & JPs: A. Barry, Henry Baker. John Lusby rec'd alienation fine from James Donnell. Rec: 9 Mar 1741. Wm. Knight, Clerk.

P. 145   Lease.   Richard Thompson of Cecil Co., gent., for yearly rents and services, to John McCreery of the same county, joiner, 100 acres of land including the marsh, part of a tract of land called Three Sisters on the north side of Bohemia Back Creek. Said land is the southernmost moiety of 200 acres which the said Richard Thompson conveyed 20 Jul 1731 to John Walker, since deceased. John Walker and the said John McCreery had agreed to divide the land. Lease is for the term of the natural lives of John McCreery and his two sons John and Robert McCreery. Rent of a bushel of winter wheat due every 10 Nov. Made 23 Nov 1741. Wit. & JPs: Wm. Rumsey, A. Barry. Ackn: 11 Mar 1741. Rec: 11 Mar 1741. Wm. Knight, Clerk.

P. 148 Deed of Gift. Benjamin Terry of Cecil Co., planter, for 5 shillings and because he is moving, to John Terry of the same county, son and heir of Augustine Terry, late of said county, deceased, a plantation and 147 acres of land called the Banks where Thomas Terry the Elder formerly lived. Made 23 Feb 1741. Wit: John Baldwin, Joshua George. Ackn: 11 Mar 1741. JPs: Pereg. Ward, Nich. Hyland. Charles Scott paid 5s.10½p alienation fine for John Terry to John Lusby. Rec: 11 Mar 1741. Wm. Knight, Clerk.

P. 149 Deed. John Baldwin of Cecil Co., gent., for 40 shillings paid to clerk William Knight on account of John Baldwin for the benefit of the town, to William Rumsey of said county, gent., 16 lots of land: lot #'s 8, 9, 11, 12, 13, 14, 32, 37, 38, 39, 40, 51, 52, 58, 59 and 60.

An Act of Assembly for erecting a town in Cecil Co. on the north side of Sassafras River at Penington Point on tracts of land called Buntington and Happy Harbor was made at an Assembly Sessions held in Annapolis 19 Mar 1735. On 12 Sep 1737 William Rumsey took up 16 lots in the town and paid Rachel Penington, administratrix of Robert Penington, 35 shillings for each lot. He began to build on some of the lots but the time period set by the Assembly elapsed before the houses were built and had brick chimneys. On 12 Sep 1739 John Baldwin took up and entered on the town's record books the same lots. Made 30 Jan 1741. Wit: Thos. Colvill, John Thompson. Ackn: same day by Baldwin and his wife Mary. JPs: Thos. Colvill, John Veazey. Rec: 16 Mar 1741. Wm. Knight, Clerk.

P. 151 Mortgage. Robert Croker of Cecil Co., planter, and Rachel his wife, for £100, to William Ellis of the same county, 158 acres of land, part of a tract called None So Good in Finland. Said land was granted to Rachel Croker by deed dated 17 Apr 1735. To be repaid on or by 6 Apr 1744. £20 of the said £100 is to be paid within 12 months. Made & Ackn: 6 Apr 1742. Wit. & JPs: John Baldwin, Wm. Rumsey. Rec: 9 Apr 1742. Wm. Knight, Clerk.

P. 152 Deed. Morris Johnson of Penns Neck, Salem Co., NJ, for £35, to David Hampton of Cecil Co., planter, 100 acres of land at Simon's Turkey Point, the northwest part of a tract called Successor originally granted by patent dated 2 May 1680 to John Browning for 500 acres in a fork of Elk River in Cecil Co. Said 100 acres formerly belonged to Simon Johnson, deceased, who died intestate and the land descended to his eldest son Andrew Johnson who also died intestate, the land descending to Morris Johnson, the surviving son of Andrew Johnson. Morris Johnson appoints his trusty friend Peter Boyer of Cecil Co. to be his attorney to acknowledge the deed. Made 4 Nov 1741. Wit: Thomas Miles, George Bristow. Ackn: in Cecil Co. 16 Nov 1741 by George Bristow and Peter Boyer. JPs: Wm. Rumsey, R'd. Thompson. David Hampton paid 4s alienation fine to John Lusby 30 Nov 1741. Rec: 13 Apr 1742. Wm. Knight, Clerk.

P. 155   Deed.   William Rumsey of Cecil Co., gent., for £45, to Richard Lewis of said county, planter, 60 acres of land by the said Lewis' land called Tryall, part of a larger tract called Concord first granted by patent dated 21 Dec 1739 to William Rumsey for 305 acres. Made 14 Dec 1741. Wit: Edward Jno. Wight, R'd. Thompson, Jr. Ackn: 21 Dec 1741 by Capt. William Rumsey and his wife Sabina. JPs: R'd. Thompson, Pereg. Ward. Lewis paid 2s.4p alienation fine to John Lusby. Rec: 13 Apr 1742. Wm. Knight, Clerk.

P. 156   Deed.   Thomas Mercer, Jr., of Cecil Co., planter, and his wife Jane, for 4,000 lbs of tobacco, to Robert Mercer of the said county, planter, land between Harmans Branch and a plantation called Mount Harman that did belong to Henry Hendrickson, deceased. Made 18 Feb 1741. Wit: Pereg. Ward, Jno. Ward, Jr. Ackn: 22 Feb 1741. JPs: John Veazey, Pereg. Ward. Alienation fine paid to John Lusby 16 Mar 1741. Rec: 26 Apr 1742. Wm. Knight, Clerk.

P. 158   Assignment of Lease.   William Cook of Cecil Co., planter, for £80, to John Harper of said county, blacksmith, 236 acres of land called Derry, part of St. Augustine Manor granted by lease dated 26 Dec 1735 to Neal Cook under yearly rent of £4.14s and 1 fat capon or 2 dunghill fowls for the term of 3 natural lives. Terms of the release remain the same for the remainder of the 3 natural lives. Rent due 26 Dec yearly. Made 6 Apr 1742. Wit: Abraham Allman, John Harper, John Seidell. Ackn: 7 Apr 1742. JP: Wm. Rumsey. Rec: 9 Apr 1742. Wm. Knight, Clerk.

P. 159   Deed.   John Severson of Cecil Co., for £205, to Benjamin Pearce of said county, gent., a tract of 140 acres of land called Severson's Delight alias Smoaky Point on the south side of Elk River. Patent in John Severson's name is dated 5 Apr 1731. Except 29 acres of the tract previously sold by John Severson. Also a moiety of a tract of land called Homely granted by patent dated 12 May 1729 to John Severson and Thomas Severson for 150 acres. Except 50 acres of this tract which John Severson sold to Garret Othoson of which a second deed was made for 20 acres to correct an error in the first deed. [Towards the end of this deed, the acreage being conveyed is stated as 136 acres.] Made 28 Apr 1742. Wit: Wm. Rumsey, John Lusby.

Ackn: same day by John Severson and his wife Sarah. JPs: John Baldwin, Wm. Rumsey. Alienation fine rec'd 30 Apr 1742 by John Lusby. Rec: 3 May 1742. Wm. Knight, Clerk.

P. 162   Deed.   Elizabeth Hendrickson of Cecil Co., spinster, and Henry Hendrickson, Jr., children of Henry Hendrickson of Cecil Co., planter, deceased, and Bartholomew Etherington of the same county, planter, for £180, to Thomas Davis of the same county, all their estate right in the middle 100 acres of a tract of land called the Level on Sassafras River near Back Creek by a tract of land formerly possessed by Thomas Lindsey but now belonging to the said Thomas Davis. Made 14 May 1742. Wit. & JPs: John Veazey, Pereg. Ward. Ackn: 4 May 1742 [sic.] John Lusby rec'd alienation fine 7 May 1742. Rec: 13 May 1742. Wm. Knight, Clerk.

P. 164   Deed.   John Winterbury of Cecil Co., planter, and his wife Rachel, for 20,000 lbs of tobacco, to James Wroth of the same county, planter, 100 acres and half the marsh, a moiety of a tract called Hendrickson's Choice lying opposite a tract formerly taken up by Mounce Anderson, which the said John Winterbury purchased by deed dated 22 Mar 1735 from Walter Shewall of New Britain, Bucks Co., PA, executor and devisee of the Last Will and Testament of Thomas Kimber of Sassafras Neck in Cecil Co., yeoman. Said moiety of land is bounded by the land of the late Roger Larramore. John Winterbury warrants the land against any claims of the descendants and heirs of Thomas Kimber, father of the said Thomas Kimber the Younger. Made & Ackn: 19 Apr 1742. Wit: Pereg. Ward, Wm. Pearce. JPs: John Veazey, Pereg. Ward. John Lusby rec'd the alienation fine from James Wroth 12 May 1742. Rec: 13 May 1742. Wm. Knight, Clerk.

P. 167   Deed of Gift.   James Morgan, Sr. of Cecil Co., planter, for the natural love and affection he has for his son Edward Morgan and for 5 shillings, all his rights to a tract of 180 acres called Shrewsbury on the north side of Sassafras River by a parcel of land called Middle Plantation formerly laid out for Andrew Woodbury of New England and by a parcel of land formerly belonging to Mounce Andrews. Said land granted by patent dated 13 Aug 1684 to Edward Jones and a part of the land was granted by deed dated 13 Mar 1693 from Edward Jones to the said James Morgan, Sr. Made & Ackn: 29 May 1742. Wit. & JPs: Pereg. Ward, John Veazey. John Lusby rec'd alienation fine for 100 acres [sic] from Edward Morgan 3 Jun 1742. Rec: 10 Jun 1742. Wm. Knight, Clerk.

P. 168   Deed.   William Sample and Esther his wife of Chester Co., PA, for £14, to John Reed of the same place, 40 acres of land in Cecil Co. on the east side of Christiana Run by the New Munster tract at the corner of James Alexander's land, part of 903 acres granted to Robert Roberts of Queen Annes Co. who by deed dated 14 Aug 1718 conveyed the land to John Stevenson of Bucks Co., PA. John Stevenson, by deed dated 15 Aug 1718 conveyed to James and Moses Alexander of Cecil Co. 92¾ acres of the 903-acre tract. James and Moses Alexander and Moses' wife Mary conveyed 40 acres of the land to William Sample by deed dated 8 Apr 1735 for £23. [Reed also spelled Read.] Made & Ackn: 5 Jun 1742. Wit: A. Barry, Mos's. Andrews. JPs: A. Barry, R'd. Thompson. Alienation fine rec'd 9 Jun 1742 by John Lusby. Rec: 10 Jun 1742. Wm. Knight, Clerk.

P. 170 Lease. John Lusby and Margaret his wife of Cecil Co., to William Morgan of the same county, the plantation and 61 acres where he now lives, part of a tract called Larramore's Neck Enlarged, near the lands of Robert Money and Thomas Severson (both of their lands part of Larramore's Neck Enlarged.) Lease is for the term of 13 years with rent of 700 lbs of tobacco and the quit rents due yearly. Morgan agrees to plant 60 apple trees. Made 13 Jan 1741. Wit: Wm. Rumsey, John Roberts, Jr. Ackn: 28 Apr 1742. JPs: Wm. Rumsey, John Baldwin. Rec: 11 Jun 1742. Wm. Knight, Clerk.

P. 172 Deed. John Ryland, Jr. of Cecil Co., innholder, for £20, to Peter and James Bayard of said county, merchants, the north half of lot #1 in Cecil Town on the south side of Bohemia River bounded by Baltimore, Leonard and Cecil streets. Made 10 Jun 1742. Wit: John Baldwin, John Lusby. Ackn: same day by John Ryland and his wife Rebecca. JPs: John Baldwin, John Veazey. Alienation fine paid 10 Jun to John Lusby. Rec: 10 Jun 1742. Wm. Knight, Clerk.

P. 173 Deed. Joseph Thomas and John Ricketts, executors of the Last Will and Testament of Roger Merrick, late of Cecil Co., deceased, for £100, according to an agreement made between Benjamin Thomas and Roger Merrick in his lifetime and mentioned in his Will dated 31 Mar 1742, convey to Benjamin Thomas of Newcastle Co., yeoman, all Merrick's plantation of 150 acres which was lately in the tenure of John Burns by other land which Roger and David Merrick sold to Joseph Thomas. Said land is part of a larger tract called Griffin which was originally surveyed in 1683 for Griffith Jones and on 10 Jun 1734 granted by Lord Baltimore's patent to David Merrick, deceased, for 1,000 acres. Made 7 Jun 1742. Wit: David Rowland, Elinor Thomas, Thomas Thomas. Ackn: 11 Jun 1742. JPs: A. Barry, Nich'ls. Hyland. On the same day Benjamin Thomas paid 3s alienation fine to John Lusby for 150 acres, part of Griffin from Christian Land and Samuel Land to

Roger Merrick by deed of release dated 19 May 1741. Rec: 11 Jun 1742. Wm. Knight, Clerk.

P. 175 Deed. Matthew Wallace of Cecil Co. and Johanna his wife, to Joseph Wallace of the same place, 128 acres of land by the corner of Samuel Willis' land. Said land is part of a tract called Wallace's Scrawl which was granted to Matthew Wallace by patent dated 6 Nov 1737 and recorded in the land office in Liber E. J. No. 2, folio 627. Made 28 May 1742. Wit. & JPs: A. Barry, Henry Baker. Ackn: next day. Rec: 11 Jun 1742. Wm. Knight, Clerk.

P. 177 Mortgage/Lease Assignment. William Croo of Cecil Co., planter, for £60, to James Bayard of said county, merchant, 120 acres of land by Wolfs Creek. Said land is part of Bohemia Manor which Ephraim Augustine Herman of Cecil Co., gent., on 2 Dec 1721 leased to William Croo for the term of the natural lives of the said William Croo, Mary Croo and Andrew Croo, the son of the said William Croo for yearly rent of £2 or its value in tobacco, winter wheat, barley or Indian Corn and 2 dunghill fowls to be paid every 10 Dec at the said Herman's dwelling house. William Croo is to repay James Bayard in 2 equal payments within 2 years time. Made 11 Jun 1742. Wit: Jno. Holland, Chas. Coatts. Ackn: same day by William Croo alias Crow. JPs: R'd. Thompson, John Veazey. Rec: 11 Jun 1742. Wm. Knight, Clerk.

P. 179 Deed. James Paul Heath of Cecil Co., merchant, for £247, to William Rumsey of Bohemia in said county, gent., 134 acres, part of a tract called Heath's Third Parcel from William Rumsey's mill pond, by land called Manwaring Hall to the cart road from Bohemia Landing. Also 7 acres which lies down lower from the mill pond which is part of the tract laid out for Rumsey's mill by virtue of a writ which is the remainder of the tract not conveyed to Dr. Hugh Matthews nor to William Knight. Heath's Third Parcel was originally granted 10 Dec 1714 by patent to James Heath, father of said James Paul Heath, for 390 acres. Also 17 acres, the south end part of 60 acres of the tract called Manwaring Hall which James Paul Heath bought from Dr. Hugh Matthews. Also 66 acres which is part of a tract called Stockton Addition lying between Heath's Third Parcel and a tract called Booker's Uppermost or Middle Parcel bounded on the southeast with part of the land sold to Michael Manycousens and on the east with a tract called Indian Range which is the remainder of Stockton Addition not already sold to the said Manycousens nor to Evert Evertson, Jr. The tract called Stockton Addition was originally granted 30 Nov 1714 by patent to Richard Bennett of Queen Annes Co. for 225 acres. Richard Bennett sold it to James Paul Heath.

Made 1 Jun 1742. Wit: John Baldwin, John Rice. Ackn: 15 Jun 1742 by Heath and his wife Rebecca. JPs: John Baldwin, John Rumsey. William Rumsey paid to John Lusby the alienation fine of 9s on 25 Jun 1742. Rec: 28 Jun 1742. Wm. Knight, Clerk.

P. 182   Deed.   Nathan Boys of Cecil Co., husbandman, and Susanna his wife, for £125, to Thomas Brown, Sr. of West Nottingham, Chester Co., PA, 150 acres of land on the east side of Susquehanna River, part of 2 tracts, one called Martin's Delight surveyed 17 Nov 1728 and conveyed to George Martin of said county by patent dated 10 Jun 1734 and recorded 4 Oct 1732 [sic] in the land office in Liber E. J. No. 4, folio 317. The other tract is George Martin's land called Martin's Enlargement recorded on page 318 of the same liber. George Martin sold the land to Hugh Boyd of said county by deed dated 11 Jun 1734 and recorded in Cecil Co. Book W. K. No. 2, folios 22-24. Hugh Boyd conveyed it to the said Nathan Boys by deed dated 29 Mar 1737 and recorded 15 Jun 1737 in Liber W. K. No. 2, folios 237-238. Made 19 Apr 1742. Wit: Henry Baker, Nich's. Hyland, Sam'l. Gilpin. Ackn: 17 Apr 1742 [sic.] JPs: Henry Baker, Nich's. Hyland. John Lusby rec'd alienation fine 29 May 1742. Rec: 14 Jul 1742. Wm. Knight, Clerk.

P. 184   Deed.   John Thompson of Cecil Co., yeoman, for £1.17s.6p, to John Baldwin of the same county, gent., lot #25 in Frederick Town. Made 12 Jul 1742. Wit: Thomas Colvill, Mary Knight. Ackn: same day by John Thompson and his wife Mary. JPs: Thomas Colvill, John Veazey. Alienation fine of 1p paid to John Lusby same day. Rec: 23 Jul 1742. Wm. Knight, Clerk.

P. 185   Deed.   Thomas Phillips, Jr., and his wife Rebecca, for £35, to Zebulon Hollingsworth, innholder, all their moiety of a tract of land called Clements' Venture. Michael Clements of Cecil Co., father of said Rebecca Phillips, on 6 Jun 1718 had surveyed and laid out for him 200 acres of land called Clements' Venture at the head of Elk River by Hog Run. Before the patent was granted he sold a moiety of the land to Robert Turnbull of said county and had the patent dated 10 Aug 1727 granted in both their names. Michael Clements died intestate and the land descended to Rebecca, his only child. Made 19 Apr 1742. Wit: Henry Baker, Nich's. Hyland, John Hyland. Ackn: same day by Thomas and Rebecca Phillips and then John Parker and Elizabeth his wife, late widow of Michael Clements, deceased, released their right to the land. JPs: Henry Baker, Nich's. Hyland. Alienation fine rec'd by John Lusby 2 May 1742. Rec: 12 Aug 1742. Wm. Knight, Clerk.

P. 188 Deed. Robert Buchannan of Kent Co., PA, for £18, to James Snell of Cecil Co., planter, 40 acres of land. Charles Lord Baltimore granted a warrant dated 12 May 1720 for 90 acres called Triangle to Anna Frisby of said county of which 40 acres were surveyed and laid out 19 May 1720 beginning at the crossroads of the old roads leading from Elk River to Bohemia and from Frenchtown to Newcastle. On 14 Jun 1720 Anna Frisby assigned the land to Rees Hinton, late of said county, who sold it by deed dated 10 Jun 1724 to the said Robert Buchannan. Made 10 Aug 1742. Wit. & JPs: Pereg. Ward, Nich's. Hyland. Ackn: 10 Aug 1742 by Buchannan and his wife Mary. Rec: 12 Aug 1742. Wm. Knight, Clerk.

P. 190 Evaluation of Estate. Lawrence Lawrenson and Samuel Bayard viewed the plantation of William Parsons, deceased, and found one square log house, 20x18 feet in good repair, a small cellar needing repair, one kitchen of square logs adjoining the house 25x14 feet in good repair with a brick chimney and old brick oven, a new round log house 15 feet covered with clapboard. The plantation in good order for fencing except one field. The land within the fencing may be cleared. The yearly rents valued at £12. Made 25 Jul 1742. JP: Nich. Hyland. Rec: 13 Aug 1742. Wm. Knight, Clerk.

P. 190 Deed. James Paul Heath of Cecil Co., merchant, for £100, to William Knight of the same county, gent., part of a tract called Heath's Third Parcel which was originally granted by patent dated 10 Dec 1714 to James Heath, father of said James Paul Heath for 393 acres on the north side of William Rumsey's mill pond by a tract belonging to the son of Charles Rumsey, deceased, and by a tract called Manwarring Hall. Made 1 Jun 1742. Wit: Jno. Baldwin, Jno. Rice, Jno. Beedle, Sr. Ackn: same day by Heath and his wife Rebecca. JPs: John Baldwin, Wm. Rumsey. Alienation fine of 5s.10p paid to Pereg. Frisby 30 Jun 1742. Rec: 2 Jun 1742. Wm. Knight, Clerk.

P. 192 Mortgage/Lease Assignment. Peter Hendrickson of Cecil Co., planter, for £20, to James Bayard of the said county, merchant, a lease of land in Bohemia Manor. Ephraim Augustine Herman, late of Cecil Co., gent., by lease dated 10 Aug 1731, leased to Peter Hendrickson 72 acres of land in Bohemia Manor for the term of the natural lives of the said Peter Hendrickson, Catharine Hendrickson his wife and their son Samuel Hendrickson for yearly rent of 27 shillings and 2 dunghill fowls due every 23 Nov. This lease is recorded in Cecil Co. Liber S. K. No. 5, folios 370-371. Peter Hendrickson is to repay Bayard within 2 years 4 months of this date. Made 30 Aug 1742. Wit: Wm. Rumsey, Wm. Rumsey, Jr. Ackn: 31 Aug 1742. JPs: Wm. Rumsey, Thos. Colvill. Hendrickson rec'd from Bayard £1.14s.6p over the stated

£20 and is subject to the terms of the mortgage/lease assignment. Rec: 6 Sep 1742. Wm. Knight, Clerk.

P. 194   Deed.   Robert Mercer of Cecil Co., planter, for £46, to William Walmsley of said county, planter, land already in Walmsley's possession on the east side and part of a tract called Mouncefield which was originally granted by patent dated 1 Jul 1663 to Mounce Anderson for 150 acres. Made & Ackn: 9 Apr 1742. Wit. & JPs: John Baldwin, John Veazey. Rec: 18 Sep 1742. Wm. Knight, Clerk.

P. 195   Deed.   Caleb Penal of Lancaster Co., PA, farmer, and Sarah his wife, for £20, to Joseph Haines of West Nottingham, Chester Co., PA, farmer, 114 acres of land, part of a tract of 225 acres called Slate Hill on the east side of Susquehanna River in Cecil Co. by a tract called Poplar Valley. Slate Hill was originally granted to Thomas Johnson, Jr. (the survey certificate is dated 2 Jun 1726.) [Penal is also spelled Pennell, Pennal. Sarah Penal made her mark with an "M".] Made 24 Sep 1742. Wit: Thomas Brown, John Gartrill. Sarah Penal, by power of attorney dated 24 Sep 1742, appointed Thomas Brown of West Nottingham to be her attorney to acknowledge this deed for her and another deed for Poplar Valley. Ackn: 25 Sep 1742. JPs: A. Barry, Henry Baker. Joseph Haines paid 4s.7p alienation fine to John Lusby on 20 Oct 1742. Rec: 21 Oct 1742. Wm. Knight, Clerk.

P. 198   Deed.   Caleb Penal of Lancaster Co., PA, farmer, and Sarah his wife, for £70, to Joseph Haines of West Nottingham, Chester Co., PA, farmer, 100 acres of land, part of a tract called Poplar Valley in Cecil Co. (the certificate of survey is dated 3 Nov 1715.) Made 24 Sep 1742. Wit: Thomas Brown, John Gartril. Sarah Penal, by power of attorney dated 24 Sep 1742, appointed Thomas Brown of West Nottingham to be her attorney to acknowledge this deed for her and another deed for Slate Hill. Ackn: 25 Sep 1742. JPs: A. Barry, Henry Baker. Alienation fine of 4 shillings paid to John Lusby 20 Oct 1742. Rec: 21 Oct 1742. Wm. Knight, Clerk.

P. 200   Power of Attorney.   Sarah Penal, wife of Caleb Penal, "being through affliction of body unable at this time to appear" appoints her trusty friend Thomas Brown of Nottingham, Chester Co., PA, her attorney to acknowledge 2 deeds for land called Poplar Valley and Slate Hill in Cecil Co., Maryland, to be conveyed to Joseph Haines of West Nottingham, Chester Co., PA. Made in Chester Co., PA 24 Sep 1742. Wit: John Gartrill, Mary Richards. Ackn: in Cecil Co., MD 25 Sep 1742 by John Gartrill, a Quaker. JP: Henry Baker. Rec: 21 Oct 1742. Wm. Knight, Clerk.

P. 201   Deed.   Colonel Thomas Colvill, Peter Bayard and Robert Carmichael, all of Cecil Co., attorneys to Jacob Rogers and Mary his wife of Great Britain, for £700 to John Read of Christiana Bridge, Newcastle-upon-Delaware Co., merchant, a tract of 700 acres of land called Kinsley, including a grist mill. Charles Lord Baltimore granted by patent dated 20 Nov 1735 to Major John Copson alias Weaver of Cecil Co., lately deceased, a tract of land called Kinsley laid out and surveyed for 700 acres. John Copson alias Weaver left only one daughter and heiress, Mary Rogers, wife of Jacob Rogers, both of Great Britain. By power of attorney dated 1 Dec, Jacob and Mary Rogers appointed as their attorneys Colonel Thomas Colvill of Cecil Co., merchant (to whom administration of the estate of Major John Copson alias Weaver had been granted by the commissary), Peter Bayard of Bohemia, merchant, and Robert Carmichael of the Parish of St. Bartholomew in London and now of Maryland, merchant, to recover for them sums of money and goods that are due them from Mary's father's estate and to sell or lease the property. Made & Ackn: 17 Sep 1742. Wit: Thomas Hughes, Wm. Rankin. JPs: A. Barry, Henry Baker. John Reed paid £1.8s alienation fine to John Lusby 30 Sep 1742. Rec: 7 Oct 1742. Wm. Knight, Clerk.

P. 205   Deed.   George Greenwood of Kent Co., planter, and his wife Barbara, for £35, to John Cooper, Jr. of Cecil Co., planter, 150 acres of land on the north side of Sassafras River at Duck Creek and Jones Creek. Said land is part of a tract of 600 acres sold by James Moore to Hezekiah Haynes and which Jervis Morgan, late of Ann Arundel Co., deceased, called Middle Neck. [Barbara's name is also spelled Barbary.] Made & Ackn: 1 May 1742. Wit. & JPs: John Baldwin, Pereg. Ward. Exchange of money was witnessed by Pereg. Ward and Jas. Holliday, Jr. John Cooper paid the alienation fine to John Lusby. Rec: 13 Oct 1742. Wm. Knight, Clerk.

P. 207   Deed.   Thady McDermott of Cecil Co., cooper, for £14, to James Paul Heath of the said county, merchant, a moiety of lot #54 with a house on it in Frederick Town bounded on the west by Frederick Street and on the south by Prince William Street. The other moiety of the lot McDermott sold to James Hughes. Made & Ackn: 13 Oct 1742. Wit. & JPs: John Veazey, Pereg. Ward. Rec: 23 Oct 1742. Wm. Knight, Clerk.

P. 208   Deed.   William Bristow and Catharine his wife of Cecil Co., for £80, to John Kankey of the said county, a moiety of a parcel of land and half the corn mill and half the saw mill at the mouth of an old mill ditch below the county road. This land Zebulon Hollingsworth purchased from Elias Everson and his wife Mary by deed dated 22 Jun 1728. Made & Ackn: 2 Dec 1742. Wit: John Hyland, Rich'd. Dobson. JPs: A. Barry, Nich's. Hyland. The

109

alienation fine of 1½p paid 15 Dec 1742 to John Lusby. Rec: 15 Dec 1742. Wm. Knight, Clerk.

P. 209 Deed. Stephen Emery, son and heir of George Emery, late of Cecil Co., weaver, deceased, for £80, to Samuel Davison of the same place, yeoman, a tract of 100 acres called Emery's Endeavor by the forest of Sherwood and Conawingo Creek. Made 2 Dec 1742. Wit: Simon Johnson, Nich's. Hyland. Ackn: 2 Sep 1742 [sic.] John Parker and his wife Sarah stated they quit claim any dowry to the land (Sarah being the relict of the deceased George Emery.) JPs: Thos. Colvill, Nic. Hyland. Alienation fine of 4s rec'd by John Lusby. Rec: 15 Dec 1742. Wm. Knight, Clerk.

P. 211 Deed of Gift. Col. John Ward of Cecil Co., gent., for natural love and affection and for 5 shillings, to his son Henry Ward of the same county, a tract of 200 acres called Chance on the north side of Sassafras River at Wheeler's Creek by land formerly taken up by John Wheeler. Made 6 Dec 1742. Wit: John Veazey, John Bellarmin, Edward Veazey. Ackn: 25 Dec 1742 before JPs John Veazey and Pereg. Ward. Rec: 8 Mar 1742. Wm. Knight, Clerk.

P. 213 Deed. John Baldwin of Cecil Co., gent., for £110, to Elihu Hall of the same county, gent., a tract of 340 acres called Baldwin's Dispatch on the east side of Susquehanna River between two tracts of land, one called Hope and the other Success. This land was originally granted to John Baldwin by patent dated 2 Feb 1726. Made 21 Sep 1742. Wit. & JPs: John Veazey, Pereg. Ward. Ackn: same day by Baldwin and his wife Mary. Alienation fine paid to John Lusby 30 Sep 1742. Rec: 10 Mar 1742. Wm. Knight, Clerk.

P. 215 Deed of Gift. Bartholomew Jacobs, Sr. of Cecil Co., yeoman, for love and natural affection, gives to his son Bartholomew Jacobs, Jr. a moiety of a tract of land called Skelton on the branches of Bohemia River. Said land Bartholomew Jacobs, Sr. purchased from Richard Bennett of Queen Annes Co. and is where the said Bartholomew Jacobs, Jr. now lives. Made & Ackn: 9 Mar 1742. Wit: John Harper, Charles Coatts. Rec: 10 Mar 1742. Wm. Knight, Clerk.

P. 216 Deed of Gift. Bartholomew Jacobs, Sr. of Cecil Co., yeoman, for love and natural affection, gives to his son Jacob Jacobs, a moiety of a tract of land called Skelton on the branches of Bohemia River. Said land Bartholomew Jacobs, Sr. purchased from Richard Bennett of Queen Annes Co. and is where the said Jacob Jacobs formerly lived. Made & Ackn: 9 Mar 1742. Wit: John Harper, Charles Coatts. Rec: 10 Mar 1742. Wm. Knight, Clerk.

P. 218 Deed. Hugh Walker of Milford Hundred, Cecil Co., farmer (and his wife Margaret,) for £60, to William Mackey of the same place, tanner, 100 acres (71½ acres of Providence and 28½ acres of Enlargement) on Contention Run and by George Robinson's land called Consent. By patent dated 2 Sep 1713, Abraham Hollingsworth was granted 500 acres of land called Providence (recorded in the land office in Lib. P. Y. No. 1, folio 115) and by another patent dated 6 Oct 1732 was granted 40 acres called Enlargement adjoining the south side of the first said tract (recorded in the land office in Lib. C. L. L. No. 8, folio 694.) Hollingsworth conveyed 287 acres, part of Providence and all 40 acres of Enlargement to Hugh Walker by deed dated 14 Sep 1732 (recorded in Cecil Co. 5 Oct 1732 in Lib. S. K. No. 5, folios 458-460.) Made & Ackn: 7 Mar 1742/3. Wit. & JPs: A. Barry, Henry Baker. John Lusby rec'd alienation fine 9 Mar 1742/3. Rec: 10 Mar 1742. Wm. Knight, Clerk.

P. 220 Deed. Joseph Steel of Milford Hundred, Cecil Co., farmer, for £200, to Robert Rowland of Kent Co., PA, farmer, 320 acres, part of a tract called Society, by Spring Run (a branch of Elk River) and by John Bristow's land. Also a tract of 70 acres called Confusion. Charles Carroll was granted 2,104 acres of land called Society on 2 Sep 1713. Carroll sold part of this tract to the said Joseph Steel by deed dated 4 Oct 1717 (recorded 6 Feb 1717 in Lib. J. D. No. 3, folios 49-51.) By deed recorded in Lib. W. K. No. 2, folio 79, Robert Holy sold to Joseph Steel 70 acres of land called Confusion which adjoins the Society tract on the north side. Made & Ackn: 8 Mar 1742/3. Wit: A. Barry, John Scott, Mich'l. Wallace. JPs: John Baldwin, John Veazey. Alienation fine paid 9 Mar 1742/3 to John Lusby. Rec: 10 Mar 1742. Wm. Knight, Clerk.

P. 222 Deed. Richard Clayton of Cecil Co., yeoman, for £50, to Samuel Bond of the same place, yeoman, 200 acres, part of Batchelor's Fun adjoining Doe Hill. By patent dated 1 Nov 1728 Charles Lord Baltimore granted to the said Richard Clayton 400 acres of land called Batchelor's Fun (adjoining George Robinson's land called Doe Hill) with quit rents of 16 shillings (recorded in patent office in Lib. P. L. L. No. 7, folio 22.) Made 4 Jan 1742. Wit: Zach. Butcher, A. Barry, Henry Baker. Ackn: 14 Jan 1742/3. JPs: A. Barry, Henry Baker. Alienation fine paid 9 Feb 1742 to John Lusby. Rec: 10 Mar 1742. Wm. Knight, Clerk.

P. 225 Deed. John Starrat of New Munster, Mary Ann Parish, Cecil Co., and Leah his wife, for £145 and because they are moving, to Robert Given of White Clay Creek, Newcastle Co., Delaware, miller, 110 acres by the land of David Alexander, deceased, by land formerly Joseph Alexander's but now James Alexander's. Said land was formerly conveyed 1727/8 by James and Moses Alexander to John Starrat. [Starrat also spelled Starat.] Made & Ackn: 18 Feb 1742/3. Wit: Henry Baker, A. Barry, James Cowdon. JPs: Henry Baker, A. Barry. John Lusby rec'd the alienation fine 9 Mar 1742. Rec: 10 Mar 1742. Wm. Knight, Clerk.

P. 227 Deed. Henry Baker of Cecil Co., and his wife Elizabeth, for £44, to James Crumley of Chester Co., PA, 100 acres, part of a tract called Kennedy's Adventure by a tract belonging to Samuel England and another tract belonging to Edward Oldham. By patent dated 12 Aug 1720, Hugh Kennedy of Ann Arundel Co., deceased, was granted 500 acres of land in Cecil Co. called Kennedy's Adventure (recorded in the land office in Liber C. E. W., folios 269-270. Henry Bennet of Queen Annes Co. and his wife Margaret, and Elizabeth Kennedy, spinster, the two daughters of the said Hugh Kennedy, conveyed the land to the said Henry Baker by deed dated 23 Oct 1740, recorded 21 Mar 1740/1 in Lib. E. J. No. 3, folio 205. Made & Ackn: 3 Feb 1742/3. Wit: Samuel Gilpin & JPs A. Barry, Nic. Hyland. John Lusby rec'd the alienation fine of 4 shillings 2 Mar 1742. Rec: 10 Mar 1742. Wm. Knight, Clerk.

P. 229 Deed. Samuel Gilpin, yeoman of Cecil Co., and his wife Jane, for £50, to John Bing of the same place, laborer, 123 acres on the North East River, part of a tract called Rumsey's Ramble, by a tract called Cox's Park and by the line which divides the lands of Samuel Gilpin and Robert Whitaker. By deed dated 18 Sep 1735, William Rumsey, gent., conveyed to Samuel Gilpin, amongst other lands, part of a tract called Rumsey's Ramble (recorded in Lib. W. K. No. 2, folios 125-127.) Made & Ackn: 14 Jan 1742/3. Wit: Zach Butcher, Henry Baker. JPs: A. Barry, Henry Baker. Alienation fine rec'd by John Lusby 12 Feb 1742. Rec: 10 Mar 1742. Wm. Knight, Clerk.

P. 231 Deed. Samuel Gilpin, yeoman of Cecil Co., and his wife Jane, for £125, to Henry Baker of the same place, gent., 15 acres, a moiety of a tract called Stony Chase, above the mill dam at the upper end of the falls by a tract called Batchelor's Fun, including a moiety of the water corn mill and saw mill. Samuel Gilpin reserves the right to build a dwelling house on the land which shall not be part of the moiety. By deed dated 18 Sep 1735, William Rumsey, gent., conveyed to Samuel Gilpin, amongst other lands, a tract of land called Stony Chase (recorded in Lib. W. K. No. 2, folios 125-127.) [Jane Gilpin is called Jean Gilpin at the signing.] Made & Ackn: 3 Feb 1742/3. Wit: A. Barry, Nic. Hyland, James Crumley. JPs: A. Barry, Nic. Hyland. John

Lusby rec'd the alienation fine 2 Mar 1742/3. Rec: 10 Mar 1742. Wm. Knight, Clerk.

P. 235   Assignment of Lease.   Enoch Jenkins, Sr., innholder, for £52.10s and rents and services, to James Boyles, laborer, 60 acres of land on the east side of the road that leads from Lawson's Mill to the head of Bohemia [river] and east of the branch that divides John Cochran's and Enoch Jenkins' land and by Newcastle Road. Said lease Enoch Jenkins, Sr. bought from Wm. Newman. Lease is for the terms of the natural lives stated in the original lease which was first granted to Walter Newman from Col. Ephraim Augustine Herman. Rent of 3 bushels of winter wheat and one dunghill fowl to be paid to Enoch Jenkins, Sr. at his dwelling house every 23 March. Made 1 Mar 1742/3. Wit: Manasseh Loage, John Cage. Ackn: 11 Mar 1742. JPs: R'd. Thompson, Nic. Hyland. Rec: 11 Mar 1742. Wm. Knight, Clerk.

P. 236   Valuation of Estate.   In viewing the lands of the orphan Richard Boulding, son of Wm. Boulding, late of Cecil Co., deceased, Robert Patton and John Bravard found the land lying on the east side of Elk River containing 200 acres called Knowlswood in middling good repair, an orchard of 40 young apple trees, a field of 8 acres out of repair and possible to clear 5 acres more of the field and another 10 acres can be cleared of the plantation. There is sufficient timber to support the plantation. There is a new log dwelling house 25x16 feet, a log dwelling house 16x16 feet with a shed, in good repair, a 30 foot tobacco house needing repair. The yearly rent of the plantation valued at £7. Another tract of land belonging to the said orphan lies on the east side of Elk River on the north side of Back Creek called Boulding's Rest containing 130 acres. The plantation and its 33 acres are in middling good repair, with a hued log house 21x16 feet with a shed on the back, brick chimney, plank floor, another house 20x15 feet, a corn crib, 3 old houses worth little, an orchard of 95 apple trees well fenced, a peach orchard, no land to be cleared except timber to be used to repair fencing. They valued the yearly rent to be £5. Made 30 Nov 1742. JP: Richard Thompson. Rec: 10 Mar 1742. Wm. Knight, Clerk.

P. 237   Lease.   Benjamin Tasker of Annapolis, esq., agent and receiver general of the Lord Proprietary and on his behalf, for rents and covenants with the consent of Gov. Thomas Bladen, to William Smith of Cecil Co., founder, 300 acres of land called Copson's Park on the North East River by lands called Copson's Intent, Small Hope and Vulcan's Delight which was leased to William Chelwynd, esq., & Co., except the 2 acres where the parish church stands. Said land was lately occupied by Major John Copson, deceased, and purchased by the said William Smith from Col. Thomas Colvill,

Peter Bayard and Robert Carmichael, attorneys for Jacob Rogers and his wife Mary of Great Britain, the only daughter and heir of the said Major John Copson. Lease is for the term of the natural lives of John, William and Sarah Smith, three children of the said William Smith. Rent of 30 shillings and two fat capons due 29 Sep yearly. Smith is to build a 30x20 foot dwelling house with a brick chimney and will plant and fence an orchard of 100 apple trees. Made 29 Sep 1742. Wit: Geo. Plater, Jno. Ross. Rec: 18 Mar 1742. Wm. Knight, Clerk.

P. 240   Deed of Gift.   David Lawson of Cecil Co., farmer, because he is moving, gives to John Lawson of the same county, planter, 100 acres, part of a tract called Providence. Said land is where he the said David Lawson now dwells which by the Last Will and Testament of Peter Sluyter alias Vorsman the said David Lawson obtained a deed from Doctor Peter Bouchell, deceased. Made & Ackn: 5 Apr 1743. Wit. & JPs: R'd. Thompson, A. Barry. Rec: 6 Apr 1743. Wm. Knight, Clerk.

P. 241   Deed.   Hugh Ross of Cecil Co., farmer, and Elizabeth his wife, for £150, to Robert Smith of Newcastle supra Delaware Co., PA, farmer, land which by deed dated 25 Mar 1738 recorded in Liber W. K. No. 2, folios 341-343, Nicholas Dorrell of Cecil Co. sold to Hugh Ross (166 acres and 106 perches) part of a tract called Newmunster on the west side of the main branch of Elk River. Hugh and Elizabeth Ross warrant the land against any claims of the said Dorrell or the heirs of John Vansant. Made 20 Apr 1743. Wit: A. Barry, Moses Andrews, Geo. Lawson. Ackn: 28 Apr 1743. JPs: A. Barry, Henry Baker; Pereg'n. Frisby rec'd from Robert Smith 3s.4p alienation fine 29 Apr 1743. Rec: 29 Apr 1743. Wm. Knight, Clerk.

P. 243   Deed of Gift.   Col. John Ward of Cecil Co., gent., for natural love and affection and for 5 shillings, to his son John Ward, Jr. of the same place, a tract of 500 acres called Strange on the west side of Bohemia River by Morgans Creek. Made 29 Apr 1743. Wit: Wm. Ellis, John Holtham, Ja. Calder. JP: Henry Hooper. Alienation fine of 10 shillings paid by John Ward, Jr. to Pereg'n. Frisby same day. Rec: 29 Apr 1743. Wm. Knight, Clerk.

P. 244   Deed.   Robert Holy and Ann his wife of Milford Hundred, Cecil Co., farmer, for £28, to James Mackey of the same place, farmer, part of a tract called Hopewell containing 27½ acres by William Hogg's land and by James Mackey's 100 acre plantation which is also part of Hopewell. By patent dated 10 Sep 1716, Matthias Vanbebber was granted 544 acres of land called Hopewell. By deed dated 15 Feb 1725, Vanbebber granted to Stephen Hollingsworth, Robert Holy and Robert Mackey 428 acres of the said tract (recorded in Lib. S. K. No. 5, folios 32-33.) The said Stephen Hollingsworth and Robert Mackey conveyed 228 acres of the land to Robert Holy by deed dated 5 May 1733 recorded in Lib. S. K. No. 5, folios 456-457. Made & Ackn: 26 Mar 1743. Wit. & JPs: A. Barry, Henry Baker. Alienation fine of 14p paid to Pereg'n. Frisby 31 Mar 1743. Rec: 29 Apr 1743. Wm. Knight, Clerk.

P. 247   Lease.   James Paul Heath of Cecil Co., merchant, for rents and services, to John Marcer of the said county, planter, and Elizabeth his wife, the plantation on which James Lattomus now lives with 200 acres bounded by Col. Ward's land on the south, Othoson's land on the east, the widow Vansant's land, the branch that Mary Twiddy lived on and on the north with the great road leading from Sassafras River to Newcastle. Lease is for the term of 21 years with rent of £25 due each 1 January. Marcer is to plant 100 apple trees. Made 20 May 1743. Wit: Hugh Matthews, Jr., John Jackson. Ackn: 31 May 1743. JPs: John Baldwin, John Veazey. Rec: 14 Jun 1743. Wm. Knight, Clerk.

P. 249   Deed.   Thomas Butler of Prince Georges Co., for £62.10s, to Jacob Giles of Baltimore Co., merchant, 150 acres of land being a moiety of a tract called Larkin's Desire in Cecil Co. on Susquehanna River by land taken up by George Holland. Made & Ackn: in Prince Georges Co. 21 May 1743. Wit. & JPs: Richard Keene, Joseph Bett, Jr. [Belt? Bell?] Confirmed by Thos. Lee, Clerk. The alienation fine of 6 shillings paid by Jacob Giles to Pereg. Frisby 4 Jun 1743. Rec: 15 Jun 1743. Wm. Knight, Clerk.

P. 250   Lease.   Benjamin Tasker, esq., agent and receiver general for and on behalf of Lord Baltimore and with the consent of Gov. Thomas Bladen, for rents and services, to Mary Storey of Cecil Co., 117½ acres of land, part of the Manor of Baltimore. Lease is for the term of the natural lives of the said Mary Storey and her children Enoch Storey and Thomas Storey. Rent of 30 shillings due every 29 September. The Storey's will build a dwelling house 30x20 feet with a brick chimney and plant and fence an orchard of 100 apple trees. Made 21 Mar 1742. Wit: Jno. Ross, G. Ross. Rec: 15 Jun 1743. Wm. Knight, Clerk.

P. 253   Deed.   Simon Johnson of Cecil Co., planter, for £40, to Benjamin Bradford of the same county, gent., a messuage at the head of Elk River, part of a tract called Succesor containing 100 acres which lately was in the possession of Jacob Poulson. Made 15 Jun 1743. Wit: Amos Fogg, Will Cummings, Jr., John Hollyday, Jr. Ackn: same day by Simon Johnson and his wife Hannah. JPs: John Baldwin, A. Barry. Alienation fine of 4s paid same day by Benjamin Bradford to Pereg. Frisby. Rec: 30 Jun 1743. Wm. Knight, Clerk.

P. 254   Deed.   Richard Bennett of St. Annes Co., gent., for £50 paid by George Hall, to John Hall, son of George Hall of Kent Co., planter, a tract of 56 acres of land in Cecil Co. called Marshfield, lately escheat to his Lordship and granted by patent to the said Richard Bennett. Made 21 May 1743. Wit: John Darnall, Greenberry Dorsey. Ackn: 25 May 1743. JP: John Darnall. Alienation fine of 2s.3p paid by John Hall to Pereg. Frisby 20 Jun 1743. Rec: 21 Jun 1743. Wm. Knight, Clerk.

P. 256   Deed.   David Lawson of Cecil Co., farmer, and his son John Lawson of the same county, planter, for £150, to Sluyter Bouchell of Cecil Co., gent., 100 acres of land (the dwelling plantation of the said David Lawson,) part of a tract of land on the north side of Bohemia River in Bohemia Manor called Providence by the land which belonged to Peter King, deceased. Said land was devised to David Lawson by Petrus Sluyter alias Vorsman, late of Cecil Co., deceased, and afterwards confirmed by deed recorded in Lib. J. D. No. 3, folio 346 and Lib. S. K. No. 5, folio 51 from Peter Bouchell, the heir and devisee of the Last Will and Testament of the said Petrus Sluyter alias Vorsman. Made & Ackn: 21 Jun 1743. Wit: Thos. Colvill, John Thompson. JPs: Thos. Colvill, John Veazey. John Lawson rec'd from Dr. Sluyter Bouchell £150 on 28 Jun 1743. Rec: 28 Jun 1743. Wm. Knight, Clerk.

P. 258   Commission.   Charles Lord Baltimore appoints as Justices of the Peace for Cecil County John Rousby, Benjamin Tasker, Philip Lee, George Plater, Edmond Jennings, James Hollyday, Charles Hammond, Levin Gale, James Harris, Samuel Chamberlain, Philip Thomas, Daniel Dulany, Thomas Colvill, Richard Thompson, John Baldwin, Andrew Berry, John Veazey, Peregrine Ward, Nicholas Hyland, William Alexander, Benjamin Chew, Henry Baker and Nathan Baker, all gents. of Cecil Co. Made 3 Jun 1743. Wit: Thomas Bladen, Gov. Rec: 17 Jun 1743. Wm. Knight, Clerk.

P. 262   Deed.   David Witherspoon of Kent Co., merchant, for £5, to John Vangezle of Newcastle, PA, sadler, a quarter part of lot #23 in Charles Town on the North East River in Cecil Co. entered in the records as taken up by the said David Witherspoon and Thomas Williams of Frederick Town in Cecil Co., merchant. Made & Ackn: 11 Aug 1743. Wit: James Paul Heath, Charles Coatts. Rec: 11 Aug 1743. Wm. Knight, Clerk.

P. 264   Deed.   Bartholomew Etherington of Cecil Co., for £10, to Edward Morgan of the said county, 5 acres and 130 perches of land, part of a tract called Jamaica by Edward Morgan's field. Made & Ackn: 10 Aug 1743.

Wit. & JPs: John Baldwin, Pereg. Ward. Alienation fine of 3p paid by Morgan to Pereg. Frisby same day. Rec: 10 Aug 1743. Wm. Knight, Clerk.

P. 265   Deed.   John Lusby of Cecil Co., with the advice and consent of his wife Margaret, for £140, to John Penington, Sr. of the said county, 132 acres of land on the east side of Elk River near the head of St. Albans Creek by land called Fryer's Hills, by land which Lusby sold to Robert Porter and by 30 acres of land laid out for Augustina Larramore's mill. Said land is the remaining part of a tract called Hazel Branch. Porter's land is also part of the tract called Hazel Branch. John and Margaret Lusby will warrant the land against any claims from the estate of Rodger Larramore, deceased father of Margaret Lusby. Made & Ackn: 18 Jun 1743. Wit: John Key, Benj. Pearce. JPs: John Baldwin, John Veazey. Rec: 9 Aug 1743. Wm. Knight, Clerk.

P. 268   Deed.   Elenor Campbell of Cecil Co., spinster and executrix of the Last Will and Testament of her father John Campbell, late of Cecil Co., gent., deceased, for £70, to John Husband of the same county, planter, 175 acres, part of a tract called Thompson's Town (which the said John Campbell bought from Charles Carroll and Joshua George) on Elk River at Pearch Creek. Made & Ackn: 15 Jun 1743. Wit. & JPs: Pereg. Ward, Nich. Hyland. John Husband paid the alienation fine of 7 shillings to Pereg. Frisby. Rec: 10 Aug 1743. Wm. Knight, Clerk.

P. 271   Deed.   Robert Miller, son and heir of Isaac Miller, lately deceased, and his widow Jane Ross of Lancaster Co., PA, for £100, to George Lawson of Cecil Co., 200 acres of land called White's Folly on the west branch of Elk River by a tract called the Society. By patent dated 19 Nov 1713, Alexander White was granted 200 acres in Cecil Co. called White's Folly. Alexander White and his wife Jane conveyed the land to Isaac Miller by deed dated 20 Mar 1728 recorded in Lib. S. K. No. 1, folios 142-143. [Jane Ross is also called Jane Miller.] Made 23 Jun 1743. Wit. & JPs: A. Barry, Henry Baker. Ackn: same day by Jane Ross and her son Robert Miller. The alienation fine of 8 shillings paid by George Lawson to Pereg. Frisby 11 Nov 1743. Rec: 9 Aug 1743. Wm. Knight, Clerk.

P. 273   Deed.   William Edmonson and his wife Mary of Chester Co., PA and John Edmonson and his wife Isabel of Cecil Co., farmer, for £52, to John McCulloch of Cecil Co., clothier, 106¾ acres of land on the west side of the west branch of Elk River. Also 4¾ acres of swamp by Rowland Chambers' land. Said land is part of 213½ acres of land and 4¾ acres of swamp in Cecil Co. which Abraham Hollingsworth sold to the said William and John Edmonson by deed dated 10 Aug 1724 recorded 11 Aug 1724 in Liber D. K. No. 1, folios 93-94. Made 9 Jun 1743. Wit: Henry Baker, James Patterson, John Hunter. Ackn: 10 Jun 1743. JPs: A. Barry, Henry Baker. Alienation fine of 4s.4p paid by John McCulloch to Pereg. Frisby. Rec: 10 Aug 1743. Wm. Knight, Clerk.

P. 275 Deed. Colonel Thomas Colvill, merchant, Peter Bayard of Bohemia, merchant, and Robert Carmichael, all of Cecil Co., attorneys for Jacob Rogers and his wife Mary of Great Britain, for £350, to William Smith of Cecil Co., founder, 13½ acres called Copson's Intent, a lease for 300 acres called Copson's Park. Except 10 acres and a grist mill which John Copson sold to Robert Storey. By a warrant from Charles Lord Baltimore to John Copson, on 12 Nov 1723 13½ acres of land called Copson's Intent was surveyed and laid out in Cecil Co. below the mill dam which was formerly Robert Jones' and granted to Copson by patent dated 13 May 1728. On 12 Apr 1723 John Copson bought a lease made by Henry Lowe to Gunning Bedford for a tract of 115 acres called Chance, part of his Lordship's Manor on the North East River. On 13 May 1729 by warrant granted to him by Matthew Tilghman, in order to renew the said lease where Copson was living, adding lands to it, John Copson had the land and adjoining vacant lands of 300 acres resurveyed and called Copson's Park. John Copson alias Weaver is lately deceased and his only daughter and heiress is the said Mary Rogers, wife of the said Jacob Rogers. By power of attorney dated 1 Dec 1741, they appointed the said Thomas Colvill, Peter Bayard and Robert Carmichael (formerly of the Parish of St. Bartholomew in London) to be their attorneys. Thomas Colvill was appointed executor of Copson's estate. Made 11 Aug 1743. Wit: Nich's. Hyland, Wm. Knight. Ackn: Aug Court 1743. Rec: 9 August 1743 [sic.] Wm. Knight, Clerk.

P. 280 Deed. John McFarland of St. Georges Hundred, Newcastle Co. upon Delaware, planter, for £36, to Samuel Bond of Cecil Co., planter, 100 acres of land, part of Rumsey's Ramble (formerly in the tenant of George Cathey) by Samuel Bond's field. By patent dated 30 Oct 1731 recorded in Lib. P. S. No. 3, folio 105, Edward Rumsey was granted a tract of 300 acres called Rumsey's Ramble in Cecil Co. in the forks of North East River adjoining two tracts called Coxes Park and Batchelor's Fund. By deed dated 3 Aug 1733, Edward Rumsey conveyed the land to William Rumsey, and the deed was acknowledged 4 Aug 1733 before Benjamin Pearce and Richard Thompson and recorded 27 Aug 1703 [sic] in Liber S. K. No. 6, folios 122-123. William Rumsey sold to John McFarland 100 acres of the land by deed dated 17 Feb 1734 acknowledged 12 Mar 1734 before John Baldwin and John Veazey and recorded 14 Mar 1734 in Lib. W. K. No. 2, folios 74-76.

John McFarland appointed his friends Thomas Reynolds and Johannes Van Ekelin, both of Cecil Co., planters, to be his attorneys. Made 20 Jun 1743. Wit: Charles Patterson, Caleb Pusey [Presey?] Ackn: 29 Jun 1743 by Thomas Reynolds and Ann McFarland, wife of John McFarland. Henry Baker witnessed the payment of the money the same day. Pereg. Frisby rec'd 4 shillings alienation money from Samuel Bond 9 Aug 1743. Rec: 11 Aug 1743. Wm. Knight, Clerk.

P. 284 Deed. Richard Foster of Cecil Co., for 2,000 lbs of tobacco, quit claims to John Foster of the same county, one half of 100 acres of land (formerly bequeathed to the said Richard Foster by his father Richard Foster, late of said county) on the west side of Elk River. Said land is part of a tract called Brereton. Made 12 Aug 1743. Wit: Joseph Lowman, George Ford. Ackn: same day by Richard Foster and his wife Sarah. JPs: A. Barry, Nicholas Hyland. Alienation fine of 2 shillings paid by John Foster to Pereg. Frisby 20 Aug 1743. Rec: 10 Nov 1743. Wm. Knight, Clerk.

P. 285 Deed. Jacob Giles of Baltimore Co., for £100, to Robert Patterson of Cecil Co., 150 acres, a moiety of a tract called Larkin's Desire in Cecil Co. on the east side of Susquehanna River by Samuel Smith's land called Heath's Adventure and by Thomas Shepherd's land who bought the other moiety of this tract. Made 20 Aug 1743. Wit: Jethro Brown & JPs Henry Baker, A. Barry. Ackn: same day by Jacob Giles and his wife Johanna. Robert Patterson paid 6 shillings alienation fine to Pereg. Frisby 1 Sep 1743. Rec: 10 Nov 1743. Wm. Knight, Clerk.

P. 287 Deed. John Gears of Cecil Co., planter, for £300, to Philip Stoops of the same county, planter, 50 acres of land called Micham and another 50 acres, part of Rook and Pill, by land called Greenfield, bounds according to his (Gears) deed dated 9 Mar 1725 and recorded in Lib. S. K. No. 5, folios 35-36. Made 5 Nov 1743. Wit. & JPs: John Baldwin, Pereg. Ward. Ackn: same day by John Gears and his wife Susannah. Philip Stoops paid 3 shillings alienation fine to Pereg. Ward 10 Nov 1743. Rec: 10 Nov 1743. Wm. Knight, Clerk.

P. 289 Lease. John Campbell of Cecil Co., sadler, for £40 and for yearly rent, to Seth Ruley of the same county, planter, 100 acres of land, part of a tract called the Devidings on the south side of Elk River and now in the possession of Mary Panthom and to remain in her possession for the rest of her natural life. Also a tract of 100 acres called Addition to Campbell's Devident on the south side of Bohemia River lying between the Devidings and a tract called True Grame and a tract called Manchester. Lease is for the term of the natural lives of the said Seth Ruley, Anthony Ruley (son of Michael Ruley of the same county) and Thomas Price (son of William Price of the said county.) Rent of 1 dunghill fowl due 10 Oct yearly. Made & Ackn: 27 Oct 1743. Wit: Pereg. Ward, Jno. Ward, Jr. JPs: John Veazey, Pereg. Ward. Rec: 10 Nov 1743. Wm. Knight, Clerk.

P. 291 Deed. Rowland Chambers of Lancaster Co., PA, farmer, for £100, to David Chambers of Cecil Co., farmer, a tract of 130 acres in Cecil Co. called Mount Joy which Rowland Chambers was granted by patent dated 20 May 1723 lying by land formerly laid out for Abraham Hollingsworth. Also a tract of 70 acres which Abraham Hollingsworth conveyed to Rowland Chambers by deed dated 14 Dec 1719 recorded in Liber J. D. No. 3, folios 147-149. This tract lies on the east side of the west branch of Elk River. Made 8 Oct 1743. Wit: Geo. Lawson, A. Barry. Ackn: by Rowland Chambers 8 Nov 1743. JPs: A. Barry, Nich. Hyland. Alienation fine of 8 shillings paid by David Chambers 10 Nov 1743 to Pereg. Ward. Rec: 10 Nov 1743. Wm. Knight, Clerk.

P. 293 Assignment of Lease. Edward Jno. Wight assigns to Thos. Ebthorp a lease made by Col. Ephraim Augustine Herman to William Hood for part of Bohemia Manor. Said lease recorded 22 Jul 1736 in Lib. W. K. No. 2, folios 175-176. Made 10 Aug 1743. Wit: Jno. Cage, Jos. Penington. Edward Jno. Wight acknowledges the assignment of the lease to Ebthorp 9 Nov. JPs: John Baldwin, A. Barry. Rec: 10 Nov 1743. Wm. Knight, Clerk.

P. 293 Deed. Thomas Clay of Chester Town, Kent Co., merchant, for 5 shillings and because he is moving to John Course of the same county, planter, a quarter part of lot #87 in Charles Town, Cecil Co., on North East River. John Course will erect a dwelling house within the time frame set out by an Act of Assembly for the building of a town at Longpoint made at a session of assembly in Annapolis 21 Sep 1742. Made & Ackn: 21 Aug 1743. Wit. & JPs: Charles Hynson, Samuel Groome, who are certified as Justices of the Peace for Kent Co. by James Smith, Clerk of Kent Co., 29 Oct 1743. Rec: in Cecil Co. 5 Jan 1743. Wm. Knight, Clerk.

P. 295 Deed. William Walmsley of Cecil Co., for £10, to Bartholomew Etherington of the same county, 5 acres and 125 perches of land, part of a tract called Shrewsbury, by a tract called Jamaica now in said Etherington's possession. Made 10 Aug 1743. Wit. & JPs: John Baldwin, Pereg. Ward. Ackn: same day by William Walmsley and his wife Sarah. Etherington paid the alienation fine of 6p to Pere. Frisby 21 Dec 1743. Rec: 7 Jan 1743. Wm. Knight, Clerk.

P. 296   Deed.   Edward Morgan of Cecil Co., for £10, to William Walmsley of the same county, 6 acres of land adjoining the Pond Creek, part of a tract called Shrewsbury already in Walmsley's possession. Made 10 Aug 1743. Wit. & JPs: John Baldwin, Pereg. Ward. Ackn: same day by Edward Morgan and his wife Elinor. Rec: 7 Jan 1743. Wm. Knight, Clerk.

P. 298   Deed.   William Barnes of Kent Co., gent., for £300, to James Paul Heath of Cecil Co., gent., land in Cecil Co., 200 acres of land on Back Creek by the land of Col. Henry Lowe of Patuxent River called Spry's Hill, part of a tract called Hackly, also called Hack's Town, on the north side of Sassafras River. The land was sold to William Barnes by Peter Hack by deed dated 8 Nov 1716. Made & Ackn: 8 Feb 1743. Wit: Pereg. Ward, John Thompson. JPs: John Baldwin, Pereg. Ward. Rec: 9 Feb 1743. Wm. Knight, Clerk.

P. 300   Bond.   William Barnes of Kent Co., gent., is bound to James Paul Heath of Cecil Co., gent., in the amount of £600. He puts his property called Hack's Town up as security for the money. William Barnes wife Ann relinquishes her right of dower to the land. Made 8 Feb 1743. Wit: Pereg. Ward, John Thompson, John Baldwin. James Paul Heath paid 4 shillings alienation fine for the land to Pereg. Frisby on 10 Feb 1743. Rec: 9 Feb 1743. Wm. Knight, Clerk.

P. 300   Mortgage.   Joseph Lowman of Cecil Co., planter, for £150, to John Kankey of the same county, planter, 500 acres of land and marsh called Bretton on the north side of Elk River at Plumb Point. Joseph Lowman's father Samuel Lowman previously granted some of the land. Joseph Lowman is to repay John Kankey within 4 years time. Made 17 Nov 1743. Wit. & JPs: Henry Baker, Nathan Baker. John Kankey paid Joseph Lowman the £150 on 7 Nov 1743. Wit: Thos. Ricketts. Ackn: 17 Nov 1743 by Joseph Lowman and his wife Elizabeth. John Kankey paid the alienation fine of 6 shillings for 300 acres [sic] to Pereg. Frisby 28 Dec 1743. Rec: 6 Mar 1743. Wm. Knight, Clerk.

P. 303   Deed.   George Welsh of Cecil Co., yeoman, and Hannah his wife, for £100, to John Ricketts of the said county, yeoman, a plantation and 70 acres of land called Smith's Discovery by John Thomas' land called Bottle east of Elk River. Said land is part of a warrant for 300 acres granted to Stephen Knight dated 2 Jun 1719. Part of the warrant was assigned to John Smith and since sold to Thomas Allison by deed dated 30 Jul 1723. The said Allison sold the land to Jane Wallace by deed dated 23 May 1727. By her

Last Will and Testament dated 26 Jan 1736, Jane Wallace bequeathed the land to the said George Welsh and his wife Hannah. Made & Ackn: 13 Mar 1743. Wit: Nath'l. Ewing, Thos. Ricketts, Francis Elliot. JPs: Pereg. Ward, Nich's. Hyland. Rec: 15 Mar 1743. Wm. Knight, Clerk.

P. 305 Commission. Charles Lord Baltimore appoints as Justices of the Peace for Cecil County John Rousby, Benjamin Tasker, Philip Lee, George Plater, Edmund Jennings, James Hollyday, Charles Hammond, Levin Gale, Samuel Chamberlain, Philip Thomas, Daniel Dulaney, Edward Lloyd, Thomas Colvill, Richard Thompson, John Baldwin, Andrew Berry, John Veazey, Peregrine Ward, Nicholas Hyland, Benjamin Chew, Henry Baker, Nathan Baker, Peter Bayard and Adam Vanbebber, all gents. of Cecil Co. Made 9 Feb 1743. Thomas Bladen, Esq.

P. 310 Deed of Gift. Philip Cazier, Sr., of Cecil Co., gent., for love, good will and natural affection, gives to his son John Cazier of the same county, cordwainer, 21 acres, part of a tract of land called Vulcan's Rest by Smith's Creek by Archibald Douglass' line and Dennis Nowland's line. Made 3 Apr 1744. Wit. & JPs: Henry Baker, Nathan Baker. Ackn: same day by Philip Cazier, Sr. and his wife Catherine. Rec: 3 Apr 1744. Wm. Knight, Clerk.

P. 311 Deed. Philip Stoops of Cecil Co., planter, for £250 and by deed dated 29 Oct 1737 recorded in Lib. W. K. No. 2, folios 315-316, to John Gears of the said county, the northern most moiety of a tract of land (87 acres) called Happy Harbor which was purchased by John Jobson from Quinton Crawford. Made 5 Nov 1743. Wit. & JPs: John Baldwin, Pereg. Ward. Ackn: same day by Philip Stoops and his wife Margaret. Alienation fine of 3s.6p paid by Gears to Pereg. Frisby. Rec: 14 Apr 1744. William Knight, Clerk.

P. 312 Deed. Philip Stoops of Cecil Co., planter, for £30 and by deed dated 5 Nov 1740 recorded in Lib. W. K. No. 9, folios 26-27, to John Gears of the said county, a tract of 31 acres of land called Corengem adjacent to the tract called Happy Harbor in Sassafras Neck by the land of Dr. John Jobson, late of this county, deceased (part of Happy Harbor.) Made 5 Nov 1743. Wit. & JPs: John Baldwin, Pereg. Ward. Ackn: same day by Philip Stoops and his wife Margaret. Alienation fine of 1s.3p paid by Gears to Pereg. Frisby. Rec: 14 Apr 1744. William Knight, Clerk.

P. 314 Deed. Jacob Vanbebber of Newcastle Co. on Delaware, and his wife Elizabeth, for £15, to Samuel McDowell of the same place, weaver, 34 acres of land in Cecil Co. on the east side of Elk River, part of a tract called

Newcastle Back Landing, by Bartholomew Johnson's land. Made 20 Jun 1744. Wit: Henry David, Joseph Watson. Ackn: 19 May 1794 [sic] by Jacob Vanbebber and his wife Elizabeth. JPs: R'd. Thompson, Adam VanBebber. Rec: 19 May 1744. Wm. Knight, Clerk.

P. 316   Release.   William Harris of Kent Co., gent. and heir of Edward Jones, late of Cecil Co., gent., deceased, for 2,000 lbs of tobacco, releases to Edward Morgan of Cecil Co., planter, all his claim to 100 acres of land now in the actual possession of the said Edward Morgan, part of a tract called Shrewsbury of 180 acres which on 13 Aug 1684 was granted by patent to the said Edward Jones. Made & Ackn: 5 May 1744. Wit. & JPs: John Baldwin, Pereg. Ward. Rec: 15 Jun 1744. Wm. Knight, Clerk.

P. 317   Deed.   David Chambers of Maryland, farmer, for £120, to Robert Holy of Cecil Co., planter, a tract of 130 acres called Mount Joy by land formerly laid out for Abraham Hollingsworth. Also a tract of 70 acres of land on the east side of the west branch of Elk River. Abraham Hollingsworth conveyed the 70 acres to Rowland Chambers of Lancaster Co., PA by deed dated 14 Dec 1719 recorded in Lib. J. D. No. 3, folios 147-149. Rowland Chambers was granted 130 acres called Mount Joy by patent dated 20 May 1723. Rowland Chambers conveyed the combined 200 acres of land to the said David Chambers by deed dated 8 Oct 1743 recorded in Lib. W. K. No. 9, folios 228-229. Made & Ackn: 5 May 1744. Wit. & JPs: Henry Baker, Nathan Baker. Robert Holy paid 8 shillings alienation fine for the 200 acres 24 May 1744 to Pereg. Frisby. Rec: 15 Jun 1744. Wm. Knight, Clerk.

P. 319   Lease.   John Campbell of Cecil Co., sadler, for £30 and annual rent, to Thomas Price of the said county, planter, a plantation where the said Thomas Price formerly dwelt on Elk River at Capt. John's Creek, part of a tract called the Dividings containing 100 acres. Lease is for the term of 99 years with annual rent of one capon and the yearly quit rents. Made & Ackn: 15 Jun 1744. Wit: Jno. Rice, David Ricketts. JPs: R'd. Thompson, Henry Baker. Rec: 15 Jun 1744. Wm. Knight, Clerk.

P. 321   Deed.   Jacob Rogers of Great Britain, clerk, and Mary his wife, for £700, to John Reed of Maryland, merchant, a grist mill and 700 acres in Cecil Co. called Kinsley. Major John Copson alias Weaver, late of Maryland, deceased, was granted by patent dated 20 Nov 1735 a tract of 700 acres in Cecil Co. called Kinsley on which he had a grist mill on the North East River below the falls. The land descended to the said Mary Rogers, the only daughter and heiress of Major John Copson alias Weaver. Jacob and Mary Rogers appoint their trusty and well beloved friends Colonel Thomas Colvill, Peter Bayard and James Bayard, all of Cecil Co., to be their attorneys to acknowledge the deed. Made in London 2 Feb 1742. Wit: Charles Hargrave, Tho. Dunn. Ackn: in London before Lord Mayor of London Robert Willimott. Thomas Dunn, clerk to William Murgatroyd of the Middle Temple of London, gent., makes oath that he was present. Ackn: in Cecil Co. 14 Jun 1744 by Peter Bayard. JP: S. Knight. Rec: 14 Jun 1744. Wm. Knight, Clerk.

P. 324 Assignment of Lease. Written on the back of a lease from Col. Ephraim Augustine Herman to John Simmons recorded in Lib. J. D. No. 3, folios 274-275, Esther Davis, late widow of Abraham Ham, deceased, for 5 shillings paid to her and her present husband David Davis, assigns the said lease to Henry Cox of Cecil Co. Lease is for the term of the natural lives expressed in the original lease. Made 27 Mar 1744. Wit: Jacob Ham, Thos. Colvill. Ackn: 13 Jun 1744. JPs: R'd. Thompson, Peter Bayard. Rec: 13 Jun 1744. Wm. Knight, Clerk.

P. 325 Assignment of Lease. William Knight of Cecil Co., gent., for £60, to Walter Scott, Sr. and Walter Scott, Jr., of Cecil Co., cordwainers, land called Scott's Tanyard with the originally lease for the terms of the natural lives mentioned in said lease. Made & Ackn: 16 Jun 1744. Wit: Silas Taylor, Jas. VBebber. JP: S. Knight. Rec: 16 Jun 1744. Wm. Knight, Clerk.

P. 326 Deed. Walter Scott, Sr. of Cecil Co., cordwainer, for £21, to William Knight of the same county, gent., 14 acres, part of a tract of land called Clifton on the south branch of Bohemia River. Made & Ackn: 16 Jun 1744. Wit: James VBebber, Silas Taylor. JP: S. Knight. On 30 Jun 1744 the alienation fine of 6½p was paid to Pereg. Frisby. Rec: 16 Jun 1744. Wm. Knight, Clerk.

P. 328 Lease. Benjamin Tasker, esq., Agent and Receiver General of Maryland, for rents and covenants and with the consent of Gov. Thomas Bladen, to Thomas Colvill, administrator of John Copson of Cecil Co., 100 acres of land called Grange, part of his Lordships manor, by land formerly surveyed for Stephen Onion called Vulcan's Tryal and by Copson's Whim. Lease is for the term of the natural lives of Benedictus Arreer, Sidney George and James Calder, Jr. Rent of 10 shillings due every 29 Sep. Tenants must build a dwelling house 30x20 feet with a brick chimney and plant and fence an orchard of 100 apple trees. Made 4 Jun 1744. Wit: Jno. Ross. Rec: 23 Jun 1744. Wm. Knight, Clerk.

P. 331 Lease. Benjamin Tasker, esq., Agent and Receiver General of Maryland, for rents and covenants and with the consent of Gov. Thomas

Bladen, to Thomas Colvill, administrator of John Copson of Cecil Co., 300 acres of land called Copson's Pasture, part of his Lordships manor on the North East River by Dutton Port's land to Broad Creek. Lease is for the term of the natural lives of Sidney George, James Calder, Jr. and Ephraim Augustine Herman paying £1.10s yearly. Tenants must build a dwelling house 30x20 feet with a brick chimney and plant and fence an orchard of 100 apple trees. Made 4 Jun 1744. Rec: 23 Jun 1744. Wm. Knight, Clerk.

P. 333   Deed.   Thomas Bouldin of Cecil Co., planter, for £250 of uncut gold coins, to William Dames of the same county, merchant, a plantation and 250 acres of land where the said Thomas Bouldin dwells, part of 2 tracts called Bristol and Bouldin's Rest, by Back Creek, by land late of Thomas Beetle's and by land lately belonging to William Bouldin, deceased, and formerly surveyed for Edward Booker. [Bouldin is also spelled Boulding.] Made 29 May 1744. Wit. & JPs: John Baldwin, John Veazey. Ackn: same day by Thomas Bouldin and his wife Ann. Alienation fine paid 15 Jun 1744 to Pereg'n. Frisby. Rec: 30 Jun 1744. Wm. Knight, Clerk.

P. 335   Deed.   Hugh Terry of Kent Co., planter, for £100 paid by Thomas Christian of Cecil Co., planter, to John Thompson of Cecil Co., gent., part of a tract of land called Addition, on the south side of Bohemia River at Omelys Creek where Hugh Terry lately dwelt and where the said Thomas Christian now dwells (all the part of this tract that the said Terry did possess on 6 Nov 1741.) Made & Ackn: 16 Feb 1743. Wit: Pere'r. Ward, Wm. Ellis. Ackn: later (no date) by Sarah, wife of Hugh Terry. JPs: Pereg'n. Ward, John Baldwin. John Thompson paid 2 shillings alienation fine for the 121 acres to Pereg'n. Frisby 16 Mar 1744. Rec: 26 Jun 1744. Wm. Knight, Clerk.

P. 337   Deed.   John Wilson of Philadelphia, PA, merchant, for 16 shillings and because he is moving, to Robert Wakely of the said city, merchant, a moiety of lot #19 in Charles Town, Cecil Co. Made 16 Apr 1744. Wit: Henry Pratt, Charles Meredith. Ackn: same day before Benjamin Shoemaker, Mayor of Philadelphia, and JP Joshua Maddox. Rec: 26 Jun 1744. Wm. Knight, Clerk.

P. 338   Deed.   Dr. Benjamin Bradford of Cecil Co., for 9,000 lbs of tobacco, to David Hampton of the said county, part of a tract of land called Successor on Elk River now in the possession of the said David Hampton and once in the possession of Simon Johnson who bought it from his brother Andrew called Turkey Point containing 100 acres. Made 15 Mar 1743. Wit:

Joshua George, James Hollyday, Jr. David Hampton paid 4 shillings alienation 12 Apr 1744 to Pereg'n. Frisby. Rec: 4 Aug 1744. Wm. Knight, Clerk.

P. 339   Assignment of Lease.   Written on the back of a lease from Col. Ephraim Augustine Herman to Peter Hendrickson recorded in Lib. S. K. No. 5, folios 370-371, for £50, Peter Hendrickson assigns the lease to John Harper, blacksmith. Made & Ackn: 13 Mar 1743. Wit. & JPs: Nicholas Hyland, Henry Baker. Rec: 9 Aug 1794 [sic.] Wm. Knight, Clerk.

P. 339   Deed.   Richard Bouldin of Cecil Co., planter, and his wife Mary, for £340, to George Ford of the same county, the western part of a plantation on the north side of Bohemia Back Creek, part of a tract of 335 acres called Richard's Chance granted by patent dated 28 May 1723 to Richard Boulding, late of the said county, father of the said Richard Bouldin. The said part of this tract was bequeathed to the said Richard Bouldin by the Last Will and Testament of his father Richard Boulding dated 28 Oct 1740. Said land is above the now dwelling house of the said Richard Bouldin. Made & Ackn: 1 Mar 1743/4. Wit: Jno. Cage, Joseph Wallace. JPs: R'd. Thompson, A. Barry. George Ford paid 8 shillings alienation fine 4 Apr 1744 to Pereg'n. Frisby. Rec: 14 Aug 1744. Wm. Knight, Clerk.

P. 341   Lease.   John Steel of Rock Run, Cecil Co., for £30 rent yearly, to John Allison and Robert Allison of the same county, a mill on Rock Run. Said mill was condemned by a Court order. John Steel will repair the mill, the dwelling house and a bake house. Lease is for the term of 12 years. Made 8 Mar 1743/4. Wit: William McKedy, Jo. Hammondorsey, Sam'l. Ingram. Ackn: 7 Aug 1744. JPs: Henry Baker, Nathan Baker. Rec: 14 Aug 1744. Wm. Knight, Clerk.

P. 343   Deed.   Gunning Bedford of Newcastle Co., PA, for £12, to Richard Norton, Jr. of Bucks Co., PA, one-third part (the southeast corner) of lot #25 in Charles Town on the North East River in Cecil Co. bounding on Conostogo Street and the ground laid out for the public key. Made & Ackn: 10 May 1744. Wit: Henry Baker. JPs: Henry Baker, Nathan Baker. Rec: 15 Aug 1744. Wm. Knight, Clerk.

P. 344   Quit Claim.   Jacob Thatcher of Cecil Co., farmer, for 5 shillings and because he is moving, to Robert Evans of Cecil Co., farmer, the only son and heir of John Evans, deceased, 300 acres of land, part of a tract called New Munster which was conveyed by Abigail Thatcher, widow of Richard Thatcher of Cecil Co., deceased, to the said John Evans by deed dated 5 Jun

1730. Made 18 Jun 1744. Wit. & JPs: Henry Baker, Nathan Baker. Ackn: 19 Jun 1744. Rec: 15 Aug 1744. Wm. Knight, Clerk.

P. 345 Deed. Robert Hodgson of Kent Co. on Delaware, son and heir of Robert Hodgson, late of Cecil Co., deceased, for £4.6s.6p, to John Mackey of Cecil Co., yeoman, 200 acres of land. In his lifetime Robert Hodgson, now deceased, agreed to sell to Joseph Houston, for £46, 200 acres of land, part of a tract called Pleasant Garden on a branch of Elk River. Joseph Houston paid £43.15s.1p to Hodgson, but the land was never actually conveyed. By several assignments this agreement has now become the right of the said John Mackey. Made 27 Jul 1744. Wit: A. Barry, Joshua George. Ackn: same day. JPs: John Baldwin, A. Barry. Alienation fine of 8 shillings paid by Mackey to Pereg'n. Frisby 14 Aug 1744. Rec: 15 Aug 1744. Wm. Knight, Clerk.

P. 347 Deed. William Few of North East River in Cecil Co., bricklayer, and his wife Mary, for £16, to Richard Norton of Charles Town in the same county, yeoman, half of lot #95 in Charles Town on the west side of North East River fronting on Market Street and lot #'s 94 and 81. Made 18 Jul 1744. Wit. & JPs: Benjamin Chew, Henry Baker. Ackn: next day. Rec: 15 Aug 1744. Wm. Knight, Clerk.

P. 349 Mortgage. John Lusby of Cecil Co., planter, and Margaret his wife, for £418.3s.9p, to James Paul Heath of the same county, merchant, Negroes named Mingo and Bess and 3 tracts of land, one called Larramore's Addition containing 109 acres surveyed 10 Sep 1716 patented to Roger Larramore, father of the said Margaret Lusby. Another tract of 50 acres called Chance, adjoining a tract called Hazel Branch, patented 10 Jul 1740 to John and Margaret Lusby. The third tract of 240 acres is the southernmost part of a track called Larramore's Neck Enlarged, adjoining the first mentioned tract. The Lusbys to repay Heath within 4 years time. Made & Ackn: 20 Aug 1744. Wit. & JPs: John Baldwin, Adam Vanbebber. Rec: same day. Wm. Knight, Clerk.

P. 351 Deed. John Hance Steelman of PA, gent., for £61.2s.7p, to John Steel of Cecil Co., 400 acres of land in Cecil Co. near Octerara Creek called Boarn's Forest. Made 15 Aug 1744. Wit: Vincent Dorsey, Luke Wyle. John Hance Steelman appoints Powell Poulson of Cecil Co., planter, to be his attorney to acknowledge the deed. Ackn: in Baltimore Co. 17 Aug 1744 by Vincent Dorsey and Luke Wyle before JPs Wm. Bond, Wm. Young, certified as JPs by Thos. Brerewood, County Clerk. Ackn: in Cecil Co. 20 Aug 1744 by Powell Poulson before JPs Henry Baker, Nathan Baker. John Steel paid

16 shillings alienation fine to Pereg'n. Frisby 21 Aug 1744. Rec: 21 Aug 1744. Wm. Knight, Clerk.

P. 353   Deed.   John Hance Steelman of Lancaster Co., PA, yeoman, for £60 sterling, £40 Maryland money and £30 Pennsylvania money, to Elihu Hall of Cecil Co., gent., and James Paul Heath of Cecil Co., merchant, 400 acres of land called Bown's Forest in Cecil Co. on Octerara Creek. Said land John Hance Steelman bought from Henry Bown. John Hance Steelman appoints as his attorneys John Baldwin, John Veazey and John Ward, Jr. Made 6 Oct 1744. Wit: Elisha Hall, Will'm. Dinsey. Ackn: 19 Oct 1744 by John Baldwin and John Veazey, Elisha Hall and William Dinsey. JPs: Benj. Chew, Nathan Baker. Alienation fine of 16 shillings paid to Pereg'n. Frisby 22 Oct 1744. Rec: 22 Oct 1744. Wm. Knight, Clerk.

P. 355   Deed.   Matthew Phillips, mariner, for £12, to Daniel Bromfield, lot #7 in Charles Town on the west side of North East River. Made 1 May 1744. Wit: Thomas Jaffray, Henry Baker. Ackn: same day. JPs: Henry Baker, Nathan Baker. Rec: 30 Oct 1744. Wm. Knight, Clerk.

P. 356   Deed.   Stephen Onion of Baltimore Co., iron master, for £250, to John Steel of Cecil Co., miller, a mill and 20 acres in Cecil Co. on the east side of Susquehanna River at Rock Run which was condemned by a writ for building water mills. To be his until the lease on the writ expires. Also 4 small islands in Susquehanna opposite Rock Run called Perk's Islands and Johnson's Islands. Made in Baltimore Co. 8 Jun 1744. Wit. & JPs: Wm. Young, W. Bond. Ackn: same day by Stephen Onion and his wife Deborah. Baltimore County Clerk Thos. Brerewood certified that William Young and William Bond are JPs. Alienation fine of 2 shillings paid by John Steel to Pereg'n. Frisby 6 Jul 1744. Rec: 30 Oct 1744. Wm. Knight, Clerk.

P. 358   Deed of Gift.   John Ryland, Sr. of Cecil Co., and Mary his wife, for love and good will, gives to their loving son Thomas Ryland of the said county, planter, the dwelling house which the said Thomas now lives in, a tobacco house and 50 acres of land, part of a tract called Mulberry Mould and Mulberry Dock and half the orchard. John Ryland, Sr. retains free access and privileges to the premises during his natural life to cut rail timbers, firewood, etc, as necessary. If John's wife Mary should be the longer liver of the two of them, then she shall inherit and possess the residue and remainder of the said lands during her natural life. Thomas Ryland shall have all the land after the death of the said John and Mary. Made & Ackn: 23 Oct 1744. Wit. & JPs: John Baldwin, Pereg'r. Ward. Rec: 30 Oct 1744. Wm. Knight, Clerk.

P. 359   Deed.   Samuel Robinet and his wife Mary of Chester Co., PA, farmer, for £111.5s, to William Boggs of Cecil Co., farmer, 151 acres of land by John Thompson's land, part of a tract of 350 acres called Providence which Samuel Robinet was granted by patent dated 8 Jun 1732. Made 13 Oct 1744. Wit: James Porter, Nath'l. Ewing. Ackn: same day before JPs A. Barry, Nathan Baker. William Boggs paid 6½ shillings alienation fine same day to Pereg'n. Frisby. Rec: 13 Nov 1744. Wm. Knight, Clerk.

P. 361   Deed.   Walter Betty and his wife Martha of Cecil Co., blacksmith, for £47, to Robert Mitchell of the same county, 80 acres of land on Christian Creek by the land of James and Moses Alexander. David Alexander conveyed to William Pollock 80 acres of land called Moyn, part of a tract called Newmunster, by deed dated 20 Apr 1727 and recorded 8 Aug 1727 in Lib. S. K. No. 5, folios 81-82. William Pollock sold it to the said Walter Betty by deed dated 2 Apr 1736, recorded in Lib. W. K. No. 2, folios 171-172. Made 20 Oct 1744. Wit: A. Barry, Joseph Thompson, Robert Tweedy. Ackn: same day. JPs: A. Barry, Nathan Baker. Mitchell paid 1s.8p alienation fine to Pereg'n. Frisby 13 Nov 1744. Rec: 13 Nov 1744. Wm. Knight, Clerk.

P. 363   Deed.   William Sherwill, Jr., late of Cecil Co., planter, and his wife Margaret, for £40, to John McCreery of the same county, yeoman, 100 acres of land by Samuel Caldwal's land. Said land is part of a tract called Three Partners, the part of the tract which Thomas Jacobs sold to William Sherwill, Sr. who sold it to William Sherwill, Jr. Made 22 Aug 1744. Wit: Henry Baker, Nathan Baker. Ackn: 24 Aug 1744. JPs: Henry Baker, Nathan Baker. McCreery paid 6 shillings alienation fine 14 Nov 1744 to Pereg'n. Frisby. Rec: 14 Nov 1744. Wm. Knight, Clerk.

P. 365   Deed.   John Mannering of Cecil Co., planter, for £150, to William Mitchell of the same place, planter, 250 acres of land called Coxes Fancy on the east side of Susquehanna River. By his Last Will and Testament, Thomas Green, late of Cecil Co., deceased, bequeathed to John Mannering and his brother Thomas Mannering (the only children of John Mannering and his wife Hannah, deceased) a tract of 250 acres called Coxes Fancy. Thomas Mannering died during his minority without issue, his only heir being his brother John. [Mannering is also spelled Manwaring.] Made 23 Oct 1744. Wit: A. Barry, G. Lawson, Jno. White. Ackn: next day. JPs: A. Barry, Nathan Baker. Alienation fine of 10 shillings paid by Mitchell 14 Nov 1744 to Pereg'r. Frisby. Rec: 14 Nov 1744. Wm. Knight, Clerk.

P. 367   Deed.   Joseph Haines of West Nottingham, Chester Co., PA, and his wife Elizabeth, for £70, to Caleb Penal of Lancaster Co., PA, 100 acres of land, part of a tract called Poplar Valley in Cecil Co. on the northeast side of Susquehanna River. Survey of this land dated 3 Nov 1715. By deed dated 24 Sep [year not given] the land was conveyed to Joseph Haines by Caleb Penal and his wife Sarah. Now Haines conveys it back to Penal. Made 13 Oct 1744. Wit: A. Barry, Nathan Baker. By Power of Attorney dated 13 Oct 1744 Elizabeth Haines appoints Thomas Brown of West Nottingham her attorney. Ackn: 13 Oct 1744 by Thomas Brown. JPs: A. Barry, Nathan Baker. Caleb Penal paid 4 shillings alienation fine 14 Nov 1744 to Pereg'r. Frisby. Rec: 15 Nov 1744. Wm. Knight, Clerk.

P. 369   Deed.   Joseph Haines of West Nottingham, Chester Co., PA, and his wife Elizabeth, for £20, to Caleb Penal of Lancaster Co., PA, 114 acres of land, part of a tract called Slate Hill, on the east side of Susquehanna River in Cecil Co. adjoining a tract called Poplar Valley. Said land is part of 225 acres originally granted to Thomas Johnson, Jr., the survey dated 2 Jun 1726. The land, having been sold to sundry persons, by deed dated 24 Sep 1742, was sold to Joseph Haines by Caleb and Sarah Penal. Haines now conveys the land back to Penal. Made 13 Oct 1744. Wit: John Gartril, A. Barry, Nathan Baker. Ackn: 13 Oct 1744 in Cecil Co. by Joseph Haines and Thomas Brown of West Nottingham, attorney for Elizabeth Haines by her power of attorney dated 13 Oct 1744 witnessed by John Waller and John Gartril before JPs: A. Barry, Nathan Baker. Alienation fine of 4 shillings paid by Caleb Penal to Pereg'n. Frisby 14 Nov 1744. Rec: 14 Nov 1744. Wm. Knight, Clerk.

P. 372   Deed.   Caleb Penal of Lancaster Co., PA, farmer, and Sarah his wife, for £120, to James Porter of Little Britain, Lancaster Co., PA, 100 acres of land, part of a tract called Poplar Valley in Cecil Co. on the northeast side of Susquehanna River. Certificate of survey for the land is dated 3 Nov 1715. Made 13 Oct 1744. Wit: John Gartril, Nath'l. Ewing. Ackn: 13 Oct 1744 by Caleb Penal and Thomas Brown of West Nottingham, Chester Co., PA, attorney for Sarah Penal by her power of attorney dated 13 Oct 1744. JPs: A. Barry, Nathan Baker. Alienation fine of 4 shillings paid by James Porter to Pereg'r. Frisby 14 Nov 1744. Rec: 14 Nov 1744. Wm. Knight, Clerk.

P. 374   Deed.   Caleb Penal of Lancaster Co., PA, farmer, and Sarah his wife, for £80, to James Porter of Little Britain, Lancaster Co., PA, 114 acres of land, part of a tract called Slate Hill in Cecil Co., on the east side of Susquehanna River adjoining the tract called Poplar Valley. The 225 acres called Slate Hill was surveyed for Thomas Johnson, Jr. by certificate of survey dated 2 Jun 1726. Made 13 Oct 1744. Wit: John Gartril, Nath'l. Ewing. Ackn: 13 Oct 1744 by Caleb Penal and Thomas Brown of West Nottingham, Chester Co., PA, attorney for Sarah Penal by her power of attorney dated 13 Oct 1744. Sarah Penal unable to appear due to infliction of body. Power of attorney witnessed by John Walker, Catherine Maghar and ackn. by John Walker. JPs: A. Barry, Nathan Baker. Alienation fine of 4s.7p paid by James Porter to Pereg'n. Frisby 14 Nov 1744. Rec: 14 Nov 1744. Wm. Knight, Clerk.

P. 378   Deed.   John Kimber of Cecil Co., planter, and Catherine his wife, for £100, to Thomas Davis of the same county, planter, a tract of 50 acres called King's Delight on the north side of Sassafras River at Back Creek by land formerly taken up by William Ward. Also a tract called Rattlesnake Neck adjoining the first tract. Made & Ackn: 14 Nov 1744. Wit. & JPs: John Veazey, Pereg'r. Ward. Alienation fine of 2 shillings paid by Davis to Pereg'n. Frisby 16 Nov 1744. Rec: 16 Nov 1744. Wm. Knight, Clerk.

P. 380   Deed.   Thomas Davis of Cecil Co., planter, and Rebecca his wife, for £20, to John Kimber of the same county, planter, a tract of 2¾ acres called the Levell by Thomas Davis' house and within the lines of a tract called Rattlesnake Neck. Also a piece of land now in Thomas Davis' possession lying between the land called Rattlesnake Neck and Back Creek and by John Kimber's landing amounting to 10 feet square, part of the tract called King's Delight, for a burial ground where John Kimber's father and one of his children are buried. Made & Ackn: 14 Nov 1744. Wit. & JPs: John Veazey, Pereg'r. Ward. John Kimber paid 1½p alienation fine 16 Nov 1744 to Pereg'r. Frisby. Rec: 16 Nov 1744. Wm. Knight, Clerk.

P. 382   Deed.   Thomas Boulding (and his wife Ann) and Thomas Beetle (and his wife Elizabeth), both of Cecil Co., to Dorothy Patton of the same county, a plantation and 107 acres on the north side of Bohemia Back Creek by land formerly taken up by Richard Boulding, late of said county, and by tracts called Boulding's Rest and Bristoll. Made & Ackn: 11 Oct 1744. Wit. & JPs: Richard Thompson, Peter Bayard. Rec: 26 Nov 1744.

P. 383   Deed.   John Currier of Cecil Co., innholder, for £280, to James Paul Heath of the same county, merchant, 300 acres of land called Helena on the North East River by land called Cavan, part of a tract called Susquehanna Manor alias Newconnaught Manor which was granted to George Talbot and by him was sold 31 May 1687 to William Currier and his wife Jane, grandparents of the said John Currier. Made 29 Oct 1744. Wit: Nicholas Hyland, Nathan Baker. Ackn: same day by John Currier and Millicent his wife. JPs: Nicholas Hyland, Nathan Baker. Rec: 30 Nov 1744. Wm. Knight, Clerk.

P. 385   Deed.   William Penington of Cecil Co., planter, for £7.10s to Sabina Rumsey during her natural life and after her death to William Rumsey, son and heir of William Rumsey, gent., deceased, part of a tract of land called Civility originally by patent dated 13 May 1679 granted to William Hill. The northernmost moiety of the land lies within the bounds of a tract called Happy Harbour and the southern line lies by a tract called Sylvania's Folly. William Penington warrants the land against claims of the heirs of William Drake, deceased. Made & Ackn: 24 Nov 1744. Wit: Pereg'r. Ward, Wm. Pearce. JPs: John Baldwin, Pereg'r. Ward. Mrs. Sabina Rumsey paid 3p.3f alienation fine 13 Dec 1744 to Pereg'r. Frisby. Rec: 21 Dec 1744. Wm. Knight, Clerk.

P. 387   Deed.   Sabina Rumsey, widow and executrix of the Last Will and Testament of William Rumsey, late of Cecil Co., gent., deceased, for £20, to Joshua George of Cecil Co., a tract of 300 acres called Rumsey's Double Parcel, a tract of 250 acres called Antego, another tract of 200 acres called Rumsey's Discovery and another tract of 300 acres called Rumsey's Range.
   Some considerable time before his death, William Rumsey made his Last Will and Testament providing lands for his then living children. His wife Sabina was pregnant at the time of his death, whose sickness was so violent and, although at intervals he plainly had a desire to alter his Will, there was not enough time to do so. Shortly after his death, Sabina gave birth to a son named John for whom there is no provision made by his father's Will. William Rumsey, providing for each of his children by name and for his widow with several tracts of land, devised the residue of the lands to be sold by the said Sabina. Sabina, believing it just that some provision be made for the said John Rumsey, puts her trust and confidence in her friend Joshua George that he shall in some good space of time convey some of the said William Rumsey's lands to the son John Rumsey. Made & Ackn: 1 Feb 1744. Wit. & JPs: John Baldwin, Adam VanBebber. Rec: 1 Feb 1744. Wm. Knight, Clerk.

P. 389   Assignment of Lease.   Written on the back of a lease from Ephraim Augustine Herman to John Hollet dated 9 Jun 1722 and recorded in Lib. J. D. No. 3, folios 295-296, John Tilton and Elizabeth his wife, for £120, assign the lease to Jacob Hosier. Made 29 Aug 1744. Wit: Thos. Colvill, Peter Bayard. Rec: 9 Jan 1744. Wm. Knight, Clerk.

P. 390   Assignment of Lease.   Written on the back of a lease from Richard Thompson to John McCreery, recorded 11 Mar 1741 in Lib. W. K. No. 9, folios 112-113, John McCreery assigns the lease to Isaac Ham. [Ham also spelled Hamm.] Made & Ackn: 15 Dec 1744. Wit: Peter Lawson, Thos. Stewart. JPs: Richard Thompson, Peter Bayard. Rec: 12 Jan 1744. Wm. Knight, Clerk.

P. 390   Lease.   Joseph Gaylard of Thomas Street, London, grocer, William Whitaker of Lime Street, London, and Matthew Testas, late of Dove Court, Lombard Street, London, merchant, assignees of the estate of Edward Warner, now or late of St. Botolph Aldgate, London, grocer, bankrupt, and Edward Warner, for 5 shillings for each, to Richard Bennett of Wye River, Queen Annes Co., Maryland, esq., a tract of 600 acres called the Hazlemore in Baltimore or Cecil Co. on the south side of Elk River by a tract of land formerly taken up by Philip Calvert called the Grove, by land formerly taken up by Mounce Andrews or Mounce Anderson and by Mr. James Frisby's land. Also the tract of 1,000 acres called the Grove on Sassafras River adjoining land laid out for Robert Burle. And all other lands which by deeds of lease and release dated 13 and 14 Nov 1740 was mortgaged by the said Edward Warner, son and heir of Edward Warner, late citizen and distiller of London, deceased, and Mary Warner, his widow and mother of the younger Edward Warner, to the said Joseph Gaylard. For an additional 5 shillings each, William Whitaker, Matthew Testas and Edward Warner convey to Bennett all the lands in Baltimore and Cecil counties which were in the possession of Edward Warner at the date of the suing for bankruptcy. Joseph Gaylard, William Whitaker, Matthew Testas and Edward Warner appoint as their attorneys Joshua George, gent., James Heath, merchant, James Calder, gent., John Baldwin, gent., and William Knight, esq., all residing in Maryland. Made 1 May 1744. Wit: Jno. Rendell, Jem. Bigg, John Dunkin, Hen. Harrison, Philip Allingham, Edward Wills, James Esten, Nath'l. Chew, Alex. Cumming. Ackn: in Cecil Co. by Capt. Philip Allingham and Alexander Cumming 16 Dec 1744. JP: Jno. Brice. Ackn: in Cecil Co. by Joshua George, James Heath, John Baldwin and William Knight, all of Cecil Co., gents. JPs: Tho. Colvill, Adam VanBebber. Rec: 21 Jan 1744. Wm. Knight, Clerk.

P. 395   Release.   Joseph Gaylord, William Whitaker, Matthew Testas and Edward Warner, for £352 and £248, to Richard Bennett, 2 tracts of land [for details of the land see previous entry P. 390.] In the original lease and release dated 13 and 14 May 1740 Joseph Gaylard paid £300 to Edward Warner for the lands called Hazelmore and the Grove. Warner was to repay Gaylord. Bankruptcy filed against Edward Warner dated 15 Jun [1743] awarded to Roger Coningsbey, Robert Salkeld, William Melmouth the

133

younger, Thomas Hutches and Conway Whithorne as Commissioners, finding that Edward Warner, for several years previous to the date of the lawsuit, had a business as a grocer and tobacconist and did become indebted to the said William Whitaker and Matthew Testas and other persons in the amount of £200 and upwards. By deed dated 27 Oct 1742 from the said Roger Coningsbey, Robert Salkeld and Conway Whithorne to William Whitaker and Matthew Testas 2 tracts of land were mortgaged to Joseph Gaylard. A deed of the same date was made by Mary Warner, widow of Edward Warner, to William Whitaker and Mathew Testas reciting the mortgage to Joseph Gaylard and the bankruptcy. The £300 was not repaid by Warner within the limited time set. Joseph Gaylard, William Whitaker, Matthew Testas and Edward Warner appoint as their attorneys Joshua George, gent., James Heath, merchant, James Calder, gent., John Baldwin, gent., and William Knight, esq., all residing in Maryland. Made 2 May 1744. Wit: Jno. Rendell, Jem. Bigg, John Dunkin, Hen. Harrison, Philip Allingham, Edward Wills, James Esten, Nath'l. Chew, Alex. Cumming. Ackn: in Cecil Co. by Capt. Philip Allingham and Alexander Cumming 16 Dec 1744. JP: Jno. Brice. Ackn: in Cecil Co. by Joshua George, James Heath, John Baldwin and William Knight, all of Cecil Co., gents. JPs: Tho. Colvill, Adam VanBebber. Richard Bennett paid £1.4s alienation fine for 600 acres called Hazlemore on 21 Jan 1744 to Pereg'r. Frisby. Rec: 21 Jan 1744. Wm. Knight, Clerk.

P. 407 Deed. Sabina Rumsey, widow and executrix of William Rumsey, gent., deceased, for £100, to Joshua George of Cecil Co., 100 acres of land, part of a tract called Sarah's Joynture which the said William Rumsey purchased from William Hill and his wife Mary and was formerly the estate of John Rennals of Cecil Co. and by him conveyed to the said Mary Hill. By his Last Will and Testament, William Rumsey directed his widow Sabina to sell all his lands not already devised by his said Will. Made & Ackn: 1 Feb 1744. Wit. & JPs: John Baldwin, Adam VanBebber. Alienation fine of 4 shillings paid to Pereg'r. Frisby 6 Feb 1744. Rec: 16 Feb 1744. Wm. Knight, Clerk.

P. 409 Lease. John Hance Steelman of Lancaster Co., PA, yeoman, for 5 shillings, to Elihu Hall and James Paul Heath of Cecil Co., gents., a tract of 400 acres which the said Steelman bought from Henry Bourn called Bourn's Forest in Cecil Co. on Octorara Creek. Steelman appoints John Baldwin, John Veazey and John Ward, Jr., all gents. of Cecil Co, to be his attorneys. Made 14 Dec 1744. Wit: Elisha Hall, Wm. Hopkins. Ackn: 30 Jan 1744 by Elisha Hall, William Hopkins, John Baldwin and John Veazey. JPs: Pereg'r. Ward, Adam VanBebber. The affirmation of Elisha Hall and William Hopkins taken before JPs Benj'a. Chew, Peter Bayard. Rec: 30 Jan 1744. Wm. Knight, Clerk.

P. 411 Release. John Hance Steelman, for £60 (£40 MD money and £30 [sic] PA money) and because he is moving, to Elihu Hall and James Paul Heath [see previous entry P. 409.] 400 acres called Bourn's Forest. Steelman appoints John Baldwin, John Veazey and John Ward, Jr., all gents. of Cecil Co, to be his attorneys. Made 14 Dec 1744. Wit: Elisha Hall, Wm. Hopkins. Ackn: 31 Jan 1744 by Elisha Hall, William Hopkins, John Baldwin and John Veazey. JPs: Pereg'r. Ward, Adam VanBebber. The affirmation of Elisha Hall and William Hopkins taken before JPs Benj'a. Chew, Peter Bayard. Alienation fine of 16s paid 14 Jan 1744 to Pereg'n. Frisby. Rec: 31 Jan 1744. Wm. Knight, Clerk.

P. 414 Deed. John Hance Steelman of Lancaster Co, PA, yeoman, for £20, to Elihu Hall of Cecil Co., gent., and James Paul Heath of Cecil Co., merchant, all the said Steelman's lands in Cecil Co. Steelman appoints John Baldwin, John Veazey and John Ward, Jr., all gents. of Cecil Co, to be his attorneys. Made 6 Oct 1744. Wit: Elisha Hall, Wm. Disney. Ackn: 19 Oct 1744 by John Baldwin and John Veazey, attorneys for Steelman, and Elisha Hall and William Disney. JPs: Benj'a. Chew, Nathan Baker. Rec: 19 Oct 1744. Wm. Knight, Clerk.

P. 417 Deed. Thomas Stratton of Kent Co., PA, because he is moving, quit claims to Martin Alexander of Cecil Co., 35 acres in Cecil Co. lying between a parcel which Thomas Stratton sold to Richard Nash, late of said county, and a large tract called Knowlwood. Made & Ackn: 4 Feb 1744. Wit: Dorithy Patton, R'd. Thompson. JPs: Rich'd. Thompson, Adam VanBebber. Rec: same day. Wm. Knight, Clerk.

P. 418 Deed. Col. Thomas Colvill of Cecil Co., for 5 shillings, to Alice George, a moiety of a lot of land in Frederick Town on Sassafras River, and the part [of the lot] not already sold to James Hughes. Made & Ackn: 14 Feb 1744. Wit: Ja. Calder. JPs: John Baldwin, A. Barry. Alienation fine paid 22 Feb 1744 to Pereg'r. Frisby. Rec: 24 Feb 1744. Wm. Knight, Clerk.

P. 419 Lease. Benjamin Tasker, Agent and Receiver General, for and on behalf of Lord Baltimore and with the consent of Gov. Thomas Bladen, for rents and services, to John Brooks of Cecil Co., 127 acres of land in Cecil Co., part of his Lordships Manor of North East. Lease is for the term of the natural lives of John Brooks, James Brooks and John Brooks [sic.] Rent of 12s.9p to be paid 29 Sep yearly. The Brooks agree to build a dwelling house 30x20 feet with a brick chimney and will plant and fence an orchard of 100 apple trees. Made 3 Feb 1743. Wit: J. Ross. Rec: 10 Feb 1744. Wm. Knight, Clerk.

P. 421 Lease. Benjamin Tasker, Agent and Receiver General, for and on behalf of Lord Baltimore and with the consent of Gov. Thomas Bladen, for rents and services, to Samuel Seal of Cecil Co., 50 acres of land, part of his Lordships Manor of North East. Lease is for the term of the natural lives of the said Samuel Seal and Mary Seal his wife, and their daughter Elizabeth Seal. Rent of 5 shillings to be paid 29 Sep yearly. The Seals agree to build a 30x20 foot dwelling house with a brick chimney and will build and fence an orchard of no less than 100 apple trees. Made 3 Feb 1743. Wit: Jno. Ross. Rec: 12 Feb 1744. Wm. Knight, Clerk.

P. 424 Deed. Joshua George of Cecil Co., for £20 and because he is moving, to John Rumsey, son of William Rumsey, and Sabina Rumsey, his mother, the following tracts of land: 300 acres called Rumsey's Double Parcel; 250 acres called Antego; 200 acres called Rumsey's Range. Lands are for Sabina Rumsey until the said John Rumsey shall become 21 years of age, should he live so long. If he should die before then Sabina Rumsey is to dispose of the lands according to the Will of her deceased husband William Rumsey. If John Rumsey lives to 21 years or before he has lawful issue then the lands are to be his. Made & Ackn: 15 Feb 1744. Wit. & JPs: Thos. Colvill, John Baldwin. Rec: 25 Feb 1744. Wm. Knight, Clerk.

P. 425 Deed. Rachel Croker of Cecil Co., widow, for £115 and 26,798 lbs of tobacco, to Peter Jones of Kent Co., 158 acres, part of a tract of land in Cecil Co. in Sassafras Neck at Back Creek called None So Good In Finland. Said land was resurveyed for her father Thomas Crouch and patented to the said Rachel and her deceased husband Robert Croker. The land has on it a mortgage which the said Robert and Rachel Croker made to William Ellis. Made 22 Oct 1744. Wit: John Veazey, John Baldwin, John Thompson. Ackn: same day. JPs: John Baldwin, John Veazey. Rec: 25 Feb 1744. Wm. Knight, Clerk.

P. 427 Lease. Benjamin Tasker, Agent and Receiver General, for and on behalf of Lord Baltimore and with the consent of Gov. Thomas Bladen, for rents and services, to James Brooks of Cecil Co., 100 acres of land, part of his Lordships Manor of North East. Lease is for the term of the natural lives of the said James Brooks, his wife Martha Brooks and his son Thomas Brooks. Rent of 10 shillings to be paid every 29 Sep. The Brooks will build a 20x30 foot house with a brick chimney and plant and fence 100 apple trees. Made 2 Feb 1744. Wit: Jno. Ross. Rec: 13 Mar 1744. Wm. Knight, Clerk.

P. 429   Lease.   Benjamin Tasker, Agent and Receiver General, for and on behalf of Lord Baltimore and with the consent of Gov. Thomas Bladen, for rents and services, to Caleb Carman of Cecil Co., 80 acres of land, part of his Lordships Manor of North East. Lease is for the term of the natural lives of the said Caleb Carman, John Brooks, son of John Brooks, and Thomas Brooks, son of James Brooks. Rent of 8s.10p to be paid every 29 Sep. The Brooks will build a 20x30 foot house with a brick chimney and plant and fence 100 apple trees. Made 17 May 1744. Wit: Jno. Ross. Rec: 13 Mar 1744. Wm. Knight, Clerk.

P. 431   Deed.   Edward Miles of White Clay Creek, Newcastle upon Delaware Co., PA, millwright and attorney for Samuel Wilds, late of said Newcastle Co., but now living in Craven Co. on Peedee River in SC, for £48.10s, to John Ricketts of Cecil Co., farmer, 100 acres of land with a grist mill on the east side of the main branch of Elk River by land called Batchelor's Hope. Said land was surveyed and laid out for John Thomas by warrant dated 3 Mar 1718. John Thomas sold the land by deed dated 1 Mar 1721 to Evan Edmond. On 24 Sep 1723 the land was sold to Griffith Nicholas who erected a grist mill on the land. By his Last Will and Testament dated 5 Dec 1726 the said Nicholas devised the land to his grandson, the said Samuel Wilds. Made 17 Jan 1744/5. Wit: John Hyland, Thomas Ricketts. John Ricketts paid the consideration money to Edward Miles 29 Nov 1744. Wit: Patrick Ferris, Thomas Ricketts, John Jenkin, Samuel Arnett. Ackn: 17 Jan 1744. JPs: A. Barry, Nicholas Hyland.

Samuel Wilds of Craven Co., SC, son of Samuel Wilds, some time ago an inhabitant on the Welsh Tract in Newcastle Co, PA, grandson of Griffith Nicholas of Cecil Co. on Elk River, and nephew to Abel Nicholas of the same place, because he is moving, appoints Edward Miles of Newcastle Co., PA, millwright, to be his attorney, to sell a tract of land called the Bottle. Made in Craven Co., SC 6 Mar 1743/4. Wit: David Lewis, John Evans before Craven Co. JP William James. Ackn: in Craven Co. by Rev. Philip James and Mr. Samuel Desaurency who swore they have both known Samuel Wilds since he was a child. Ackn: in Cecil Co. by David Lewis 3 Dec 1744. JP: A. Barry. Rec: 13 Mar 1744. Wm. Knight, Clerk.

P. 436   Lease.   John Campbell of Cecil Co., sadler, for covenants and agreements, to Andrew Price of the said county, planter, a plantation and 100 acres on Elk River where the said Andrew Price now lives at the mouth of Capt. John's Creek, part of a tract called the Dividings. Lease is for the term of the natural lives of the said Andrew Price, his wife Elizabeth Price and his son Nicholas Price. Rent of one dunghill fowl and the yearly quit rents. Made 7 Jan 1744. Wit: Robert Walmsley, Jno. Rice. Ackn: 10 Jan 1744 before JPs John Baldwin and John Veazey.

On 15 Jun last, Thomas Price of Cecil Co. bought the said 100 acres for the term of 99 years from John Campbell. Now Thomas Price, for £40 and 2,220 lbs of tobacco, assigns the lease to Andrew Price. Made 7 Jan 1744. Wit: Jno. Campbell, Jno. Rice. Ackn: 15 Mar 1744. JPs: John Baldwin, John Veazey. Rec: 15 Mar 1744. Wm. Knight, Clerk.

P. 438   Deed.   Simon Johnson, Jr. of Millford, Cecil Co., planter, and his wife Catherine, for £30, to Thomas Booth of the same place, blacksmith, 50 acres of land, part of the 100 acres in Millford Hundred, part of a larger tract called Successor, which Paul Poulson sold [to Simon Johnson, Jr.] by deed dated 12 Jan 1740/1 and recorded in Lib. W. K.. No. 9, folio 52. Made & Ackn: 9 Feb 1744/5. Wit. & JPs: A. Barry, Nathan Baker. Rec: 15 Mar 1744. Wm. Knight, Clerk.

P. 440   Deed.   William Stooby of Newcastle Hundred, Newcastle Co. upon Delaware, weaver, and his wife Ann, for £51, to Peter Poulson of the said place, yeoman, 100 acres on the west side of Elk River by Simon Deny's land. By deed dated 26 Sep 1710, Margaret Lindsey of West New Jersey, spinster, sold 300 acres called Feddart on the west side of Elk River in Cecil Co. to Henry Johnson (recorded in Lib. W. K. No. 1, folio 116.) By his Last Will and Testament, Henry Johnson bequeathed 100 acres to Michael Johnson who, by deed dated 22 Jul 1727 recorded in Lib. S. K. No. 5, folio 91, sold the 100 acres to Suleff Stedham. Suleff Stedham and his wife Ann, by deed dated 14 Jul 1738, sold the 100 acres to the said William Stooby. Made 21 Sep 1744. Wit: Henry Colesberry Goldsmith, Edward Folwell. Ackn: in Cecil Co. 17 Jan 1744/5. JPs: A. Barry, Nicholas Hyland. Rec: 15 Mar 1744. Wm. Knight, Clerk.

P. 443   Lease.   Thomas Hitchcock the Younger of Cecil Co., planter, to Michael Lum of said county, planter, for yearly rents and covenants, 99 acres of land lying between Elk River and the main road, part of a tract of 200 acres belonging to said Hitchcock. Lease is for the term of 22 years. Rent of 1 ear of Indian corn yearly. Made & Ackn: 15 Mar 1744. Wit: Charles Coatts, Wm. Knight. JPs: Nicholas Hyland, Nathan Baker. Rec: 15 Mar 1744. Wm. Knight, Clerk.

P. 444   Assignment of Lease.   Catherine Wood, widow and executrix of Robert Wood, late of Cecil Co., deceased, and Robert Wood of the same place, for 5 shillings, to Thomas Cox of the said county, all their rights and title to the annexed lease land and premises. Land is one moiety of the lease bequeathed Robert Wood by his deceased father Robert Wood. Made & Ackn: 11 Mar 1744. Wit. & JPs: R'd. Thompson, Peter Bayard. Note: the above assignment is for a lease from Col. Eph'm. Augt'n. Herman to Joseph Woods and Robert Woods for land in Bohemia Manor dated 4 Jun 1722. Rec: 15 Mar 1745. Wm. Knight, Clerk.

P. 445 Valuation of Estate. James Wroth and Robert Walmsley have viewed the plantation and land belonging to Joseph Clements, orphan, now in the possession of his guardian Francis Bonner, and found the premises out of repair of fencing, 2 very old small dwelling houses are leaky, 16 old apple trees needing to be trimmed. They allow the guardian to cut timber to repair the houses and to build a tobacco house. Also he may clear a strip of ground called Dogwood Field for rails for the fences. They value the land and plantation at 500 lbs of tobacco a year. Made 8 Dec 1744. Wit: John Veazey. Rec: 15 Mar 1744. Wm. Knight, Clerk.

P. 445 Assignment of Lease. Written on the back of a lease from Eph'm. Aug. Herman to John Ham, Jr. for land in Bohemia Manor, Walter Devan assigns the lease to Garret Johnson for the terms of the natural lives stated in the lease. Made 27 Aug 1743. Wit: Benjamin Lancaster, Thomas Ebthorp. Ackn: 6 Feb 1743/4. JPs: Tho. Colvill, John Veazey. Rec: 23 Feb 1743. Wm. Knight, Clerk.

P. 446 Release. Alexander White of Lancaster Co., PA, yeoman, son of Alexander White, deceased, and Jean White of Chester Co., PA, widow and executrix of Alexander White, deceased, to Samuel Thompson of Cecil Co., yeoman, because of his affinity with Elizabeth White, daughter of the deceased Alexander White who had assigned the tract of land to the said Samuel Thompson as part of a child's part, 183 acres of land by Joseph Carter's land called Kinly. Alexander White of Chester Co., PA, deceased, yeoman, conveyed to his son the said Alexander White his patent dated 1738, recorded in Lib. E. J. No. 2, folio 794 for land in Cecil Co. called Gorry. [Jean White is also called Jane White.] Made 28 Mar 1745. Wit: A. Barry, Jno. White. Ackn: 29 Mar 1745. JPs: A. Barry, Nathan Baker. Samuel Thompson paid 7s.4p alienation fine to Pereg. Frisby 2 Apr 1745. Rec: 24 Apr 1745. Wm. Knight, Clerk.

P. 448 Deed. William Harris of Kent Co., gent., for 5 shillings, to Charles Hynson of the same county, gent., 300 acres of land called Salem on Bohemia River in Cecil Co. by land formerly taken up by Capt. George Goldsmith. Said land originally granted to Hugh Woodberry. Made 23 Mar 1744. Wit: John Brown, R'd. Loyd. Ackn: in Kent Co. same day. JPs: John

Brown, Richard Loyd, certified by James Smith, Kent Co. Clerk. On 1 Apr 1745 Charles Hynson by the hands of Joshua George paid 12 shillings alienation fine to Pereg'r. Frisby. Rec: 15 Apr 1745. Wm. Knight, Clerk.

P. 449   Deed.   William Harris of Kent Co., gent., for 5 shillings, to James Paul Heath of Cecil Co., gent., a tract of 340 acres called Mesopotamia on the north side of Sassafras River by land formerly laid out for Andrew Woodbury called the Middle Plantation, by a tract called Woodbury formerly laid out for Edward Jones, by a tract formerly laid out for Mounce Andrews, by a tract called Hendrick's Choice formerly laid out for Hendrick Hendrickson and by a tract called Larramore's Neck Enlarged formerly laid out for Roger Larramore. Said 340 acres was first granted to Edward Jones by patent dated 10 Aug 1684 and by several conveyances became the estate of John Price. Except the 80 acres already sold to James Wroth and 112 acres sold to John Roberts. Made 23 Mar 1744. Wit: John Brown, R'd. Loyd. Ackn: in Kent Co. same day. JPs: John Brown, R'd. Loyd. Pereg'r. Frisby was paid 5s11p alienation fine by James Paul Heath on 1 Apr 1745. James Smith, Clerk of Kent Co., certified John Brown and Rich'd. Loyd as JPs. Rec: 15 Apr 1745. Wm. Knight, Clerk.

P. 451   Deed.   William Harris of Kent Co., gent., for 5 shillings, to William Husband of Cecil Co., gent., 125 acres, a half-part of 250 acres of land called Prosperity on the east side of Elk River at the head of St. Alban's Creek by a tract called Larramore. Made 23 Mar 1744. Wit: John Brown, R'd. Loyd. Ackn: in Kent Co. same day. JPs: John Brown, R'd. Loyd. James Smith, Clerk of Kent Co., certified John Brown and Richard Loyd as JPs. Alienation fine of 5 shillings paid by Joshua George for William Husband to Pereg'r. Frisby on 1 Apr 1745. Rec: 15 Apr 1745. Wm. Knight, Clerk.

P. 453   Deed.   William Harris of Kent Co., gent., for 5 shillings, to James Wroth of Cecil Co., planter, 80 acres of land, part of a tract called Mesopotamia, by Stony Run Branch and Pond Creek (except for 2 acres of marsh.) Made 23 Mar 1744. Wit: John Brown, R'd. Loyd. Ackn: in Kent Co. same day. JPs: John Brown, R'd. Loyd. James Smith, Clerk of Kent Co., certified John Brown and Richard Loyd as JPs. Alienation fine of 3s.10½p paid by Joshua George for James Wroth to Pereg'r. Frisby on 1 Apr 1745. Rec: 15 Apr 1745. Wm. Knight, Clerk.

P. 454   Deed.   William Harris of Kent Co., gent., for 5 shillings, to John Roberts of Cecil Co., planter, 112 acres of land called Montgomery, part of a tract called Mesopotamia formerly belonging to Edward Jones, on the north side of Sassafras River by John Price's late dwelling plantation. Made 23

Mar 1744. Wit: John Brown, R'd. Loyd. Ackn: in Kent Co. same day. JPs: John Brown, R'd. Loyd. James Smith, Clerk of Kent Co., certified John Brown and Richard Loyd as JPs. Alienation fine of 4s.6p paid to Pereg'r. Frisby on 1 Apr 1745. Rec: 15 Apr 1745. Wm. Knight, Clerk.

P. 456   Release.   William Harris of Kent Co., gent., for 5 shillings, to John Beddle of Cecil Co., planter, 150 acres, a moiety of 300 acres called Abraham's Promise on Elk River on the south side of Capt. John's Creek. Made & Ackn: 2 Apr 1745. Wit. & JPs: John Baldwin, R'd. Thompson. John Beddle paid 6 shillings alienation fine to Pereg'r. Frisby. Rec: 15 Apr 1745. Wm. Knight, Clerk.

P. 457   Lease.   James Paul Heath of Cecil Co., merchant, for rents and agreements, to Prince Snow of the said county, carpenter, 2 lots in Warwick, both lots called #12. The first lot of ½ acre bounds on Chesapeake Street and Bohemia Street, the other lot of 5 acres lies along Bohemia Street and by the 200 acres of the commons laid out by said James Paul Heath. Lease is for the term of the natural lives of Nathaniel Cleave, Benjamin Cleave and Nathan Cleave, Snow's sons-in-law. Rent of 50 shillings due 24 Mar yearly after 4 years have past. Within the 4 years, they are to build on the ½ acre lot a dwelling house. Made 25 Mar 1745. Wit: Hercules Real, Robert Marcer. Ackn: 1 May 1745. JPs: John Baldwin, John Veazey. Rec: 9 May 1745. Wm. Knight, Clerk.

P. 460   Lease.   James Paul Heath of Cecil Co., merchant, for rents and agreements, to Hercules Real, now or late of Newcastle Co. on Delaware, 2 lots in Warwick, both lots called #43. One is ½ acre on Delaware and Cecil Streets, and the other lot of 5 acres on Cecil Street and the privilege of the Commons. Lease is for the term of the natural lives of the said Hercules Real and his wife Rebecca, and during the life of Joseph Rue, son of Matthew Rue of Newcastle Co. on Delaware. Rent of 50 shillings due every 25 Mar after 4 years have past. Within those 4 years they are to build a dwelling house on the ½ acre lot. Made 25 Mar 1745. Wit: Ja. Caulk, Chas. Heath. Ackn: 2 May 1745. JPs: John Baldwin, John Veazey. Rec: 9 May 1745. Wm. Knight, Clerk.

P. 463   Lease.   Benjamin Tasker, Agent and Receiver General, for and on behalf of Lord Baltimore and with the consent of Gov. Thomas Bladen, for rents and services, to James Paul Heath, 1,000 acres of land, part of his Lordships Manor of Susquehanna alias New Connaught or Talbott's Manor, by the North East River and by land lately surveyed for John Wallace, merchant. One-fourth part of this land is to always remain uncleared. Lease is for the natural lives of the said James Paul Heath, his wife Rebecca and their son Daniel Charles Heath. Rent of £5 to be paid 25 Mar yearly. Heath is to build a dwelling house 30x20 feet and plant and fence an orchard of 100 apple trees. Made 25 Mar 1745. Wit: Thomas Bladen, Benjamin Chew, Walter Dulany. Rec: 28 May 1745. Wm. Knight, Clerk.

P. 467 Deed. Hugh Matthews of Philadelphia Co., PA, chirurgeon, for £500, to William Knight of Cecil Co., gent., and his wife Rachel, a tract of land called Manwaring Hall in Cecil Co. on Bohemia River, except the part which was formerly conveyed by the said Hugh Matthews to James Paul Heath. Hugh Matthews bought the land from Dr. Richard Hill of Ann Arundel Co. The 400 acres of land was formerly patented to Richard Hill, grandfather of Dr. Richard Hill. Also part of a tract called Devidend which was resurveyed for Nicholas Sewall of St. Marys Co., esq., which lies northward of the main east branch of Bohemia River. This part of Devidend was bought by Hugh Matthews from George Douglass of Cecil Co., gent., and his wife Susannah. Also 200 acres of land which Matthews bought from James Paul Heath, actually part of 2 tracts called Heath's Third Parcel and Addition to Heath's Third Parcel, between the tract called Manwaring Hall and Indian Branch also called Harper's Branch. Hugh Matthews appoints his trusty and well beloved friends James Paul Heath and Peter Bayard, both of Cecil Co., to be his attorneys. Made 28 Jan 1744. Wit: Patrick Matthews, John Nelson, John Harper. Ackn: 30 May 1745 by John Nelson and John Harper. JPs: Tho. Colvill, Peter Bayard. Ackn: 10 Jun 1745 by James Paul Heath and Peter Bayard. JPs: Thos. Colvill, Adam VanBebber. William Knight paid £1.2s.7p alienation fine to Pereg'r. Frisby 10 Feb 1744. Rec: 10 Jun 1745. Wm. Knight, Clerk.

P. 471 Deed. James Penington and his wife Elizabeth of Cecil Co., planter, for 2,000 lbs of tobacco and £10, to David Ricketts of the same county, planter, part of a tract called Pains Lt on the west side of Hen Island Creek, which is part of the tract bequeathed to James Penington by John Atkey's Last Will and Testament. Made & Ackn: 4 Apr 1745. Wit. & JPs: John Baldwin, Pereg'r. Ward. Rec: 12 Jun 1745. Wm. Knight, Clerk.

P. 473 Deed. Abel Williams of Cecil Co., schoolmaster, and his wife Mary, one of the daughters of Griffith Nicholas, son of Griffith Nicholas, both deceased, for £30, to Henry Baker, 2 tracts of land called Landuel and Contention. Griffith Nicholas the Elder was granted by patent a tract of 240 acres of land called Landuel on the west side of little North East Creek by a tract called Kinsley. Griffith Nicholas the Younger was granted by patent a tract of 66 acres called Contention on the east side of the east branch of Elk River by a tract called Newmunster. Made 24 Dec 1744. Wit: Samuel Gilpin,

Zach Butcher. Ackn. and transfer of money made 10 Jan 1744 before JPs Nicholas Hyland and Benjamin Chew. Pereg'r. Ward rec'd 2s.8p alienation fine 24 Jan 1744. Rec: 13 Jun 1745. Wm. Knight, Clerk.

P. 475   Deed.   James Bayard and Peter Bayard of Cecil Co., gents., for £250, to Peter Lawson of the same place, innholder, a mill and land on Back Creek where Peter Lawson now lives. Made & Ackn: 13 Jun 1745. Wit. & JPs: John Veazey, Pereg'r. Ward. Rec: 14 Jun 1745. Wm. Knight, Clerk.

P. 477   Deed.   Peter Lawson of Cecil Co., innholder, for £260, to Sluyter Bouchell of the same county, physician, a grist mill called Back Creek Mill with 10 acres of land on the south side of Back Creek including use of the landing adjoining the mill and privilege of dirt for support of the mill dam towards Lawson's house. The mill was formerly held by Howell James. Made & Ackn: 14 Jun 1745. Wit. & JPs: John Veazey, Pereg'r. Ward. Rec: 14 Jun 1745. Wm. Knight, Clerk.

P. 478   Deed.   Philip Cazier, Sr. of Cecil Co., farmer, for £12.18s.9p, to Dennis Nowland of the same place, planter, 5¾ acres, part of a tract called Coxes Forrest by the line separating the land of Philip Cazier and Colonel John Ward. Made 1 Mar 1744. Wit: Philip Cazier, Jr., Richard Cazier. Ackn: 10 Jun 1745. JPs: Tho. Colvill, Nathan Baker. Rec: 18 Jun 1745. Wm. Knight, Clerk.

P. 480   Quit Claim.   John McKnitt of Cecil Co., because he is moving, quit claims to Andrew Alexander, 30 acres, the west end of a tract of land called Glasgow formerly taken up by John McKnitt, late of said county, grandfather of the first said John McKnitt, on Back Creek by land originally taken up by Nicholas Painter called Highspaniola. Made, Ackn. & Rec: 14 Jun 1745. Wit. & JPs: Peter Bayard, Pereg'r. Ward. Wm. Knight, Clerk.

P. 481   Valuation of Estate.   At the request of JP Richard Thompson, Andrew Zelafroe and Peter Bouchell have viewed the lands belonging to Thomas Boulding, son of Richard Boulding, late of Cecil Co., deceased. The said orphan Thomas is now under the guardianship of Robert Veazey. They found 180 acres, 25 acres of it cleared and 7 acres of the cleared land fenced. No house, no orchard. They give the yearly rent valued as 50 shillings. They allow 10 acres each year to be cleared. Made 11 Apr 1745. Rec: 11 Jun 1745. Wm. Knight, Clerk.

P. 482   Lease.   James Paul Heath of Cecil Co., merchant, for rents and services, to Andrew Wayt of the said county, gent., 2 lots in Warwick, both called lot #49, one a ½ acre fronting on Delaware Street and back to Baltimore Street. The other lot is 5 acres, and includes privilege of the commons. Lease is for the natural lives of the said Andrew Wayt, Charles Heath (son of Charles Heath of Cecil Co.) and John Ward (nephew of the said J.P. Heath.) After the first 4 years, rent of 50 shillings to be paid to James Paul Heath at Warwick on 25 Mar each year. Within the first 4 years, tenants are to build a house on the ½ lot. [Andrew Wayt is also called Andrew Wyat.] Made 25 Mar 1744. Wit: Cha. Heath, Benjamin Town. Ackn: 6 Jun 1745. JPs: John Baldwin, John Veazey. Rec: 6 Jun 1745. Wm. Knight, Clerk.

P. 485   Lease.   Andrew Alexander of Cecil Co., for rents and services, to John Croazier of the same county, the plantation where the said John Croazier now lives near Elk River. Lease is for 21 years. Rent of 700 lbs of tobacco due 25 Mar yearly. Croazier will acquire and plant 50 apple trees and another 50 apple trees which Alexander will provide. [Croazier also spelled Crozier.] Made, Ackn. & Rec: 12 Jun 1745. Wit. & JPs: A. Barry, Pereg'r. Ward. Wm. Knight, Clerk.

P. 486   *Cecil County to wit: I hereby certify that the aforegoing pages from folio 1 to 486 (inclusive) are truly transcribed from Liber W. K. No. 11. Test: Jo. Baxter, Clerk, Cecil County.*

[The preceding was abstracted from *Cecil County Court Land Records 1734- 1745* microfilm #MSA WK 944-45 photographed by the Genealogical Society, Salt Lake City, Utah, 1948.]

Deed Book No. 7
1745 - 1753

P. 1   Deed.   Nicholas Vandyke of Cecil Co., blacksmith, and Sarah his wife, for £80, to Thomas Mills of the same county, blacksmith, 65 acres by Long Creek, the easternmost part of a tract of 400 acres called Jones' Green Springs formerly laid out for William Harris of Kent Co., by land belonging to the heirs of Henry Ward, by the road leading from Andrew Alexander's to the fording place of Broad Creek and by land called Charles' Camp. [Vandyke is also spelled Vandike.] Made, Ackn. & Rec: 9 Aug 1748. Wit. & JPs: John Baldwin, John Veazey. Francis Lee, Clerk, received the alienation fine of 2s.7½p on the same day.

P. 3   Lease.   Benjamin Tasker, Agent and Receiver General, for and on behalf of Lord Baltimore and with the consent of Gov. Thomas Bladen, for rents and services, to Richard Rutter of Cecil Co., planter, a parcel of 100 acres called Old Field Lot, part of his Lordship's manor, on the west side of Elk River. Lease is for the term of the natural lives of the said Richard Rutter, Mary Rutter and Moses Rutter. Rent of 10 shillings and 2 fat capons due 29 Sep yearly. The Rutters are to build a house 30x20 feet with a brick or stone chimney and will plant and fence an orchard of 100 apple trees. Made 25 May 1745. Wit: John Veazey, Thomas Price. Rec: 10 Aug 1748. Francis Lee, Clerk.

P. 6   Release.   John Mercer of Cecil Co., planter, for £65, to his brother Robert Mercer of the same county, 60 acres of land, part of 2 tracts called Mount Herman and Indian Range. Said land was granted to John Mercer by deed of gift from his father Thomas Mercer, deceased. Made 28 Mar 1740. Wit. & JPs: John Baldwin, John Veazey. Ackn: same day by Robert Mercer and his wife Elizabeth. Alienation fine of 2s.5p paid 10 Aug 1748. Rec: 10 Aug 1748. Francis Lee, Clerk.

P. 8   Deed.   John Edmondson and Isabella his wife of Cecil Co., for £78, to Michael Wallace of the same place, part of 2 tracts of land, one called Lidia's Jointure (69 acres and 36 perches), and the other tract of 30 acres and 124 perches called Good Will which was granted to Martin Cartmill by patent dated 1716. Lidia's Jointure was granted to Martin Cartmill by deed dated 20 May 1727. By deed dated 16 Nov 1738 and recorded in Lib. W. K. No. 2, folios 398-399, Martin Cartmill sold the said 2 tracts to John Edmondson. The land lies on the north side of the land where the said John

Edmondson now lives, by John McCullach's plantation and by Joseph Thompson's land. Made & Ackn: 6 Aug 1748. Wit: A. Barry, James Baxter. Alienation fine of 4 shillings paid 10 Aug 1748. Rec: 10 Aug 1748. Francis Lee, Clerk.

P. 11 Deed. John Chambers of Frederick Town, Cecil Co., yeoman, and his wife Rachel, for £3, to Ann Webster of the same place, widow, lot #17 in Frederick Town. Made & Ackn: 6 Aug 1748. Wit: John Veazey, Pereg'r. Ward. The receipt of the £3 acknowledged by John Chambers, Jr. Rec: 15 Aug 1748. Francis Lee, Clerk.

P. 12 Deed. Jacob Young and John Young of Cecil Co., planters, for £100, to John Currier of the said county, planter, 100 acres, a moiety of a tract of land called Poplar Neck, part of a tract called Clay Fall, by the land of George Simco. Said land was left to them by their late father by his Last Will and Testament dated Apr 1727. Made & Ackn: 7 May 1748. Wit: John Hyland, Francis Mauldin, Robert Low. Signed and acknowledged only by Jacob Young. JPs: Nathan Baker, James Baxter. Alienation fine of 4 shillings paid 23 Aug 1748. Rec: 23 Aug 1748. Francis Lee, Clerk.

P. 14 Lease. Benjamin Tasker of Annapolis, Agent and Receiver General, for rents and services on behalf of Lord Baltimore and with the consent of Gov. Samuel Ogle, to Tobias Amspoker of Cecil Co., 78 acres of land in his Lordships manor of Susquehanna alias New Connach, by a tract of land called Holland now claimed by Samuel Smith. Lease is for the term of the natural lives of the said Tobias Amspoker, Sarah Amspoker and Elizabeth Amspoker. Rent of 23 shillings due every 1 January. Tenants will build a house 30x20 feet with chimney and plant and fence and orchard of 100 apple trees. Made 21 Jul 1747. Wit: Benjamin Chew, Nath. Broughton. Rec: 19 Aug 1748. Francis Lee, Clerk.

P. 18 Deed. John Currer of Charles Town, Cecil Co., planter, and his wife Meliscent, for £180, to the Vestry of St. Mary Anns Parish in Cecil Co. in trust for the use of Rev. John Hamilton and his successors, a moiety of a tract of land called Poplar Neck, 100 acres, part of a tract called Clay Fall by the land of George Simco. Said land was granted to John Currier by Jacob Young by deed dated 7 May 1748 which was left to him by his deceased father's Will dated Apr 1727. Made & Ackn: 7 Jun 1748. Wit: Peter Boyer, Mich'l. Hackett, William Currer. JPs: Nathan Baker, James Baxter. Rec: 23 Aug 1748. Francis Lee, Clerk.

P. 20 Assignment of Lease. John Chick, Jr. of Cecil Co., yeoman, for £65, to Alexander Lewis of Newcastle Co. upon Delaware in the Territories of PA, farmer, a lease for 140 acres of land. Matthias VanBebber of Cecil Co., gent., on behalf of himself and Samuel Chew, Jr. and his wife Hennrietta, the daughter and heiress of Philemon Lloyd, esq., deceased, and also on behalf of Edward Jennings, esq., during the minority of Thomas Bordley, Jr., by deed dated 12 Nov 1735, leased to John Chick 140 acres of land called Chick's Enlargement, part of St. Augustine's Manor, by Chick's land called Chick's Choice and by Galasshot's land. Lease was for the term of the natural lives of Nathaniel Chick, John Chick, Jr. and Susanna Chick, three of the children of the said John Chick. Rent of £2.16s due 26 Dec yearly to be paid to Benjamin Chew, Jr., Thomas Bordley, Jr. and Matthias VanBebber at VanBebber's dwelling house. By deed of gift dated 1740, John Chick, Sr. assigned the lease to his son John Chick, Jr. Made & Ackn: 9 Mar 1747. Wit: Thomas Rose, William Rose. JPs: Nich. Hyland, Nathan Baker. Rec: 8 Sep 1748. Francis Lee, Clerk.

P. 23 Deed. Simon Wilmore of Kent Co., gent., and Rebecca Wye of Cecil Co., widow, for £430, to Robert Hart of Kent Co., planter, 460 acres, part of a larger tract called Triumph (formerly in Baltimore Co., now in Cecil Co.) on Fishing Creek and Elk River by the part of this tract belonging to Thomas Crouch and by a tract called Wademous Neck. Thomas Johnson, late of Cecil Co., gent., in his lifetime owned a tract of land called Triumph in Cecil Co. on the north side of Elk River. In his Last Will and Testament he devised the land to his then wife, the said Rebecca during her natural life and after her death to his son Edward. It was stated Rebecca may sell the land to pay his debts if necessary. By deed dated 11 Jun 1740, Rebecca sold the tract of land to Simon Wilmore. Made 20 Aug 1748. Wit. & JPs: Beddingfield Hands, Daniel Chirton. Ackn: same day in Kent Co. by Simon Wilmore and his wife Mary and Rebecca Wye. Kent County Clerk James Smith certified the JPs 22 Aug 1748. Robert Hart paid 9 shillings alienation fine 30 Sep 1748. Rec: 30 Sep 1748. Francis Lee, Clerk.

P. 27 Mortgage. Manadaw Phillips of Cecil Co., for £50, to Ann Kankey of the same county, widow, 400 acres of land on the north side of Elk River by the cleared lands of John Gesigne and Peter Classons. Manadaw to repay Kankey by Aug 1752. Made & Ackn: 11 Aug 1748. Wit: Nich's. Hyland, Nathan Baker, Mich'll. Lum. JPs: Nich's. Hyland, Nathan Baker. Ann Kankey paid Phillips the consideration money 10 Aug 1748. Rec: 14 Sep 1748. Francis Lee, Clerk.

P. 30   Deed.   Samuel Land of Christien Creek, Newcastle Co., executor to Francis Land, deceased, for £39.16s.10p, to Robert Holy of Cecil Co., 140 acres of land by the land of Roger Lawson. Said land was sold to Francis Land by deed dated 1733 from Morgan Patton. The land is part of 300 acres which Charles Carroll of Annapolis sold to the said Patton. Patton sold 150 acres of the land to Roger Lawson and 10 acres was condemned for a mill. Made 20 Aug 1748. Wit: Walter Ker, John Land. Samuel Land empowers William Bristow of Cecil Co. to acknowledge the deed for him, giving him a warrant dated 20 Aug 1748. Ackn: by Walter Carr 22 Aug 1748. JPs: Nathan Baker, James Baxter. Robert Holy paid 5 shillings alienation fine 30 Sep 1748. Rec: 30 Sep 1748. Francis Lee, Clerk.

P. 32   Deed of Partition.   Richard Bennett of Queen Annes Co., esq., has lately resurveyed several tracts of land in Cecil Co. near the mouth of Sassafras River called the Grove, Hazelwood and the Rambles. Before the survey was completed some disputes arose concerning the place where the first line of a tract called Burley's Journey owned by Peregrin Frisby of Cecil Co., gent., should be. They were also concerned with the southern bounds of the tract called Hazelmore[sic.] They referred to Mr. James Tilghman of Talbot Co. and determined the boundary lines, marking a locust post with R.B. on two sides and P.F. on two sides. Concerning the limits of Hazelmore they agreed to draw the line by the east line of Mounts Andrews' land called Mounts Field to the southeast line of Frisby's Addition. Frisby quit claims to Bennett his interest in land lying westward and northward of the division line for which Bennett paid Frisby 5 shillings. Made & Ackn: 27 Apr 1749. Wit: John Veazey, Richard Tilghman. JP: Richard Tilghman. Recorded by Francis Lee, Clerk.

P. 34   Assignment of Lease.   Thomas Harper states that some years previous he leased to his son Jacob Harper 100 acres, part of a tract leased to him. He now assigns the lease to his son John Harper. Made & Ackn: 3 Sep 1748. Wit. & JPs: John Baldwin, Pt. Bayard. Rec: 18 Feb 1748/9. Francis Lee, Clerk.

P. 35   Deed.   William Price and his wife Sarah of Talbot Co., for £300, to James McCombes of Cecil Co., 192 acres and 115 acres of land in Cecil Co., both parcels part of a tract called Indian Range by a tract called Stockton. Said land formerly laid out for 500 acres and by a later survey found to be 307 acres. Made 20 Oct 1748. Wit: Wm. Price, Tho. Colvill, Adam VanBebber. Ackn: 21 Nov 1748. JPs: Tho. Colvill, Adam VanBebber. Alienation fine of 12s.3½p paid 21 Nov 1748. Rec: 21 Nov 1748. Fra. Lee, Clerk.

P. 38   Deed of Gift/Lease.   Margaret Reynolds, for love and affection, gives to her eldest son Richard Reynolds a lease of land. Made & Ackn: 9 Nov 1748. Wit. & JPs: R'd. Thompson, Adam VanBebber. Rec: 21 Nov 1748. Fra. Lee, Clerk. Memo: this lease is recorded in Lib. W. K. No. 2, folios 387-389.

P. 39   Deed of Gift.   Bartholomew Jacobs, Sr. of Cecil Co., planter, for natural love and affection and because he is moving, gives to his son Henry Jacobs who has obligated himself to pay a bond due from Bartholomew Jacobs, Sr. to Richard Bennett, esq., of Queen Annes Co., 500 acres of land called Stockton where he the said Bartholomew Jacobs, Sr. now lives. The father will continue to have possession of the land for the rest of his natural life. Made 8 Dec 1748. Wit: Elizabeth Eveartson, Evert Everson, Step'n. Gudgeon. Ackn: 9 Dec 1748. JPs: John Baldwin, Pereg'r. Ward. Rec: 9 Dec 1748. Fran. Lee, Clerk.

P. 40   Deed.   John Cooley of Kent Co., PA, yeoman, and his wife Ruth, for £10, to William Henry of the same county, yeoman, a tract of land in the said county called Caffanrwry [sp?] and another tract in the same county, part of a tract called Black Marsh. Both tracts are now in the occupation of the said William Henry. Made 15 Jun 1748. Wit: J. Hamilton, Nathan Baker, James Baxter. Ackn: in Cecil Co. by John and Ruth Cooley before JPs Nathan Baker and James Baxter. Rec: 13 Dec 1748. Fran. Lee, Clerk.

P. 42   Assignment of Lease.   Written on the back of a lease recorded in W. K. No. 9, folios 330-331, Benjamin Tasker states he received from Mr. Jno. Brooke, by the hands of Mr. Geo. Rock, £1.5s.6p for 2 years rent of this lease granted to the said Jno. Brooke. The said sum is the fine for his leave to assign the within lease. Made 19 Apr 1745. On 31 Jan 1745 John Brooks and Cathran his wife acknowledge assigning the lease to George Rock before JPs Nich. Hyland, Nathan Baker. Rec: 11 Jan 1748. Francis Lee, Clerk.

P. 42   Valuation of Estate.   William Pearce and Otho Penington have sworn before Capt. Peregrine Ward that they have viewed the land called Coxes Forest in the possession of Maj. John Veazey, guardian to John Ward, son of John Ward, deceased. They judge the yearly value to be £7.10. The property is a large plantation but 1 old log dwelling house, an old log corn house, an old tobacco house and about 40 apple trees. They have marked out lines they feel necessary to cut and occupy for support of the plantation. Made 10 Dec 1748. Rec: 14 Mar 1748/9. Fran. Lee, Clerk.

P. 43   Deed.   Daniel Pecow of Cecil Co., planter, for £30, to Johannes Arnest of the same place, cordwainer, 130 acres on the north side of Elk

River, part of St. John's Manor, joining Nathan Philips' and Mannado Philips' plantations. Made & Ackn: 25 Feb 1748/9. Wit. & JPs: Benja. Chew, James Baxter. Alienation fine of 5s.2p paid 6 May 1749 to Alex'r. Baird. Rec: 15 Mar 1748/9. Fran. Lee, Clerk.

P. 44 Deed. Thomas Money of Cecil Co., for £100, to John Money of Cecil Co., planter, 40 acres of land, part of a tract called Larramore's Neck by Robert Walmsley's land. Said land Thomas Money's father Robert Money bequeathed him. Made 14 Mar 1748/9. Wit. & JPs: John Baldwin, Adam VanBebber. Ackn: same day by Thomas Money and his wife Elizabeth. John Money paid 9p.3f alienation fine 15 Mar 1748. Rec: 15 Mar 1748. Fran. Lee, Clerk.

P. 46 Lease. Henry Baker of Cecil Co., for rents and services, to William Smyley of said county, 55 acres, part of a tract called Landue, including the place where William Phillips now lives. Lease is for the natural life of the said William Smyley. Rent of 50 shillings due 1 Mar yearly. Tenant will plant an orchard of 100 apple trees. Made & Ackn: 17 Mar 1748/9. Wit: John Smith, Benj. Starratt. JPs: Nathan Baker, James Baxter. Rec: 17 Mar 1748/9. Fra. Lee, Clerk.

P. 47 Lease. Benjamin Tasker of Annapolis, Agent and Receiver General, for rents and services on behalf of Lord Baltimore and with the consent of Gov. Samuel Ogle, to Richard Patten of Cecil Co., 115 acres of land called Patten's Desire, part of his Lordship's Manor of North East by land called Round Stone on the southeast side of North East River. Lease is for the term of the natural lives of Amelia Patten, Rebecca Patten and William Patten, son of James Patten. Rent of 11 shillings due 29 Sep yearly. The Patten's will build a 30x20 foot dwelling house with a brick chimney and will plant and fence an orchard of 100 apple trees. [Patten is also spelled Patton.] Made 13 Nov 1748. Wit: Wm. Roberts, Geo. Lawson. Rec: 21 Mar 1748/9. Fra. Lee, Clerk. Examined by M. Bordley, Clerk.

P. 50 Deed. Edward Comegys of Kent Co., planter, and Mary his wife, for £51, to John Stockton of Cecil Co., farmer, land where the said John Stockton now dwells called New Garden in Cecil Co. (the survey was made for Rebeckah Campbell) between Sassafras River and Bohemia River. Made 16 Nov 1748. Wit. & JPs: Jerves Spencer, William Hynson. Ackn: in Kent Co. same day. James Smith, Clerk of Kent Co., certifies Jerves Spencer and William Hynson as JPs. John Stockton paid 7s7p alienation fine to Alex'r. Baird 19 Mar 1748/9. Rec: 1 Apr 1749. Fra. Lee, Clerk.

P. 52 Assignment of Lease.   Ephraim Augustine Herman leased land to Lydia Tyler, Frederick Wolbough and Christopher Wolbough. Lease is recorded in Lib. S. K. No. 6, pgs 142-143. Now Lydia Tyler, for £4 to be paid to her annually during her natural life by her son Frederick, assigns the lease to her said son Frederick Ellberry. Made & Ackn: 5 Nov 1748. Wit: Adam VanBebber, Waller Diven. JPs: Adam VanBebber, R'd. Thompson. Rec: 1 Apr 1749. Fra. Lee, Clerk.

P. 53 Assignment of Lease.   Ephraim Augustine Herman leased land to Rene' Tulien [Julien.] Lease is recorded in Lib. S. K. No. 5, pgs 138-139. Now, among other assignments, Dr. Hugh Matthews, Jr., doctor, and Teresa Allman, admin. of Joseph Allman of Cecil Co., deceased, for £190.12s, assigns the lease of land called Noble Town to Cornelius Wooliston. Made & Ackn: 7 Mar 1748/9. Wit: William Harper, Adam VanBebber. JPs: R'd. Thompson, Adam VanBebber. Rec: 8 Apr 1749. Fra. Lee, Clerk.

P. 53 Deed.   Catharine Harker, wife of Samuel Harker, Sr., of Salem Co., West New Jersey, and Samuel Harker, Jr., son of said Catharine, of the same place, yeoman, for £40, to James Knox of Cecil Co., yeoman, 125 acres in Cecil Co., part of a tract of land on the east end of a tract called Coxes Prevention. Said land was formerly owned by Thomas Green, deceased. Made 18 Mar 1748/9. Wit: Aron Hill, James Ewing. Ackn: same day by Aron Hill and James Ewing before Isaac Sharp, JP for Salem Co., NJ. Ackn: in Cecil Co. 24 Apr 1749 by William Mitchell of Cecil Co., attorney for Catharine Harker and Samuel Harker, Jr. before JPs Nich. Hyland, Benja. Chew. James Nox [sic] paid 5s.1p alienation fine 28 Apr 1749 to Alex'r. Baird. Rec: 28 Apr 1749. Fran. Lee, Clerk.

P. 56 Power of Attorney.   Cathrine Harker, wife of Samuel Harker, Sr. of Salem Co., West New Jersey, and Samuel Harker, Jr., son of said Cathrine, of the same place, yeoman, appoint their trusty friend William Mitchell of Cecil Co. their attorney to acknowledge a deed of conveyance of a tract of land called Coxes Prevention in Cecil Co. to James Knox. Made 18 Mar 1748/9. Wit: Aron Hill, James Ewing. Ackn: in Salem Co. same day by Hill and Ewing. JP: Isaac Sharp. On 20 Mar 1748 Nich. Gibbon, Clerk of Salem Co., certifies that Isaac Sharp is a JP. Ackn: in Cecil Co. 24 Apr 1749 by James Ewings. JPs: Nich. Hyland, Benja. Chew. Rec: 28 Apr 1749. Fra. Lee, Clerk.

P. 58 Deed.   David Whit and Easter his wife of "Chaster County in pencelveney", yeoman, for £52.10s, to Inat and Martha Thomson of Cecil Co., 150 acres of land in Cecil Co. on the southwest side of Stony Run by the path from David Rus to Thomas Phillips. Alexander Whit of Chester Co.,

151

PA, deceased, yeoman, sold his patent dated 1720 recorded in Lib. P. S. No. 5, folio 956, to Alexander Whit [sic] for land in Cecil Co. called Raccoon Point. David Whit and his wife Easter are the heirs of their father Alexander Whit's Last Will and Testament proved or dated 27 May 1743. [Whit is spelled White at the end of the deed. Easter is also spelled Ester. Inat is spelled Iennett, Ianat and Thomson is also spelled Thompson.] Made 20 Mar 1748/9. Wit: James Baxter, Benja. Chew, Philip Cazier, Jr. Ackn: same day by David White. JPs: Benja. Chew, James Baxter. Inat and Martha Thompson paid 6 shillings alienation fine to Alex'r. Baird 8 Apr 1749. Rec: 6 May 1749. Fra. Lee, Clerk.

P. 60 Deed. John Kimber of Cecil Co., planter, for £50 and because he is moving, to Thomas Davis of Cecil Co., planter, the upper 25 acres of a tract called Rattlesnake Neck near Back Creek on the north side of the main road leading from St. Stephen's Church to Frederick Town. [Kimber is spelled Kimlar, Kimbar at the end of the deed.] Made 28 Apr 1749. Wit. & JPs: John Veazey, Pereg'r. Ward. Ackn: same day by John Kimber and his wife Catharine. Thomas Davis paid 1 shilling alienation fine 11 May 1749 to Alex'r. Baird. Rec: 11 May 1749. Fra. Lee, Clerk.

P. 63 Deed of Partition. Richard Bennett of Queen Annes Co., esq., has lately resurveyed several tracts of land near the mouth of Sassafras River called the Grove, Hazelmore and the Rambles. Some disputes arose between Bennett and Peregrine Frisby of Cecil Co., gent., concerning the line of a tract called Burley's Journey owned by Frisby and also the southern bounds of the tracts called the Grove, Hazelmore. Mr. James Tilghman of Talbot Co. was called upon to aid in settling the dispute. A locust post was marked RB on 2 sides and PF on 2 sides. The parties agreed to draw a line from Mounts Andrews land called Mountsfield to the end of the land called Frisby's Addition and from the middle of that line to the end of the line of Burley's Journey, creating a northern and southern boundary and an eastern and western boundary. Richard Bennett, for £40, releases to Peregrine Frisby the land lying eastward and southward of the new division lines. Made & Ackn: 20 Mar 1748. Wit: R'd. Tilghman, James Tilghman. JP: R'd. Tilghman. Rec: 2 Jun 1749.

P. 66 Lease. Rebecca Heath of Cecil Co., executrix of James Paul Heath, late of said county, deceased, for rents and services, to Nicholas Price of said county, blacksmith, 2 lots: one is lot #9 in Warwick, a ½ acre on Chesapeake Street and Smith Street; the other 5 acres along Smith Street with the privilege of the 200 acres of commons laid out by the said James Heath. Lease is for the natural lives of Margaret Price (wife of said Nicholas,) Hugh Price and Elizabeth Price (children of the said Nicholas Price.) Rent of 50 shillings due 25 Mar yearly. Within 4 years time the tenants shall build a house on the ½ acre lot. Made 25 Mar 1749. Wit: Pr. Bayard, Adam VanBebber. Ackn: 1 May 1749. JPs: Adam VanBebber, Pr. Bayard. Rec: 12 Jun 1749. Fran. Lee, Clerk.

P. 69 Deed. Edward Johnson of Cecil Co., for £50, to Thomas Johnson of the same place, 110 acres of land called Purchase on the north side of Elk River by a tract called Brewerton and by land formerly laid out for Peter Clauson. Made & Ackn: 16 Mar 1748. Wit: Mich'l. Lum, William Bristow, Henry Baker. JPs: Nich's. Hyland, Nathan Baker. Rec: 14 Jun 1749.

P. 71 Deed. Isaac Freeman of Kent Co., farmer, for £150, to William Abbott of Cecil Co., bricklayer, 100 acres, part of a tract called Daniel's Denn in Cecil Co. on the north side of Sassafras River at Back Creek by Richard Rumsey's plantation. Made & Ackn: 13 Jun 1749. Wit. & JPs: John Veazey, Pereg. Ward. Rec: 14 Jun 1749. Fra. Lee, Clerk.

P. 73 Deed. Nathaniel Moor of Milford Hundred, Cecil Co., planter, and Rachel his wife, for £40, to Robert Evans of the same place, tanner, 2 tracts of land lying southward of John Wield's land and east of the land of David Miller. Thomas Moor, father of the said Nathaniel Moor, was granted 100 acres of land called St. John's Town in Milford Hundred by Gov. Charles Calvert by patent dated 13 Aug 1725 recorded in Lib. P. L. No. 6, folio 148. By deed dated 1 Aug 1739 James Archibald Armstrong conveyed to the said Thomas Moor 50 acres called Addition in Milford adjoining the first mentioned tract. This deed recorded in Lib. W. K. No. 2, folios 445-446. Thomas Moor made his Last Will and Testament dated 21 Jan last past, bequeathing the 2 tracts of land to the said Nathaniel Moor, in the last clause of the said Will in the words: "all the rest and residue of my estates both personal and real estate goods and chattels I give and bequeath unto my well beloved son Nathaniel Moor whome I appoint my full and sole executor of my last will and testament." He soon after died. Made 27 Mar 1749. Wit: John Smith, Nathan Baker, James Baxter. Ackn: 24 Apr 1749. JPs: Nathan Baker, James Baxter. Nathaniel Moor paid the 6 shillings alienation fine 13 Jun 1749 to Alex'r. Baird. Rec: 14 Jun 1749. Fra. Lee, Clerk.

P. 77 Mortgage. Nathaniel Moor and his wife Rachel will repay Robert Evans £32.10s with 2 parcels of land called St. John's Town and Addition held as security following a set payment schedule with a final payment due 27 Mar 1754 to be paid at the dwelling house of Robert Evans in Milford Hundred. The Moor's will continue to occupy the land unless payment is defaulted. Nathaniel Moor may have at any time within one year £15 more with the same security. Made 27 Mar 1749. Wit: James Baxter, Nathan Baker, John Smith. Rec: 14 Jun 1749.

P. 80 Deed. Richard Norton and Unity his wife of Charlestown, Cecil Co., innholder, for £156, to William Maffit of the same place, planter, 300 acres, part of a tract called VanBebber's Forrest. Matthias VanBebber was granted a tract of 850 acres called VanBebber's Forrest by patent dated 8 Oct 1720 recorded in the land office in Lib. C. E. No. 1, folios 275-276. By deed dated 18 Nov 1729, Matthias VanBebber conveyed the land to Christian Peters. Said deed recorded 2 Apr 1730 in Lib. S. K., folios 235-237. By his Last Will and Testament dated 13 Jun 1748, Christian Peters made his wife Unity Peters executrix and empowered her to give a months public notice and sell to the highest bidder part of the said tract to pay off a mortgage Peters contracted with James Bayard. This was done and William Maffit was the highest bidder. Richard Norton is now the lawful husband of the said Unity Peters. Made & Ackn: 6 May 1749. Wit: Henry Baker, Robert Allison, Jno. Scott. JPs: Nicho. Hyland, Benja. Chew. William Maffitt paid 12 shillings alienation fine to Alex'r. Baird 2 Jun 1749. Rec: 15 Jun 1749. Fran. Lee, Clerk.

P. 83 Deed. William Alexander of Prince Fredericks Co., yeoman, for £40, to Thomas Weir of Cecil Co., farmer, 2 tracts of land in Cecil Co. of 131 acres and 67 acres, part of a tract called New Munster. The first tract is part of 903 acres purchased by Arthur Alexander from Thomas Stevenson by deed dated 15 Aug 1718, assignee of Robert Roberts by deed dated 14 Aug 1718. Said land bounds on William Longwill's corner. The other tract adjoining the first is part of 1,150 acres which Arthur Alexander and Company bought from Thomas Stevenson by deed dated 18 May 1714, assignee of Robert Roberts by deed dated 1 Apr 1714. This land is bounded by the lands of John McCoy and William Longwill. [Stevenson is also spelled Stephenson.] Made 1 Mar 1748/9. Wit: James Alexander, Amos Alexander. Ackn: 4 Mar 1748. JPs: Nathan Baker, Geo. Rock. Alienation fine of 2s.8p paid by Weir to Alex'r. Baird. Rec: 15 Jun 1749. Fra. Lee, Clerk.

P. 85 Lease. John Veazey of Cecil Co., gent., for rents and services, to James Robb of the same county, cordwainer, 60 acres of land, part of a tract called True Gaim by tracts called Salem, New Garden and Strange and by Capt. John's Creek. Lease is for the natural lives of the said James Robb, his wife Jane Robb and their son James Robb. Rent of £3 due 1 Dec yearly. Within 2 years time the Robb's will plant an orchard of 50 apple trees.

[Robb also spelled Rob.] Made & Ackn: 15 Jun 1749. Wit. & JPs: R'd. Thompson, John Baldwin. Rec: 15 Jun 1749.

P. 87 Deed. Timothy Roberts of New Munster, Mary Anns Parish, Cecil Co., miller, and Mary his wife, for £300, to John Passmore of the same county and Timothy Griffith of Pencader Hundred, Newcastle Co., gent., 110 acres of land in Newmunster, Cecil Co., on the east side of the main fresh of Elk River near the land of David Alexander, deceased, and the land that is now James Alexander's, including the mills and mill dams. Made 18 Apr 1749. Wit: Wm. Jones, Henry John, James Broom. James VBebber added and crossed out various words in the deed. Ackn: 9 May 1749. JPs: Nathan Baker, James Baxter. John Passmore paid 2s.2½p alienation fine 14 Jun 1749 to Alex'r. Baird. Rec: 15 Jun 1749. Fra. Lee, Clerk.

P. 90 Lease. Edward Taylor of Cecil Co., innholder, for yearly rents and services, to John Gibson of the said county, planter, 160 acres of land on the north side of Elk River south of James Veazey's land, formerly called Jones' Land. Lease is for 8 years. Rent of £12 and 60 gals of cider due 25 Mar yearly. [Taylor also spelled Tailor.] Made & Ackn: 15 Jun 1749. Wit: Mich'l. Lum, Johanes Arrants. JPs: Nathan Baker, Benj'a. Chew. Rec: 5 Aug 1749.

P. 92 Release. Robert Ritchy and Margaret his wife of Cecil Co., releases to James Ritchy of the same place, farmer, 150 acres of land lying between the branches of Elk River already in the actual possession of James Ritchy, part of a tract called Sligo which Robert Ritchy bought jointly with his brother John Ritchy, now deceased, who by his Last Will and Testament left the land to his son James Ritchy. A temporary division of the land was made between the two brothers. Said land is bounded on one corner by the land of Joseph Wallace. Made & Ackn: 14 Apr 1749. Wit: Geo. Rock, Joseph Wallace, Rich'd Norton, Jr. JPs: Geo. Rock, Nathan Baker. Rec: 8 Aug 1749. Fra. Lee, Clerk.

P. 93 Deed. William Edmondson and Mary his wife of Chester Co., PA, and John Edmondson and Isabella his wife of Cecil Co., for £79, to Michael Wallace of the same place, 106½ acres of land, part of a tract of 213 acres in Cecil Co. conveyed [to the Edmondson's?] by Abram Hollingsworth by deed dated 10 Aug 1724 recorded in Lib. D. K. No. 1, folios 93-94. [Edmondson is also spelled Edmiston.] Made & Ackn: 6 Aug 1748. Wit. & JPs: A. Barry, James Baxter. Alienation fine of 4s.3p paid 10 Aug 1748. Rec: 10 Aug 1748. Francis Lee, Clerk. Note: this deed should have been recorded on page 11 immediately after the deed from John Edmondson and wife to Michael Wallace.

P. 95 Deed. Robert Ritchy and Margret his wife of Cecil Co., farmer, to Joseph Wallace of the same county, blacksmith, for £139 and because they are moving, 2 tracts of land between the branches of Elk River. One tract is part of a tract called Sligo which was the estate of Ninian Dunlap by patent granted 10 Oct 1708 and was conveyed by Dunlap to David Miller by deed of gift dated 17 Apr 1714. David Miller sold the 50 acres to the said Robert Ritchy and his brother John Ritchy by deed dated 16 Nov 1725. The other tract of land called Monon was formerly the estate of the said Ninian Dunlap by patent granted 2 Sep 1714 and conveyed by Dunlap to David Miller by the above cited deed of gift. Miller sold the 100 acres to Robert and John Ritchy. Made & Ackn: 13 Apr 1749. Wit: Tho's. Alexander, James Alexander, Rich'd. Norton, Jr. JPs: Nathan Baker, Geo. Rock. Joseph Wallace paid 6 shillings alienation fine to Alex'r. Baird 5 May 1749. Rec: 8 Aug 1749. Fran. Lee, Clerk.

P. 99 Valuation of Estate. David Hampton and Thomas Ruketts, at the request of Joseph Wallace, viewed the dwelling house and plantation of Francis Elliott, deceased, and value the yearly rents at £5.10s. Made 4 Aug 1749. JP: James Baxter. Rec: 8 Aug 1749.

P. 99 Valuation of Estate. Henry Baker and Robert Alison met at Little Elk at the estate of Thomas Booth, deceased, and found a dwelling house in good repair, a smith's shop in tolerable good order, an old house fit for no use, a small young orchard and garden and meadow of 2 or 3 acres not well fenced, a field of 12 acres plowed, an old mill entirely out of order. The guardian should clear no more land and cut timber only for repair of fences, houses, et cetera. Yearly value set at £12. Made 1 Apr 1749. JP: Nathan Baker. Rec: 8 Aug 1749.

P. 99 Assignment of Lease. Aron Latham of Cecil Co., innholder, for yearly rents, because he is moving and for natural affection and fatherly love, gives to his daughter Ann Haltham, now wife of Jno. Haltham of the same place, land near the court house on Elk River by the line of John Condal, deceased, by William Rumsey's line, and by William Thomas' boundary tree which washed away. Also a lot between the court house prison and the house of James Forster, deceased. Lease is for the term of the natural lives stipulated in the original lease from Col. Eph'm. Aug't. Herman "provided that her present husband (or any other husband if it should so happen) doth not quarrel nor abuse me nor my family nor at any time disturbe my creatures."

Rent of £2 due 10 Nov yearly. Made 21 Oct 1737. Wit: Thos. Forster [Foster?], Jno. Cage. JPs: Tho. Colvill, R'd. Thompson. Rec: 19 Aug 1749. Fra's. Lee, Clerk.

P. 102   Deed.   George Simcoe and his wife Elizabeth, Richard Stedman and his wife Anne, for £30, to John Hyland, 200 acres called Kemston's Delight at Bryery Point on the north side of Mudey Creek at Garrit Cove Creek and Elk River. George and Elizabeth Simcoe and Richard and Ann Stedman hold the land as heirs of John Kempston, deceased, and the said John is heir of his brother Richard Kempston, Jr., and the said Richard heir to his father Richard Kempston the Elder. Made 12 May 1749. Wit: Henry Baker, John Currer. Ackn: 13 May 1749. JPs: Nicho. Hyland, Nathan Baker. Rec: 21 Oct 1749. M. Bordley, Clerk.

P. 104   Articles of Agreement.   George Hamilton of Prince Georges Co., gent., to Abram Miller of Newcastle Co., PA, who has paid to the said George Hamilton £85, part of the purchase money for a tract of land near the head of Elk River on the old county road in Cecil Co. called Simmes Forest containing 400 acres. George Hamilton agrees to give to Abram Miller a bond within 11 years from this date, promising to convey to him the 400 acres within 10 years after the 11 years have ended. Abram Miller has promised George Hamilton that he will give him a like bond within 11 years to pay to the said Hamilton the £85 within 10 years after the 11 years have expired. They bind themselves with a penal sum of £340. [Abram also called Abraham.] Made 13 May 1749. Wit: Rees Thomas, Martin Alexander. Rec: 9 Nov 1749. M. Bordley, Clerk.

P. 104   Deed.   Hugh Lawson of Lunenburgh Co., VA, esq., for £115, to James Allison of Cecil Co., farmer, 150 acres of land where the said Allison now lives which Morgan Patton had surveyed out of a tract of 300 acres and granted to said Patton 6 Aug 1719 by Charles Carroll of Annapolis. Said land part of a tract called the Society containing 2,104 acres assigned by James Carroll of a survey made by Simon Willmore, then surveyor of said county, 10 Mar 1701. Afterwards on 14 May 1713 Henry Hollingsworth, then surveyor of said county, completed the survey. The said 150 acres, part of the Society, was then granted by Morgan Patton to Rodger Lawson by deed dated 20 Oct 1719 and by Rodger Lawson by deed of gift dated 4 May 1733 conveyed to the said Hugh Lawson. Made 25 Aug 1749. Wit: A. Barry, Moses Andrews, Alex McDowel. Ackn: 4 Sep 1749 by Hugh Lawson. JPs: Nicho. Hyland, Benja. Chew. James Elison paid 6 shillings alienation fine 16 Nov 1749 to Alex'r. Baird. Rec: 15 Nov 1749. M. Bordley, Clerk.

P. 107 Bond. Hugh Lawson of Lunenburgh Co., VA, esq., and George Lawson of Cecil Co., merchant, are bound to James Allison of Cecil Co., for £50 to be paid to said Allison. The condition is that Margaret, wife of the said Hugh Lawson, does not disturb or molest the said James Allison in the possession of 150 acres of land, part of the tract called Society which Allison bought from Hugh Lawson, and the said Margaret abides by the conveyance which her husband has done as if she herself had been there and acknowledged the deed with her husband, then this obligation will be void. Made 29 Aug 1749. Wit: A. Barry, Moses Andrews, Alex McDowel. Rec: 15 Nov 1749. M. Bordley, Clerk.

P. 108 Deed. John Wallace of Lancaster Co., PA, yeoman, for £36, to Samuel Scott of the same place, yeoman, 50 acres, part of a tract called New Munster in Cecil Co., at the west end of John Vansant's land. John Wallace bought this land from Thomas Stevenson. Made & Ackn: 19 Jul 1749. Wit: Nathan Baker, James Baxter, Anne Miller. JPs: Nathan Baker, James Baxter. Rec: 15 Nov 1749. M. Bordley, Clerk.

P. 110 Deed. John Baxter of Lancaster Co., PA, yeoman, for £60, to his son Andrew Baxter of the same place, yeoman, a tract of 100 acres called Largent's Neck in Cecil Co. Richard Bennett of Queen Annes Co. conveyed the land to John Baxter by deed dated 2 Oct 1730 recorded in Lib. W. K. No. 2, folios 203-204 (247-248.) Made & Ackn: 15 Nov 1749. Wit. & JPs: James Baxter, Henry Baker. Andrew Baxter paid 4 shillings alienation fine 16 Nov 1749 to Alex'r. Baird. Rec: 15 Nov 1749.

P. 112 Lease. Joseph Wood of Cecil Co., for £220.5s and yearly rents and services, to William Armstrong of Cecil Co., 225 acres of land on the north side of Back Creek by Jacob Young's cart road at the corner of Howel James' land, part of a tract called the Three Sisters which was formerly devised by Augustine Herman to his daughter Franciana. Lease is for the term of the natural lives of the said William Armstrong, his wife Jane and his son Robert. Rent of 4s.6p and a dunghill fowl due 20 Oct yearly. Made 20 Oct 1749. Wit: R'd. Thompson, John Miller, Francis Alexander. Ackn: 27 Oct 1749. JPs: R'd. Thompson, Adam VanBebber. Rec: 15 Nov 1749. M. Bordley, Clerk.

P. 114 Deed. Samuel Scott of Lancaster Co., PA, yeoman, for £36, to George Lawson of Cecil Co., 50 acres, part of a tract of land called New Munster in Cecil Co. at the west end of John Vansant's land. John Wallace bought the land from Thomas Stevenson and Wallace sold it to Samuel Scott. Made & Ackn: 15 Nov 1749. Wit: A. Barry, Tho. Burch, Thomas

Sharp. JPs: Nicho. Hyland, James Baxter. Rec: 15 Nov 1749. M. Bordley, Clerk.

P. 117 Deed. James Bayard of Cecil Co., merchant, for £37.6s.5p and £23 and £92.3s.8½p, to Richard Norton of Charles Town, Cecil Co., innholder, 850 acres called VanBebber's Forest. Christian Peters, late of said county, deceased, by deed of mortgage dated 11 Aug 1738, conveyed to James Bayard a tract of 850 acres called VanBebber's Forrest with a condition that the conveyance was void when Christian Peters paid James Bayard £37.6s.5p and £23 by a certain date. Made & Ackn: 5 Sep 1749. Wit. & JPs: Adam VanBebber, Pr. Bayard. Rec: 17 Nov 1749. M. Bordley, Clerk.

P. 118 Deed. Peter Carmack of Salem, NJ, for £170, to Edward Johnson of Cecil Co., farmer, 427 acres of land in Cecil Co. called Nevan in St. John's Manor on the west side of Elk River by land which belonged to Thomas Johnson, deceased, and by the land of Peter Manadore. [Carmack also spelled Carmick.] Made & Ackn: 5 Jun 1749. Wit. & JPs: John Veazey, Pereg'r. Ward, Sidney George. Rec: 17 Nov 1749. M. Bordley, Clerk.

P. 120 Deed. Aaron Alexander of Lancaster Co., PA, farmer, for £5, to John Alexander of London Brittan, Chester Co., PA, farmer, 28 acres of land, part of a tract called New Munster at Christiana Creek by Robert Mitchell's land. Said land formerly belonged to David Alexander of Cecil Co., "and now conveyed to John Alexander by Aaron Alexander being the righteous heir at law of the said David Alexander." Made 15 Nov 1749. Wit: Zebulon Alexander, Sam'l. Steel. Ackn: 28 Nov 1749 by James Alexander, attorney for Aaron Alexander. JPs: R'd. Thompson, Tim'o. Roberts. Rec: 29 Nov 1749. M. Bordley, Clerk.

P. 121 Power of Attorney. Aaron Alexander of Lancaster Co., PA, farmer, because he is moving, appoints his well beloved and trusty friend James Alexander of Cecil Co., to acknowledge a deed to John Alexander. Made 15 Nov 1749. Wit: Zebulon Alexander, Sam'l. Steel. Ackn: 28 Nov 1749 by Zebulon Alexander and Sam'l. Steel. JPs: R'd. Thompson, Tim'o. Roberts. Rec: 29 Nov 1749. M. Bordley, Clerk.

P. 122 Deed. Benjamin Benson of Cecil Co., planter, for £85, to Philip Stoops of the same county, planter, 55 acres of land, part of a tract called Pain's lot on the north side of Sassafras River east of Heniland Creek. Said land was devised by John Atkey, late of Cecil Co., deceased, to James Penington who conveyed the land to Benjamin Benson. Made: 14 Aug 1749. Wit. & JPs: John Baldwin, John Veazey. Ackn: same day by Benjamin and his wife

Mary Ann Benson. Philip Stoops paid 2s.2½p alienation fine to Alex'r. Baird 27 Nov 1749. Rec: 4 Dec 1749. M. Bordley, Clerk.

P. 124 Lease. Ariana Margaretta Harris of Kent Co., widow, for rents and services, to John Wallace of Cecil Co., planter, land in Cecil Co. where the said John Wallace now dwells and the adjoining land lying between the Old Town Road and the Irish Road. Said land formerly leased by William Harris in his lifetime to Thomas Etherington and Gavin Hutcheson. Lease is for 14 years. Rent of £8 due 1 Jan yearly. Wallace will build a dwelling house on the land and will plant and fence an orchard of 100 apple trees. Made 25 Nov 1749. Wit: Th. Ringgold, Anna Maria Ringgold. Ackn: same day in Kent Co. before JPs Paul Whichcote, William Hynson. James Smith, Clerk of Kent Co., certifies the JPs. Rec: in Cecil Co. 1 Jan 1749. M. Bordley, Clerk.

P. 126 Deed. John Cazier of Cecil Co., and his wife Rebecca, for £120, to Bryan Riley, late of Newcastle Co. on Delaware, 28 acres of land where John Cazier did live on Smith's Creek, part of a tract called Vulcan's Rest by land lately held by Archibald Douglass which is part of the same tract, and by Dinis Nowland's land. Made 5 Oct 1749. Wit: Adam VanBebber, Ja. VBebber. Ackn: 6 Oct 1749. JPs: Adam VanBebber, R'd. Thompson. Briant Reyley paid 13½p alienation fine to Alex'r. Baird 8 Jan 1749/50. Rec: 8 Jan 1749. M. Bordley, Clerk.

P. 128 Assignment of Lease. Joseph Chicke, house carpenter and joiner of Cecil Co., for £150, to James Bayard of the same place, gent., a lease of land called Chick's Choice. Matthias VanBebber of Cecil Co., gent., now deceased, for himself and empowered by and on behalf of Samuel Chew the Younger who married Henrietta, daughter and heiress of Philemon Lloyd, esq., deceased, and on behalf of Edmond Jennings, esq., for and during the minority of Thomas Bordley, Jr., on 12 Nov 1736 leased to John Chicke, Sr., father of the said Joseph Chicke, 175 acres of land called Chick's Choice, part of St. Augustine's Manor, on the north side of a branch of Back Creek. Lease was for the natural lives of James Hattery, Joseph Chick and Tabitha Chick, daughter of the said John Chick. John Chick assigned the lease to Joseph Chick for £50 because the said John Chick was moving. If Joseph Chicke should repay James Bayard in a series of payments with final payment due on or by 10 Jan 1752 then this assignment void. Made & Ackn: 5 Feb 1749. Wit: P. Bayard, John Bayard. JPs: Tho. Colvill, P. Bayard. Rec: 19 Feb 1749. M. Bordley, Clerk.

P. 133   Bill of Sale.   Joseph Chicke of Cecil Co., for £49, to James Bayard of said county, gent., 4 black cows 4 years old, 3 red cows about 3 years old, 1 black horse branded "JM" [or "IM"] about 8 years old, 1 bay horse about 9 years old, 1 black mare about 7 years old, 1 black horse colt 3 years old, 1 bright bay horse about 7 years old: all valued to £55 and delivered to the said James Bayard in the presence of William Paul who left the animals in the care of said Chicke. If Joseph Chicke should repay on or before 10 Dec next then this bill of sale is void. Made & Ackn: 5 Feb 1749/50. P. Bayard, John Bayard. JP: P. Bayard. Rec: 19 Feb 1749. M. Bordley, Clerk.

P. 135   Deed of Gift.   Peregrine Ward of Cecil Co., gent., to comply with his father's Will and for natural love and affection and for 5 shillings, to James Chattam Ward of the same county, 300 acres, the northwest end of a tract called Greenfield. John Ward, late of the said county, father of Peregrine Ward and grandfather of James Chattam Ward, by his Last Will and Testament dated 25 May 1745, devised (among other things) to the said Peregrine the dwelling plantation of the said John Ward, and the tracts of land belonging to it: Ward's Knowledge, Ward's Addition, part of Pain's Lott, 100 acres part of Colleton, 100 acres on the proviso that Peregrine make a deed to James Chattam Ward for 300 acres, part of a tract called Greenfield where the said Peregrine then lived. The said 300 acres to be laid out on the west side of the main road leading from Cecil Town to Frederick Town with the plantation where Jeremiah Grindley formerly lived. John Ward bequeathed to the said James Chattam Ward these 300 acres. If James Chattam Ward should die without heirs, then the land goes to John Ward, son of Henry Ward and his wife Hannah. Made: 13 Feb 1749. Wit. & JPs: P. Bayard, Adam VanBebber. Ackn: same day by Peregrine Ward and his wife Mary. Rec: 26 Feb 1749/50. M. Bordley, Clerk. Peregrine Ward paid 12s alienation fine on 16 Nov 1751.

P. 138   Assignment of Lease.   Written on the back of a lease from Matthias VanBebber for Cornelius Wooliston, Robert Faris and Robert Ford assign their lease to James McCoy. Made & Ackn: 8 Nov 1740. JPs: John Baldwin, Adam VanBebber. Rec: 26 Feb 1749/50. M. Bordley, Clerk.

P. 138   Deed.   Anthony Smith of Cecil Co., gent., for £200, to William Hutchman of the same county, gent., 150 acres, part of a tract called Holland on the east side of Susquehanna River. Made 19 Feb 1749/50. Wit: David Creswell, Messor Brown, Randell Death. Ackn: same day by Anthony Smith and his wife Jean. JPs: Benja. Chew, John Smith. William Hutchman paid 6 shillings alienation fine to Alex'r. Baird 9 Mar 1749/50. Rec: 9 Mar 1749/50.

P. 141   Deed.   James Donnell, miller, and his wife Jean of Cecil Co., for £100, to James Rowland, farmer, and his sons William Rowland, miller, and Robert Rowland, farmer, 100 acres on the east side of Susquehanna River, part of a tract originally taken up by Richard Gray 11 Apr 1678 called the Glass House. Richard Gray and his wife Rachel sold the land 1 Feb 1684 to Cornelius Comegys. Since that time the land was conveyed to Paul Poulson and Randell Death. On 22 Mar 1736/7, 200 acres of the tract was conveyed to Thomas Coulson. On 1 Mar 1741/2, 100 acres of the tract was conveyed to James Donnell. [Jean Donnell is also called Jane Donnell.] Made & Ackn: 23 Sep 1749. Wit: Nicho. Hyland, Nathan Baker, Matthias Johnson. JPs: Nicho. Hyland, Nathan Baker. James Rowland paid 4 shillings alienation fine 14 Mar 1749/50 to Alex'r. Baird. Rec: 9 Mar 1749/50.

P. 144   Deed.   Joseph Brown and his wife Hannah of West Nottingham, Chester Co., PA, planters, for £50, to Richard Griffee of Cecil Co., planter, 100 acres on the east side of Susquehanna River. This land is part of a tract originally taken up by Richard Gray 11 Apr 1678 called the Glass House. The tract was sold 1 Feb 1684 by Richard Gray and his wife Rachel to Cornelius Comegys. Since then the tract was conveyed to Paul Poulson and Randell Death who conveyed 200 acres of the land 2 Mar 1736/7 to Thomas Coulson. The said Coulson, on 6 Oct 1741 sold 100 acres to Joseph Brown. Made & Ackn: 11 Dec 1749. Wit: Vg. Rigbie, Jr., Edward Ricketts. JPs: Benja. Chew, John Smith. Rec: 9 Mar 1749/50. M. Bordley, Clerk.

P. 146   Deed.   Jedediah Alexander (son and heir of Elias Alexander) and Anna his wife of Lancaster Co., PA, yeoman, for £6, to James Porter of Cecil Co., yeoman, 15 acres of land called Slate Hill on the east side of Susquehanna River by a tract called Poplar Valley. Made & Ackn: 15 Aug 1749. Wit: C. Shepherd, L. Hill, H. Gibbon, Nathan Baker. JPs: Nathan Baker, Benja. Chew. Rec: 13 Mar 1749/50. M. Bordley, Clerk.

P. 149   Lease.   Benjamin Tasker of Annapolis, Agent and Receiver General, for rents and services on behalf of Lord Baltimore and with the consent of Gov. Samuel Ogle, to Margaret Brumfield of Cecil Co., 100 acres of land, part of his Lordship's Manor of Susquehanna alias New Connah, by land surveyed for James Paul Heath. Lease is for the term of the natural lives of the said Margaret Brumfield, Elizabeth Cox and Sarah Brumfield. Yearly rent of 20 shillings. Tenants to build a house 30x20 feet with a brick or stone chimney and plant and fence an orchard of 100 apple trees. Made 18 Sep 1749. Wit: Benja. Chew, Elizabeth Chew. Rec: 13 Mar 1749/50. M. Bordley, Clerk.

P. 152 Deed. Robert Mitchell of Cecil Co., weaver, for £67, to Hugh Longwool of the same county, 80 acres at Christiana Creek by the lands of James and Moses Alexander, part of a tract called Newmunster, formerly granted to William Pollock by deed dated 24 Apr 1727 from David Alexander. Pollock sold the land to Walter Beaty who sold it to the said Robert Mitchell by deed dated Oct 1744. Made 6 Oct 1749. Wit: William Longwell, Nathan Baker, James Baxter. Ackn: 7 Oct 1749 by Robert Mitchell and his wife Mary. JPs: Nathan Baker, James Baxter. Rec: 15 Mar 1749/50. M. Bordley, Clerk.

P. 153 Deed. Thomas Sharp, Jr. of Cecil Co., farmer (executor of the Last Will and Testament of his father Thomas Sharp, lately deceased) for £290, to Moses Andrews of the same place, miller, 261 acres called Guill Glass, part of a tract called the Society, in Millford Hundred. Thomas Sharp was conveyed the land from Charles Carroll of Annapolis by deed dated 27 Dec 1723 recorded in Lib D. K. No. 1, folios 58-59. Sharp sold 14 acres of the tract to Alex'r. Loggan by deed dated 12 Dec 1735. Made 15 Dec 1749. Wit: A. Barry, Geo. Lawson, Robert Evans. Isabella Sharp, wife of the deceased Thomas Sharp, Sr., releases her right to the land. Ackn: same day by Thomas Sharp, Jr. and his wife Elizabeth. JPs: Nathan Baker, Tim'o. Roberts. Moses Andrews paid 10s.5½p alienation fine 16 Mar 1749 to Alex'r. Baird. Rec: 16 Mar 1749/50. M. Bordley, Clerk.

P. 155 Deed. Moses Andrews of Cecil Co., for £290 and because he is moving, to Thomas Sharp of the same place, land called Guill Glass [see previous entry P. 153.] Made 16 Dec 1749. Wit: A. Barry, Geo. Lawson, Robert Evans. Ackn: same day by Moses Andrews and his wife Latitia. JPs: Nathan Baker, Tim'o. Roberts. Thomas Sharpe paid 10s5p alienation fine to Alex'r. Baird. Rec: 16 Mar 1749/50. M. Bordley, Clerk.

P. 157 Deed. Thomas Sharpe, Jr. of Cecil Co., farmer, (executor of the Last Will and Testament of his father Thomas Sharp, lately deceased) for £50, to Moses Andrews of the same place, 75 acres, part of a tract called Confusion in Milford Hundred and by a tract called the Society. Said land Robert Holy sold to Thomas Sharp, Sr. by deed dated 10 Mar 1735 recorded in Lib. W. K. No. 2, folios 77-78. Made 15 Dec 1749. Wit: A. Barry, Nathan Baker, Robert Evans. Isabella Sharp, wife of the deceased Thomas Sharp, Sr., releases her right to the land. Ackn: same day by Thomas Sharp, Jr. and his wife Elizabeth. JPs: Nathan Baker, Tim'o. Roberts. Moses Andrews paid 3 shillings alienation fine to Alex'r. Baird. Rec: 16 Mar 1749/50. M. Bordley, Clerk.

P. 158   Deed.   Moses Andrews of Cecil Co., for £50 and because he is moving, to Thomas Sharp of the same place, 75 acres, part of a tract called Confusion [see previous entry P. 157 for land description. Same dates and people as entry P. 155.]

P. 160   Deed.   Colonel Nathan Rigbie of Baltimore Co., and his wife Sabina, executrix of the Last Will and Testament of William Rumsey of Cecil Co., gent., deceased, for £95.5s, to Henry Baker of Cecil Co., 69 acres of land called Philips' Neglect and 31 acres from a tract called Ant Castle adjoining the first said tract.   William Rumsey was granted by patent 69 acres in Cecil Co. on a branch of Elk River called Stony Run by a tract called Raccoon Range. Also a tract called Ant Castle and another called Philips' Neglect, adjoining each other and containing 500 acres. By his Last Will and Testament, William Rumsey appointed his well beloved wife Sabina his executrix to sell these tracts of land. Made 16 Feb 1749. Wit: John Philips, Wm. Rumsey, John Driscoll. Ackn: 10 Mar 1749 by Nathan and Sabina Rigbie. JPs: Pereg'r. Ward, Adam VanBebber. Rec: 17 Mar 1749/50. M. Bordley, Clerk.

P. 162   Assignment of Lease.   Written on the back of a lease from Ephraim Augustine Herman to Cornelius Eliason recorded in Lib. S. K. No. 5, folios 97-99, Cornelius Eliason assigns the lease to his sons Elias Eliason and Cornelius Eliason. Made & Ackn: 5 Apr 1750. Wit. & JPs: P. Bayard, Nich'o. Hyland. Rec: 5 Apr 1750. M. Bordley, Clerk.

P. 162   Deed.   James Thompson and his wife Martha of Philadelphia, for £102, to Benjamin Benson of Cecil Co., land on the north side of Sassafras River at Back Creek called Moneyworth where Robert Thompson, deceased, used to live. Also part of an adjoining tract called Daniel's Denn which was bequeathed to James Thompson by the Last Will and Testament of his father Robert Thompson. Made & Ackn: 19 Mar 1749. Wit: Wm. Pearce, John Cooper. JPs: R'd. Thompson, Adam VanBebber. Benjamin Benson paid 7 shillings alienation fine to Alex'r. Baird on 10 Apr 1750. Rec: 7 Apr 1750. M. Bordley, Clerk.

P. 164   Deed.   James Allison of Cecil Co., farmer, for £140, to William Whan of Newcastle Co., weaver, 150 acres of land which was ordered by Morgan Patton to be surveyed out of a tract of 300 acres granted to him 6 Aug 1719 by Charles Carroll of Annapolis, which was part of a tract of 2,104 acres called the Society. Land was assigned to Charles Carroll by James Carroll and surveyed by Simon Willmore 10 Mar 1701. On 14 May 1713 Henry

Hollingsworth, then the county surveyor, completed the survey. The 150 acres was then granted by Morgan Patton to Rodger Lawson by deed dated 20 Oct 1719. Lawson granted the land to Hugh Lawson by deed of gift dated 4 May 1733. Hugh Lawson granted it to James Allison by deed dated 5 Aug 1749. Made 5 Jan 1749/50. Wit: Geo. Rock, Wm. Pennock. Ackn: 6 Jan 1749 by James Allison and his wife Mary. JPs: Geo. Rock. Timo. Roberts. William Whan paid 6 shilling alienation fine to Alex'r. Baird 9 Apr 1750. Rec: 19 May 1750. M. Bordley, Clerk.

P. 166   Deed.   Timothy Roberts of New Munster, Mary Anns Parish, Cecil Co., miller, for £250, to Jacob VanBebber of Redlyon Hundred, Newcastle Co. on Delaware, yeoman, who has agreed to discharge Roberts' debt, the 110 acres which on 18 Apr 1749 Timothy Roberts mortgaged to John Passmore and Timothy Griffith for £300. His 110 acre plantation in New Munster on the east side of the main branch of Elk River near David and James Alexander's lands was mortgaged with the proviso that the land still remain in his the said Timothy Roberts' possession. Roberts' was to repay Passmore and Griffith. Made & Ackn: 12 May 1750. Wit: P. Bayard, Antony Noones. JPs: P. Bayard, Adam VanBebber. Rec: 28 Apr 1750. M. Bordley, Clerk.

P. 169   Deed.   Simon Johnson, Jr. of Cecil Co., planter, and Catren his wife, for £42, to Robert Evans of the said county, tanner, 50 acres of land on the south side of Little Elk River by Thomas Booth's land, part of a larger tract called Successor and part of 100 acres which was conveyed to Simon Johnson by Paul Poulson by deed dated 12 Jan 1741 recorded in Lib. W. K. No. 9, folio 52. [Catren is also called Catharine.] Made & Ackn: 23 Jan 1749. Wit: Zeb. Hollingsworth, Thos. Ricketts, Jesse Hollingsworth. JPs: Nich'o. Hyland, Tim'o. Roberts. Robert Evans paid 2 shillings alienation fine to Alex'r. Baird 9 Apr 1750. Rec: 13 Jun 1750. M. Bordley, Clerk.

P. 171   Deed.   Nathaniel Williams of Newcastle Co., PA, and Ann his wife, for £150 and because they are moving, to Joseph Wood of Cecil Co., 225 acres of land on the north side of Back Creek by Jacob Young's cart road and the easternmost corner of John Altham's land, part of a tract called Three Bohemia Sisters (called Francina by a late resurvey.) Part of this was formerly devised by Augustine Herman to his daughter Francina. Joseph Wood, son of the said Francina, sold it to John Evans who sold it to William Rees, father of the above said grantor. William Rees devised the land to his son Elias who died without issue and said land descended to the said Nathaniel as lawful heir. Said land already in the actual possession of the said

Joseph Wood. Made & Ackn: 13 Jun 1750. Wit. & JPs: Tho. Colvill, Pereg'r. Ward. Rec: 13 Jun 1750. M. Bordley, Clerk.

P. 174 Deed. William Smith, son and heir of James Smith, once of Maryland but now of York Co., PA, and Mary Smith, also of York Co., widow of the said James Smith, deceased, for £120, to Nicholas White of Cecil Co., yeoman, 200 acres of land by a tract called Batchelor's Fund at the corner of John McFarland's land and Robert Whitacres land, part of 2 tracts called Rumsey's Ramble and Coxes Park. By deed dated 18 Sep 1735 recorded in Lib. W. K. No. 2, folios 127-130, Samuel Gilpin sold this land to Edward Taylor who by deed dated 30 Dec 1738 recorded in Lib. W. K. No. 2, folios 396-397 sold it to the said James Smith, now deceased. [McFarland is also spelled McFarlin.] Made & Ackn: 8 Feb 1749. Wit: Nathan Baker, Geo. Rock, Isabella Best. JPs: Nathan Baker, Geo. Rock. Nicholas White paid 8 shillings alienation fine to Alex'r. Baird 11 Apr 1750. Rec: 13 Jun 1750. M. Bordley, Clerk.

P. 176 Lease. Benjamin Tasker of Annapolis, Agent and Receiver General, for rents and services on behalf of Lord Baltimore and with the consent of Gov. Samuel Ogle, to John Dempster of Cecil Co., 1,000 acres of land called Swaile on the south side of Elk River adjoining the land laid out for George Thompson. Lease is for the term of the natural lives of the said John Dempster's son David Dempster and David's son John Dempster and the natural life of John Whittington. Rent of £10 due 29 Sep yearly. Tenants will build a house and plant 100 apple trees. Made 16 Dec 1749. Wit: Jno. Ross, James Keith. Rec: 13 Jun 1750. M. Bordley, Clerk.

P. 178 Deed. Joseph Chick and Mary his wife, Francis Reynolds and Johanna his wife, and Sarah Alcock, spinster, all of Cecil Co., for £60, to William Maffit of the same county, 100 acres of land called Tilly Broom for which the certificate of survey is dated 5 Oct 1720. Rowland Chambers, late of Cecil Co., yeoman, on 2 Jul 1739 obtained a patent for a tract of 100 acres called Tilly Broom in Cecil Co. and he sold this tract to Humphrey Alcock, now deceased, of the same county, yeoman, for £30, but Humphrey Alcock did not obtain a deed for the land. So Rowland Chambers made a deed for the land dated 10 Jul 1739 to John Alcock, son and heir of Humphrey. John Alcock died intestate and without issue and the land descended to the said Mary Chick, Johanna Reynolds and Sarah Alcock by the death of their beloved brother John Alcock. Their father Humphrey Alcock's Last Will and Testament was dated 28 May 1733. Made & Ackn: 5 Apr 1750. Wit. & JPs: P. Bayard, Adam VanBebber. William Maffit paid 4 shillings alienation fine to Alex'r. Baird 11 Apr 1750. Rec: 13 Jun 1750. M. Bordley, Clerk.

P. 181   Deed.   James Ewing of Cecil Co., planter, for £241.10s, to George Gillespie of the same place, planter, 145 acres of land, part of a tract which James Ewing's father Alexander Ewing bought from William Vestal of the same place, which itself was part of a tract called the Levell on the east side of Susquehanna River. Except for 7 acres in the southwest corner which the said James Ewing sold to William Husband. Made 7 Mar 1750. Wit: James Porter, Joss Ewing, James Knox. Ackn: same day by James Ewing, John Ewing and William Ewing and also Rebeckah Ewing, mother of the said James, John and William Ewing. JPs: Benj'a. Chew, Nathan Baker. George Gillespie paid 5s.10p alienation fine to Alex'r. Baird 13 Jun 1750. Rec: 14 Jun 1750. M. Bordley, Clerk.

P. 183   Deed.   James Ewing of Cecil Co., planter, for £42.10s, to John Ewing and William Ewing, of Cecil Co., planters, 56 acres of land, part of a tract called the Levell's Addition on the west side of Octerrara Creek at the dividing line between James Ewing's and William Husband's parts of the tract called the Levell. Made & Ackn: 7 Mar 1749/50. Wit: James Porter, Joss Ewing, Jas. Knox. JPs: Benj'a. Chew, Nathan Baker. John and William Ewing paid 2s.3p alienation fine to Alex'r. Baird 13 Jun 1750. Rec: 14 Jun 1750. M. Bordley, Clerk.

P. 185   Deed.   Andrew Hall of Cecil Co., wheelwright, for £100, to his son Richard Hall, a tract of 100 acres called Hollingsworth's Second Parcel by lands formerly belonging to Abraham Hollingsworth and Martin Cartmill. Charles Lord Baltimore, by the hands of Gov. Samuel Ogle, granted 100 acres to Zebulon Hollingsworth by patent dated 10 Jun 1734 recorded in the land office in Lib. J. N. No. 1, folio 231. Zebulon Hollingsworth sold the said land to Andrew Hall for £60 paid to Joseph Hollingsworth, uncle of the said Zebulon, and £10 paid to Zebulon. This deed is recorded in Lib. W. K. No. 2, folio 420. Made 24 May 1750. Wit: William Maffit, Nathan Baker, Geo. Rock. Ackn: same day by Andrew Hall and his wife Elliason. JPs: Nathan Baker, Geo. Rock. Richard Hall paid 4 shillings alienation fine to Alex'r Baird 14 Jun 1750. Rec: 14 Jun 1750. M. Bordley, Clerk.

P. 187   Lease.   Benjamin Tasker of Annapolis, Agent and Receiver General, for rents and services on behalf of Lord Baltimore and with the consent of Gov. Samuel Ogle, to Moses Jones of Cecil Co., planter, 100 acres of land called White Point at Plum Creek, part of his Lordship's Manor in Cecil Co. Lease is for the term of the natural lives of the said Moses Jones, his wife Margaret Jones and their daughter Sarah Jones. Rent of 20 shillings due 29 Sep yearly. Tenants will build a house and plant an apple orchard. Made 20

Apr 1750. Wit: John Veazey. Rec: 16 Jun 1750. M. Bordley, Clerk. Matt's. Bordley received 12s5½p alienation fine for this land from the within named James Evans [sic] 16 Jun 1750. Rec: 11 Sep 1751.

P. 190 Valuation of Estate. Robert Holy, late of Cecil Co., deceased, Willed to Stephen Smallwood 2 adjoining tracts of land. One is the tract which Rowland Chambers formerly lived on and the other is where Morgan Patton lived. Stephen Smallwood, not yet of age, has chosen John Passmore as his guardian and Passmore has asked that the land be viewed and valued. Samuel Bond and Richard Cleyton, appointed by Nathan Baker, have viewed the land and believe the value to be worth £6.10s a year. On the plantation where Chambers lived they find 1 log house, an orchard with a few trees, a cleared field of about 7 acres, the fences tolerable. On the place which was Pattons there is 1 log house much decayed, and a tolerable good orchard. Made 8 Jun 1750. Rec: 16 Jun 1750.

P. 192 Bill of Sale/Mortgage. Francis Maybury of Cecil Co., hammer man, for £200, to Nich'o. H. Carew Bart & Co., owners of the Princip'o. Iron Works, the plantation of 120 acres where he the said Francis Maybury now lives adjoining the said Company's land called Vulcan's Delight where the North East Forge stands, which was conveyed to him by lease dated 26 May 1746, along with 2 grey mares, 2 brown horses, 4 cows, 2 heifer yearlings, 2 calves, 4 hogs, 1 cart and iron bound wheels, 1 plow and gears, 1 clock made by Anthony Ward, 1 chest of drawers, 1 desk, 1 oval table, 3 square tables, 6 flag bottom chairs, 3 feather beds and furniture and 4 iron pots and household goods he is now in possession of. Maybury is to repay the Company on or by 20 Jun 1753 to void this writing. Made 20 Jun 1750. Wit: James Baxter, William Baxter. Ackn: 23 Jun 1750. JP: James Baxter. Rec: 30 Jun 1750. M. Bordley, Clerk.

P. 193 Release. Ann Kankey of Cecil Co., widow, obtained from Manadow Phillips of said county, farmer, a mortgage deed dated 11 Aug 1748 for a plantation in Cecil County. Ann Kankey has since married Edward Taylor of said county, farmer. Edward Taylor and Ann his wife, for £50 plus the interest, release the plantation to Manadow Phillips. Made 10 Jun 1750. Wit: Nich'o. Hyland, Jno. Smith, Alexander Mekine. Rec: 7 Jul 1750. Fran's. Key, Clerk.

P. 194 Deed. Francis Farra, widow, for £17, to John Chisholm, lot #48 in Frederick Town with the houses and improvements made by said Francis. [Her name is spelled Francis in the male form of the name throughout the deed but for two places, but they are clearly referring to a woman in this deed.] She signed and sealed the deed with "Francis Ann Farra." Made & Ackn: 1 Sep 1749. Wit. & JPs: John Veazey, Pereg'r. Ward. Rec: 1 Aug 1750. M. Bordley, Clerk.

P. 195   Bond.   Jedediah Alexander of York Co., PA, yeoman, bound for £300 to James Caldwell of Lancaster Co., PA, yeoman, agrees to make a deed of conveyance for a tract of land called Slate Hill in Cecil Co. to said Caldwell to secure the debt. Said land is the remaining part of the tract adjoining the 15 acres which the said Alexander sold to James Porter. Made 13 Nov 1749. Wit: Isaac Sanders, John Daniel. Ackn: 18 Jun 1750 in Lancaster Co. before James Gillespie by Isaac Sanders and John Daniel. Thos. Cookson, Clerk of Lancaster Co., certifies James Gillespie as JP 22 Jun 1750. Rec: 6 Aug 1750. M. Bordley, Clerk.

P. 197   Deed of Partition.   James Baxter of Cecil Co., merchant, owns 273 acres, part of a tract called Anna Catharina Neck. George Simco of the same county, farmer, owns 200 acres, the residue of the same tract. Some doubts had arisen concerning the boundaries of the lines. The two agree to new boundary lines, Baxter's land to the south of Simco's. Made & Ackn: 21 Jul 1750. Wit: Peacock Beggar, I. Hamilton, Nicholas Discon. JPs: Benj'a. Chew, John Smith. Rec: 6 Aug 1750. M. Bordley, Clerk.

P. 200   Deed of Partition.   James Baxter of Cecil Co., merchant, to George Simcoe of the same county, farmer [same land and bounds as in previous entry P. 197.]

P. 202   Assignment of Lease.   Ephraim Augustine Herman made a lease of land to Walter Newman, recorded in Lib. J. D. No. 3, folios 336-337. James Bayard, administrator of the estate of Enoch Jenkins, late of Cecil Co., assigns this said lease to Edward Means. Made & Ackn: 15 Jun 1750. Wit. & JPs: John Veazey, Pereg'r. Ward. Rec: 23 Aug 1750. M. Bordley, Clerk.

P. 203   Assignment of Lease.   On the back of a lease is the endorsement of Enoch Jenkins, who assigns the lease to Abraham Allman (lease recorded in Lib. W. K. No. 2, pgs 274-276.) Thomas Stuart, for £110, assigns the same lease to Nicholas Wood. Made 14 Mar 1749/50. Wit: R'd. Thompson, Jr., Walter Diven. Ackn: 19 Mar 1749/50 by Thomas Stewart and his wife Margaret, who was formerly the wife of Abraham Allman and executrix of his estate. JPs: R'd. Thompson, Adam VanBebber. Rec: 27 Mar 1750. M. Bordley, Clerk.

P. 203 Deed. Joseph Lowman of Cecil Co., planter, and his wife Elizabeth, for £100, to Hannah Johnson of the same county, 100 acres near Pents Creek on the east side of Elk River by land belonging to Martin Alexander called Alexandria. Said land was granted to Adam Wallace, late of said county, by patent dated 13 Aug 1731 and descended to his son James Wallace who conveyed it to the said Joseph Lowman by deed dated 6 Sep 1746. Also 15 acres adjoining the 100 acres which were sold to James Wallace, late of North Carolina, by the said Martin Alexander and sold to the said Joseph Lowman by Robert Wallace, the son and heir of James Wallace, late of Carolina. Made & Ackn: 24 Jul 1750. Wit: [Z?] Bouchell, Richard Bouldin. JPs: P. Bayard, Adam VanBebber. Rec: 30 Aug 1750.

P. 205 Deed. Bryan Reyley of Cecil Co., yeoman, for £120, to Dennis Nowland of the said county, planter, 28 acres of land on Smith's Creek, part of a tract called Vulcan's Rest, by land lately held by Archibald Douglas which is part of the same tract, and by Dennis Nowland's line. Bryan Reyley bought this land from John Cazier by deed dated 5 Oct 1749. [Reyley also spelled Riley.] Made 14 Aug 1750. Wit: Joseph Lilly, James Nowland. Ackn: same day by Bryan Reyley and his wife Mary. JPs: Tho. Colvill, R'd. Thompson. Dennis Nowland paid 1s.1p alienation fine to Alex'r. Baird 6 Sep 1750. Rec: 10 Sep 1750. M. Bordley, Clerk.

P. 207 Deed. Robert Money of Cecil Co., planter, for £160, to Robert Walmsley of the said county, planter, 80 acres of land, part of 300 acres called Larramore's Neck Enlarged, by John Money's land which is part of the same tract. Said land was bequeathed to the said Robert Money by his deceased father Robert Money in his Last Will and Testament. Rodger Larramore conveyed the land to Robert Money the father. Made 5 Sep 1750. Wit: Mich'l. Earle, Ben Pearce. Ackn: 1 Sep 1750 [sic] by Robert Money and by Marg't. Money, widow of Robert Money, deceased. JPs: John Veazey, Pereg'r. Ward. Alex'r. Baird received 1s.7p alienation fine 25 Sep 1750. Rec: 25 Sep 1750. M. Bordley, Clerk.

P. 209 Deed. Robert Walmsley of Cecil Co., planter, for £75, to Robert Money of the said county, planter, 37½ acres of land, the uppermost part of Larramore's Neck Enlarged. Said land Robert Money, deceased, conveyed to Thomas and Catharine Walmsley, deceased. Made 1 Sep 1750. Wit: Mich'l. Earle, Ben Pearce. Ackn: same day by Robert Walmsley and his wife Elizabeth. JPs: John Veazey, Pereg'r. Ward. Robert Money paid 9 pence alienation fine to Alex'r. Baird 25 Sep 1750. Rec: 1 Oct 1750.

P. 211 Lease. Benjamin Pearce and Margaret his wife of Cecil Co., for rents and services, to Richard Beedle of the said county, a plantation of 100 acres on the north side of the head of Broad Creek which was the division between Hance Patton's and John Gullick's lands near Thomas Price's land, part of a tract called Three Bohemia Sisters. Lease is for 21 years. Rent of £9.4s due 10 Mar yearly. Made 23 May 1750. Wit: James Eruen [Erwen?], Michael Cartwright. Ackn: 1 Sep 1750. JPs: John Veazey, Pereg'r. Ward. Rec: 10 Oct 1750. M. Bordley, Clerk.

P. 213 Lease. Benjamin Pearce and Margaret his wife of Cecil Co., for rents and services, to John Weylie of the said county, a plantation of 100 acres (where Hance Patton lately dwelt) near Broad Creek at the main road leading to Elk River by the lands of John Gullick, James Smith and William Price, part of a tract called Three Bohemia Sisters. Lease is for 14 years. Rent of £8.4s due 10 Mar yearly. Made 23 May 1750. Wit: James Euren [sic], Michael Cartwright. Ackn: 1 Sep 1750. JPs: John Veazey, Pereg'r. Ward. Rec: 10 Oct 1750. M. Bordley, Clerk.

P. 214 Deed. Jacob Anderson, John Anderson and James Anderson of St. George's Hundred, Newcastle Co., for £100, to Robert Evans of Cecil Co., tanner, a plantation of 94 acres in the forks of Elk River, part of a tract called Successor (6 acres of the plantation was sold to Mr. Hollingsworth.) Made 13 May 1750. Wit: Jno. Holland, George Hardman, John Smith. Ackn: 13 Jun 1750 by Jacob and John Anderson. JPs: John Veazey, Nich'o. Hyland. Robert Evans paid 4 shillings alienation fine to Alex'r. Baird 17 Oct 1750. Rec: 19 Oct 1750. M. Bordley, Clerk.

P. 216 Assignment of Lease. George Rock of Cecil Co., merchant, for £225, to Edward Lloyd of Talbot Co., 20 acres on North East Creek with the grist mill, plating mill, houses, etc. Said land was, by Writ to the then Sheriff of the county, laid out and condemned for Robert Jones and by deed dated 29 Sep 1746 was conveyed to George Rock for 80 years from 2 May 1711. George Rock is to repay Edward Lloyd on or by 17 Oct 1752 to void this deed. Made & Ackn: 17 Oct 1750. Wit: E. Dorsey, H. Woodward. JP: Geo. Stewart. Rec: 22 Oct 1750. M. Bordley, Clerk.

P. 219 Mortgage. Matthias Harris of Kent Co., gent., for £114.5s, to Edward Lloyd of Talbot Co., the undivided fourth parts of several tracts of land in Cecil Co: 1 tract called Brownly of 100 acres, 1 tract called Coasters Harbour of 300 acres, 1 tract called Wheeler's Warren of 100 acres, one tract called Locust Neck of 120 acres, 1 tract called Pasture Point of 18 acres, 1 tract called High Park of 200 acres and part of a tract called

Warmast of 90 acres. Herculus Coatts sold these land to the said Matthias Harris by deed dated 27 Aug 1746. Herculus Coatts held the land by right of his mother Jane, one of the daughters and coheirs of Matthias Vanderheyden, late of Cecil Co., deceased. Matthias Harris is to repay Edward Lloyd on or by 30 Apr 1750 to void this deed. Made in Kent Co. 30 Oct 1750. Wit. & JPs: B. Hands, Cha. Scott. Ackn: same day by Matthias Harris and his wife Mary. James Smith, Clerk of Kent Co., certifies that Bed Hands and Charles Scott are JPs. Rec: 13 Nov 1750. M. Bordley Clerk.

P. 222 Deed. Manadow Philips of Cecil Co., planter, for £260, to Nicholas Hyland of the said county, gent., 270 acres of land lying behind the cleared ground formerly belonging to John Cusine by that part of the same tract that Peter Picoe bought from Peter and Paternella Manadow, by the line of the land formerly belonging to Peter Clauson and by the land of Johannes Arinst which he bought from Daniel Picoe, the heir of the said Peter Picoe. Said land is part of a tract called Carr's Manor. Capt. John Carr, late of Cecil Co., deceased, by his Last Will and Testament, devised all his estate to his wife, his son and four daughters to be equally divided among them. One of his daughters, Paternella, afterwards married Peter Manadow. Their only daughter Elizabeth Manadow married Samuel Philips, and the said Manadow Philips is their eldest son. Paternella and her husband Peter Manadow have always held her share of her father's land which was laid out to her by the other devisees as her part of a tract of land on Elk River called Carr's Manor. Made 30 Aug 1750. Wit: Tho. Colvill, Nath'n. Baker, Geo. Rock. [Nicholas Hyland is called Capt.] Ackn: same day by Manadow Philips and his wife Rodey. JPs: Tho. Colvill, Geo. Rock. Nicholas Hyland paid 9 shillings alienation fine to Alex'r. Baird 13 Nov 1750. Rec: 13 Nov 1750. M. Bordley, Clerk.

P. 224 Deed. Andrew Barry, gent. of Cecil Co., for £271, to Alexander McDowell, clerk, of the same place, 3 tracts of land. 115 acres, part of a tract called the Society. Also 45 acres (part of a tract called Confusion surveyed for Robert Holy 26 Jul 1723) being the northernmost end of the dividing line between Holy's land and Barry's tract. Also a tract of 10 acres called Barry's Meadow lying between the Society tract and another tract now in the possession of James Mackey, which was surveyed by warrant dated 17 Jan 1744 and granted to James Porter for 400 acres. Porter conveyed it to Barry. The 115 acres was granted to Charles Carroll of Annapolis, deed recorded in Lib. J. D. No. 3, folios 145-146. By deed dated 6 Aug 1719 Charles Carroll conveyed the land to John Seegar who by deed dated 30 Apr 1731 recorded in Lib. S. K. No. 5, folio 336 conveyed the land to Andrew Barry. Made & Ackn: 4 Oct 1750. Wit: Geo. Lawson, James Mackey. JPs: Nathan Baker, James

Baxter. Alexr. Baird received from Alexander McDowell 6s.4½p alienation fine 13 Nov 1750. Rec: 13 Nov 1750. M. Bordley, Clerk.

P. 227   Deed.   John Kimber of Cecil Co., planter, for £200, to Thomas Davis of the said county, 4 tracts of land: 75 acres, the remainder of a tract called Rattlesnake Neck at the dividing of Back Creek; 20 acres, part of Cockatrice on the south side of a branch of Back Creek at Rattlesnake Point adjoining Rattlesnake Neck (conveyed by Matthias Hendrickson to John Atkeson 13 Sep 1686); 2¾ acres, part of the tract called the Levell near Thomas Davis' house within the lines of Rattlesnake Neck; and 7 acres of land between Rattlesnake Neck and Back Creek by John Kimber's landing. All 4 tracts except the 20 square feet where the burying ground now is. Made 12 Nov 1750. Wit: Peter Noxon, John Veazey. Ackn: same day by John Kimber and his wife Catharine. JPs: John Veazey, P. Bayard. Thomas Davis paid 4s.4p alienation fine to Alex'r. Baird 14 Nov 1750. Rec: 14 Nov 1750. M. Bordley, Clerk.

P. 230   Valuation of Estate.   Otho Penington and John Ryland, both of Cecil Co., at the request of Peter Noxon, guardian of Charles Heath, James Heath and Rebecca Heath, orphans of the said county, viewed the lands of the said orphans and found 1 good frame house with 2 brick chimneys and a square log kitchen, 1 smoke house & corn house, 1 old log stable, corn crib, 3 old tobacco houses much out of repair, a few apple trees, 2 log barns. They give the yearly value to be £27. Made 14 Oct 1750. JP: Adam VanBebber. Rec: 14 Nov 1750. M. Bordley, Clerk.

P. 230   Deed.   Anna Alexander, widow and executrix of Jedediah Alexander, deceased, late of Cecil Co., for £150, to James Caldwell of the same place, planter, 85 acres of land, part of Slate Hill, by the land Jedediah sold to James Porter. In his lifetime, Jedediah Alexander, son and heir of Elias Alexander, deceased, borrowed £150 from James Caldwell and secured the loan with a parcel of land, part of a tract called Slate Hill by deed dated 13 Nov 1749. By his Last Will and Testament filed in the registers office of York, PA, Jedediah Alexander ordered the land to be released to James Caldwell. Made 2 Aug 1750. Wit: Robert Leslie, Rich'd. Beder, Isaac Sanders. Ackn: same day by Anna Alexander and John McDonald. JPs: Geo. Rock, Nathan Baker. James Caldwell paid 3s.5½p alienation fine to Alex'r. Baird 18 Oct 1750. Rec: 15 Nov 1750. M. Bordley, Clerk.

P. 233   Mortgage.   John Dempster of Cecil Co., planter, for £200, to James Bayard of the same place, gent., 193 acres on the north side of Bohemia Back Creek by _____ Beedle's land called Bristol. Said land is part of a tract called Bolding's Rest formerly conveyed by William Bolding to his son Thomas Bolding, who along with Richard Bolding, conveyed it to William Dames who conveyed it to the said John Dempster in exchange for a tract of land in Queen Annes Co. called Shepherd's Fortune. John Dempster must repay Bayard within 3 years to void the deed. Made & Ackn: 16 Nov 1750. Wit. & JPs: John Veazey, P. Bayard. Rec: 17 Dec 1750. M. Bordley, Clerk.

P. 235 Mortgage. John Drummond of Cecil Co., merchant, and Augustina his wife, for £220, to Alexander Lunan and James McNabb of the same county, merchants, a tract of 300 acres called Larramore's Neck, where the Drummonds now live, lying between Sassafras and Bohemia Rivers near the mouth of Bohemia River (except for about 12 acres, the part that Thomas Severson has claim to and has a suit of ejectment pending in the provincial court.) The Drummonds are to repay Lunan and McNabb on or by 17 Dec 1753 to void this deed. Made & Ackn: 17 Dec 1750. Wit. & JPs: Tho. Colvill, P. Bayard. Rec: 22 Dec 1750. M. Bordley.

P. 237 Deed. James Crumly of Chester Co., PA, and Katharine his wife, for £80, to William Robinson and Martha Robinson of the same place, 100 acres of land, part of a tract called Kennedy's Adventure, by Samuel England's tract and by a tract now possessed by Edward Oldham. By patent dated 12 Aug 1720 recorded in Lib. E. W., folios 269-270, Hugh Kennedy of Ann Arundel Co., deceased, was granted a tract of 500 acres called Kennedy's Adventure. Henry Bennett of Queen Annes Co., the husband of Margaret, one of the daughters and coheirs of the said Hugh Kennedy, and Elizabeth Kennedy, spinster, the other daughter of the said Hugh, conveyed to Henry Baker the said tract by deed dated 23 Oct 1740 recorded 20 Mar 1640 in Lib. E. I. No. 3, folio 205. [Katharine also spelled Catherine.] Made & Ackn: 25 Aug 1750. Wit: Rich'd. Patten, Thomas Archer, Ed Mitchell. JPs: Benja. Chew, Nathan Baker. Rec: 29 Dec 1750. M. Bordley, Clerk.

Addendum: On 12 Sep 1750, William Robinson and Esbiarl [sic] Robinson assigned all their interest and title of the land to James Gallt. Wit: Hugh Allison. Rec: 29 Dec 1750. M. Bordley. Alienation fine received 3 May 1751.

P. 240 Mortgage. John Smith of Cecil Co., gent., for £450, to James Baxter of the same county, merchant, 425 acres on Susquehanna River called Holland and Heath's Adventure where he the said John Smith now lives by the line of division made between the said John Smith and his brother Anthony Smith. John Smith to repay Baxter on or by 24 Aug 1754 to void this deed. Made 23 Aug 1750. Wit: Nathan Baker, Wm. Baxter, Geo. Rock.

Ackn: same day by John Smith and his wife Grace. JPs: Nathan Baker, Geo. Rock. Rec: 9 Jan 1750. M. Bordley, Clerk.

P. 242   Deed.   Andrew Wallace of Cecil Co., for £60, to Andrew Alexander of the same county, 71¼ acres by a tract called Blankesteen's Park which was patented to Andrew Wallace last year. Made & Ackn: 19 Jul 1750. Wit: John Edwards, William Price. JPs: John Veazey, Adam VanBebber. Rec: 9 Jan 1750. M. Bordley, Clerk.

P 243   Deed.   Michael Lum of Elk River Hundred, planter, and Mary his wife, for £150, to John Lewis of the same place, eldest son of John Lewis, deceased, 115 acres land (part of 400 acres) in Elk River Hundred adjoining the land of John Cossine. At a provincial court held in Annapolis on 20 Oct "third year of the Dominion of the Right Hon. Charles Absolute Lord Proprietor of the Province", Michael Lum recovered 400 acres of land against Thos. Hitchcock. By deed dated 29 Apr 1748 recorded in Lib. W. K., No. [?], folio 242-243, Michael Lum and Thomas Hitchcock agreed the land was the property of the said Michael Lum. Made 3 Aug 1750. Wit: Nich'o. Hyland, Johanus Arrants, Nath'n. Baker. Ackn: 18 Aug 1750. JPs: Nich'o. Hyland, Nathan Baker. Rec: 29 Dec 1750. M. Bordley, Clerk. Alienation fine of 4s.7p.1f paid to Matt's. Bordley. Rec: 12 Feb 1750/51. M. Bordley, Clerk.

P. 246   Deed.   Roger Dyer of Augusta Co., VA, yeoman, and Hannah his wife, for £54, to Edward Dougherty of Lancaster Co., PA, yeoman, 100 acres called Duck Neck. Charles Lord Baltimore, by deed dated 20 Jul 1704, granted to William Smith 100 acres called Duck Neck in Cecil Co. by Elk River near French Town. William Smith died intestate and the land descended to the said Hannah, now wife of Roger Dyer. Made 27 Jul 1750. Wit: James Baxter, Nath'n. Baker, Robert Alison. Ackn: 28 Jul 1750 by Roger Dyer and Hannah his wife. JPs: Nath'n. Baker, James Baxter. Rec: 24 Jan 1750. Edward Dougherty paid 4 shillings alienation fine 23 Dec 1752. Rec: 23 Dec 1752. Matt Bordley.

P. 249   Deed.   Thomas Beetle and Thomas Boulding, Sr., by his attorney James Boulding, and Thomas Boulding, Jr., of Cecil Co., for £50, to Andrew Alexander of Cecil Co., a plantation and 100 acres on the north side of Bohemia Back Creek by land formerly taken up by Richard Boulding, late of said county, and by tracts called Bouldin's Rest and Bristol. [Boulding is also spelled Bouldin.] Made & Ackn: 4 Feb 1751. Wit: Richard Beedle, John Hall, Isaac Alexander. JPs: Nich'o. Hyland, Adam VanBebber. Rec: 8 Feb 1750/51. M. Bordley, Clerk.

P. 251   Deed.   George Rock of Cecil Co., merchant, for 5 shillings, to Reese Meredith of Philadelphia, PA, merchant, a lot on 5th Street in Philadelphia, late in the possession of James Wagg; 117½ acres of land at the head of North East River called Dutton Port granted to Mary Storey; a tract of 127 acres called Brooks Range granted to John Brooks who assigned the land to George Rock, on the southeast side of North East River; and 20 acres condemned for building a grist mill on the main branch of North East River and the mill, forge, buildings on the land, which land is now mortgaged to Edward Lloyd for £300 due 5 Oct 1752 which George Rock is to repay and within 12 months after the death of his wife Mary Rock (to whom the interest of the said £800 is appointed to be paid during her natural life) George Rock must satisfy the payment to Reese Meredith to void this deed.
    Deans Cox, widow of William Cox of Philadelphia, merchant, deceased, in Sep 1745 make a bond to the said Reese Meredith for £800. George Rock, with the consent of Deans Cox, took out letters of administration on the estate of the said William Cox and became accountable to Meredith for the money. Made 11 Apr 1751. Wit: Nath'n. Baker, Wm. Pennock. Ackn: 15 Apr 1750 [sic] by George Rock and his wife Mary. JPs: Nath'n. Baker, James Baxter. Rec: 15 Apr 1751. M. Bordley, Clerk.

P. 254   Valuation of Estate.   Robert Porter and Benjamin Benson have viewed the plantation of Jacob Jones, orphan and heir of Peter Jones of Cecil Co., late deceased. Joseph Redgrave is the orphans guardian. They find about 160 acres of cleared and cultivated land, fences in "midlan good" repair, 1 old frame dwelling house 20x20 with a brick chimney, 1 log kitchen, a milk house, corn house, meet house, hen house and tobacco house. They laid out and marked for support until "sad orphan comes to age" the woodland adjoining the plantation up by the main road that leads from St. Stephens Church to Frederick Town by Sassafras and by a branch of Back Creek. Yearly value of £10. Made 19 Feb 1750. JP: John Veazey. Rec: 15 Apr 1751.

P. 255   Assignment of Lease.   Wm. Hood of Cecil Co., gent., assigned his lease to Thomas Roose [Reese? Rose?] of the same place, weaver, for land where the said Roose now lives at Herrin Creek by Patrick Burks field and by Bennett's old field. Lease was for the term of the natural lives of William Hood and his wife Alee and the natural life of Siddne George, son of Joshua George, attorney. After the first 2 years, rent of 600 lbs of tobacco due every 10 Dec for the 1st 7 years, and thereafter 35 bushels of winter wheat. The original lease was granted by Col. Eph'm. Aug't. Herman. Made 31 Jan 1738/9. Wit: Jer'h. Larkin, Margarett Hamilton. The original lease is recorded in Lib. W. K. No. 2, pgs 415-416. The present assignment of the same lease is from Thomas Castevans and Sarah Crage, widow of George

Crage, late of said county, deceased, joint administrators of the said George Crage's estate, for £60.15s, to John Carty. Made & Ackn: 12 Mar 1750/51. Wit. & JPs: R'd. Thompson, P. Bayard. [Castevans is also spelled Custephs.] Rec: 15 Apr 1751. M. Bordley, Clerk.

P. 256   Deed.   Robert Jones of Cecil Co., cooper, and Elizabeth his wife, for £90.10s, to James Frazier of the same place, farmer, 100 acres called Buck Head on the west branch of Elk River by the plantation of Matthias Johnson. A warrant dated 2 Jun 1719 was granted to Stephen Knight, late of Cecil Co., gent., for 600 acres. The warrant was renewed 20 Oct next ensuing and assigned to Mrs. Ariana Frisby on 8 Mar 1719. Ariana Frisby assigned 100 acres of the warrant to John Jones 10 Mar 1719 and the surveyor surveyed the tract called Buck Head for the said John Jones. Made & Ackn: 22 Dec 1750. Wit: Thomas Ricketts, John Hedrick, Nathan Baker, Tim'o. Roberts. JPs: Nath'n. Baker, Tim'o. Roberts. On 21 Jan 1750 James Frazier paid 4 shillings alienation fine to Matthias Bordley. Rec: 15 Apr 1751. M. Bordley, Clerk.

P. 260   Assignment of Lease.   Written on the back of a lease from Ephraim Augustine Herman to Abraham Allman for land called Allman's Privilege dated 6 Mar 1728, Iseable Elison who was the widow of Thomas Bird of Cecil Co., for £14.5s, assigns the lease to Alexander Stewart. She has power of attorney from her husband Thomas Elison to make over the one third part of the lease. Made & Ackn: 28 Sep 1750. She makes her mark as Elizabeth Elison. Wit. & JPs: Tho. Colvill, P. Bayard. Rec: 15 Apr 1751. M. Bordley, Clerk.

P. 260   Deed.   William Jones of Cecil Co., for £94, to Benjamin Benson of the said county, 75 acres of land on the north side of Sassafras River called Jones' Venture. Made & Ackn: 13 Mar 1750. Wit: Ben Pearce, Peter Noxon. JPs: Pereg'r. Ward, Benj'a. Chew. Alienation fine of 3 shillings paid 14 Mar 1750/51 to Matt Bordley. Rec: 15 Apr 1751.

P. 262   Lease.   David Weatherspoon of Newcastle Co., PA, gent., for yearly rents and services, to John McDowell of Cecil Co., cooper, land that is part of the Indian Range on the head branch of Bohemia River by the lands of William Rumsey, gent., deceased, by land now in the possession of Mary Knaresborough and by the land of Andrew Peterson, gent., deceased. Lease is for the term of the natural lives of the said John McDowell and his wife Elioner. If they should die before the end of 8 years, then John McDowell's son-in-law Philip McGlaughlin should have the land for the rest of the term of the lease. Rent of £6 due 24 Dec yearly. [McDowell also spelled

McDowal.] Made 24 Dec 1750. Wit: D'tt. Bryane, Walter Diven. Ackn: 14 Mar 1750/51. JPs: John Smith, R'd. Thompson. Rec: 15 Apr 1751. M. Bordley, Clerk.

P. 264 Deed. Emanuel Grubb, Sr. of Brandywine Hundred, Newcastle Co. on Delaware, for £250, to Emanuel Grubb, Jr. of the same place, 150 acres of land called Repensation in Cecil Co. by a tract called Poplar Valley originally surveyed for Nicholas Hiland and by a tract called Slate Hill surveyed for Thomas Johnson, Jr. Said land was conveyed to Emanuel Grubb, Sr. by deed dated 1734 from George Martin who had a patent for the land. Made 10 Nov 1750. Signed by Emanuel Grubb; Ann Grubb made her mark. Wit: Peter Grubb, William Saftlawe. Ackn: 13 Mar 1750 in Cecil Co. by Emanuel Grubb before JPs Nath'n. Baker and Geo. Rock. Emanuel Grubb, Jr. paid 6 shillings alienation fine 15 Mar 1750/51 to Matt Bordley. Rec: 15 Apr 1751. M. Bordley, Clerk.

P. 266 Deed. Michael Earle of Cecil Co., gent., and Mary his wife, for £35, to John McDermont of the same place, innholder, a one-fifth part of 2 lots in Frederick Town, lot #'s 49 and 50, which by his Last Will and Testament, William Hutcheson devised to the daughters of Dominick Carrol, deceased. Made & Ackn: 23 Feb 1750/51. Wit. & JPs: Tho. Colvill, John Veazey. Rec: 15 Apr 1751. M. Bordley, Clerk.

P. 267 Deed. John McDermont of Cecil Co., innholder, for £40, to Michael Earle of the same county, gent., a one-fifth part of 2 lots [see previous entry P. 266. Same dates, witnesses, justices. McDermont is also spelled McDermott.]

P. 269 Deed. Juliana Carroll of Cecil Co., spinster, one of the daughters of Dominick Carroll, deceased, for £20, to Michael Earle of the same Co., gent., her one-fifth part of lot #'s 49 and 50 in Frederick Town, which William Hutcheson devised to the daughters of Dominick Carroll by his Last Will and Testament. Made & Ackn: 23 Feb 1750/51. Wit. & JPs: Tho. Colvill, John Veazey. Rec: 15 Apr 1751. M. Bordley, Clerk.

P. 270 Power of Attorney. Aron Alexander of Petersburgh, Cumberland Co., PA, farmer, appoints his trusty and well beloved friend Moses Alexander of Milford Hundred, Cecil Co., farmer, to be his attorney to acknowledge a deed dated 11 Nov 1750 to William Langwill of Milford Hundred for a tract of land that is part of a tract called Newmunster formerly in the possession of David Alexander. Made 11 Nov 1750. Wit: Andrew Moor, Tho's. Reese. JP: Nath'l. Alexander. Ackn: in Cecil Co. 18 Mar 1750 [/51] by Andrew Moor and Thomas Reese before JPs Geo. Rock and Nath'n. Baker. Rec: 15 Apr 1751. M. Bordley.

P. 271   Deed.   Aaron Alexander of Cumberland Co., PA, farmer, for £41, to William Langwill of Cecil Co., merchant, 152 acres and 95 perches of land in Cecil Co., part of a tract called Newmunster, on the east side of Elk River by Hugh Langwall's line. It is the land which Aron Alexander enjoyed as the heir of his father David Alexander who bought the land from Thomas Stevenson of Bucks Co., PA, gent., by deed dated 18 May 1714, the assignee of Robert Roberts of Queen Annes Co., glover. Signed by Aaron Alexander and Ann Alexander made her mark. [Langwill also spelled Longwall, Longwill.] Made 11 Dec 1750. Wit: Andrew Moor, Tho's. Rees. Ackn: 18 Mar 1750/51 by Moses Alexander, attorney for Aaron Alexander. JPs: Nath'n. Baker, Geo. Rock. Rec: 15 Apr 1751. M. Bordley, Clerk.

P. 273   Deed.   Robert Money of Cecil Co., planter, for £67.12s.6p, to John Money of the same place, planter, 37½ acres of land, part of a tract called Larymore's Neck Enlarged which Roger Larrimore sold to Robert Money, father of the above said Robert Money. Robert Money the father sold the land to Catherine Walmsley. Her son Robert Walmsley sold it to Robert Money the son. Made & Ackn: 16 Mar 1750. Wit. & JPs: John Veazey, P. Bayard. John Money paid 9p alienation fine 4 Apr 1751 to Matt's. Bordley. Rec: 15 Apr 1751. M. Bordley, Clerk.

P. 275   Deed.   William (alias Bosen) Price, Jr., of Cecil Co., planter, for £150, to Peter Bayard of the same place, merchant, 150 acres of land in Sassafras Neck called Abraham's Promise. William Price bought the land from James Harris, esq., deceased, and it was determined that James Harris had not sufficient right to sell the land. Application was made by Price to William Harris, son and heir of James Harris, who released the land to him 26 Apr 1748. Made & Ackn: 5 Apr 1751. Wit. & JPs: R'd. Thompson, Benj'a. Chew. Rec: 15 Apr 1751. M. Bordley, Clerk.

P. 277   Deed.   William Penington of Newcastle Co. on Delaware, cordwainer, and his wife Elizabeth, for £130, to Thomas Beard of Cecil Co., planter, 100 acres, the lower half of a tract called Norland. In his lifetime James Heath of Cecil Co. held a moiety of a 100 acres of a tract called Norland (the lower half) on the north side of the head of Sassafras River which was divided by deed of release from Heath to the heirs of John Wheeler. James Heath conveyed the land to Otho Othoson of Cecil Co., carpenter, deceased, by deed recorded 18 Nov 1725 in Lib. D. K. No. 1, folios 196-199. Otho Othoson conveyed the land to William Penington by deed of gift recorded 11 Feb 1743 in Lib. W. K. No. 8, folios 67-68. [Beard is also spelled Baird.] Made & Ackn: 3 Dec 1750. Wit: Pereg'r. Ward, John Latham. JPs: R'd. Thompson, Pereg'r. Ward. Alienation fine of 4 shillings paid 6 Apr 1751 to Matt Bordley. Rec: 15 Apr 1751. M. Bordley, Clerk.

P. 279 Deed. John Brice of Annapolis, for £5, to John Veazey of Cecil Co., a moiety of a marsh which is included in a tract of land called the Addition to the Forest lately granted to the said John Brice and adjoins a tract called Frisby's Farm now occupied by John Veazey but recently in the tenure of Daniel Cheston. Made 18 Apr 1751. Wit: Geo. Dent, James Smith. Ackn: same day by John Brice and his wife Sarah. JP: Geo. Dent. Rec: 23 Apr 1751. M. Bordley, Clerk.

P. 280 Bond. John Hamilton of Cecil Co., clerk, to secure an obligation, for 5 shillings and because he is moving, to Nicholas Hyland and James Baxter of the said county, gents., 450 acres called Copson's Pasture and a 150 acres called Hamilton's Lott. Also the lot in Charles Town where John Hamilton's dwelling house is built and the half lot adjoining it. Also a moiety of a lot in the said town where Robert Good has built a house. Also lot #'s 120 and 121 in the said town. Plus all the household goods, implements, chattels listed on a schedule annexed here. If Hamilton meets his obligations, then this writing is void. Made 17 May 1751. Wit: Add'n. Murdock, Dan Dulaney. The list of goods is added to the end of the deed, and includes a female slave named Cate. Ackn: 18 May 1751. JP: Robert Gordon. Ackn: again on 5 Jun 1751. JPs: Nath'n. Baker, Geo. Rock. Rec: 5 Jun 1751. M. Bordley, Clerk.

P. 283 Deed. Vincent Dorsey of Ann Arundel Co., gent., and John Hammond Dorsey of Baltimore Co., for £80 (already paid by John Steel, deceased,) to Walter Steel of Cecil Co., heir of John Steel, deceased, 100 acres of land, part of a tract called Success, by a tract called Bourn's Forest. The tract called Success on the east side of Susquehanna River was resurveyed and laid out for John Hammond of Cecil Co. by special warrant dated 25 Apr 1732 which was originally surveyed 3 Nov 1683 and laid out for Thomas Lightfoot for 300 acres. Made & Ackn: in Baltimore Co. 25 Mar 1751. Wit: Jared Nilson, John Dorsey. JPs: W. Young, Jno. Paca. Talbot Risteau, clerk of Baltimore Co., certifies William Young and John Paca as Justices. Rec: in Cecil Co. 5 Jun 1751. M. Bordley, Clerk.

P. 285 Deed. Vincent Dorsey of Ann Arundel Co., and John Hammond Dorsey of Baltimore Co., for £320 already paid by John Steel, to Walter Steel of Cecil Co., son and heir of John Steel of said county, deceased, a tract of 400 acres called Boren's Forest which Zachariah Maccubbin of Ann Arundel Co., gent., by deed dated 5 Oct 1732, sold to John Hammond of Cecil Co. Made 25 Mar 1751. Wit: John Dorsey, Jared Nilson. Ackn: same day in Baltimore Co. before JPs W. Young and Jno. Paca. Clerk of Baltimore Co. Talbot Rusteau [sic] certified William Young and John Paca as Justices. Rec: in Cecil Co. 5 Jun 1751. M. Bordley, Clerk.

P. 287   Assignment of Lease.   James Harper of Cecil Co., cordwainer, for £13.5s.6p, assigns his share of a lease to his brother John Harper of the same county, farmer. By lease dated 29 Jan 1731 and recorded in Lib. S. K. No. 5, folios 422-424, Col. Ephraim Augustine Harman leased this land to Thomas Harper of the said county. Thomas Harper assigned the lease to his sons John Harper, William Harper and James Harper (except 100 acres which he leased to his son Jacob Harper) which assignment is recorded in Lib. W. K. No. 9, folio 89. And for £20 James Harper assigned his share of the lease to his brothers John Harper and William Harper by assignment recorded in Lib. W. K. No. 10, folios 254-255. By his Last Will and Testament, the said William Harper devised his share of the lease to his brother James Harper on the condition that James pay a sum of money to cover a debt he the said William owed. Made 13 May 1751. Wit: Walter Diven, James Smith. Ackn: same day by James Harper and his wife Sarah. JPs: R'd. Thompson, Adam VanBebber. Rec: 12 Jun 1751. M. Bordley, Clerk.

P. 289   Assignment of Lease.   John Campbell assigned a lease for land on Elk River (part of a tract called the Dividings) to Andrew Price and this assignment was recorded in Lib. W. K. No. 9, folios 341-342. Now the said Andrew Price assigns the lease to Anthony Lynch. Ackn: 14 Mar 1751. JPs: R'd. Thompson, John Veazey. Rec: 14 Jun 1751. M's. Bordley, Clerk.

P. 290   Deed of Gift.   John Baldwin of Cecil Co., gent., because he is moving and for 5 shillings and for the natural love and affection he has for his daughter Catharine and her husband George Milligan of Chester Town, Kent Co., merchant, gives to George Milligan and his wife Catharine, 240 acres called Macgregory's Delight in Cecil Co. on the south side of Bohemia River at St. Augustine's Branch. The certificate of survey is dated 25 Jul 1689 and was originally granted to Hugh Macgregory. John Baldwin retains use of the land for the remainder of his natural life and after his decease the land is for the benefit of his daughter the said Catharine, wife of the said George. Made & Ackn: 15 Jun 1751. Wit. & JPs: John Veazey, Adam VanBebber. Rec: 22 Jun 1751. M's. Bordley, Clerk.

P. 292   Mortgage.   Sarah Savin of Cecil Co., widow of William Savin, late of said county, deceased, and John Savin, son of the said William Savin, for

£160, to James Bayard of the same county, merchant, 100 acres on the north side and near the head of Sassafras River, part of a tract called Green Spring which William Hill, son and heir of the patentee Samuel Hill, and his widow Elizabeth Hill, conveyed by their deed dated 5 May 1703 to William Savin. By his Last Will and Testament, William Savin devised the land to his son the said John Savin, to be his after the death of his mother the said Sarah Savin. Sarah and John are to repay Bayard within 3 years. Made 17 Jun 1751. Wit. & JPs: P. Bayard, Adam VanBebber. Ackn: same day by Sarah Savin, John Savin and his wife Esther Savin. Rec: 27 Jun 1751. M's. Bordley, Clerk.

P. 295 Lease. Benjamin Tasker of Annapolis, Agent and Receiver General, for rents and services on behalf of Lord Baltimore and with the consent of Gov. Thomas Bladen, to Samuel White of Cecil Co., 86 acres of land, part of his Lordship's Manor of Susquehanna, by Robert Mills' land. Lease is for the term of the natural lives of William White, Samuel White, Jr., and Benjamin Chew, Jr. Rent of 21s.6p due 1 Jan yearly. Tenants will build a house with a brick or stone chimney and plant and fence an orchard of 100 apple trees. Made 10 Jun 1745. Wit: Benjamin Chew. Rec: 1 Jul 1751. M's. Bordley, Clerk.

P. 298 Last Will and Testament. Samuel White of Cecil Co., indisposed in body but of perfect mind, gives to his son William White 5 shillings and no more; to his beloved wife Hannah White one third part of the rents and profits of his plantation in Cecil Co where he now lives, she to enjoy the same during her natural life and he gives to her one third part of his moveable goods, chattels, money, debts, during her natural life and at her decease to be returned to his executor; he gives to his son Samuel White the remaining two thirds part of the plantation and the other third part of the plantation and his moveable goods after the death of his wife Hannah. Also to his son Samuel White all his titles and interests in all other lands in Maryland or elsewhere. He appoints his son Samuel White to be his executor. Made 30 May 1750. Wit: John Johnson, David Kerr. Rec: 1 Jul 1751. M's. Bordley, Clerk.

P. 299 Deed. Anthony Smith of Cecil Co., gent., for £500, to James Evans of Chester Co., PA, gent., his undivided moiety of 2 tracts of land (except 150 acres, part of the moiety already sold by the said Anthony Smith to William Hitchman.) Samuel Smith, late of Ann Arundel Co., deceased, by his Last Will and Testament bequeathed to his two sons John Smith and the said Anthony Smith his 2 tracts of land on the north side of Susquehanna River in Cecil Co., one called Heath's Adventure and the other adjoining tract called Holland, to be divided equally between them. Made 12 Apr 1751. Wit: John Howard, John Watkins, John Hall. Witnesses to the exchange of money were Benja. Crockett and Henry Baker. Ackn: in Ann Arundel Co. 12 Apr 1751 by Anthony Smith and his wife Jane. JP: Geo. Dent. Rec: in Cecil Co. 6 Aug 1751. M's. Bordley, Clerk.

P. 301   Deed.   Peter Lawson of Cecil Co., innholder, for £260, to Sluyter Bouchel of the same county, physician, a grist mill and its' land called Back Creek Mill (which was formerly in the possession of Howell James) on the north side of Back Creek and the 10 acres of land on the south side of the creek. Also the privilege of dirt for the mill dam (convenient next to the mill towards Lawson's house.) Lawson reserves for Col. Thomas Colvill the liberty of being hopper free during his life. Made & Ackn: 14 Jun 1745. Wit. & JPs: John Veazey, Pereg'r. Ward.
   Sluyter assigns this deed to Thomas Ogle of Whiteley Creek Hundred in Newcastle Co. on Delaware, gent. Made 30 Jul 1751. Wit. & JPs: R'd. Thompson, Adam VanBebber. Ackn: 31 Jul 1751. Rec: 14 Aug 1751.

P. 304   Deed.   Benjamin Sluyter of Augustine Parish, Cecil Co., for 400 lbs of tobacco and because he is moving, to the Vestry of Augustine Parish for the use of the Rev. Hugh Jones and his successors, 2 acres, part of the tract where Augustine Church now stands on the south side of the road from Bohemia Ferry to Newcastle. Made & Ackn: 6 Aug 1751. Wit. & JPs: R'd. Thompson, Adam VanBebber. Rec: 13 Aug 1751. M. Bordley, Clerk.

P. 305   Deed of Gift.   William Beedle, Sr. of Cecil Co., for natural love and affection, to his sons Thomas Beedle and John Beedle, the tract of land where he the said William now lives called Collecton containing 200 acres to be equally divided between them. The westernmost part of the land to Thomas and the easternmost part to John, to be theirs after the decease of the said William their father, and all the adjoining lands. [Beedle is also spelled Beetle, Bettel.] Made Aug 1751. Wit. & JPs: Nich'o. Hyland, R'd. Thompson. Ackn. & Rec: 13 Aug 1751. M. Bordley, Clerk.

P. 306   Valuation of Estate.   Robert Porter and Benjamin Benson, with JP John Veazey and the orphan's guardian Thavanta? [page torn] Penington, have viewed the lands of Ebenezer Penington, orphan of William Penington, late deceased, and find that 110 acres of the cultivated land in good repair of fence, about 35 apple trees, a dwelling house with a kitchen which Benjamin Sluyter covered with joint shingles, an old tobacco house and another good tobacco house, a log meet house, hen house, a well, a brick oven. They have laid out an adjoining woodland near the lands of William Jones and John Geers by Benjamin Cox, Jr.'s land called Sivility for the use of the said orphan to support the plantation until he comes of age. Yearly value of the place set at £12.10s. Made 5 Aug 1751. Rec: 17 Aug 1751.

P. 307   Deed of Partition.   John Smith of Cecil Co., planter, owns 428 acres, part of 2 tracts called Heath's Adventure and Holland and Anthony Smith of the same county, planter, owns 4?? [page torn], the residue of the said tracts. Some doubts have arisen about the boundaries of the tracts. Anthony Smith and John Smith agree on a boundary line between each person's share of the land. Made 1 Mar 1750/51. Wit: Ellneer Poulson, John Wood, Isaac Jones. Ackn: 27 Jul 1751. JPs: Nath'n. Baker, James Baxter. Rec: 20 Aug 1751.

P. 309   Agreement.   Angelica Coppin, Mary Ricketts and David Ricketts agree that the remainder of a tract of land where John Atkey of Cecil Co., planter, lived and died and which by his wife he bequeathed to his two daughters the said Angelica and Mary after the decease of his wife Ann Atkey, now lately dead, to be equally divided between them be divided as soon as the bounds of an equal division can be settled. The upper part joining the lands now in the possession of the Widow Elizabeth Frisby and Mr. Peregrine Ward will belong to the eldest daughter Angelica and the other part will be the youngest daughter Mary's, wife of David Ricketts. Made 16 Mar 1750/51. Wit: Th. Jones, Thos. Spencer, Robert Porter, Michell Ruley. Rec: 31 Aug 1751.

P. 309   Assignment of Lease.   Richard Thompson, Sr. and his son Richard Thompson, Jr., of Cecil Co., gents., for rents and covenants, to Robert Thompson, 237 acres and 20 perches, part of a tract called Three Bohemia Sisters, on the north side of Back Creek at the mouth of Broad Creek, by the property of Isaac Ham which Richard Thompson, Sr. conveyed to John McCreary. Richard Thompson, Sr. formerly granted this lease dated 23 Nov 1741 to Richard Thompson, Jr. Lease is for the term of the natural lives of the said Richard Thompson, Jr. and his wife Mary and for the natural life of Samuel, the son of Mary, the daughter of Rene Julian, late of Cecil Co. Yearly rent of 20 shillings and two dunghill fowls. Made & Ackn: 31 Aug 1751. Wit. & JPs: Tho. Colvill, P. Bayard. Rec: 9 Sep 1751. M's. Bordley, Clerk.

P. 312   Lease.   Benjamin Tasker of Annapolis, Agent and Receiver General, for rents and services on behalf of Lord Baltimore and with the consent of Gov. Samuel Ogle, to John Kirkpatrick of Cecil Co. 96 acres, part of his Lordship's Manor of Susquehanna, by the commons of Charles Town on the north side of the main road leading to the lower ferry. Lease is for the term of the natural lives of John Kirkpatrick, Jr., James Kirkpatrick and Mary Kirkpatrick. Rent of 19s.6p due 1 Jan yearly. Tenants will build a dwelling house and plant and fence an apple orchard. Made 20 May 1751. Wit: Benj'a. Chew, Jno. Ross. Rec: 9 Sep 1751. M's. Bordley, Clerk.

P. 315 Deed. Henry Cox of Newbury, York Co., PA, farmer, and Mary Cox, for £5, to John Ham, son of Ephearm Ham, land called the Lone Tree on the east side of Elk River in Cecil Co. Made 5 Jun 1751. Wit: William Beals, William Bennett. Rec: 21 Sep 1751. M. Bordley, Clerk.

P. 315 Deed. Elenor Taylor of Cecil Co., widow, for £10, to John Hamm, son of Ephraim Hamm, land called Lone Tree on the east side of Elk River. Made 20 Jun 1751. Wit: Robert Veazey, Jr. Ackn: 23 Aug 1751 by Ellen Taylor. JPs: Tho. Colvill, P. Bayard. Rec: 21 Sep 1751. M. Bordley, Clerk.

P. 316 Deed. John Terry of Cecil Co., planter, and Ann his wife, in exchange for a tract of land in Kent Co. called Suffolk conveyed to John Terry by George Milligan, to the said George Milligan of the same county, merchant, 147 acres, part of a tract called Banks in Cecil Co. on the south side of Bohemia River by Hugh Watson's part of the same tract at the dividing line between Watson's part and Thomas Terry's land who formerly held the part of the tract now being conveyed. Made & Ackn: 1 Oct 1751. Wit: Tho's. Colvill, Tittuir [sic.] JPs: Tho's. Colvill, Adam VanBebber. Rec: 4 Oct 1751. M's. Bordley, Clerk.

P. 318 Deed. Thomas Mills of Cavel Co., [sic], blacksmith, for £45, to William Wallace of the same place, farmer, 65 acres on Long Creek near Bohemia Back Creek by land belonging to the heirs of Henry Ward and by the road leading from Andrew Alexander's to the fording place at Broad Creek, part of a tract of 400 acres called Joan's Green Spring which was formerly granted to William Harris of Kent Co. [Mills also spelled Milles.] Made & Ackn: 16 Sep 1751. Wit: Benj'a. Chew, Nath'n. Baker, Benj'a. Crockett. JPs: Benj'a. Chew, Nath'n. Baker. Rec: 4 Oct 1751. M. Bordley, Clerk. Alienation fine of 2s.7½p paid.

P. 320 Deed. James Redus and Catharine his wife, of Cecil Co., planter, for £40 and because they are moving, to John Holtham of the same county, innholder, 102 acres which was formerly called Collet's Land but now called Blanford and is part of a tract called Town Point or Cecil Town and lies on the east side of Elk River by the land called Cecil Town belonging to the heirs of William Parsons and by John Jawert's land called Jawert's Delight now occupied by George Lewis. Parsons' land was sold to him by Casparus Herman, esq. [Redus also spelled Reddus.] Made & Ackn: 5 Oct 1751. Wit: Tho's. Foster, Adam VanBebber. JPs: R'd. Thompson, Adam VanBebber. Rec: 7 Oct 1751. M's. Bordley, Clerk.

P. 322 Bill of Sale. James McLacklan of Cecil Co., merchant, to John Drummonds of the said county, merchant, a Negro man named Jack. Made 23 Oct 1751. Wit: Wm. Hedges, Rebecca Hedges. Rec: 26 Oct 1751. M's. Bordley, Clerk.

P. 323 Bill of Sale. John Drummond of Cecil Co., merchant, to William Hedges of the same county, a Negro man named Jack. Made 25 Oct 1751. Wit: John Walker, Jas. Schee. Rec: 26 Oct 1751. M's. Bordley, Clerk.

P. 323 Bill of Sale. David Crosby of Maryland, husbandman, for £40 and because he is moving, to Baptist Scott of the same province, planter, a 7 year old mare, a bay mare, a natural pacer 12 years old, a quantity of corn in 37 acres (of which one third of it belongs to Crosby), an Indian house, a cow, a stack of flax, a pot, and a bed and bedding. Made 8 Oct 1751. Wit: Wm. Webby, Thomas Ellot. Ackn: same day in Cecil Co. by David Crosby. JP: Nath'n. Baker. Rec: 26 Oct 1751. M's. Bordley, Clerk.

P. 324 Deed. Charles Carroll of Annapolis, esq., for £50, to James Elliot, son and heir of William Elliot, late of Cecil Co., farmer, 200 acres of land called Kittavilly in Cecil Co. Made 27 May 1751. Wit: Dan'l. Carroll, Wm. Baker. JP: Jno. Price. Alienation fine of 8 shillings paid by James Elliott 30 Oct 1751. Rec: same day. Ms. Bordley, Clerk.

P. 325 Power of Attorney. Matthias Matthiason of Biddeford, Devonshire, England, mariner, and Ann his wife, own the land called Corncalson and another tract called Freeman's Land, both on the north side of Sassafras River in Cecil Co. and now in the possession of his tenant John Fulingham. Matthias and Ann Matthiason empower Francis Bonner of Sassafras to sell the tracts of land to the best purchaser. Made 1 Mar 1750. Wit: Jno. Bartlett, Jno. Lovering, Peter Saintwell. Ackn: 30 Oct 1751 in Cecil Co. by John Lovering and Peter Saintwell. JPs: John Veazey, Pereg. Ward. Rec: 8 Nov 1751. M's. Bordley, Clerk.

P. 327 Lease. Peter Augustine Bouchell and John Lawson, for yearly rents and services, to John Cage, 50 acres of land in Bohemia Manor. Lease is for the term of the natural lives of the said John Cage and his sons James

Cage and John Cage. Rent of 20 shillings due 10 Mar yearly. Made 24 Aug 1751. Wit: James McLachlan, Jonathan Hodgson. Ackn: 31 Aug 1751. JPs: R'd. Thompson, P. Bayard. Rec: 12 Nov 1751. M's. Bordley, Clerk.

P. 328   Assignment of Lease.   Jacob Hoser of Cecil Co., now married to Anne Neide, widow of Michael Neide, late of said county, deceased, for £146, to Joseph Neide, a lease of land. [Jacob Hoser is also called Jacob Ozier.] Made & Ackn: 22 Aug 1751. Wit. & JPs: Tho's. Colvill, P. Bayard. Rec: 14 Nov 1751. M's. Bordley, Clerk. Memo: the above assignment is endorsed on the back of a lease from Ephraim Augustine Herman to Michael Neide recorded in Lib. D. K. No. 1, pgs 159-161.

P. 329   Deed.   Alexander Lunan of Cecil Co., merchant, for £220, to John Wallace of Kent Co., merchant, the mortgage on a tract of 300 acres of land called Larramore's Neck. By deed dated 17 Dec 1750, John Drummond of Cecil Co., merchant, and his wife Augustina, mortgaged to the said Alexander Lunan and James McNabb, late of Cecil Co., merchant, now deceased, a tract of 300 acres called Larramore's Neck (which was then the dwelling plantation of the said John and Augustina Drummond) in Cecil Co. lying between Sassafras and Bohemia Rivers (except 12 acres, the part of the land which Thomas Severson claims.) The Drummonds were to repay £212 on or by 17 Dec 1753. The money has not been paid to the said Lunan or James McNabb in his lifetime nor since his death. Made 25 Sep 1751. Wit: John McDermott, John Baine. £220 paid by Wallace to Lunan next day. Wit. & JPs: Tho's. Colvill, P. Bayard. Ackn: 13 Nov 1751. Rec: 16 Nov 1751. M's. Bordley, Clerk. Wallace paid 12 shillings alienation fine 9 Nov 1751. Rec: 8 Jan 1752. M's. Bordley, Clerk.

P. 332   Assignment of Lease.   Richard Thompson, Sr. and his son Richard Thompson, Jr., both of Cecil Co., gents., for rents and services, to Ephraim Thompson, 217 acres and 20 perches of land, part of a tract called Three Bohemia Sisters on the north side of Back Creek by the land of Isaac Hams (which the said Richard Thompson, Sr. conveyed to John McCreary) and by Jacob Young's cart road and his landing on Back Creek. Richard Thompson, Sr. made this lease to Richardson Thompson, Jr. by lease dated 23 Nov 1741. Lease is for the terms of the natural lives of the said Richard Thompson, Jr. and his wife Mary and for the natural life of Samuel, the son of Mary, the daughter of Rene Julien, late of Cecil Co. Made & Ackn: 14 Nov 1751. Wit: D'd. Witherspoon, George Rock. JPs: P. Bayard, Geo. Rock. Rec: 18 Nov 1751. M's. Bordley, Clerk.

P. 334   Deed.   Charles Carroll of Annapolis, son of Charles Carroll, late of said city, deceased, for £16.10s and to correct a previous land division and because he is moving, quit claims to Robert Rowland of Cecil Co., farmer, 354 acres of land, part of a tract called Society. By deed dated 4 Oct 1717, Charles Carroll the father, in his lifetime, conveyed to Joseph Steel of the said county, planter, a tract of 320 acres of land in Cecil Co. called Society on the east side of Spring Run (a branch of the west branch of Elk River) by John Bristow's land. By deed dated 8 Mar 1743, Joseph Steel conveyed the land to the said Robert Rowland. The land was resurveyed and found that part of the 320 acres lies out of the bounds of the tract called Society. Made 20 Nov 1751. Wit: Thomas Sharp, Geo. Lawson. Ackn: 22 Nov 1751. JP: Geo. Stewart. Rowland paid Carroll 23 Nov 1751. Rec: 23 Nov 1751. M's. Bordley, Clerk.

P.336   Deed.   Charles Carroll of Annapolis, son of Charles Carroll, late of said city, deceased, for 5 shillings and because he is moving, quit claims to Alexander McDowell of Cecil Co., gent., 115 acres of land, part of the tract called Society on the northwest side of Spring Run near where it enters Little Elk Creek. By deed dated 6 Aug 1719, Charles Carroll the father conveyed to John Seagar 115 acres in Cecil Co., part of a tract called Society. Seagar conveyed the land to Andrew Barry by deed dated 30 Apr 1731. The said Barry granted the land to the said Alexander McDowell by deed dated 4 Oct 1750. Made 22 Nov 1751. Wit: Geo. Lawson, Tho's. Sharp. Ackn: same day. JP: Geo. Stewart. Rec: 23 Nov 1751. M's. Bordley, Clerk.

P. 338   Deed.   Charles Carroll of Annapolis, son of Charles Carroll, late of said city, deceased, for £35.10s and to correct an earlier survey error and because he is moving, to Thomas Sharp of Cecil Co., planter, 315 acres, part of the Society tract. Charles Carroll the father, by deed dated 20 May 1719, conveyed to Thomas Sharp, deceased father of the said Thomas Sharp, a tract of 244 acres of land called Guil Glass, part of a tract called Society, by John Bishop's land. Charles Carroll the son, by deed dated 27 Dec 1723, granted to Thomas Sharp the father another 261 acres of the Society tract. By his Last Will and Testament, Thomas Sharp the father authorized his executors to sell the land, which they did by deed dated 14 Dec 1749 to Moses Andrews of said county, miller. By deed dated 15 Dec 1749, Moses Andrews conveyed the land to the said Thomas Sharp the son. There was an early mistake made in the survey of the Society tract. Made 2 Nov 1751. Wit: Geo. Lawson, Robert Rowland. Ackn: 22 Nov 1751. JP: Geo. Stewart. Rec: 23 Nov 1751. M's. Bordley, Clerk.

P. 341   Lease.   Benjamin Tasker of Annapolis, Agent and Receiver General, for rents and services on behalf of Lord Baltimore and with the consent of Gov. Samuel Ogle, for rents and services, to Garrett McKenny of Cecil Co., farmer, a marsh called Kenny's Meadow, part of Elk River Manor, on the west side of the river adjoining two parcels called Old Field Lot and Hopewell. Lease is for the term of the natural lives of the said Garrett McKenny, his wife Margaret McKenny and their son John McKenny. Rent of 5 shillings due every 29 Sep. [Garratt also spelled Gerratt and McKenny also spelled McKinna.] Made 17 Oct 1751. Wit: Josiah Wilson, John Veazey. Rec: 25 Nov 1751. M's. Bordley, Clerk.

P. 342   Deed.   John Holland of Cecil Co., gent., for £3, to James Bayard and Peter Bayard, both of said county, gents., a ½ acre lot called Holland's Point on Bohemia River where the ferry is kept. Said lot was laid out by the Justices of Cecil Co. for building and use of an Inspection House for tobacco. Made 25 Nov 1751. Wit: R'd. Thompson, John Veazey, Peter Lawson. Ackn: same day by John Holland and his wife Mary. JPs: R'd. Thompson, John Veazey. Rec: 29 Nov 1751. M's. Bordley, Clerk.

P. 344   Bill of Sale.   John McClen of Cecil Co., planter, for 2,250 lbs of tobacco, to Andrew Barratt of the said county, gunsmith, 1 brown mare branded with "WS", 3 cows, 1 bull and all the tobacco on the plantation he now lives on. Made 14 Nov 1751. Wit: James Worth, Elez Worth [he made his mark with an "O".] Ackn: next day by John McClean. JP: John Veazey. Rec: 2 Dec 1751.

P. 345   Deed.   Nathaniel Chapman, attorney for Sir Nicholas Hackett Carew, Baronet Osgood Gee, esq., Thomas Russell and John Price, merchants of Great Britain and owners of Principio Iron Works in Maryland, for £50, to John Stump of Cecil Co., farmer, 50 acres of land being a moiety of a tract called Gotham Bush in Cecil Co. on the east side of Susquehanna River adjoining the other moiety of the land formerly conveyed to Edward Jackson and now in the possession of Jackson's heirs. Made 18 Nov 1751. Wit: James Baxter, Nath'n. Baker, George Poughfer. Ackn: next day. JPs: Nath'n. Baker, James Baxter. Rec: 3 Dec 1751. M's. Bordley, Clerk. John Stump paid 2 shillings alienation fine 17 Dec 1751 to Matt's. Bordley.

P. 347   Release.   Charles Carroll of Annapolis, esq., for 5 shillings and because he is moving, to George Lawson of Cecil Co., merchant, 337 acres, part of a tract called Society formerly granted to Roger Lawson by Charles Carroll, father of the above said Charles Carroll, by deed dated 28 May 1718. Roger Lawson conveyed the land to the said George Lawson by deed of gift.

Made 22 Nov 1751. Wit: Will'm. Baker, Moses Andrews. Ackn: 21 Nov 1751 [sic.] JP: Geo. Stewart. Rec: 4 Dec 1751. M's. Bordley, Clerk.

P. 349   Lease.   Benjamin Tasker of Annapolis, Agent and Receiver General, on behalf of Lord Baltimore and with the consent of Gov. Samuel Ogle, for rents and services, to Thomas Rose of Cecil Co., farmer, 74 acres of land called Rose's Choice (part of North East Manor) on the south east side of North East River by the land of James Brooks, by a tract surveyed for George Rock called Peredice and by a tract belonging to the Iron Works Company. Lease is for the term of the natural lives of the said Thomas Rose, his daughter Jane Rose and Peregrine Rose, son of the said Thomas Rose and Jane Rose [sic.] Rent of 7s.6p due every 29 Sep. Tenants are to build a dwelling house and plant an orchard of 70 apple trees. Made 7 Aug 1751. Wit: Josiah Wilson, Edward Veazey. Rec: 9 Dec 1751. M's. Bordley, Clerk.

P. 351   Deed.   Nathaniel Cartmell of Frederick Co., VA, son and heir of Martin Cartmell, deceased, for £60, to Joseph Cochran of Cecil Co., farmer, 100 acres of land in Milford Hundred, Cecil Co., part of a tract called Fair Hill granted by patent to John Hollingsworth, deceased, and by John Hollingsworth's son and heir granted to Martin Cartmell. Also another tract of 24 acres called Cartmell's Addition adjoining the first said tract and granted to Martin Cartmell by patent in 1724. Also 2 tracts, one called Good Will and the other part of Lydia's Joynture (except 110 acres sold by Martin Cartmell to John McCullock.) Made 1 Nov 1751. Wit: Nich'o. Hyland, Nath'n. Baker, Francis Mauldin. Ackn: next day. JPs: Nich's. Hyland, Nathan Baker. Alienation fine of 8 shillings paid 13 Dec 1751 to Matts. Bordley. Rec: 13 Dec 1751. Ms. Bordley, Clerk.

P. 353   Power of Attorney.   John Aug't. Lawson of Cecil Co. and his wife Mary appoint their trusty friend and brother Peter Lawson of the same place to be their attorney to recover all debts due them. Made 10 Dec 1751. Wit: Daniel Ryon, Adam VanBebber, Elisabeth Frasher. Ackn: same day. JP: Adam VanBebber. Rec: 23 Dec 1751. M's. Bordley, Clerk.

P. 355   Bill of Sale.   John Drummond of Cecil Co., merchant, to William Hedges of the same county, a Negro man named Jack (which the said John Drummond recently bought from James McLacklan of Cecil Co.) William Hedges and James McLacklan have "superseded" for John Drummond in a lawsuit filed by Henry Harrison of Philadelphia against Drummond. Also another suit brought by Michael Neidy against Drummond. James McLacklan has entered a bond to the said John Drummond for £230 and Drummond is to pay the several charges mentioned on or by 10 Feb next. When the obligation is settled then this bill of sale will be void. Made 22 Oct 1751. Wit: John Walker, James Schee. Rec: 30 Dec 1751. M's. Bordley, Clerk.

P. 356   Assignment of Lease.   Written on the back of a lease from Ephraim Augustine Herman to Francis Forster and recorded in Lib. S. K. No. 5, pgs 5-6, Tho's. Forster assigns his interest in half of the leased land to Robert Thompson. Said land was bequeathed to Thomas Forster by his father Francis Forster's Last Will and Testament. Made & Ackn: 9 Sep 1751. Wit. & JPs: P. Bayard, Adam VanBebber. Rec: 3 Jan 1752. M's. Bordley, Clerk.

P. 356   Lease.   Benjamin Tasker of Annapolis, Agent and Receiver General, for rents and services on behalf of Lord Baltimore and with the consent of Gov. Samuel Ogle, for rents and services, to Andrew Gibson of Cecil Co., 60 acres, part of his Lordship's Manor of Susquehanna alias New Connah. Lease is for the term of the natural lives of the said Andrew Gibson, Elizabeth Gibson and Thomas Gibson. Rent of 12 shillings due every 1 Jan. Tenants are to build a dwelling house and plant and fence an orchard of 100 apple trees. Made 15 Sep 1749. Wit: Benj'a. Chew. Rec: 8 Jan 1752. M's. Bordley, Clerk.

P. 359   Lease.   Jane Thompson of Cecil Co., for rents and services, to Lydia Houston of the same place, 69 acres of land, part of a tract called the Addition on the south side of Bohemia River (which was formerly conveyed by Hugh Watson to Augustine Terry, both of Cecil Co.) by the main road leading from Bohemia Ferry to the head of Sassafras. Lease is for the term of the natural life of the said Lydia Houston. Rent of 1 bushel of wheat due 10 Mar yearly and a year of Indian corn for the acknowledgement. Made 16 Jan 1752. Wit: Mary Taylor, John Brown. Rec: 8 Jan 1752.

P. 360   Assignment of Lease.   Richard Patton of Cecil Co., shipwright, for £15, to John Simpass, all his interest in a lease. Made 9 Nov 1751. Wit: Henry Baker, Nathan Baker. Ackn: same day by Richard Patton and his wife Rebecca. JPs: Nath'n. Baker, Nich'o. Hyland. John Simpass paid £50 [sic] to Richard Patton the same day. Memo: this was endorsed on the back of a lease "recorded on page 47 of this book" [see pg 150, entry P. 47.] Rec: 28 Jan 1751. M's. Bordley, Clerk.

P. 361   Bill of Sale.   George Johnson of Cecil Co., cordwainer, for £11.5s, to Andrew Barrett of the said county, 1 bed and its furniture, a pot and pot rack, a parcel of pewter (10 plates, 2 dishes, 2 basins), a chest and 2 chairs and a brass mortar. Made 7 Feb 1752. Wit: W. Husbands, Jr., Grace Smith. Ackn: same day. JP: John Smith. Rec: 10 Feb 1752. M's. Bordley, Clerk.

P. 361 Lease. Peter Aug't. Bouchell of Cecil Co., gent., and his wife Catharine, daughter of Col. Ephraim Augustine Herman, deceased, and John Aug't. Lawson of said county, gent., and his wife Mary, also daughter of the said Col. Ephraim Augustine Herman, for yearly rents and services, to John Carnan of the said county, 300 acres of land between the head of Cedar Branch and Indian Branch, part of Bohemia Manor, by the ancient highway. Lease is for the term of the natural lives of the said John Carnan and his sons William Carnan and John Carnan, Jr. Rent of £2.8s and 2 dunghill fowls due every 10 Dec. Made & Ackn: 27 Jan 1752. Wit. & JPs: Tho's. Colvill, P. Bayard. Rec: 19 Feb 1752. M's. Bordley, Clerk.

P. 365 Deed. Nathan Worley of Charles Town, Cecil Co., for 5 shillings, to John Lacky of the same place, yeoman, the southernmost half of lot #106 in Charles Town on Baltimore and Cecil Streets, distinguished in the plan by the letter "N" and bordering on lot #92. Made 8 Feb 1752. Wit: Philip Cazier, Jr., Hukel Guilder. Ackn: same day. JPs: Benj'a. Chew, John Smith. Rec: 19 Feb 1752. M's. Bordley, Clerk.

P. 366 Bill of Sale. William Grace of Cecil Co., planter, for £10, to Jethro Brown, 1 black horse with a brown nose, 1 feather bed, 2 iron pots, 4 pewter dishes, 12 pewter plates, 2 guns, 3 porringers, and all other of his household goods. Made & Ackn: 7 Feb 1752. Wit. & JP: Nathan Baker. Rec: 23 Feb 1752. M's. Bordley, Clerk.

P. 366 Deed of Gift. Benjamin Pearce of Cecil Co., and his wife Margaret, daughter of Henry Ward, late of Cecil Co., deceased, for natural love and affection, leases to their son William Pearce, land called Three Bohemia Sisters, part of a tract bequeathed by Augustine Herman to his daughter Anna Margaretta, lying between Broad Creek and Long Creek by Nath'l. Chick's mill dam on Broad Creek. Lease is for the term of the natural lives of the said William Pearce, Henry Ward Pearce and Andrew Pearce, sons of the said Benjamin and Margaret Pearce. Rent of 20 shillings due every 25 March. Made & Ackn: 28 Aug 1751. Wit. & JPs: John Veazey, Adam VanBebber. Rec: 27 Feb 1752. M's. Bordley, Clerk.

P. 367 Deed. Frances Ann Farra of Philadelphia, widow, for £17, to John Chisholm of Cecil Co., gent., lot #48 in Frederick Town in Cecil Co. Frances Ann Farra appoints her trusty friends James Calder, James Hollyday and Thomas Ringold her attorneys. Made 27 Feb 1752. Wit: Alex'r. Lunan, Rob't. Stratlett [sp?,] Mayor of Philadelphia. Ackn: 11 Mar 1752 by Alexander Lunan of Cecil Co. and Thomas Ringold, attorney. Rec: 11 Mar 1752. M's. Bordley, Clerk.

P. 369 Deed. Isaac Daws of Charles Town, Cecil Co., tanner, and his wife Mary, for £60, to Edward Mitchell of the same place, merchant, one half of lot #94 in Charles Town on Conestogo St., conveyed to Isaac Daws by Hugh Foster who was conveyed the lot from Edward Johnson who originally owned the lot. Made & Ackn: 7 Mar 1752. Wit: by JPs James Baxter, Nich'o. Hyland and by Elisha Hughes. Rec: 11 Mar 1752. M's. Bordley, Clerk.

P. 370 Deed. Joseph Bass of Cecil Co., planter, by power of attorney from Peter Hance of Fredrec Co. dated 20 Feb 1752, for 30 shillings, to William Husbands of Cecil Co., planter, 5 acres of land, part of a tract called Bourn's Walnut Thickett in Cecil Co. on the east side of Conewowango [sic] Creek. Made: 7 Mar 1752. Wit: James Baxter, Nath'n. Baker, Will. Husband, Jr. Ackn: same day by Joseph Bass by power of attorney witnessed by George Johnson. JPs: Nath'n. Baker, James Baxter. Rec: 11 Mar 1752. M's. Bordley, Clerk.

P. 371 Power of Attorney. Peter Hance of Fredrec Co., farmer, because he is moving, appoints as his attorneys his trusty friends Joseph Bass and John Death, both of Cecil Co., to make over a deed of 5 acres to William Husbands of Cecil Co. Made 12 Feb 1752. Wit: George Johnson. Ackn: by George Johnson 7 Mar 1752. JPs: Nath'n. Baker, James Baxter. Rec: 11 Mar 1752. M's. Bordley, Clerk.

P. 372 Deed of gift. Peter Bayard of Cecil Co., gent., son and heir of Samuel Bayard, late of said county, deceased, for natural love and affection and for 5 shillings, to his brother James Bayard of the same place, gent., the southern moiety of 868 acres of land on Bohemia River, part of a tract called Second Neck laid out of Bohemia Manor where the said James Bayard now lives and which he possesses for life by devise of his father Samuel Bayard. Made & Ackn: 10 Mar 1752. Wit. & JPs: R'd. Thompson, Adam VanBebber. Rec: 11 Mar 1752. M's. Bordley, Clerk.

P. 373 Division of Land. Samuel Bayard of Cecil Co., gent., releases to James Bayard of the same county, merchant, the southernmost moiety of a tract of 858 acres of land on which the great house stands. James Bayard releases to Samuel Bayard the northernmost moiety of the said tract of land. Samuel Bayard, deceased father of the said Samuel and James Bayard, owned the 858 acres, part of a tract of 1,700 acres called Second Neck formerly laid out of Bohemia Manor. Samuel Bayard the father, by his Last Will and Testament, devised one half of his then dwelling plantation jointly to his said sons to be shared equally, the other half of the said tract of Second Neck being given to his brother-in-law Henry Sluyter. Made & Ackn: 10 Mar 1752. Wit. & JPs: R'd. Thompson, Adam VanBebber. Rec: 11 Mar 1752. M's. Bordley, Clerk.

P. 376 Agreement. Benjamin Sluyter of Cecil Co., gent., for the premises and for £5, to James Bayard of the same place, gent., an annuity of 4s9p from the moiety of the Second Neck tract now possessed by Benjamin Sluyter, to be paid on the feast of St. Michael every year at the great house. By deeds of division dated 30 Aug 1722, Benjamin Sluyter and James Bayard hold several separate moieties of a tract of 1,700 acres called Second Neck, being part of Bohemia Manor. Said land was formerly jointly owned by Samuel Bayard and Henry Sliter [Sluyter,] fathers of the said Benjamin Sluyter and James Bayard. James Bayard is the present owner of the great house and his holding is subject to annual rent of £7. Made & Ackn: 10 Mar 1752. Wit. & JPs: R'd. Thompson, Adam VanBebber. Rec: 11 Mar 1752. M's. Bordley, Clerk.

P. 378 Deed of Gift. Peter Bayard of Cecil Co., gent., son and heir of Samuel Bayard, late of Cecil Co., deceased, for 5 shillings and for the natural love and affection he has for his brother Samuel Bayard of the same place, gent., releases to Samuel Bayard all his rights to the northern moiety of a tract of 868 acres called Second Neck on Bohemia River, being the land where the said Samuel Bayard now dwells and possesses for life by the devise of his father Samuel Bayard. Made & Ackn: 10 Mar 1752. Wit. & JPs: R'd. Thompson, Adam VanBebber. Rec: 11 Mar 1752. M's. Bordley, Clerk.

P. 379 Bill of Sale. James O'Bryan of Cecil Co., farmer, for £109.13s.6p, to James Bayard of the same county, merchant, 1 cow and it's calf, 4 cows, 2 yearlings, 1 heifer, 1 sow and 8 pigs, 8 shoats six months old, 1 breeding sow, 7 ewes and lambs, 4 old sheep and a 12 year old black mare, 1 bright bay horse 10 years old, 1 small bay 5 years old, 1 sorrel 9 years old, 1 grey horse 6 years old, an old iron cart, 1 plough, 1 plow shear and colter, 1 iron tooth harrow, 20 bushels of wheat unthrashed, three fourths of the field of wheat sowed on the plantation where O'Bryan lives, supposedly 45 acres, 2 mattocks, 4 narrow axes, 2 broad hoes, 1 narrow hoe and 1 servant man named Cornelius Cliff who has about 3 years to serve. These goods to be sold at public auction and O'Bryan is obliged to pay to James Bayard any amount of money that the sale of the goods brings short of the above said sum of money. Made & Ackn: 4 Mar 1752. Wit: P. Bayard, Wm. Wheland. JP: P. Bayard. Rec: 11 Mar 1752. M's. Bordley, Clerk.

P. 380 Lease. Peter Aug't. Bouchell and John Aug't. Lawson of Cecil Co., gents., for yearly rents and services, to Francis Ozier of the same place, yeoman, 70 acres of land lying between James Bayard's patent line and Henry McCoy's manor lease and down to Back Creek. Lease is for the term of the natural lives of the said Francis Ozier, his wife Mary and Sarah Lusk, spinster, who the said Ozier brought up from a child. Rent of £1.5s and 2 dunghill fowls due every 10 Dec. Made & Ackn: 20 Dec 1751. Wit. & JPs: Tho. Colvill, P. Bayard. Peter Lawson signed as attorney for John Aug't. Lawson. Rec: 11 Mar 1752. M's. Bordley, Clerk.

P. 382 Lease. James Douglass of Cecil Co., for rent and services, to Hartley Sappington of the same county, land on the south side of Bohemia River adjoining the river on the east side of Smith's Creek, part of a tract called Vulcan's Rest. Lease is for 11 years. Hartley Sappington agrees to repair the existing dwelling house, tobacco house and the fencing. Sappington can take 1 tenant under him for a yearly rent. Sappington will pay yearly every 5 Mar £17. Made & Ackn: 25 Feb 1752. Wit. & JPs: John Veazey, Pereg'r. Ward. Rec: 11 Mar 1752. M's. Bordley, Clerk.

P. 383 Lease. Peter Aug't. Bouchell and John Aug't. Lawson of Cecil Co., gents., for yearly rents and services, to Richard Ford, yeoman, 200 acres of land, part of Bohemia Manor, formerly leased to John Husbands of the said county, called Husband's Choice on the north side of Newcastle Road by a corner that was Ann Hughes' land and by Herring Creek. Lease is for the term of the natural lives of Richard Ford's wife Mary Ford and their sons Richard Boulding Ford and Edward Ford. Rent of £3 and 2 dunghill fowls due 1 Feb yearly. Made & Ackn: 7 Feb 1752. Wit. & JPs: Tho's. Colvill, P. Bayard. Catharine Bouchell, wife of Peter Aug't. Bouchell, also acknowledged the lease. Rec: 11 Mar 1752. M's. Bordley, Clerk.

P. 385 Lease. Joseph Wood of Cecil Co., gent., for yearly rents and services, to Thomas Stewart of the same place, 161 acres of land, part of the tract called Three Bohemia Sisters, on the north side of Back Creek by Jacob Young's landing and cartway. Three Bohemia Sisters was formerly Willed by Augustine Herman to his daughter Francinea, grandmother to the said Joseph Wood (by a recent survey the land has been named Francinea.) Lease is for the term of the natural lives of the said Thomas Stewart's children William Stewart and Ann Stewart and his nephew John Scott. Rent of 7s.6p and 2 dunghill fowls due every 27 Oct. The tenants have free access to the

Colvill's and Young's landings on Back Creek. Made & Ackn: 11 Jan 1752. Wit. & JPs: R'd. Thompson, Adam VanBebber. Rec: 11 Mar 1752. M's. Bordley, Clerk.

P. 387 Lease. Samuel Davis of Fairfax Co., VA, planter, and Williminchie his wife, for £50 and yearly rents and covenants, to Richard Griffith of Cecil Co., farmer, 55 acres of land, the eastern part of a tract belonging to Paul Poulson, deceased, called the Glass House and given by the said Paul Poulson in his lifetime to the said Williminchie by deed of gift. Lease is for 99 years. Made 26 Sep 1751. Wit: John Bond, John Davis. Rec: 11 Mar 1752. M's. Bordley, Clerk.

P. 388 Bill of Sale. Thomas Fankett of Cecil Co., planter, for £10.17s.10p, to James Bayard of the same county, merchant, 3 cows, 2 mares and all his household goods. Made 19 Feb 1752. Wit: P. Bayard, Wm. Wheeland. JP: P. Bayard. Rec: 11 Mar 1752.

P. 389 Lease. Peter Aug't. Bouchell and John Aug't. Lawson of Cecil Co., gents., for yearly rents and services, to Robert Mansfield of Kent Co., 125 acres, part of Bohemia Manor, on the northwest side of Hogg Creek by land that was leased to Solomon Bowen and by Herring Creek. Also land on the said Manor which was once occupied by Bennet Jump bounded by land once possessed by Humphrey Alcock. Said land once possessed and occupied by James Moody, now belonging to James Bayard, by Nicholas Vandegriff and McCoy's lands. Lease is for the term of the natural lives of Sidney George (son of Joshua George) and Robert Mansfield's sons John Mansfield and James Mansfield. Rent of £6 and 2 dunghill fowls due every 10 Dec. Made & Ackn: 7 Feb 1752. Wit. & JPs: Tho's. Colvill, P. Bayard. Also acknowledged by Catharine Bouchell, wife of Peter Aug't. Bouchell. Rec: 12 Mar 1752. M's. Bordley, Clerk.

P. 391 Deed. James Elliott of Cecil Co., farmer, for £60, to Thomas Ricketts of the same place, blacksmith, 50 acres, part of a tract of 200 acres called Kittavilly which Charles Carroll conveyed to James Elliott by deed dated 27 May 1751. Made & Ackn: 13 Mar 1752. Wit: Nich'o. Hyland, Nath'n. Baker, Daniel Neide. JPs: Nich'o. Hyland, Nath'n. Baker. Alienation fine of 2 shillings paid same day. Rec: 13 Mar 1752. Matt's. Bordley, Clerk.

P. 392 Deed. Matthias Matthiason of Biddeford, England, and his attorney Francis Bonner of Cecil Co., for £200, to John Cox of the same county, 100 acres of land in Cecil Co. called Matthiason's Point on the north side of Sassafras River and the west side of Wheeler's Creek. Also 140 acres of land called Corneliason by Hendrick Matthiason's land. Also 30 acres called Matson's Range on the west side at the northern most fork of Matson's Creek. Except 100 acres out of the 3 tracts which was sold to John Baldwin of Cecil Co., gent., by the said Matthias Matthiason's father. In a power of attorney dated 1 Mar 1750 and recorded in Lib. F. L. No. 13, pgs 267-268, Matthias Matthiason appointed Francis Bonner as his attorney. Made & Ackn: 12 Mar 1752. Wit. & JPs: John Veazey, Benja. Chew. Rec: 13 Mar 1752. M's. Bordley, Clerk.

P. 394 Deed. Jacob Anderson, John Anderson and James Anderson, all of St. Georges Hundred, Newcastle Co. on Delaware, yeomen, for £10, to Robert Evans of Millford Hundred, Cecil Co., tanner, a marsh on the west side and near the head of Elk River contained within the west line of a tract called Price's Venture. The Andersons will warrant the land against any claims of John Campbell or his heirs and _____ Prichot and his heirs. Made 27 Sep 1751. Wit: R'd. Thompson, Dane Wills [Daniel Wills?.] Ackn: 28 Sep 1751 by Jacob and John Anderson. JPs: R'd. Thompson, Tho's. Colvill. Alienation fine of 5p paid 20 Mar 1752 to Matt's. Bordley. Rec: 12 Mar 1752.

P. 395 Bill of Sale. Daniel Gelder of Cecil Co., laborer, for £6, to Richard Barnaby of the same place, planter, 1 brown horse branded with an "SH". [Gelder is also spelled Golder.] Made 6 Mar 1752. Wit: John Ricketts, Tho's. Ricketts. Rec: 21 Mar 1752.

P. 396 Deed. James Boulding, farmer, and his wife Elizabeth, for £30.8s, to Johanas Arrants, cordwainer, a moiety of a tract of land on Elk River. By his Last Will and Testament dated 24 May 1748, Nathan Philips, late of Cecil Co., deceased, devised to his two sons-in-law James Boulding and Johanas Arrants, land on the north side of Elk River. [Boulding is also spelled Bouldin.] Made 2 Dec 1751. Wit: Adam VanBebber, Jno. Cage. Note: Capt. Zebulon Hollingsworth and Capt. Nicholas Hyland divided the said tract of land which was part of St. John's Manor laid out for 26 acres. Ackn: 5 Dec 1751. JPs: R'd. Thompson, Adam VanBebber. Rec: 24 Mar 1752. M's. Bordley, Clerk.

P. 397 Deed. Thomas Jacobs of Cecil Co., yeoman, and Martha his wife, for 5 shillings, to Zebulon Hollingsworth of the same county, innholder, a marsh of 35 acres on the west side of Elk River, part of a 70 acre tract called Jacob's Chance which Charles Lord Baltimore granted by patent dated 30 Jul 1713 to Thomas Jacobs. Made 26 Mar 1752. Wit: Geo. Rock, Nich'o. Hyland, Geo. Cattoe. Thomas Jacobs has right to pass through the marsh.

Ackn: same day. JPs: Nich'o. Hyland, Geo. Rock. Alienation fine of 17p paid same day by Hollingsworth to Matt's. Bordley. Rec: 26 Mar 1752.

P. 399   Deed.   Charles Carroll of Annapolis, esq., for £95 and because he is moving, to Moses Andrews of Cecil Co., 225 acres of land in Cecil Co., part of a tract called Society. Made & Ackn: 21 Nov 1751. Wit: Geo. Lawson, Robert Rowland. JP: Geo. Stewart. Moses Andrews paid 9s alienation fine to Matt's. Bordley 27 Mar 1751. Rec: same day.

P. 400   Deed.   Zebulon Hollingsworth of Cecil Co., innholder, and Mary his wife, for £200, to James Frier of the same place, farmer, 300 acres of land. Henry Hollingsworth, surveyor of Cecil Co., deceased, on 20 Jan 1713 bought 300 acres (part of a tract called New Munster) from Peter Massey and his wife Sarah. Zebulon Hollingsworth, son and surviving executor of the said Henry Hollingsworth, on 27 Mar 1746 met on the premises and fixed the boundaries for 300 acres of land. Made & Ackn: 26 Mar 1752. Wit: Geo. Cattto, Matt's. Bordley, Robert Evans. JPs: Nich'o. Hyland, Geo. Rock. James Frier paid 6s alienation fine to Matt's. Bordley. Rec: 27 Mar 1752. M's. Bordley, Clerk.

P. 402   Release.   Charles Carroll of Annapolis, esq., for 5 shillings and because he is moving, releases to William Whan of Cecil Co., farmer, 150 acres of land in Cecil Co. by George Lawson's land. Said land is part of a tract called Society formerly granted by Charles Carroll of Annapolis, father of the said Charles Carroll, to Morgan Patton by deed dated 6 Aug 1719. By deed dated 29 Oct 1719, Morgan Patton conveyed the land to Roger Lawson who conveyed it to his son Hugh Lawson by deed of gift. Hugh Lawson conveyed it to James Allison who conveyed the land to William Whan. Made & Ackn: 21 Nov 1751. Wit: Geo. Lawson, Robert Rowland. JP: Geo. Stewart. Rec: 4 Apr 1752. M's. Bordley, Clerk.

P. 403   Deed.   Peter Boyer and Hester his wife and John Lewis and his wife Mary of Cecil Co., farmers, for £140, to Michael Lum of the said county, farmer, 115 acres of land (part of St. John's Manor) on the west side of Elk River near the mouth of Cockerells Creek. [Hester Boyer is also called Ester Boyer.] Made & Ackn: 15 Nov 1752. Wit: Nich'o. Hyland, Matt's. Bordley, Nath'n. Baker. JPs: Nich'o. Hyland, Nath'n. Baker. Michael Lum paid 4 shillings alienation fine 4 Apr 1752 to county clerk Matt's. Bordley who recorded the deed on the same day.

P. 406   Receipt.   Some years ago Hance Rudulph made over to William Hitchman a servant man named Nicholas Crowly in exchange for Hitchman paying to Rudulph 9,000 trunnels to be delivered to Mr. George Adams at Christeen Bridge. Rudulph acknowledges receipt of full satisfaction from George Adams on account of said William. Made 4 Apr 1751. Wit: Joh's. Arrants, Edward Phillips. Rec: same day.

P. 406   Assignment of Lease.   Endorsed on the back of a lease from Ephraim Augustine Herman to Francis Forster, an assignment from Thomas Forster to Robert Thompson is recorded on pg 356 of this book [see pg 199, entry P. 356.] Memo made 21 Mar 1752: Robert Thompson of Cecil Co. assigns the lease to Charles Ford for the sum of £60. Wit & JPs: R'd. Thompson, P. Bayard. Ackn: same day. Rec: 11 Apr 1752. M's. Bordley, Clerk.

P. 406   Deed.   William Boggs of Cecil Co., for £150, to John Bailey of Newcastle Co. on Delaware, 150 acres, part of a tract called Providence, by John Thompson's tract. By patent dated 8 Jun 1732 from Samuel Robins, William Boggs was granted a tract of 350 acres called Providence in Cecil Co. Made & Ackn: 25 Jan 1752. Wit: by JPs Geo. Rock and Nath'n. Baker and by Rosanna Maybury. John Bailey paid 6s½p alienation fine 14 Apr 1752 to Matt's. Bordley, clerk, who recorded the deed the same day.

P. 408   Bill of Sale.   George Rock of Cecil Co., for 5 shillings, to Robert Cumings of the said county, all his goods and chattels listed on the annexed inventory. If George Rock should pay to Enoch, Thomas and Mary Mory, the 3 youngest children of Robert Mory, deceased, the full sum that is due them as dividends of their father's estate on or by 25 Mar next then this bill of sale is void. [Should Mory be Money?] Made 13 Apr 1752. Wit: Nathan Baker, Joyce Baker. Rec: 24 Apr 1752. M's. Bordley, Clerk.

P. 409   Inventory.   The following is the list of goods and chattels which George Rock gives as security to Robert Cumings for payment of £308.8s to the three youngest children of Robert Mory, deceased. Inventory made 13 Apr 1752 and witnessed by Nathan Baker. Ackn: by George Rock 15 Apr 1752 before Nathan Baker. The inventory consists of a very long and specific list of household goods including a mulatto slave called Jo and a Negro called Ragoo now in the hands of _____ White and _____ Harrison. Rec: 24 Apr 1752. M's. Bordley, Clerk.

P. 410   Deed.   John Chisholm of Charles Town, Cecil Co., schoolmaster, for £17, to Michael Earle of Frederick Town, Cecil Co., gent., lot #48 in Cecil Town. Made 9 Apr 1752. Wit: Thomas Elliot, Jno. Hyland, Jr. The consideration sum was paid to John Chisholm 30 Apr 1752. Wit: Nath'n. Baker,

Matt's. Bordley. Ackn: 1 May 1752. JPs: James Baxter, Nath'n. Baker. Rec: same day. M's. Bordley, Clerk.

P. 411   Deed of Gift.   Mary Stump of Cecil Co., for natural love and affection and because she is moving, gives to her son Henry Stump all her goods, chattels, leases, debts, plate, jewels, etc., in the annexed list. Made 29 Apr 1752. Wit: B'a. Chew, Jr., John Welsh, William Welsh. Mary Stump gave to Henry Stump 1 pewter dish and 1 pewter tankard in good faith for the rest of the list of goods. Ackn: 1 May 1752. JP: Benj'a. Chew. Rec: 4 May 1752. M's. Bordley, Clerk.

P. 412   Deed of Gift.   David Ricketts of Cecil Co., for natural affection and because he is moving, gives to his daughter-in-law Rachel Penington 1 Negro girl named Patt about 2 years old. Made 18 Apr 1752. Wit: Wm. Pearce, B. Penington. Rec: 4 May 1752.

P. 413   Indenture.   John Dillon of Cecil Co., laborer, agrees to bind himself to Benedict Penington of Cecil Co., planter, to be Penington's servant at the rate of £6 per year until the amount discharges all debts he the said Dillon now owes. John Dillon will not absent himself nor marry during the time of his servitude without the consent of Benedict Penington who will provide for Dillon meat, drink, washing, lodging and apparel. Made 1 Apr 1752. Wit: Thomas Kees, Rebecca Penington, Rachel Penington. Rec: 4 May 1752.

P. 413   Deed.   John Holtham of Cecil Co., innholder, for £100, to Thomas Ogle of Newcastle Co., Territories of PA, land now occupied by the said John Holtham, part of a tract condemned by a Writ by Thomas Colvill of Cecil Co., gent., near the head and on the north side of Bohemia Back Creek near the mill house occupied by the said Thomas Ogle. Said land was bought by John Holtham from Peter Lawson of Cecil Co. at public auction, not including the land leased by Howel James from Joseph Wood, who are both now deceased. Made & Ackn: 21 Mar 1752. Wit. & JPs: R'd. Thompson, P. Bayard. Rec: 7 May 1752. M's. Bordley, Clerk.

P. 414   Assignment of Lease.   Cornelius Wooliston of Cecil Co., farmer, for £120, to Anthony Fartado of the same county, a lease of land in Bohemia Manor. Ephraim Augustine Herman, late of Cecil Co., gent., on 1 May 1728 leased to Rene' Julien land in Bohemia Manor which was a vacancy between Newcastle Road and the lands of Charles Mullins, Henry Dehoof and John Sidler. The lease was for the term of the natural lives of the said Rene' Julien and his sons Stephen Julien and Peter Julien. Rent of £2 and 2 dunghill fowls due every 23 Nov. This lease was recorded in Lib. S. K., No. 5, folios

138-139. For £40, Rene' Julien sold the lease to Henry McCay of the said county and it was recorded in Lib. W. K., No. 2, folios 337-338. For £70, Henry McCay sold the lease to Abraham Allman which was recorded in Lib. W. K. No. 9, folio 19. Abraham Allman, for natural love and affection, transferred the land by deed of gift dated 15 Oct 1740 to his son Joseph Allman. Teresa Allman, widow, and Dr. Hugh Matthews, Jr., assignees and appointed executors of the estate of Joseph Allman, for £190.12s, sold the lease to the said Cornelius Wooliston and the transaction was recorded in Lib. F. L. No. 13, folios 40-41. Made & Ackn: 3 Apr 1752. Wit. & JPs: R'd. Thompson, Adam VanBebber. Rec: 9 May 1752. M's. Bordley, Clerk.

P. 416 Record of Mark. Oliver Miller records his mark for cattle, hogs and sheep as a hole in the near ear and a cross and 2 slits in the off ear. Made and Rec: 9 May 1752.

P. 417 Notice of Stray. Hartley Sappington, Deputy Ranger in Sassafras has 2 strays: a black horse with saddle spots branded on the near buttock "RI" and a black mare with star on her forehead, no brand. Rec: 15 May 1752.

P. 417 Bill of Sale. Christopher Hollands of Cecil Co., planter, to Jethro Brown, for £27.3s.4p, 1 sorrel horse, 1 mare, a brown cow, 2 ewes: one red and the other brown, 2 black prize heifers 2 years old, 3 feather beds, a black walnut chest, and other household goods. Made 1 May 1752. Wit: Nath'n. Baker. Ackn: next day before JP Nath'n. Baker. Rec: 16 May 1752. M's. Bordley, Clerk.

P. 417 Deed. Mary Ross and Rebecca Mackenna of Frederick Co., for £9.7s and because they are moving, to Thomas Meek of the same place, 81 acres of land called New Munster in Cecil Co. on Elk River. Made 6 Nov 1751. Wit: Nath. Wickham, John Stone Hawkins. Ackn: 26 Nov 1751. JPs: Nath. Wickham, Nath. Alexander. Jno. Darnall, Frederick County Clerk, certifies that Nathaniel Wickham and Nathaniel Alexander are JPs for Frederick Co. on 26 Nov 1751. Rec: 19 May 1752.

P. 419 Deed of Gift. Cornelius Eliason, Sr., of Cecil Co., farmer, for natural love and affection, gives to his loving son-in-law Abraham Williams of Newcastle Co., PA, farmer, a Negro woman named Hannah. Made & Ackn: 23 May 1752. Wit: Henry Penington and JPs Adam VanBebber, P. Bayard. Rec: same day.

P. 419   Deed of Gift.   Cornelius Eliason, Sr., of Cecil Co., farmer, for natural love and affection, gives to his well beloved son Elias Eliason of the said county, farmer, a Negro man named Bohemia, a Negro woman named Patience and a Negro boy named George. Made (_?_) May 1752. Wit: P. Bayard, Rich'd. Canter. Ackn: 23 May 1752. JPs: P. Bayard, Adam VanBebber. Rec: same day. M's. Bordley, Clerk.

P. 420   Deed of Gift.   Cornelius Eliason, Sr., of Cecil Co., farmer, for natural love and affections, gives to his well beloved son Cornelius Eliason of the said county, farmer, a Negro man named Tom. Made (_?_) May 1752. Wit: P. Bayard, Rich'd. Canter. Ackn: 23 May 1752. JPs: P. Bayard, Adam VanBebber. Rec: same day. M's. Bordley, Clerk.

P. 420   Deed of Gift.   Cornelius Eliason, Sr., of Cecil Co., farmer, for natural love and affection, gives to his loving son-in-law John Woods of Kent Co., PA, farmer, and his wife Rebecca, a Negro woman named Sall and her child named Peter. [In the acknowledgement, the child Peter is called Toney.] Made (_?_) May 1752. Wit: P. Bayard, Rich'd. Canter. Ackn: 23 May 1752. JPs: P. Bayard, Adam VanBebber. Rec: same day. M's. Bordley, Clerk.

P. 421   Deed.   William Wallace and Ketrine his wife of Cecil Co., for £64.10s, to John Faires of Pencader Hundred, Newcastle Co. on Delaware, 65 acres of land by land belonging to the heirs of Henry Ward, by the road leading from Andrew Alexander's to Broad Creek and by a tract called Charlosis Camp. Said land is the easternmost part of a tract of 400 acres called Jones' Spring Green in Cecil Co. which was formerly granted to William Harris of Kent Co. Made 1 Apr 1752. Wit: John Faires, Sam'l. Adaer. Ackn: 3 Apr 1752 by William and his wife Cath. JPs: R'd. Thompson, Adam VanBebber. Alienation fine of 2s7p paid to Matt's. Bordley by John Faires 27 May 1752. Rec: same day.

P. 423   Lease.   Richard Kennard of Kent Co., farmer, for 10 shillings, to William Bordley of Cecil Co., gent., 500 acres of land called Pullen's Refuge in Cecil Co. by land laid out for Nicholas Painter at the head of Sassafras River and by the Indian path from the river to Appoqueniman Creek. For the term of 1 year. [Kennard is also spelled Kenword, Kenward.] Made & Ackn: 3 Dec 1751. Wit. & JPs: John Veazey, Pereg'r. Ward. Rec: 30 May 1752. M's. Bordley, Clerk.

P. 424   Release.   Richard Kennard of Kent Co., farmer, for 8,000 lbs of tobacco, to William Bordley of Cecil Co., gent., 500 acres of land called

Pullen's Refuge [see previous entry P. 423.] Richard Kennard warrants the land against any claims by or for Richard Pullen, grandfather of the said Richard Kennard, to whom Pullen's Refuge was first granted by patent. Made & Ackn: 3 Dec 1751. Wit: John Veazey, Pereg'r. Ward, Wm. Pearce, Edward Furroner. Ackn. and receipt for 8,000 lbs of tobacco dated 4 Dec signed by Richard Kinword [sic.] JPs: John Veazey and Pereg'r. Ward. Alienation fine of 20 shillings paid by William Bordley to Matt's. Bordley 14 Dec 1751. Rec: 13 May 1752.

P. 427   Bill of Sale.   Attached to a bill of sale from Daniel Johnson to Edward Ricketts which was recorded in Lib. W. K. L. No. 8, pgs 266-267: Edward Ricketts, for £11, to Andrew Barratt of Cecil Co., blacksmith, the said bill of sale and the listed household goods and implements. Made & Ackn: 4 Jun 1752. Wit: John Smith, Grace Smith. JP: John Smith. Rec: 5 Jun 1752. M's. Bordley, Clerk.

P. 427   Notice of Stray.   John Taylor found a black "ronish" horse near Principio Iron Works on 4 Jun 1752. Owner may claim horse at John Taylor's place 8 Jun 1752. Rec: 8 Jun 1752.

P. 427   Lease.   Peter Aug't. Bouchell and John Aug't. Lawson of Cecil Co., gents., for yearly rents and services, to Thomas Ogle of Newcastle Co. on Delaware, gent., 140 acres of land on Back Creek, part of Bohemia Manor, near Thomas Moor's plantation. Said land was granted by Ephraim Aug't. Herman to Walter Newman by lease dated 15 Nov 1722 and lately in the possession of Edward Means. Lease is for the term of the natural lives of the said Thomas Ogle, Sr. and his children Thomas Ogle and Mary Ogle. Rent of £2.10s and 2 dunghill fowls due every 10 Dec. Peter Lawson acting as attorney for John Aug. Lawson. Made & Ackn: 14 May 1752. Wit. & JPs: R'd. Thompson, P. Bayard. Rec: 10 Jun 1752. M's. Bordley, Clerk.

P. 429   Lease.   Peter Bouchell and John Lawson of Cecil Co., for yearly rents and services, to John Latham of the same county, innholder, land on Elk River, part of Bohemia Manor, between the lands of William Sinklar, William Thomas (deceased), Charles Dermott, Robert Veazey and Richard Taylor. Excepting only 78 acres already leased to Martin Nicholas. Lease is for the term of the natural lives of the said John Latham and his now wife Susannah Latham and the life of Sarah Latham. Rent of 50 shillings and one dunghill fowl due every 10 June. Made & Ackn: 1 Jun 1752. Wit. & JPs: R'd. Thompson, P. Bayard. Rec: 10 Jun 1752. M's. Bordley, Clerk.

P. 430   Deed.   Nathan Brown of Chester Co., PA, yeoman, and his wife Margaret, for 20 shillings, to Thomas Brown of Cecil Co., planter, 104½ acres and 38 perches of land on the east side of Susquehanna River, part of 2 tracts called Martin's Delight and Martin's Enlargement. Said tracts were granted to Thomas Brown, father of the said Nathan Brown and Thomas Brown, by Nathan Boys by deed dated 19 Apr 1742 and recorded in Lib. W. K. No. 9, folios 141-142. Nathan Brown is the eldest son and heir of Thomas Brown the father, now deceased. Made 15 Feb 1752. Wit: James Allen, John [Ehzod?], Rachel Adams. Ackn: _____ 1752. JPs: Nath'n. Baker, Geo. Rock. Thomas Brown paid 4s.3p alienation fine 10 Jun 1752 to Matt's. Bordley, who recorded the deed the same day.

P. 431   Deed.   Thomas Brown of Cecil Co., planter, and his wife Rachel, for £130, to James Allen of Chester Co., PA, 104½ acres and 38 perches of land on the east side of Susquehanna River, part of 2 tracts called Martin's Delight and Martin's Enlargement. Said land was granted to the said Thomas Brown by his brother Nathan Brown by deed dated 15 Feb last. Made & Ackn: 11 Apr 1752. Wits: Gco. Rock, Nath'n. Baker, Hower Greenland. JPs: Geo. Rock, Nath'n. Baker. James Allen paid 4s.3p alienation fine 10 Jun 1752 to M's. Bordley, who recorded the deed the same day.

P. 431   Bill of Sale.   Armwell Bayley, weaver, for £7.9s, to Cornelius Cray, farmer, 1 mouse colored mare and a gelding of the same color. If Bayley repays Cray by or on 1 Oct next then this obligation is void. [Armwell Bayley also spelled Aurmaell Baily.] Made 1 Jun 1752. Wit: John Lackey. Ackn: 13 Jun 1752. JP: Benj'a. Chew. Rec: 12 Jun 1752. M's. Bordley, Clerk.

P. 432   Assignment of Lease.   John Walker, son of John Walker, deceased, for £15, assigns this lease to Robert Thompson. Made & Ackn. 26 Mar 1752. Wit. & JPs: P. Bayard, Adam VanBebber. Rec: 13 Jun 1752. M's. Bordley, Clerk. Note: this lease recorded in Lib. S. K. No. 5, pgs 364-365.

P. 432   Lease.   Peter Aug't. Bouchell and Catharine his wife and John Aug't. Lawson and Mary his wife, all of Cecil Co., gents., for yearly rents and services, to Nicholas Wood of the same place, farmer, 200 acres in Bohemia Manor on the north side of the main road to Newcastle near the dwelling house of Abraham Allman, near Back Creek and by the line dividing the lands of John Cochran and Thomas Ogle. Lease is for the term of the natural lives of the said Nicholas Wood and his son Nicholas Wood and the life of Joseph Bouchell, son of Dr. Sluyter Bouchell. Rent of £2.10s and 2 dunghill fowls due every 10 Dec. Made & Ackn: 14 May 1752. Wit. & JPs: Thomas Collvill, P. Bayard. Rec: 20 Jun 1752.

P. 434 Deed. John Hance of Newcastle Co., PA, farmer, for £232.10s, to John Jackson, physician, of Cecil Co., 2 parcels of land in Cecil Co. The first tract is the remaining 200 acres of a tract called Daniel's Den on the south side of the easternmost branch of Back Creek adjoining tracts called Hackley and Civility on the west and Hill's Adventure on the south. The second tract is 68 acres called Hill's Adventure on the north side of Hack's Creek by ____ Hack's land. Except that part of Daniel's Den enclosed in the tract called Civility belonging to Thomas Penington. Made 25 Apr 1752. Wit. & JPs: R'd. Thompson, Adam VanBebber. Ackn: same day by John Hance and his wife Elonar. Rec: 16 Jul 1752. M's. Bordley, Clerk.

P. 435 Assignment of Lease. John Dunn of Cecil Co., mariner, for £11.14s.9p, to William Currer, 40 acres, Dunn's part of a lease for a tract called Copson's Park purchased by Wm. Smith from Maj. John Copson, being the upper part of the said tract adjoining John Read's land. Agreement void when John Dunn repays William Currer on or by 22 Jul next. Made & Ackn: 22 Jul 1752. Wit: Nich'o. Hyland, John Hyland. JPs: Nich'o. Hyland, James Baxter. Rec: 23 Jul 1752. M's. Bordley, Clerk.

P. 436 Deed. Alexander Kennedy of Cecil Co., smith, for a £22 bond to be paid by John Bonar, to John Bonar of the same place, smith, a plantation of 50 acres at the Chapel in Susquehanna New Connough Manor. Made 21 Jul 1752. Wit: Andrew Campbell, William Cuningham. Rec: 27 Jul 1752.

P. 436 Notice of Stray. A small bay mare has been found slightly injured and can be claimed by the owner at the plantation of Henry Stidham on Elk River. Made 28 Jul 1752 by Nich'o. Hyland. Rec: 29 Jul 1752. M's. Bordley, Clerk.

P. 436 Lease. Peter Aug'n. Bouchell and Catharine his wife and John Aug'n. Lawson and Mary his wife, all of Cecil Co., gents., for yearly rents and services, to Andrew Croo of the same place, planter, 125 acres of land in Bohemia Manor at the head of Herring Creek and on the west side of Hogg Creek. Lease is for the term of the natural lives of the said Andrew Croo, his wife Margaret Croo, and their son Andrew Croo. Rent of £3 and 2 dunghill fowls due every 10 Dec. Made & Ackn: 14 May 1752. Wit. & JPs: Tho. Collvill, P. Bayard. Rec: 1 Aug 1752. M's. Bordley, Clerk.

P. 437 Lease. Joseph Wood of Cecil Co., for yearly rents and services, to John Holtham of the said county, 91 acres on the north side of Back Creek by the mill and Jacob Young's cart road (except the mill land which was condemned.) Said land is part of Three Bohemia Sisters which was formerly Willed by Augustine Herman to his daughter Francine, grandmother to the said Joseph Wood, and later resurveyed and named Francina. John Holtham has liberty to divide 10 acres to Thomas Mills. Lease is for the term of the natural lives of John Haltham's son Spencer Haltham, his daughter Mary Mills and the life of John Veazey, son of John Veazey the son of Robert Veazey. Rent of 7s.6p and 2 dunghill fowls due every 27 Oct. [John Holtham is also called John Altham.] Made & Ackn: 30 Jul 1752. Wit. & JPs: Adam VanBebber, Geo. Rock. Rec: 3 Aug 1752. M's. Bordley, Clerk.

P. 439 Valuation of Estate. Henry VanBebber, guardian of William Parson, along with Adam VanBebber, one of the County Commissioners, Robert Veazey, Sr. and Charles Ford entered the lands of the said orphan and viewed the property on 18 Apr 1752. They found a dwelling house and kitchen "very much wrecked" with a cellar "all fallen in", a well framed tobacco house 40x12, and a straggling orchard of about 30 bearing apple trees and 10 or 12 young trees planted amongst them, 80 acres of cleared land with half of it fenced and probably 50 acres more cleared adjoining the plantation. They estimate the annual value of the place to be £8.10s. Made 2 Jun 1752. Rec: 11 Aug 1752.

P. 439 Bond. John Driscoll of Cecil Co., tailor, for security to Adam VanBebber of said county, gent., who has this day become special bail for Driscoll in an action brought against Driscoll in county court by Ignatias Wheeler for £12, to the said Adam VanBebber 1 brown horse 8 years old, a red & white spotted cow and calf, a feather bed and bedstead with bolsters, pillows and 2 blankets, and 2 tables. Void when John Driscoll repays VanBebber. Made 12 Aug 1752. Wit: Jas. Holliday, Chas. Gordon. Ackn: same day. JP: Nich'o. Hyland. Rec: same day.

P. 439 Notice of Stray. Richard Thompson has in his custody a bay mare branded with "ET". Owner may claim mare by proving the property and paying the charges. 13 Aug 1752. Rec: 14 Aug 1752.

P. 439 Deed. John Bavington of Cecil Co., for £20, to Sidney George of the said county, 50 acres of land, part of a tract called Addition, with half the plantation and all of the house thereon. By deed dated 5 Nov 1722, the 50 acres was conveyed by Hugh Terry, late of Cecil Co., deceased, to the said John Bavington. Made 13 Aug 1752. Wit. & JPs: Nich'o. Hyland, Thos.

Savin, John Canasque [it is not clear here if John Canasque was a witness or if he signed the deed as grantor along with John Bavington.] Ackn: by John Bavington and his wife Mary. Rec: 17 Aug 1752. Fran's. Key, Clerk.

P. 440 Notice of Stray. There is a stray on the plantation of William Mainly near Turkey Point on Elk River. The stray is a small brown horse branded with "TB". Said horse has been in that neighborhood for three months. Notice taken 16 Aug 1752 by JP Nich'o. Hyland. Rec: 20 Aug 1752. M's. Bordley, Clerk.

P. 440 Notice of Stray. Nich'o. Hyland reports there is a stray on the plantation of Joseph Lowman near Turkey Point. It is a small black horse branded with an "I" [or "J".] The horse was doing poorly when he came into the neighborhood where he has been for three months. Notice taken 17 Aug 1752. Rec: 22 Aug 1752. M's. Bordley, Clerk.

P. 440 Lease. Benjamin Tasker of Annapolis, Agent and Receiver General, for and on behalf of Lord Baltimore and with the consent of Gov. Samuel Ogle, for rents and services, to James Buchannan of Cecil Co., 50 acres of land, part of his Lordship's Manor of Susquehanna alias New Connah. Lease is for the term of the natural lives of the said James Buchannan, Eleanor Buchannan and John Buchannan. Rent is 10 shillings a year due every 1 Jan. James Buchannan will build a dwelling house and plant and fence an orchard of 100 apple trees. Made 20 Sep 1747. Wit: Benj'a. Chew, James Laper. Rec: 22 Aug 1752. M's. Bordley, Clerk.

P. 442 Release. Written on the back of a deed from Jacob Anderson and John Anderson to Robert Evans, which was recorded in this book on pgs 214-216 [see pg 171, Entry P. 214,] Elizabeth Carson of Newcastle Co., on 23 Jul 1752, made over to Robert Evans all her rights to the mentioned tract of land. She acknowledged her action before JPs John Baxter and Geo. Rock. Rec: 29 Aug 1752. M's. Bordley, Clerk.

P. 442 Deed. Philip Cazier, Jr., of Cecil Co., joiner, for £65 and because he is moving, to Henry Baker of the said county, gent., 45 acres which is part of several tracts called Smith's Addition, Vulcan's Rest and a tract called Venture in St. Stephens Parish on the west side of Smith's Creek by the road from Bohemia to Sassafras Neck. Made & Ackn: 30 Mar 1752. Wit: Nich'o. Hyland, Nath'n. Baker, John Arrants. JPs: Nich'o. Hyland, Nath'n. Baker. On 9 Apr 1752, Mary Cazier, wife of Philip Cazier, Jr., acknowledged the deed before JPs Nich'o. Hyland and Geo. Rock. Rec: 9 Aug 1752. M's. Bordley, Clerk.

P. 443   Mortgage.   Moses Jones of Cecil Co., for £60, to Nicholas Hyland of the same county, yeoman, 297 acres of land on the north side of Elk River by the land of John Hyland, Nicholas Hyland's brother, and by the line of St. John's Manor. Certificate of survey dated 23 Aug 1751. Moses Jones is to repay Nicholas Hyland on or by 20 Aug 1759. Made & Ackn: 31 Aug 1752. Wit. & JPs: Nath'n. Baker, Geo. Rock. On the same day Capt. Nicholas Hyland paid £60 to Moses Jones and he paid 11s.11p alienation fine to Matt's. Bordley who recorded the deed the same day.

P. 444   Bill of Sale.   George Vickers of Charlestown, joiner, for £20, to William Pennock of Charlestown, attorney, 2 feather beds and furniture, 2 chests, 1 table, 1 cow and all the said George Vickers carpenters tools and joiners tools. Made 15 Sep 1752. Wit: John Baine, John Parks. Rec: 25 Sep 1752. M's. Bordley, Clerk.

P. 444   Bill of Sale.   Thomas Watts, Jr. of Cecil Co., for £8, to Benjamin Chew, Jr. of said county, carpenter, all his the said Watts' part of a crop of Indian corn now growing on the plantation of the said Benjamin Chew. Made & Ackn: 2 Sep 1752. Wit: Benjamin Chew, Aquilla Johns. JP: Benj'a. Chew. Rec: 28 Sep 1752. M's. Bordley, Clerk.

P. 445   Lease.   John Smith of Cecil Co., gent., for 5 shillings, to William Graham of the said county, farmer, 428 acres, part of 2 tracts of land called Holland and Heath's Adventure on Susquehanna River. For 1 year. Made 25 Aug 1752. Wit. & JPs: Benj'a. Chew, Nath'n. Baker. Ackn: 26 Aug 1752. Rec: 3 Oct 1752. M's. Bordley, Clerk.

P. 445   Release.   John Smith of Cecil Co., gent., for £850 and because he is moving, to William Graham of the said county, farmer, 428 acres, part of 2 tracts of land called Holland and Heath's Adventure on Susquehanna River. [See previous entry P. 445.] The land has attached to it a mortgage of £450 dated 23 Aug 1750 to James Baxter which will expire on 24 Aug 1754. Made 26 Aug 1752. Wit: Nath'n. Baker, Benj'a. Chew, Sidney George. Ackn: same day by John Smith and his wife Grace Smith. JPs: Benj'a. Chew, Nath'n. Baker. Rec: 3 Oct 1752. M's. Bordley, Clerk.

P. 447   Bill of Sale.   Thomas Watts, Jr. of Cecil Co., planter, for £9, to Mathias Seal, 1 black horse called Dimond branded "IY" [or "JY"] with 1 bridle and saddle. Made & Ackn: 10 Oct 1752. Wit: Benj'a. Chew, William Watts. JP: Benj'a. Chew. Rec: 11 Oct 1752. M's. Bordley, Clerk.

P. 447   Power of Attorney.   William Ramsey and his wife Hannah Ramsey appoint Moses Andrews of Milford Hundred, Cecil Co., their attorney to convey possession of land and property pertaining to it which was granted to Robert Arthur by article dated 13 Sep 1740. Made 31 May 1752 in Cumberland Co., PA. Wit: Sam'l. Smith, Wm. Allison, Robert Arthur. Ackn: in Cecil Co. 28 May 1752 by Robert Arthur. JPs: James Baxter, John Smith. Rec: 1 Oct 1752. M's. Bordley, Clerk.

P. 448   Deed.   William Ramsey of Prince George Co., and Hannah his wife, late of Cecil Co., and Jacob Thatcher and Abigail Thatcher, for £125 and because they are moving, to Moses Faires of Cecil Co., 209 acres of land on Elk River, part of 1,200 acres which is part of 6,000 acres called New Munster. A tract of 6,000 acres called New Munster in Cecil Co. was surveyed and laid out for Edmond O'Dweyer by certificate dated 29 Aug 1683. Edward [sic] O'Dweyer conveyed the land to Daniel Toes, Sr., late of Maryland, mariner, who bequeathed the New Munster tract to his children Daniel, John and Sarah Toes. Sarah Toes later married Peter Massey and the two of them conveyed 1,200 acres on the south end of New Munster to Richard Thatcher, now deceased. To gain a clear title, an Act of Assembly was made 26 Feb 1721, investing the land as an estate of inheritance in fee simple to the said Richard Thatcher. Jacob Thatcher, Abigail Thatcher, William Ramsey and his wife Hannah Ramsey are heirs and legatees of the said Richard Thatcher. [Thatcher is also spelled Tatcher. Faires is also spelled Faris.] Made 30 Jan 1748. Wit: Thos. Trather [Thatcher?], Mar'n. Moran. William Ramsey acknowledged receipt of £131.12s from Moses Faires. Ackn: 30 Jan 1748/9 by William Ramsey before Thomas Trather and Mar'n. Moran. Ackn: in Cecil Co. 28 May 1752 by Moses Andrews. JPs: James Baxter, John Smith. Moses Faires paid 4s.4p alienation fine 21 Oct 1752 to Matt's. Bordley who recorded the deed 1 Oct 1752.

P. 449   Release.   Anne Holy, widow and executrix of Robert Holy, late of Cecil Co., deceased, for £6.8s, releases to Alexander McDowell of the said county, gent., 45 acres of land. A vacant piece of land was discovered on the north end of a tract called Society owned by Thomas Sharpe, Joseph Steel, John Seagar and the said Robert Holy. The men agreed that Robert Holy should get the land surveyed and patented to him and then release to each of the other men the part of the land he had possessed before which adjoined the Society tract. Each of the other men would pay to Holy a sum of money in consideration of his costs and trouble in taking up the land. Accordingly, Holy had the land surveyed under the name of Confusion on 6 Jul 1723 and subsequently laid out to each of the men their respective parts of the tract now called Confusion. John Seagar got the part he had possessed and occupied before on the west by north line of Society containing 45 acres. John Seagar conveyed the 45 acres to Andrew Barry by deed dated 30 Apr 1731. The said Andrew Barry conveyed the land to the said Alexander McDowell by deed dated 4 Oct 1750. However, Robert Holy died before he made a release of the land to the said John Seagar. By Robert Holy's Last Will and Testament, Anne Holy is his sole heir to the lands called Society and Confusion. Made 6 Jun 1752. Wit: William Bristow, Walter Ker. Ackn: 30 Oct 1752. JPs: Nich'o. Hyland, Benj'a. Chew. Rec: 30 Oct 1752. M's. Bordley, Clerk.

P. 450   Lease.   Peter Aug'n. Bouchell of Cecil Co., gent., and Catharine his wife and John Aug'n. Lawson of the same county, gent., and Mary his wife, for yearly rents and services, to Jacob Ozier of the same county, yeoman, 130 acres of land on the north side of the road from Bohemia Ferry to Newcastle and to the intersection of the road leading to the courthouse on Elk River. Lease is for the term of the natural lives of Jacob Ozier's son Jacob Ozier and daughter Sarah Ozier and the natural life of Benedict Beetle, son of Samuel Beetle. Rent of £1.12s and 2 dunghill fowls due every 10 Dec. Made & Ackn: 14 May 1752. Wit. & JPs: Tho. Colvill, P. Bayard. Rec: 4 Nov 1752. M's. Bordley, Clerk.

P. 451   Lease.   Peter Aug'n. Bouchell of Cecil Co., gent., and Catharine his wife and John Aug'n. Lawson of the same county, gent., and Mary his wife, for yearly rents and services, to Jacob Ozier of the same county, yeoman, 150 acres of land in Bohemia Manor on the south side of the road leading from the chapel to the courthouse on Elk River and by Andrew Larrence's fence and by yhe lands of Jacob Ozier and Richard Ford. Lease is for the term of the natural lives of Jacob Ozier's son Stephen Ozier and daughter Elizabeth Ozier and for the life of John Vanhorne, son of Barnett Vanhorne. Rent of £2.10s and 2 dunghill fowls due every 10 Dec. Made & Ackn: 14 May 1752. Wit. & JPs: Tho. Colvill, P. Bayard. Rec: 4 Nov 1752. M's. Bordley, Clerk.

P. 453   Deed of Gift.   Thomas Jacobs of Cecil Co., clothier, for natural affection and because he is moving, gives to his son Joseph Jacobs of the same county, 574 acres of land, part of a tract called the Three Partners, by the path leading from Abraham Penington's to Conestoga in the line of a tract called Comwell Addition belonging to Emanuel Grubb. Also another tract of 96 acres in Lancaster Co., PA in Little Brittain township formerly taken up by the said Thomas Jacobs. Made & Ackn: 8 Nov 1752. Wit: Zeb. Hollingsworth, Tobias Rudulph, Fra. Catto. JPs: John Veazey, Geo. Rock.

Joseph Jacobs paid 23 shillings alienation fine 9 Nov 1752 to M's. Bordley, Clerk, who recorded the deed the same day.

P. 454 Deed. Elizabeth Jones and William Jones of Cecil Co., executors of Thomas Jones, late of said county, deceased, and by the power of the Last Will and Testament of the said Thomas Jones dated 22 Nov 1748, for £32 paid to the said Thomas Jones in his lifetime, to Philip Stoops, 16 acres of land in Sassafras Neck called Jones' Addition by land granted to John Brice, William Harris and Daniel Cheston on 12 Jul 1743 called Frisby's Neglect. Made & Ackn: 4 Nov 1752. Wit. & JPs: John Veazey, Thomas Savin. Philip Stoops paid 8p alienation fine 15 Nov 1752 to County Clerk Matt's. Bordley. Rec: same day.

P. 454 Notice of Strays. Richard Thompson, Jr. reports he has in his custody a small mare branded "IB" [or "JB"] and a young iron gray mare. Owner may claim strays by proving their property. Made 20 Oct 1752. Rec: 15 Nov 1752. M's. Bordley, Clerk.

P. 455 Bill of Sale. John Drummond of Cecil Co., for £50, to Richard Graham of Kent Co., 3 horses, 3 mares and a colt, 2 cows, 2 calves, 1 steer, 2 heifers, 19 sheep, 4 feather beds, 1 desk, 1 chest of drawers, 57 lbs wood, 1 iron kettle, 1 large iron pot, 1 small iron pot. Void if and when John Drummond repays Richard Graham on or by 1 Nov next. Made 14 Nov 1752. Wit: James McLachlan, George Fulton. Ackn: in Kent Co. 16 Nov 1752. JPs: S. Wilmer, Jacob Jones. Rec: 18 Nov 1752.

P. 455 Register of Mark. Thomas Marr of Cecil Co., blacksmith, makes the mark of his cattle and hogs as 2 holes and an underkeel in the right ear. Rec: 22 Nov 1752.

P. 455 Register of Mark. Catharine Chambers of Cecil Co. makes the mark of her cattle and hogs as 1 hole and an underkeel in the right ear and 2 holes in the left ear. Rec: 22 Nov 1752.

P. 455 Bill of Sale. James Redus, for £20, to Peter Bayard, a Negro boy called Nead. Void when James Redus repays Peter Bayard on or by 6 months from this date. [Redus also spelled Reiduih.] Made 17 Nov 1752. Wit: Thomas Barnum, Grace McComb. Ackn: 20 Nov 1725. JP: Nich'o. Hyland. Rec: 27 Nov 1752. M's. Bordley, Clerk.

P. 455 Notice of Strays. John McCay posts notice that he has a small sorrel mare on his plantation on Elk River near William Longwill's. The owner may claim by proving his property and paying charges. Rec: 16 Dec 1752.

P. 455 Deed. Thomas Weir of Cecil Co., yeoman, for £70, to William Ferguson of the same place, tailor, 67 acres of land by Thomas Weir's land and near John Alexander's place. Said land is part of a tract of 903 acres called New Munster purchased by Arthur Alexander from Thomas Stephenson by deed dated 15 Aug 1718, the assignees of Robert Roberts by deed dated 14 Aug 1718. Made 1 Dec 1752. Wit: William Longwill, Edward Weir, James Alexander. Ackn: 16 Dec 1752. JPs: Nath'n. Baker, Geo. Rock. Matt's. Bordley recorded the deed and rec'd from Ferguson the alienation fine of 16½p on 16 Dec 1752.

P. 456 Bill of Sale. Hukill Guilder of Cecil Co., smith, for sundry services, debts paid, and having become security for his appearance at next March Court in two suits by Henry Baker, to the said Henry Baker 3 horses, (1 with no brand, 1 branded "NH" and the other "TS",) 3 feather beds, one cow and calf, a 2 year old heifer, 11 sheep and all his other household goods and chattels with 2 sets of smith tools, one of which is now in the possession of James Manley. If Henry Baker comes to no damage by being security and if all debts are paid or if Baker becomes security as well to Capt. Jethro Brown or others within 6 months then bill of sale is void. Made & Ackn: 16 Dec 1752. Wit. & JP: Nathan Baker. Rec: 18 Dec 1752. M's. Bordley, Clerk.

P. 457 Bill of Sale. Jared Nellson of Cecil Co., miller, for £100, to Robert Alison of Charles Town, Cecil Co., gent., 1 wagon and 4 geldings (the team belonging to the wagon,) 1 bay mare 7 years old, 3 milk cows and 2 two year old heifers, 12 sheep, 3 feather beds, bedding and furniture and all the gears and furniture belonging to the wagon and team. Made 18 Dec 1752. Wit: Wm. Pennock, Thos. Pryer. Rec: 18 Dec 1752. M's. Bordley, Clk.

P. 457 Notice of Strays. Nich'o. Hyland makes notice that at John Mainley's plantation there has been taken up as a stray a small bay horse about 3 years old branded with "IR" [or "JR".] Said horse came into the neighborhood last May. Owner may claim by proving property. Made 13 Nov 1752. Rec: 18 Dec 1752.

P. 457 Deed. Robert Rowland of Millford Hundred, Cecil Co., farmer, for £6 and because he is moving, to Thomas Sharpe of the same [place], farmer, 4 acres of land by Alexander Logan's upper meadow, part of a tract called Confusion which Joseph Steel conveyed to the said Robert Rowland. Made 13 Nov 1752. Wit: John Caldwell, Isabella Rowland, Edmund Castle.

Ackn: 23 Dec 1752. JP: James Baxter, Nath'n. Baker. Alienation fine of 2p paid by Thomas Sharpe 23 Dec 1752 to Matt's Bordley. Rec: same day.

P. 458 Deed. Robert Rowland of Millford Hundred, Cecil Co., farmer, for £15 and because he is moving, to Thomas Sharpe of the same [place], 1 acre, 1 rood and 18 perches of land on the south line of the said Robert's and Thomas' Society land. Said land is part of a tract called Society and was conveyed to Rowland by deed dated 20 Nov 1751 from Charles Carroll of Annapolis. Made 20 Nov 1752. Wit: John Caldwell, Isabella Rowland, Edmund Castle. Ackn: 23 Dec 1752. JP: James Baxter, Nath'n. Baker. Alienation fine of 6p paid by Thomas Sharpe 23 Dec 1752 to Matt's Bordley. Rec: same day.

P. 459 Deed. Edward Dougherty of Cecil Co., yeoman, and Ann his wife, for £65 [?, torn], to Robert Evans of said county, tanner, 100 acres of land by Elk River near French Town. Charles Lord Baltimore, by deed dated 20 Jul 1704, conveyed to William Smith a tract of 100 acres of marsh and highland called Duck Neck in Cecil Co., recorded in Lib. C. D. The said William Smith died intestate and the tract of land descended to his daughter Hannah, wife of Roger Dyer. Hannah and her husband Roger Dyer, on 27 Jul 1750, conveyed the land to Edward Dougherty. Made & Ackn: 30 Oct 1752. Wit: Benj'a. Chew, Nath'n. Baker, Benj'a. Crockett. JPs: Benj'a. Chew, Nath'n. Baker. Robert Evans paid 4 shillings alienation fine 23 Dec to clerk Matt's. Bordley, who recorded the deed the same day.

P. 460 Indenture. Philip Connor of Baltimore, obligated and indebted to Charles Dolan of Baltimore for £12, agrees to serve John Hays, surveyor of Charles Town, Cecil Co., as an indented servant for 2 years from this date. John Hays will provide for the said Philip Connor drink, washing, lodging and apparel. Made & Ackn: 14 Dec 1752. Wit: D. Fanings, James Cummings. JP: Nath'n. Baker. Rec: 2 Jan 1753. M's. Bordley, Clerk.

P. 461 Deed. Isaac Rew of Frederick Co., farmer, and Elizabeth his wife, for £30, to James Evans of Chester Co., PA, gent., all their interests and rights in part of a tract of land called Glass House in Cecil Co. which Paul Poulson, the father of the said Elizabeth, owned when he died intestate. Made & Ackn: 17 Jul 1752 in Frederick Co. Wit: John Darnall, Mary Darnall. JP: John Darnall. Rec: 4 Feb 1753. M's. Bordley, Clerk.

P. 462 Deed. Luke Bernard and his wife Margaret of Frederick Co., for £5, to James Evans of Chester Co., PA, gent., all their interests and rights in part of a tract of land called Glass House in Cecil Co. which Paul Poulson, the grandfather of the said Margaret, owned when he died intestate. Made &

Ackn: 17 Jul 1752 in Frederick Co. Wit: John Darnall, Mary Darnall. JP: John Darnall. James Evans paid the £5 to Luke Bernard 31 Jul 1752 and on the same day James Evans paid another £5 to Isaac Rew. Rec: 4 Feb 1753. M's. Bordley, Clerk.

P. 463   Deed.   James Death and John Death of Cecil Co., planters, both sons and heirs of Randall Death, late of the same county, deceased, for £5, to James Evans of Cecil Co., farmer, 95 acres of land in Cecil Co. called the Glass House which was originally laid out and granted to Richard Gray. Made & Ackn: 12 Aug 1752. Wit. & JPs: Thos. Colvill, Nathan Baker. Ackn. again 31 Oct 1752 by Sophia, wife of James Death, and Hannah, wife of John Death. JPs: Nath'n. Baker, James Baxter. Rec: 4 Jan 1753. M's. Bordley, Clerk. Alienation fine of 3s10p sterling paid 24 Feb 1753.

P. 464   Release.   On the back of the previous deed was written that Honor Death, widow and relict of Randall Death, for 10 shillings and because she is moving, releases to James Evans her interest in the said 95 acres called the Glass House. Made & Ackn: 31 Oct 1752. Wit. & JPs: James Baxter, Nath'n. Baker. Rec: 4 Jan 1753. M's. Bordley, Clerk.

P. 465   Mortgage.   Hukill Guilder of Cecil Co., blacksmith, for £57.2s.4p, to Alexander Lunan of Philadelphia, merchant, a tract of 100 acres called Guilder's Forest in Cecil Co. in Turkey Point Neck at the back end of a tract called Bayley. Also a 50 acre tract which was leased to Samuel Seal by deed dated 3 Feb 1743 and is part of his Lordship's Manor of North East. Void if Guilder repays Lunan on or by 1 Jun 1753. Made 9 Dec 1752. Wit: Matt's. Bordley, Sidney George. Ackn: 11 Dec 1752. JPs: James Baxter, Nath'n. Baker. Rec: 6 Jan 1753. M's. Bordley, Clerk.

P. 467   Bill of Sale.   John Dunn of Charles Town, Cecil Co., mariner, to Ruth Smith of the same county, spinster, for £50 and her agreement to satisfy a debt due Thomas Ellot, a one-third part of a shallop called *the Nancy*. On 24 Jul 1752, for £18.11½p and for security of this loan, John Dunn gave to Thomas Ellot of the same town, innholder, one-third part of the shallop called *the Nancy*. One-third of the boat is held by Samuel Rankin and the other third is held by Robert Allison, both of the said place. John Dunn has not repaid the loan. This bill of sale to be void when John Dunn repays Ruth Smith on or by 10 Feb next. Made & Ackn: 5 Jan 1753. Wit: John Smith, Edward Philips. JP: John Smith. Rec: 8 Jan 1753. M's. Bordley, Clerk.

P. 468   Lease.   Daniel Cheston of Bristol but late of Kent Co., Maryland. merchant, and Franscina Augustina his wife and daughter of the late Arriana

Jennings, wife of the Honorable Edmond Jennings, esq., of Annapolis, for 5 shillings, to John Veazey of Cecil Co., 373 acres, part of 2 tracts of land lying between Sassafras and Bohemia Rivers in Cecil Co. called Frisby's Farm or Frisby's Prime Choice, by Scotchman's Creek, by Thomas Davis' land called the Level and by a tract called King's Aim. Made 31 Aug 1752. Wit: Thos. Luntley, Jno. Hope. Rec: 20 Jan 1752. M's. Bordley, Clerk.

P. 469   Release.   Daniel Cheston and his wife Franscina Augustina, for £323, to John Veazey, 373 acres [see previous entry P. 468.] Made 1 Sep 1752. Wit: Jno. Hope, Thos. Luntley. James Terry, Mayor of Hereford in Great Britain and Thomas Williams and John Hunt, two alderman of the said city, certify that on 1 Sep 1752 Daniel Cheston and his wife Franscina Augustina, being persons well known to the 3 men, signed, sealed and delivered the deed in their presence. John Hope and Thomas Luntley, also well known to them, were present. Attested by Jno Weare, Clerk of Hereford. A public notary of Hereford, Richard Moore, notarized the document. Rec: in Cecil Co. 20 Jan 1753. M's. Bordley, Clerk.

P. 473   Deed.   George Lawson of Cecil Co., merchant, for £25, to Robert Evans of the said county, farmer, 50 acres of land by the land of John Vansandt, part of a tract called New Munster. Thomas Stephenson sold this land to John Wallace and Wallace conveyed the land to Sam'l. Scott who conveyed it to the said George Lawson. Lawson warrants the land against any claims of Sam'l. Scott and Will'm. Keltham. Made 24 Jan 1753. Wit: John Veazey, Robert Smith. Ackn: 26 Jan 1753. JPs: Benj'a. Chew, James Baxter. Rec: 27 Jan 1753. M's. Bordley, Clerk. Alienation fine of 1 shilling paid by Robert Evans 26 Feb 1753 to Matt's. Bordley.

P. 475   Deed.   Andrew Alexander of Cecil Co., for £60, to Isaac Alexander of the same county, 71¼ acres of land by a tract called Blancestine's Park which was patented to Andrew Wallace in 1749. Made 2 Sep 1752. Wit: Wm. Wheland, Thomas Bouldin. Ackn: same day by Andrew Alexander and his wife Lewey. JPs: P. Bayard, Adam VanBebber. Rec: 29 Jan 1753.

P. 476   Deed.   David Witherspoon of New Castle Co. on Delaware, esq., and his wife Esther, for £429, to Barnet Vanhorn of Cecil Co., 197 acres of land on the head branch of Bohemia River, part of a tract called Indian Range, by old Bartholomew Jacob's land called Stockton. [Esther is also spelled Hester.] Made & Ackn: 15 Dec 1752. Wit. & JPs: R'd. Thompson, Adam VanBebber. Alienation fine of 7 shillings paid 3 Feb 1753. Rec: 30 Mar 1753. M's. Bordley, Clerk.

P. 477   Deed of Gift.   James Baxter of Cecil Co., for natural love and affection, gives to his grandson James Smith, son of his daughter Grace Smith, a Negro woman named Pender and 2 children called Philis and Jane. Made & Ackn: 25 Jan 1753. Wit: Geo. Rock, Nath'n. Chapman. JPs: George Rock, Nathan Baker. Rec: 10 Feb 1753. M's. Bordley, Clerk.

P. 478   Lease.   Benjamin Tasker of Annapolis, Agent and Receiver General, for and on behalf of Lord Baltimore, for rents and services, to William Graham of Cecil Co., 150 acres of land by a tract called Holland, part of his Lordship's Manor of Susquehanna alias New Connach. Lease is for the term of the natural lives of the said William Graham, Ann Shepard and Phineas Chew. Rent of 30 shillings due every 19 Oct. Tenants will build a dwelling house and plant and fence an orchard of 100 apple trees. Made 19 Oct 1752. Wit: Benj'a. Chew, John Smith. Rec: 26 Feb 1753. M's. Bordley, Clerk.

P. 480   Deed.   William Rumsey of Cecil Co., gent., to William Pearce, Jr., son of Wm. Pearce, late of Fredrick Town, innholder, deceased, for £2.10s already paid to Wm. Rumsey, deceased father of the said William Rumsey, and to honor some promises and agreements made between the said William Rumsey's deceased father William Rumsey, late of Cecil Co., and the said William Pearce, deceased, the northern moiety of lot #46 in Frederick Town by lot #47, including the dwelling house thereon. Made 3 Jan 1753. Wit. & JPs: P. Bayard, Adam VanBebber. Ackn: same day by William Rumsey and his wife Susanna. Alienation fine paid and deed recorded 5 Mar 1753. M's. Bordley, Clerk.

P. 481   Deed.   William Pearce, Jr. of Cecil Co., son of William Pearce, late of Frederick Town, innholder, deceased, for £50, to Samuel Beedle of the said county, gent., the northern moiety of lot #46 in Frederick Town on Frederick Street by lot #47. Made 3 Jan 1753. Wit. & JPs: P. Bayard, Adam VanBebber. Ackn: same day by Samuel Beedle and Sarah Penington, mother of the said William Pearce. Alienation fine paid and deed recorded 6 Mar 1753. M's. Bordley, Clerk.

P. 483   Release.   Richard Eavenson of Thornbury, Chester Co., PA, for 5 shillings, to his well beloved brother Nathaniel Eavenson of the same place, all his estate rights and title of survivorship in a lot in Charlestown, Cecil Co., at Long Point on the Northeast River which by virtue of an Act of Assembly passed at Annapolis in Sep 1742 and balloted the next 10th of May wherein lot #127 fell jointly to the two brothers. They agree to divide the lot and release their claims to each other's half of the lot. Nathaniel Eavenson's moiety of the lot begins at the corner of Richard Eavenson's lot on Conestogoe Street. Made, Ackn. & Rec: 10 Mar 1753. Wit: Henry Good, Zach Butcher, Samuel Gilpin. JPs: George Rock, John Smith.

P. 484   Release.   Nathaniel Eavenson of Thornbury, Chester Co., PA, for 5 shillings, releases to his well beloved brother Richard Eavenson his rights to half of lot #127 in Charlestown [see previous entry P. 483.] Richard Eavenson's moiety of the lot begins at a post on Conestogoe Street adjoining the public square. Made, Ackn. & Rec: 10 Mar 1753. Wit: Henry Good, Zach Butcher, Samuel Gilpin. JPs: George Rock, John Smith.

P. 486   Bill of Sale.   Patrick Harris of Cecil Co., farmer, for £33, to James Congetton of Newcastle Co. on Delaware, farmer, 2 cows, 1 yearling, 2 cows which Harris bought at the Vendue of Effects of Dr. John Musgang, 1 gray mare, 1 bright bay mare, 1 dark bay mare and 10 head of sheep. The animals will remain in the care of the said Patrick Harris until 1 Nov 1754 by which time Harris should have repaid James Congetton. Void when repaid. Made & Ackn: 6 Mar 1753. Wit: P. Bayard, R'd. Blake. JP: P. Bayard. Rec: 15 Mar 1753. Fran's. Key, Clerk.

P. 488   Deed.   Thomas Etherington of Cecil Co., planter, for £15, to Philip Stoops of said county, planter, 10 acres of a tract of 12 acres called Hendrickson's Oversight by a tract called None So Good In Finland. [Etherington also spelled Eathrington, Edthrington.] Made, Ackn. & Rec: 16 Mar 1753. Wit. & JPs: Pereg'r. Ward, Thomas Savin. Exchange of money witnessed by Wm. Pearce. Alienation fine of 6 pence paid same day to Matt's Bordley, Clerk.

P. 489   Bill of Sale.   Philip Cazier, Jr., for the consideration of Henry Baker becoming security for him in several suits, to Henry Baker 1 Negro girl named Nan about 12 or 13 years old who is now in the possession of said Cazier's father from whom she was sold to me. Also 1 tobacco box. Void when Baker is repaid the cost and damages. Made & Ackn: 26 Feb 1753. Wit: Benj'a. Chew, Thomas Downton. [In the acknowledgement he is called Philip Conor, Jr.] JP: Benj'a. Chew. Rec: 17 Mar 1753. M's. Bordley, Clerk.

P. 490   Lease.   John Campbell of Cecil Co., son and devisee of John Campbell, late of said county, deceased, for £20 and yearly rent, to Seth Ruley of the same place, planter, 100 acres of land, part of a tract called the Dividing which John Campbell the Father (devised by his Last Will and Testament to his son John) bought from Nicholas Ridgeley. Lease is for the term of the natural life of the said Seth Ruley. Rent of 1 dunghill cock due every 10 Dec. Made, Ackn. & Rec: 17 Mar 1753. Wit: John Veazey, Tho's. Savin, Rich'd. Price. JPs: John Veazey, Tho's. Savin.

P. 491 Assignment of Lease. John Smith of Cecil Co., saddler, for £150, to William Currer of Cecil Co., innholder, a lease for land called Copson's Park. This endorsement was written on the back of a lease for the land called Copson's Park, part of his Lordship's Manor of North East River, from Thomas Bladen and Benjamin Tasker to William Smith and recorded in Lib. W. K. No. 9, folios 187-189. Made 10 Mar 1753. Wit. & JPs: James Baxter, Nath'n. Baker. Ackn: same day by John Smith and his wife Sarah. Rec: 19 Mar 1753. M's. Bordley, Clerk.

P. 492 Deed. John Smith of Cecil Co., saddler, for £24, to William Currer of the same county, innholder, 13½ acres of land called Copson's Intent near the head of North East River below the mill dam which was formerly Robert Jones'. Made 10 Mar 1753. Wit. & JPs: James Baxter, Nath'n. Baker. Ackn: same day by John Smith and his wife Sarah. Alienation fine of 6½p paid by William Currer to Matt's. Bordley on 23 Mar 1753. Rec: same day.

P. 495 Bill of Sale. James Roberts of Cecil Co., planter, for £26.6s.11p, to Francis Mauldin of Cecil Co., farmer, 1 Negro man named Davi. Roberts to repay Mauldin within 12 months time to void this writing. Made & Ackn: 10 Mar 1753. Wit: Nich'o. Hyland, Zasaerus Granger. JP: Nicholas Hyland. Rec: 24 Mar 1753. M's. Bordley. Discharge of this bill of sale recorded in Lib. W3 [M3?], pg 128.

P. 497 Deed. James Porter of Cecil Co., yeoman, for £130, to Thomas Love of the same place, yeoman, 235 acres of land, part of two tracts called Hopewell and Levell's Addition. James Porter reserves the liberty of having a wagon road leading from his dwelling house through the granted land to where the school house now stands. Made 26 Mar 1753. Wit: Wm. Husbands, Jr., John Ewing, John Smith. Ackn: same day by James Porter and Elinor his wife. JPs: John Smith, Nath'n. Baker. Thomas Love paid 9s.6p alienation fine to Matt's. Bordley 26 Mar 1753. Rec: same day.

P. 499 Deed. William Wallace of Cecil Co., yeoman, and Catharine his wife, for £346, to Joseph Wallace of said county, 140 acres of land, part of a larger tract of 500 acres called Castle Finn taken up by Andrew Wallace by 2 warrants dated 15 Jun 1713 and 31 Oct following and recorded in Lib. C. E. No. 6, folios 19-20. Andrew Wallace and his wife Elennor conveyed the 140 acres to the said William Wallace by deed dated 28 Apr 1732. Also an adjoining tract of 62 acres called Gardner's Gift which was patented to William Wallace and signed by Gov. Charles Calvert dated 3 May 1723. Made 14 Mar 1753. Wit: Nath'n. Baker, James Baxter, Joseph Watkins. Matt's. Bordley rec'd 20 Mar 1753 from Joseph Wallace 8s.1p alienation fine. Ackn: 23 Mar 1753. Nath'n. Baker, James Baxter. Rec: 3 Apr 1753.

P. 502   Bill of Sale.   Joseph Lowman of Cecil Co., farmer, for 860 lbs of tobacco, to William Mainly of said county, farmer, 1 bed and furniture, 2 tables, 2 iron pots, 4 pewter dishes, 6 plates, 1 poplar chest, 1 griddle and 1 iron pot rack. Made 16 Mar 1753. Wit: Patrick Dougherty. Ackn: 19 Mar 1753. JP: R'd. Thompson. Rec: 4 Apr 1753. M's. Bordley, Clerk.

P. 503   Mortgage.   Joseph Young of Cecil Co., carpenter, for £40, to Henry Baker, an undivided equal fifth part of a tract of land called Clayfall where the said Joseph Young now lives. The land was devised to Joseph Young by the Last Will and Testament of his father Joseph Young, deceased. Void if Joseph Young repays Henry Baker within 2 years time. Made & Ackn: 4 Nov 1752. Wit: Geo. Rock, Amos Fogg, Nath'n. Baker. JPs: Geo. Rock, Nath'n. Baker. Rec: 6 Apr 1753. M's. Bordley, Clerk.

P. 505   Deed.   Joseph Wallace of Cecil Co., smith, and Mary his wife, for £316, to James Finley of said county, gent., 191 acres, part of 2 tracts of land called Castle Fin and Gardner's Gift. The tract of 500 acres called Castle Fin was taken up by Andrew Wallace and surveyed and patented to him by 2 warrants dated 15 Jun 1713 and 31 Oct 1713, recorded in Lib. E. E. No. 6, folios 19-20. The land descended to Joseph Wallace at the death of Andrew Wallace except for 140 acres which was conveyed by Andrew and his wife Elinor in his lifetime to William Wallace by deed dated 28 Apr 1732. William Wallace and his wife Catharine conveyed it to the said Joseph Wallace by deed dated 14 Mar 1753. William and Catharine Wallace also conveyed to Joseph Wallace by deed dated 14 Mar 1753 an adjoining tract of 60 acres called Gardner's Gift which was surveyed by warrant dated 3 Aug 1723 and patented by Gov. Charles Calvert to the said William Wallace (recorded in Lib. P. L. No. 6, folio 139.) Made 6 Apr 1753. Wit: Theo's. Alexander, Wm. Wallace, Thomas Sharp. Ackn. & Rec: next day. JPs: Nath'n. Baker, Geo. Rock. James Finley paid that day 7 shillings alienation fine to Matt's. Bordley.

P. 508   Release.   Joseph Price of Kent Co. on Delaware, farmer, and Jane his wife, late widow of Philip Barratt of Cecil Co., deceased, for 10 shillings and because they are moving, quit claims to Andrew Barratt of Cecil Co., blacksmith and son and heir of the said Philip Barratt by his wife the said Jane, all the lands and tenements which the said Philip Barratt possessed when he died. Made & Ackn: 2 Nov 1752. Wit. & JPs: Nath'n. Baker, James Baxter. Rec: 13 Apr 1753. M's. Bordley, Clerk.

P. 510 Deed. Thomas Lindsey, late of Cecil Co., planter, for £75, to John Foulton of the same place, planter, 75 acres of land called Dougherty's Endeavor on the east side of Susquehanna River on the north west side of a tract of land which Abraham Penington bought from William Teague and near Penington's dwelling plantation. [Lindsey also spelled Linsey.] Made 11 Apr 1753. Wit: Samuel Fulton, Hugh Rea, Isaac Sanders. Ackn: 13 Apr 1753. JPs: Benj'a. Chew, Nath'n. Baker. John Foulton paid 3 shillings alienation fine 13 Apr 1753. Rec: same day. Matt's. Bordley, Clerk.

P. 512 Bill of Sale. Peter Noxon of Cecil Co., for £135, to William Hedges of the same county, a Negro man named Will aged 20 and a Negro lad named Isaac aged between 17 and 18 years. Made 7 Apr 1753. Wit: John Drummond, Wm. Walmsley. Rec: 14 Apr 1753. M's. Bordley, Clerk.

P. 513 Lease. Onorah Death, wife of Randell Death, lately deceased; James Death and his wife Sophia; and John Death and his wife Hannah, all of Cecil Co., planters, for £5, to Richard Griffee of Chester Co., PA, farmer, a 55 acre tract of land called Glasshouse. Term is for 98 years. [Onorah also spelled Honor.] Made & Ackn: 31 Oct 1752. Wit: James Baxter, Nath'n. Baker. JP: Nathan Baker. Rec: 19 Apr 1753. M's. Bordley, Clerk.

P. 516 Bill of Sale. Alexander Macintosh of Cecil Co., for £10 and because he is moving, to John Ogg of the said county, 1 feather bed and its furniture and 1 sorrel mare branded "TB". Made Apr 1753. Wit: Edward Veazey, John Veazey. Ackn: 5 Apr 1753. JP: John Veazey. Rec: 21 Apr 1753.

P. 517 Bill of Sale. William Nevill of Cecil Co., weaver, for £4.1s, to John Hyland, Jr., of the same county, 1 weaver's loom, a quil wheel, 5 slays and 5 good pairs of gears belonging to said loom. Made & Ackn: 12 Apr 1753. Wit: Edward Johnson and JP Nich'o. Hyland. Rec: 25 Apr 1753.

P. 518 Lease. Benjamin Tasker of Annapolis, Agent and Receiver General, for and on behalf of Lord Baltimore, for rents and services, to Patrick Hamilton of Cecil Co., 80 acres of land, part of his Lordship's Manor of Susquehanna alias New Connah. Lease is for the term of the natural lives of Patrick Hamilton, Matthias Bordley and John Currer, Sr. Rent of 16 shillings due every 25 Dec. Tenants to build a dwelling house and plant and fence an orchard of 100 apple trees. [Hamilton is also spelled Hambelton.] Made 21

Feb 1753. Wit: Matt's. Bordley, Benj'a. Chew, Frances Tasker, Sarah Bickerton. Rec: 26 Apr 1753. M's. Bordley, Clerk.

P. 521   Lease.   Benjamin Pearce of Cecil Co., for yearly rents and services, to John Beedle, Jr. of the said county, a plantation where John Penington now dwells, part of a tract called Poplar Neck, by the road leading to the church where it intersects William Beedle's land called Colleton. Lease is for 14 years. First year's rent £7.5s and 950 lbs of tobacco; thereafter £15.5s and 1,000 lbs of tobacco. Beedle will build a dwelling house. Made 29 Dec 1752. Wit: John Clark, Michael McDaniel. Ackn: 24 Apr 1753 by Benjamin Pearce and Marg't. his wife. JPs: John Veazey, Tho's. Savin. Rec: 26 Apr 1753. M's. Bordley, Clerk.

P. 523   Bill of Sale.   Henry Baker of Cecil Co., for £74.17s.9p money of Great Britain and £10.17s.9p Maryland money, to Patrick Hamilton, 1 Mulatto man named Jam and 1 Negro man named Lincoln. Bill of Sale is void when Henry Baker discharges Patrick Hamilton from a judgement obtained against him in Court. Wit: Nath'n. Baker, Matt's. Bordley. Ackn: 12 Apr 1753. JP: Nath'n. Baker. Rec: 26 Apr 1853. M's. Bordley, Clerk. Receipt and discharge recorded in Lib. M3, pg 51.

P. 524   Deed.   Captain Zebulon Hollingsworth of Cecil Co., gent., for £100, to Thomas Jacobs of the said county, clothier, 100 acres, part of a tract called Friendship on the north side and near the head of Elk River by 50 acres (part of the same tract) belonging to Simon Johnson and by another part of the same tract belonging to the heirs of William Alexander and now possessed by George Catto. Made 28 Mar 1753. Wit: Joseph Wallace, Sam'l. Hall, Adam Dobson. Ackn: same day by Zebulon Hollingsworth and his wife Mary. JPs: Nich'o. Hyland, Geo. Rock. Matt's. Bordley received 4 shillings alienation fine from Thomas Jacobs 27 Apr 1753. Rec: same day.

P. 527   Bill of Sale.   John Hyland and William Bristow, both gents. of Cecil Co., became bound for the administration of the estate of John Kankey, late of said county, deceased, by his widow and administratrix Ann Kankey, who has since married Hance Rudolph of the said county. To secure the bond, Hance Rudolph is willing to mortgage sundry goods and chattels. Thus, Hance Rudolph, for 5 shillings, to John Hyland and William Bristow, 1 Negro man named Bristow, 1 Negro man named Cuff, another named Harry, 1 Mulatto man named Will, 1 Mulatto girl or young woman named Jenny and her child, 1 Mulatto woman named Nell, 1 Negro boy named Pompey, another named Cesar, 1 Mulatto boy named Gabriel, 1 Mulatto girl named Suckey, 1 Negro boy named Bobb, 1 Negro boy named Isaac, 1 old brown horse, 1 old white horse, 1 black mare, 1 crooked backed bay horse, 1 black mare with a white face, 1 old black horse, 1 roan mare, 1 bay mare, 1 mare with white mane and tail, 1 brown horse, 2 bay mare yearling colts [sic], 1 brown horse colt, 1 bay horse colt, 1 with white main and tail 2 years old, 1 colt, 1 black mare, another black mare, 14 milk cows, 1 black bull, 2 steers three years old, 3 yearling heifers, 1 red pied heifer two years old, 23 ewes and lambs, 5 weathers [sic], 2 rams, 1 copper kettle, 132 lbs weight, 1 clock, 2 desks, 1 old desk, 10 beds and furniture, 1 old case of drawers, 1 old oval table, 1 old wagon, 2 old carts and back bands. Void when Hance Rudolph and his wife Ann fully settle the estate of the said John Kankey and give full accounting for the balance of the estate to whom it belongs at the next (Nov) sitting of the court. The goods remain in the custody of Hance Rudolph. A viewing and description of the goods and chattels amounting to £750.3s was made "yesterday" by Robert Hart and Francis Mauldin. Made & Ackn: 4 May 1753. Wit: Ja. Hollyday, Tho's. Ringgold. JPs: John Veazey, Adam VanBebber. Rec: same day. M's. Bordley, Clerk.

P. 529 Mortgage. James Morgan (son and heir to Hugh Morgan, deceased) and his wife Rachel of Cecil Co., farmer, for £44, to Joseph Wallace of the same place, blacksmith, a tract of 150 acres called Zebulon's Fancy on the west branch of Elk River. Zebulon Hollingsworth was granted by patent dated 1 Oct 1733 the 150 acres called Zebulon's Fancy which was recorded in Book L. L. No. 8, folio 772. Zebulon conveyed this land to Hugh Morgan by deed recorded 14 Nov 1733 in Book S. K. No. 6, folios 153-156. Morgan is to repay Wallace on or by 1 Apr 1756 and will remain in possession of the land unless he defaults on the loan. Made & Ackn: 7 Apr 1753. Wit: Nath'n. Baker, Henry Horah, Geo. Rock. JPs: Nath'n. Baker, Geo. Rock. Rec: 17 May 1753. M's. Bordley, Clerk.

P. 532 Bill of Sale. Thomas Shepherd of Cecil Co., planter, to Anthony Smith of the same place, for £61.19s.6p, the Negroes named Sudy, Moll, Toby and Parraway. Made & Ackn: 10 May 1751. Wit: John Holtham and JP Nath'n. Baker. Rec: 18 May 1753.

P. 533 Bill of Sale. William Currer of Cecil Co., planter, £3.18s.6p, to Oliver Miller, 6 acres of wheat growing on the plantation that formerly belonged to John McClannan. Made: not given. Wit: Tho. Kirkpatrick, Joseph Kinsey. Ackn: 19 May 1753. JP: Geo. Rock. Rec: same day.

P. 533 Bill of Sale. Joseph Coart, for £40, to Henry Baker, 1 flea bitten horse branded "H" [or "tt"], 1 young black mare branded "IR" [or "JR"], 1 bay horse, 3 cows, 12 old hogs and some young ones, 2 feather beds and furniture, 1 desk, 1 large bible, and all his other utensils, pewter, brass, iron, cast iron, bead cloths, and plantation implements, goods and chattels. [Coart also spelled Coarf, Coars.] Made & Ackn: 11 May 1753. Wit: John Smith, William Currer. JP: Nath'n. Baker. Rec: 24 May 1753. M's. Bordley, Clerk.

P. 534 Bill of Sale. William Buttrum of Frederick Co., for £4, to James Burns, a dark brown horse branded "MS". [Buttrum also spelled Butturm.] Made 19 May 1753. Wit: Thomas Wiles [Miles?], Rid. Ridgway. Rec: 28 May 1753. M's. Bordley, Clerk.

P. 534 Mortgage. Philip Cazier the Younger of Charles Town, Cecil Co., joiner, for £17.4s.11p, to Edward Mitchell of the same place, merchant, a fourth part of the northwestern corner of lot #22 in Charles Town bounded by Caroline Street. Cazier to repay Mitchell on or by 1 Mar next. Made 19 May 1753. Wit: Nath'n. Baker, Oliver Miller, Geo. Rock. Ackn: same day by Philip Cazier, Jr. and his wife Mary. JP: Nath'n. Baker, Geo. Rock. Rec: 31 May 1753. M's. Bordley, Clerk.

P. 536 Bill of Sale. Philip Cazier the Younger of Charles Town, Cecil Co., joiner, for £15.15s, to Edward Mitchell of the same place, merchant, 3 feather beds and furniture, 3 iron pots, 1 bell "mettle" skillet, 1 corner cupboard, 1 oval walnut table, 5 pewter dishes and 12 pewter plates. Void when Cazier repays Mitchell on or by 1 Mar next. Made & Ackn: 19 May 1753. Wit. & JPs: Nath'n. Baker, Geo. Rock. Rec: 31 May 1753. M's. Bordley, Clerk.

P. 538 Bill of Sale. John Jones of Cecil Co., planter, for £19.19s, to Edward Mitchell of Charles Town, Cecil Co., 1 dark brown horse branded "DB", another dark brown horse branded "I" [or "J"], 1 bay mare, 1 red cow, a red & white heifer big with calf, 1 black heifer and a red & white yearling heifer. Jones to repay Mitchell on or by 1 Mar next to void this bill of sale. Made & Ackn: 19 May 1753. Wit: Matt's. Bordley, Nath'n. Baker. JP: Nath'n. Baker. Rec: 31 May 1753. M's. Bordley, Clerk.

P. 540 Bill of Sale. Benjamin Bradford of Cecil Co., chirurgeon, for £41.6p and 1,258 lbs of tobacco, to Edward Mitchell of Cecil Co., merchant, and Robert Alison of the same place, gent., 1 Mulatto slave named Sarah and her child, a 3-pint silver cup and server, 1 silver can, 1 large silver scalloped dish, 1 silver sugar bowl, 3 silver table spoons, 2 best beds and their furniture, 1 silver watch, 1 cow and 1 horse. Benjamin Bradford to repay Mitchell and Alison on or by 1 Dec next to void this bill of sale. Made & Ackn: 29 May 1753. Wit: James Baxter, Matt's. Bordley. JP: James Baxter. On the back of this bill of sale was written: Robert Alison, for £20.10s.3p and 629 lbs of tobacco, quit claims to Edward Mitchell his share of this bill of sale. Made 29 May 1753. Wit: Matt's. Bordley. Rec: 31 May 1753. M's. Bordley, Clerk.

P. 542 Deed. Simon Johnson of Cecil Co., farmer, for £105, to Zebulon Hollingsworth of the same county, innkeeper, 50 acres, part of a tract called Friendship on the north side of Elk River by the west corner of a large marsh claimed by the heirs of William Alexander, gent., and east of old Simon Johnson's place. Made & Ackn: 5 May 1753. Wit: John Hyland and JPs Geo. Rock, Nich'o. Hyland. [Zebulon Hollingsworth called "Captain." Simon's name also spelled Symon.] Hollingsworth paid 2 shillings alienation fine to Matt's. Bordley 5 Jun 1753. Rec: same day.

P. 543 Deed. William Robinson, now of Augusta Co., VA, but late of Chester Co., PA, yeoman, and Isabella his wife, for £80, to James Galt of said Chester Co., yeoman, 100 acres, part of a tract called Kennedy's Adventure. By patent dated 12 Aug 1720, Lord Baltimore conveyed a tract of 500 acres in Cecil Co. called Kennedy's Adventure to Hugh Kennedy of Ann Arundel Co. (recorded in patent office in Lib. C. E. W., folios 269-270. Henry Bennet and his wife Margaret and Elizabeth Kennedy, daughters of the deceased Hugh Kennedy, conveyed the land to Henry Baker by deed dated 23 Oct 1740 and recorded 20 Mar 1741/2 in Lib. E. J. No. 3, folio 205. Henry Baker and his wife Elizabeth conveyed 100 acres of the land to James Crumley by deed dated 3 Feb 1742, recorded 10 Mar 1742 in Lib. W. K. No. 9, folios 178-180. James Crumley and his wife Catharine conveyed the land to the said William Robinson by deed dated 25 Aug last past. William Robinson and his wife Isabella appoint John Smith and his wife Margaret to be their attorney to ackn. this deed. Made 9 Dec 1752. Wit: Neal McCaskey, Thomas McCuistion. Ackn: in Cecil Co. 24 Apr 1753 by Neal McCaskey, John Smith and his wife Margaret Smith before JPs Nich'o. Hyland, Nath'n. Baker. Galt paid 4 shillings alienation fine 6 Jun 1753 to Matt's. Bordley. Rec: same day.

P. 546 Deed. Jacob VanBebber of Redlyon Hundred, Newcastle Co. on Delaware, yeoman, and Timothy Griffith of the same county, gent., for £650, to John Passmore of Cecil Co., yeoman, a plantation and 110 acres of land in Newmunster, Cecil Co., on Elk River near the lands of David Alexander and James Alexander. VanBebber and Griffith will warrant the land against any claims of Tim. Roberts and his heirs. Made & Ackn: 15 Dec 1752. Wit. & JPs: R'd. Thompson, Adam VanBebber. John Passmore paid 2s.2½p alienation fine 8 Jun 1753 to M's. Bordley. Rec: same day.

P. 547 Cecil County, to wit: I hereby certify that the aforegoing pages from folio 1 to 547 (inclusive) are truly transcribed from Liber F. L., No. 13. Test: Jo. Baxter, Cl.

[The preceding was abstracted from *Cecil County Court Land Records 1748-1758* microfilm #MSA WK 945-46 photographed by the Genealogical Society, Salt Lake City, Utah, 1948.]

Notes

INDEX

Abbott, Mary, 85
  William, 85, 153
Adaer, Sam'l., 202
Adams, George, 199
  Rachel, 204
Aikin, James, 17
Alcock, Elizabeth, 6
  Humphrey, 6, 29, 37, 166, 196
  Johanna, 166
  John, 6, 166
  Mary, 6, 166
  Sarah, 166
Alexander, Aaron, 159, 179
  Amos, 154
  Andrew, 59–60, 72, 83, 92, 143–145, 175, 185, 202, 215
  Ann, 179
  Anna, 162, 173
  Araminta, 95
  Aron, 178–179
  Arthur, 154, 212
  David, 14, 17, 29, 83, 112, 129, 155, 159, 163, 165, 178–179, 224
  Elias, 162, 173
  Francis, 79, 158
  Isaac, 175, 215
  James, 14, 23, 29, 32, 83–84, 90, 104, 112, 129, 154–156, 159, 163, 165, 212, 224
  James, Capt., 14
  Jean, 83
  Jed'ah., 47
  Jedediah, 162, 169, 173
  Jedidiah, 47
  John, 159, 212
  Joseph, 90, 112
  Lewey, 215
  Margaret, 90
  Martin, 2, 4–5, 9, 17, 135, 157, 170
  Mary, 14, 104

Alexander *cont'd*
  Moses, 14, 29, 32, 104, 112, 129, 163, 178–179
  Nath., 201
  Nathaniel, 201
  Nath'l., 178
  Paul, 2, 4–5
  Robert, 53
  Samuel, 7, 9, 17, 59
  Sophia, 84
  Susannah, 9
  Theo's., 219
  Tho's., 156
  Will, 61, 66
  William, 29, 39, 53, 65–66, 75, 95, 116, 154, 221, 224
  Zebulon, 159
Alison, *see also* Allison, Elison
  Robert, 156, 175, 212, 223–224
Allen, James, 96, 204
Allingham, Philip, 133–134
  Philip, Capt., 133–134
Allison, *see also* Allison, Elison
  Hugh, 174
  James, 157–158, 164–165, 198
  John, 126
  Mary, 165
  Robert, 126, 154, 214
  Thomas, 121
  Wm., 209
Allman, Abraham, 84, 102, 169, 177, 201, 204
  Joseph, 151, 201
  Margaret, 169
  Teresa, 151, 201
Alman, Abraham, 11, 45, 49
Altham, *see also* Haltham, Holtham
  John, 165, 206
Amspoker, Elizabeth, 146

Amspoker *cont'd*
  Sarah, 146
  Tobias, 146
Anderson, Jacob, 47–48, 171, 197, 207
  James, 47–48, 171, 197
  John, 47–48, 171, 197, 207
  Mounce, 26–27, 90, 103, 108, 133
Andrews, Latitia, 163
  Moses, 53, 114, 157–158, 163–164, 188, 190, 198, 209
  Mos's., 104
  Mounce, 86, 92, 103, 133, 140
  Mounts, 148, 152
Annis, Julian, 30
Archer, Jacob, 83
  Thomas, 174
Arinst, *see also* Arnest, Arrants
  Johannes, 172
Armstrong, Archibald, 54, 75
  James, 14, 54, 75
  James Archibald, 153
  Jane, 158
  Robert, 158
  William, 158
Arnest, *see also* Arinst, Arrants
  Johannes, 149
Arnett, Samuel, 137
Arrants, *see also* Arinst, Arnest
  Johanas, 197
  Johanes, 155
  Johanus, 175
  John, 207
  Joh's., 199
Arreer, Benedictus, 124
Arthur, Matthew, 81
  Robert, 209
Atkeson, John, 173

Atkey, Angelica, 184
Angellica, 43
Ann, 42-43, 184
John, 42-43, 62, 67, 142,
 159, 184
Mary, 43, 184
Attwood, Peter, 1
Auelman, Sarah, 42
Avelman, Sarah, 42-43
Bailey, *see also* Baily, Bayley
John, 199
Baily, *see also* Bailey, Bayley
Aurmaell, 204
Baine, John, 187, 208
Baird, *see also* Beard
Alex'r., 150-158, 160-
 167, 170-173
Alexr., 173
Mary, 32
Thomas, 32, 179-180
Baker, Ann, 34
Ann (Christian), 11, 35
Elizabeth, 112, 224
Henry, 10, 97, 100, 105-
 106, 108-109, 111-
 112, 114-119, 121-
 123, 126-129, 142,
 150, 153-154, 156-
 158, 164, 174, 183,
 191, 207, 212, 217,
 219, 221-222, 224
Joyce, 199
Mary, 10
Nathan, 116, 121-123,
 126-132, 135, 138-
 139, 143, 146-150,
 153-158, 162-163,
 166-168, 172-175,
 177, 190-192, 199,
 212, 214, 216
Nath'n., 172, 175-176,
 178-180, 184-186,
 189-190, 193, 196,
 198-201, 204, 207-
 208, 212-214, 218-
 223
Thomas, 11, 34-35
Will'm., 190
Wm., 186
Baldwin, Catharine, 181
Jno., 107

Baldwin *cont'd*
John, 7, 10, 12-13, 15-
 16, 19, 21-31, 36-37,
 53, 55, 62, 65-66, 68,
 83-90, 92, 94-95, 97,
 99, 101, 103-104,
 106-111, 115-123,
 125, 127-128, 132-
 136, 138, 141-142,
 144-145, 148-150,
 155, 159, 161, 181,
 197
Mary, 85, 101, 110
_____, 44
Barnaby, Richard, 197
Barnes, Ann, 121
William, 121
Barnum, Thomas, 211
Barr, David, 95
Barratt, Andrew, 189, 203,
 219
Jane, 219
Philip, 219
Barrett, Andrew, 191
Philip, 50
Barry, *see also* Berry
A., 2-4, 6, 8-9, 12-17,
 19, 21, 25, 29, 32, 35-
 36, 39-40, 45, 47, 53-
 56, 58, 66-70, 73, 75,
 77-80, 88, 90-91, 96,
 98, 100-101, 104-
 105, 108-109, 111-
 112, 114-115, 117-
 120, 126-127, 129-
 131, 135, 137-139,
 144, 146, 155, 157-
 158, 163
Andrew, 7, 16, 28, 49,
 55, 97, 172, 188, 210
Andrew, Mr., 8
Andw., 24
Mary, 39, 54
Bartlet, Benjamin, 45
Frances, 45
Bartlett, Jno., 186
Bass, Joseph, 193
Bassett, Arnold, 67
Bateman, John, 87-88
William, 87
Bavington, John, 206-207

Bavington *cont'd*
Mary, 207
Baxter, Andrew, 158
Grace, 216
James, 70, 72, 146, 148-
 150, 152-156, 158-
 159, 163, 168-169,
 173-176, 180, 184,
 189, 193, 200, 205,
 208-209, 213-216,
 218-220, 223
Jo., 80, 144, 225
John, 33, 158, 207
William, 168
Wm., 174
Bayard, James, 29, 42, 55,
 61, 63-64, 68-69, 78,
 86, 91, 93, 104-105,
 107, 124, 143, 154,
 159-161, 169, 173-
 174, 182, 189, 193-
 196
John, 160-161
P., 160-161, 164-166,
 170, 173-174, 177,
 179, 182, 184-185,
 187, 191-192, 195-
 196, 199-205, 210,
 215-217
Peter, 41, 76, 104, 109,
 114, 118, 122, 124,
 131-135, 139, 142-
 143, 179, 189, 193-
 194, 211
Peter, Capt., 76, 93
Pr., 153, 159
Pt., 148
Samuel, 55, 107, 193-
 194
Bayley, *see also* Baily, Bailey
Armwell, 204
Beals, William, 185
Beard, *see also* Baird
Mary, 32
Thomas, 32, 34-35, 179
Beastin, *see also* Beasting,
 Beaston
Elizabeth, 92
William, 47, 86, 88, 91-
 92

Beasting, *see also* Beastin,
Beaston
William, 36
Beaston, *see also* Beastin,
Beasting
Elizabeth, 85
William, 38, 85
Beaty, *see also* Betty
Walter, 163
Beck, J., 33, 50
John, 23
Beddle, *see also* Beedle,
Beetel, Beetle
John, 141
Beder, Rich'd., 173
Bedford, Gunning, 118, 126
Beedle, *see also* Beddle,
Beetel, Beetle
Elizabeth, 49
Jno., Sr., 107
John, 53, 183
John, Jr., 221
Richard, 171, 175
Samuel, 216
Thomas, 49, 183
William, 49, 92, 221
William, Sr., 183
____, 173
Beetel, *see also* Beddle,
Beedle, Beetle
John, 17
Beetle, *see also* Beddle,
Beedle, Beetel
Benedict, 210
Elizabeth, 131
Samuel, 210
Thomas, 2, 4–5, 59, 125, 131, 175
Beezley, Wm., 6
Beggar, Peacock, 169
Bell, Joseph, Jr., 115
Bellarmin, John, 110
Belt, Joseph, Jr., 115
Bennet, Henry, 112, 224
John, 48, 62
Margaret, 112
Margaret (Kennedy), 112, 224
____, 70
Bennett, Elizabeth, 83, 91
Henry, 174

Bennett *cont'd*
John, 83, 91
Margaret (Kennedy), 174
Richard, 23–24, 33, 50, 90, 99, 105, 110, 116, 133–134, 148–149, 152, 158
William, 185
____, 176
Benson, Benjamin, 159, 164, 176–177, 183
Daniel, 30, 35, 38
Mary, 38
Mary Ann, 160
P., 4
Pervy, 4
Bentham, Rich'd., 9
Bernard, Luke, 213–214
Margaret, 213
Berry, *see also* Barry
Andrew, 89, 116, 122
Best, Isabella, 166
Bett, Joseph, Jr., 115
Bettel, *see* Beedle, Beetle
Betty, *see also* Beaty
Martha, 129
Walter, 29, 129
Bickerton, Sarah, 221
Bigg, Jem., 133–134
Bing, John, 112
Bird, Iseable, 177
J., 31
Thomas, 177
Bishop, John, 188
Blacke, John, 3
Bladen, Thomas, 122, 142, 218
Thomas, Gov., 113, 115–116, 124–125, 135–137, 141, 145, 182
Blaidenburgh, Benjamin, 41
Blakey, R'd., 217
Susanah, 73
Blakiston, Ebenezer, 43
Blany, Katherine, 63
Bledenburgh, Judith, 64
Blidenburgh, Judith, 52
Boalding, *see* Bolding, Bouldin, Boulding
Boarn, *see also* Bourn

Boarn *cont'd*
Wm., 4
Boggs, William, 129, 199
Bolding, *see also* Bouldin, Boulding
Richard, 174
Thomas, 174
William, 174
Bollen, John, 4
Bonar, John, 205
Bond, John, 196
Samuel, 12, 111, 118–119, 168
W., 128
William, 128
Wm., 127
Bonner, Francis, 63, 74, 139, 186, 196–197
Mary, 74
Booker, Edward, 5, 125
____, 2, 4
Booth, Thomas, 138, 156, 165
Bordley, M., 150, 157–181, 183, 185
Matt, 175, 177–178, 180
Matthias, 177, 220
Matt's., 168, 175, 179, 189, 196, 198–200, 202–204, 208–209, 211–213, 215, 217–221, 223–224
Matts., 190
M's., 182–224
Thomas, Jr., 147, 160
William, 202–203
Borom, Anry, 95
Bostick, Thomas, 70, 88, 92
Bouchel, Sluyter, 183
Bouchell, Catharine, 195–196, 204–205, 210
Catharine (Herman), 192
Joseph, 204
Peter, 55, 116, 143, 203
Peter Aug'n., 205, 210
Peter Aug't., 192, 195–196, 203–204
Peter Augustine, 186
Peter, Dr., 114
Sluyter, 77, 116, 143
Sluyter, Dr., 116, 204

Bouchell *cont'd*
  Z.(?), 170
Bouldin, *see also* Bolding,
    Boulding
  Ann, 125
  James, 12
  Mary, 126
  Richard, 126, 170
  Thomas, 2, 4, 125, 215
  William, 125
  Wm., 95
Boulding, *see also* Bolding,
    Bouldin
  Alexander, 4, 59–60
  Ann, 131
  Elizabeth, 30, 197
  James, 30, 175, 197
  Mary, 60
  Richard, 6, 13, 40, 60, 90,
    113, 126, 131, 143,
    175
  Thomas, 2, 4, 14, 55,
    131, 143
  Thomas, Jr., 175
  Thomas, Sr., 175
  Thos., 4
  William, 2, 4–6, 13–14,
    30, 50
  William, Jr., 2, 14, 30, 50
  William, Sr., 2, 4, 14
  Wm., 113
Bourn, *see also* Boarn
  Henry, 134
Bowen, Charles, 6
  Soloman, 29
  Solomon, 196
Bower, *see also* Bowers,
    Bowyer, Boyer
  Esther, 51
  Peter, 51
Bowers, *see also* Bower,
    Bowyer, Boyer
  Easter, 31
  Esther, 31
  Isaac, 8, 11, 26, 31
  Isaak, 31
Bowyer, *see also* Bower,
    Bowers, Boyer
  Augustine, 11
  Esther, 50–51
  Peter, 50–51

Bowyer *cont'd*
  Rebecca (Christian), 11
Boyd, Hugh, 39, 106
  Mary, 39
Boyde, Hugh, 6
Boyer, *see also* Bower,
    Bowers, Bowyer
  Augustine, 34–35
  Ester, 198
  Esther, 51
  Hester, 198
  Peter, 51, 102, 146, 198
  Rebecca, 34
  Rebecca (Christian), 35
Boyles, James, 113
Boys, Nathan, 39, 106, 204
  Susanna, 106
Bozman, Risd'n., 4
  Risdon, 4
Bradford, Ben, 83
  Ben., 35, 66, 72
  Benjamin, 35, 78, 115,
    223
  Benjamin, Dr., 94, 125
Bradley, James, 34
Bravard, *see also* Brevard
  Jno., Jr., 74
  John, 96, 113
  John, Jr., 72, 96
  John, Sr., 96
Breading, *see also* Breeding,
    Brideing
  Thomas, 19
Breeding, *see also* Breading,
    Brideing
  Isaac, 29
  Jane, 19
  Thomas, 19
Brerewood, Thos., 127–128
Brevard, John, 9
Brice, J., 97
  Jno., 97, 133–134
  John, 180, 211
  Sarah, 180
Brideing, *see also* Breading,
    Breeding
  Jane, 64
  Thomas, 64
Briding. *see* Breading,
    Breeding, Briding
Bristoll, William, Jr., 16

Bristow, Catharine, 109
  George, 102
  John, 111, 188
  William, 24, 32, 109,
    148, 153, 210, 221
  William, Jr., 15–16, 23
Brittain, Benjam., 32
Brockers, William, 41
Brokers, William, 87
Brokus, William, 41
Bromfield, Daniel, 128
Brooke, Jno., 149
Brooks, Cathran, 149
  James, 135–137, 190
  John, 135, 137, 149, 176
  Martha, 136
  Thomas, 136–137
Broom, James, 155
Broughton, Nath., 146
Browkus, William, 87
Brown, Charles, 11
  Hannah, 162
  Henry, 128
  Jethro, 119, 192, 201
  Jethro, Capt., 212
  John, 139–141, 191
  Joseph, 97, 162
  June D., 10, 52, 61, 75,
    79
  Margaret, 204
  Martha, 49
  Messor, 161
  Nathan, 204
  Rachel, 204
  Thomas, 108, 130–131,
    204
  Thomas, Sr., 106
  William, 49
Browne, Ch., 29
  Jethro, 10, 20
Browning, John, 59, 101
  Thomas, 38
Brumfield, Margaret, 162
  Sarah, 162
Bryane, D'tt., 178
Bubenheim, John, 42, 61,
    64, 69
Buchannan, Eleanor, 207
  James, 207
  John, 207
  Mary, 107

Buchannan *cont'd*
  Robert, 107
Buck, John, 16, 37, 41–42
Bull, James, 1
  Thomas, 1
Bullen, Thos., 4
Burch, Tho., 158
Burk, ____, 86
Burks, Patrick, 176
Burksfield, Patrick, 70
Burle, Robert, 133
Burns, James, 223
  John, 104
Butcher, Zach, 143, 217
  Zach., 111–112
Butler, Thomas, 115
Buttrum, William, 223
Butturm. *see* Buttrum
Cage, James, 186–187
  Jno., 120, 126, 157, 197
  John, 66, 113, 186–187
Calder, Ja., 114, 135
  James, 57, 133–134, 192
  James, Jr., 124–125
  Jas., 7
Caldwal, Samuel, 129
Caldwell, James, 169, 173
  John, 212–213
  Samuel, 31
Calvert, Benedict Leonard, Gov., 17
  Charles, Gov., 20, 153, 219
  Charles, Governor, 81
  Philip, 133
Calwall, *see also* Caldwell
  William, 68
Calwell, *see also* Caldwell
  Sam., 31
Campbell, Andrew, 205
  Elenor, 117
  Jno., 29, 138
  John, 10, 15, 26, 35, 64, 82, 87, 89, 117, 119, 123, 137–138, 181, 197, 217
  Rebeckah, 150
  ____, 35
Canasque, John, 207
Canter, Rich'd., 202
Carew, Nich'o. H., 168

Carew. *cont'd*
  Nicholas Hackett, Sir, 189
Carmack, Peter, 159
Carman, Caleb, 137
Carmichael, Robert, 109, 114, 118
Carmick. *see* Carmack
Carnall, Ann, 58
  Daniel, 58
  Deborah, 58
  Mary, 58
Carnan, John, 61, 192
  John, Jr., 192
  William, 192
Carr, *see also* Ker, Kerr
  John, 23–24
  John, Capt., 23–24, 172
  Paternella, 172
  Walter, 148
Carroll, Antho., 26
  Charles, 54, 93, 111, 117, 148, 157, 163–164, 172, 186, 188–189, 196, 198, 213
  Daniel, 4
  Dan'l., 186
  Dom, 10, 13
  Dominick, 13, 178
  James, 157, 164
  Juliana, 178
Carson, Elizabeth, 207
Carter, Joseph, 20, 24, 139
  Sarah, 20
Cartmell, Esther, 69
  Martin, 69, 190
  Nathaniel, 190
Cartmill, Esther, 66
  Martin, 66, 69, 71, 145, 167
Cartwright, Michael, 171
Carty, John, 177
Castevans, Thomas, 176
Castevens, Thomas, 75
Castle, Edmund, 212–213
Caswell, Richard, 34
Cathey, George, 12, 118
Catto, Fra., 210
  George, 221
Cattoe, Geo., 197–198
Caulk, Ja., 141

Cazier, Catherine, 45, 122
  John, 122, 160, 170
  Mary, 207, 223
  Philip, 44–45, 143
  Philip, Jr., 143, 152, 192, 207, 217, 223
  Philip, Sr., 122, 143
  Philip The Younger, 223
  Rebecca, 160
  Richard, 143
Chamberlain, Samuel, 116, 122
Chamberlaine, Sam., 90
Chamberlin, John, 41
  John, Jr., 82
  Rachel, 82
  Samuel, 89
  William, 41
Chambers, Catharine, 211
  David, 120, 123
  James, 82
  John, 77, 82, 146
  John, Jr., 146
  Mr., 82
  Rachel, 77, 82, 146
  Rowland, 117, 120, 123, 166, 168
Chapman, Nathaniel, 189
  Nath'n., 216
Cheek, *see also* Chick, Chicke
  John, 49
Chelwynd, William, 113
Cherry, Susana, 77
Cheston, Daniel, 180, 211, 214–215
  Franscina Augustina, 214–215
Chew, B'a., Jr., 200
  Benj., 128, 150–151
  Benj'a., 134–135, 155, 167, 169, 177, 179, 185, 191–192, 200, 204, 207–208, 210, 213, 215–217, 220–221
  Benja., 93, 152, 154, 157, 161–162, 174, 197
  Benjamin, 116, 122, 127, 142–143, 146, 182, 208

Chew cont'd
  Benjamin, Jr., 147, 182,
    208
  Elizabeth, 162
  Henrietta (Lloyd), 147,
    160
  Nath'l., 133–134
  Phineas, 216
  Samuel, Jr., 147
  Samuel The Younger,
    160
Chick, see also Chicke,
    Cheek
  John, 147, 160
  John, Jr., 147
  John, Sr., 147
  Joseph, 160, 166
  Mary, 166
  Mary (Alcock), 166
  Nathaniel, 147
  Nath'l., 192
  Susanna, 147
  Tabitha, 160
Chicke, see also Chick,
    Cheek
  John, Sr., 160
  Joseph, 160–161
Childs, Benjamin, 9, 87, 92
  Martha, 92
Chirton, Daniel, 147
Chisholm, John, 168, 192,
    199
Christian, Ann, 11, 35
  Rebecca, 11, 35
  Sarah, 35
  Sarah (Wheeler), 11
  Thomas, 11, 35, 125
Clark, John, 52, 221
Classons, Peter, 147
Clauson, Peter, 153, 172
Clay, Thomas, 120
Clayton, Richard, 111
Cleave, Benjamin, 141
  Nathan, 141
  Nathaniel, 141
Cleghorn, Susanah, 79
Clements, Abraham, 74
  Ann, 67
  Cornelius, 67
  Elizabeth, 106
  Isaac, 67

Clements cont'd
  Jacob, 74
  Joseph, 139
  Michael, 14, 74, 106
  Rebecca, 106
Cleyton, Richard, 168
Cliff, Cornelius, 194
Coarf. see Coart
Coars. see Coart
Coart, Joseph, 222
Coatts, see also Coutts
  Charles, 23, 41, 78, 93,
    110, 116, 138
  Chas., 105
  Herculus, 172
  Jane (Vanderheyden),
    172
Cochran, John, 78, 113, 204
  Joseph, 78, 190
  Moses, 78
Cole, John, 86
Collet, John, 78, 82, 85
  Richard, 78
Collvill, Thomas, 205
Colvill, John, 44
  John, Capt., 44
  Tho., 1, 7, 17, 36, 54–55,
    57, 65, 78, 133–134,
    139, 142–143, 148,
    157, 160, 166, 170,
    172, 174, 177–178,
    184–185, 195, 210
  Thomas, 28, 44–45, 49,
    55–56, 76, 89, 93,
    106, 116, 118, 122,
    124–125, 200
  Thomas, Col., 76, 93,
    113, 135, 183
  Thomas, Colonel, 109,
    118, 123–124
  Tho's., 187, 192, 195–
    197
  Thos., 1, 3–4, 7, 10–11,
    20–21, 27, 29–30, 32,
    35, 41–42, 44, 46, 61,
    68, 70, 76, 85, 88, 92–
    95, 101, 107, 110,
    116, 124, 132, 136,
    205, 214
  _____, 196
Comegies, William, 24

Comegys, Cornelius, 39, 97,
    100, 162
  Edward, 150
  Mary, 150
Commins, see also Cumings,
    Cummine, Cummings
  Robert, 70
Condal, John, 156
Condon, Edward, 75
  John, 75
Congetton, James, 217
Coningsbey, Roger, 133–
    134
Connor, Philip, 213
Conor, Philip, Jr., 217
Cook, Neal, 102
  William, 102
Cookson, Thos., 169
Cooley, John, 149
  Ruth, 149
Cooper, John, 109, 164
  John, Jr., 109
Copen, Angelico, 42
  John, 67
Copin, John, 67
Coppen, Angelica, Mrs., 41
  Angellica (Atkey), 43
  John, 67
Coppin, Angelica (Atkey),
    184
  John, 52
Copson, Jno., 1, 6, 10, 12,
    15, 17, 20–24, 26, 28–
    29, 31–32, 34, 39, 45–
    48, 51, 59–61, 66–67,
    70–73, 81
  John, 7, 17, 20–22, 24,
    28, 36, 61, 118, 124–
    125
  John, Maj., 25, 205
  John, Major, 109, 113–
    114, 123
  Mary, 109, 114, 118, 123
Cory, see also Curry
  Robert, 37
Cosden, Alphonso, 2, 41, 43,
    79
Cossine, see also Cusine
  John, 175
Coulson, Martha, 97, 100
  Robert, 73, 91

Coulson *cont'd*
  Sarah (Richardson), 73,
    91
  Thomas, 39, 97, 100, 162
Coulter, Mich'a., 39
  Mich'l., 39
Course, John, 120
Coursey, Mary, 66
Coutts, *see also* Coatts
  Hercules, 38
Cowan, Rosanah, 53
  Rosannah (McCay), 57
  Thomas, 53, 57
Cowdon, James, 112
Cowen, John, 32
Cox, Abraham, 37
  Abram, 37
  Benjamin, 50
  Benjamin, Jr., 184
  Deans, 176
  Elizabeth, 162
  Henry, 124, 185
  John, 5, 48, 196
  Mary, 185
  Thomas, 138
  William, 17, 176
Crafford, *see also* Crawford
  Quinton, 51
Craford. *see* Crawford
Crage, George, 177
  Sarah, 176
Craig, James, 37, 78
  Thomas, 40
Crawford, *see also* Crafford
  Quinton, 122
  Samuel, 47
Cray, Cornelius, 204
Creswell, David, 161
Croazier, John, 144
Crocker, *see also* Croker
  Rachel, 21
  Robert, 21
  Thomas, 21
Crockett, Benj'a., 185, 213
  Benja., 183
  Gilbert, 34
Croker, *see also* Crocker
  Rachel, 37, 101, 136
  Rachel (Crouch), 136
  Robert, 33, 37, 101, 136
Croo, *see also* Crow

Croo *cont'd*
  Andrew, 105, 205
  Margaret, 205
  Mary, 105
  William, 105
Crosby, David, 186
Crouch, Margaret, 84
  Rachel, 136
  Thomas, 2, 136, 147
  Thomas, Jr., 84
Crow, *see also* Croo
  John, 6, 49
  William, 105
Crowly, Nicholas, 198
Crozier, John, 144
Crumley, Catharine, 224
  James, 112, 224
Crumly, Catherine, 174
  James, 174
  Katharine, 174
Cumings, *see also* Commins,
    Cummine, Cummings
  Robert, 199
Cummine, *see also* Commins,
    Cumings, Cummings
  James, 17
Cumming. *see* Cummings
Cummings, *see also*
    Commins, Cumings,
    Cummine
  Alex., 66, 133-134
  Alexander, 133-134
  James, 213
  Robert, 24, 72-73, 199
  Will, Jr., 115
Cummins. *see* Cummings
Cuningham, William, 205
Currer, *see also* Currier
  John, 81, 146, 157
  John, Sr., 220
  Miliscent, 146
  William, 73, 146, 205,
    218, 222-223
Currier, *see also* Currer
  Jane, 131
  John, 131-132, 146
  Millicent, 132
  Mr., 97
  William, 55, 90, 131
Curry, *see also* Cory
  Robert, 38

Curry *cont'd*
  Tenent, 38
Cusine, *see also* Cossine
  John, 172
Custephs. *see* Castevans
Dallam, Wm., 34
Dames, William, 125, 174
Daniel, John, 169
Dare, William, 1
  William, Jr., 1
  William, Sr., 1
Darnall, Jno., 201
  John, 116, 213-214
  Mary, 213-214
David, Henry, 123
Davidge, John, 78
Davis, David, 124
  Esther, 124
  Fouch, 52, 62, 69
  John, 196
  Rachel, 72
  Rebecca, 65, 69, 131
  Rebecca (McGregory),
    82
  Samuel, 196
  Thomas, 18, 52, 65, 69,
    74, 82, 91, 103, 131,
    152, 173, 215
  William, 72
  Williamincher (Polston),
    75
  Williminchie, 196
  Wm., 52
Davison, Samuel, 98, 110
Dawkins, Simon, 24
Daws, Isaac, 193
  Mary, 193
Dawson, James, 4, 58
  Mary, 4
  Mary (Carnall), 58
Dearmott, *see also* Dermott,
    Dirmot, Dorment
  Charles, 6
Death, Hannah, 214, 220
  Honor, 214, 220
  Honour, 39
  James, 214, 220
  John, 193, 214, 220
  Onorah, 220
  Randall, 39, 97, 214
  Randell, 100, 161-162,

233

Death, Randell cont'd
220
Sophia, 214, 220
Dehoff, Henry, 200
John, 57
Delamontange, Jesse, 68
Nicholas, 68
Dempster, David, 166
John, 166, 173–174
Denny, David, 97
Simon, 71
Dent, Geo., 180, 183
Deny, Simon, 138
Deoran, Will., 25, 29, 45
William, 25, 39, 69
Willm., 20, 22, 28, 32, 47–48
Wm., 21
Dermott, see also Dearmott, Dirmot, Dorment
Charles, 6, 203
Desaurency, Samuel, 137
Devall. see Duvall
Devan, Walter, 139
Dillon, John, 200
Dinsey, see also Disney
William, 128
Will'm., 128
Dirmot, see also Dearmott, Dermott, Dorment
Charles, 24
Discon, Nicholas, 169
Disney, see also Dinsey
William, 135
Wm., 135
Diven, Waller, 181
Walter, 169, 178, 181
Dobson, Adam, 221
Rich'd., 109
Dolan, Charles, 213
Donnel, William, 68
Donnell, James, 100, 162
Jane, 162
Jean, 162
William, 67
Dorment, see also Dearmott, Dermott, Dirmot
Charles, 16
Dorrell, Elizabeth, 56
Nicholas, 56, 88, 114
Dorsey, E., 171

Dorsey cont'd
Greenberry, 116
John, 180–181
John Hammond, 180
Vincent, 127, 180
Dorson, Samuel, 78
Dougherty, Ann, 213
Edward, 175, 213
Nathaniel, 9–10, 49
Patrick, 219
Douglas, Archibald, 170
George, 81
Susannah (Sewall), 81–82
Will'm, 41
Douglass, Archibald, 122, 160
George, 81, 142
James, 195
Susanah, 142
Susannah (Sewall), 81
Dowdall, John, 42, 63, 89
John, Maj., 31, 35, 52
John, Major, 10, 82
Richard, 10, 30–31, 42, 53, 82, 89
Downton, Thomas, 217
Drake, William, 132
_____, 23
Drewry, Edward, 1, 50
Driscoll, John, 164, 206
Drummond, Augustina, 174, 187
John, 174, 186–187, 190, 211, 220
Drummonds, John, 186
Drury. see Drewry
Dulaney, Dan, 180
Daniel, 116, 122
Dulany, Walter, 142
Dunkin, John, 133–134
Dunlap, Ninian, 156
Dunn, John, 205, 214
Tho., 124
Dushene, Anthony, 14–15, 47–48
Jemima, 47–48
Dushone, Antoney, 15
Duvall, John, 91
Samuel, 91
Dye, John, 16

Dyer, Hannah, 175
Hannah (Smith), 213
Roger, 175, 213
Eagleson, Bryan, 52
Earle, Mary, 178
Michael, 178, 199
Mich'l., 170
Eathrington. see Etherington
Eavenson, Nathaniel, 216–217
Richard, 216–217
Ebthorp, Thomas, 139
Thos., 120
Ebthrop, Thomas, 10
Edmiston. see Edmondson
Edmond, Evan, 137
Edmondson, Isabella, 145, 155
John, 66, 145–146, 155–156
Mary, 155
William, 155
Edmonson, Isabel, 117
John, 117
Mary, 117
William, 117
Edthrington. see Etherington
Edwards, John, 12, 27, 175
Mary, 27
Philip, 61
Phillip, 27
Ehzod?, John, 204
Eldersly, Elizabeth, 91
Henry, 91
Parnell, 91
Eliason, Cornelius, 164, 202
Cornelius, Sr., 201–202
Elias, 164, 202
Elison, see also Alison, Allison
Elizabeth, 177
Iseable, 177
James, 157
Thomas, 177
Ellberry, Frederick, 151
Elleer, Geo., 39
George, 39
Elliot, see also Ellot
Francis, 122

Elliot *cont'd*
  James, 186
  Thomas, 199
  William, 186
Elliott, Francis, 156
  James, 196
Ellis, Edward, 28, 67–68
  William, 27, 72, 101, 136
  Wm., 37, 114, 125
Ellot, *see also* Elliot
  Thomas, 186, 214
Emery, George, 110
  Sarah, 110
  Stephen, 110
England, Samuel, 112, 174
English, Ephesus (Tyliard), 22
  George, 22
Eruen, James, 171
Erwen, James, 171
Esten, James, 133–134
Etherington, Bartholomew, 103, 116, 120
  Thomas, 5, 160, 217
Euren, James, 171
Evans, Henry, 38
  James, 168, 182, 213–214
  John, 126, 137, 165
  Robert, 95, 126, 153, 163, 165, 171, 197–198, 207, 213, 215
Eveartson, Elizabeth, 149
Everdson, Evert, Jr., 1
  Jacob, 34, 64
Everson, Elias, 32, 109
  Evert, 149
  Job, 98
  Mary, 32, 109
Evertson, Elizabeth, 99
  Evert, 2, 73, 99
  Evert, Jr., 2, 99–100, 105
  Job, 49
Ewing, Alexander, 167
  Alex'r., 4
  James, 151, 167
  John, 167, 218
  Joss, 167
  Nath., 32
  Nathaniel, 97
  Nath'l., 4, 122, 129–131

Ewing *cont'd*
  Rebeckah, 167
  William, 167
Faires, *see also* Faris
  John, 202
  Moses, 209
Fanings, D., 213
Fankett, Thomas, 196
Faris, *see also* Faires
  Robert, 161
Farra, Frances, 82, 168
  Frances Ann, 192
  Francis, 168
  Francis Ann, 169
Fartado, Anthony, 200
Ferguson, William, 212
Ferris, Patrick, 137
Few, Mary, 127
  William, 127
Finley, James, 219
Flale, Henry, 30
Fogg, Amos, 115, 219
Folwell, Edward, 138
Ford, Charles, 199, 206
  Edward, 195
  George, 119, 126
  Mary, 195
  Richard, 195, 210
  Richard Boulding, 195
  Robert, 161
Forster, Francis, 191, 199
  James, 156
  Thomas, 35, 191, 199
  Tho's., 191
  Thos., 157
Foster, Hugh, 193
  James, 3–4, 14, 90, 96
  John, 96, 119
  Mary, 3
  Richard, 3, 119
  Sarah, 119
  Tho's., 186
  Thos., 157
  William, 3, 7, 72, 96
Foulton, *see also* Fulton
  John, 220
Frasher, Elisabeth, 190
Frazier, *see also* Frezar
  James, 177
  Joseph, 31
Freeman, Hannah, 71

Freeman *cont'd*
  Isaac, 71, 153
  Matthias, 62
  Richard, 13
  Susannah, 71
  William, 71, 85, 100
Frezar, *see also* Frazier
  Joseph, 31
Frier, James, 198
Frisby, Anna, 107
  Ariana, 177
  Elizabeth, Widow, 184
  James, 58, 133
  Jane, 84
  Pere., 120
  Pereg., 89, 93, 107, 115–119, 121, 123–124, 139
  Pereg'n., 60, 114–115, 125–131, 135
  Pereg'r., 130, 132, 134–135, 140–142
  Peregrin, 148
  Peregrine, 14, 58, 152
Fulingham, John, 186
Fulton, *see also* Foulton
  George, 211
  Samuel, 220
Furroner, Edward, 203
Gale, Betty, 74
  Levin, 82, 89, 116, 122
  Sevin, Col., 74
Gallasbie, *see also* Gillespie
  George, 4
Gallashot, _____, 147
Gallt, James, 174
Galt, James, 224
Gardner, Rob't., 90
Garison, *see* Garrison
Garrison, *see also* Geirison, Geerison
  Peter, 38, 67–68
  Sarah, 38
Gartril, John, 108, 130–131
Gartrill, John, 108
Gater, Ann (Ruley), 97
  John, 97
Gaylard, Joseph, 133–134
Gears, *see also* Geers
  John, 119, 122
  Susannah, 119

Gee, Osgood, Baronet, 189
Geerison, *see also* Garrison,
  Geirison
  Peter, 28
Geers, *see also* Gears
  John, 184
Geirison, *see also* Garrison,
  Geerison
  Peter, 28
  Sarah, 28
Gelder, Daniel, 197
Gelfton, Samuel, 23
George, Alice, 29, 135
  Jos., 42, 55, 76
  Joshua, 17, 19, 29–30,
    35, 44–46, 61, 70, 76–
    78, 81, 87, 89, 94,
    101, 117, 126–127,
    132–134, 136, 140,
    176, 196
  Siddne, 176
  Sidney, 29, 70, 124–125,
    159, 196, 206, 208,
    214
Gesigne, John, 147
Gibbon, H., 162
  Nich., 151
Gibbons, John, 94
Gibson, Andrew, 191
  Elizabeth, 191
  John, 155
  Jonathan, 98
  Robert, 24
  Thomas, 191
Giles, Jacob, 91, 115, 119
  Johanna, 119
Gilesland, John, 15
Gillespie, *see also* Gallasbie
  George, 167
  James, 169
Gilpen, Jane, 32
  Samuel, 32
Gilpin, Jane, 20, 22, 112
  Jean, 112
  Sam'l., 106
  Samuel, 20–23, 66, 89,
    112, 142, 166, 217
Given, Robert, 111
Glens, James, 79
  Robert, 79
Glover, William, 8

Glover *cont'd*
  Wm., 31
Godment, Miles, 52
Golder. *see* Gelder
Goldsmith, George, 23, 85
  George, Capt., 139
  Henry Colesberry, 138
Good, Henry, 217
  Robert, 180
Gordon, Chas., 206
  Robert, 23–24, 33, 54,
    81–82, 94, 180
Grace, William, 192
Graham, John, 2–3, 6, 43–
    44, 49, 97
  Richard, 211
  William, 208, 216
Granger, Zasaerus, 218
Gray, Rachel, 39, 97, 100,
    162
  Richard, 39, 97, 100, 162,
    214
Green, Hester (Tyliard), 22
  Rachel, 47
  Rachell, 47
  Thomas, 47, 129, 151
Greenland, Hower, 204
Greenwood, Barbara, 109
  Barbary, 109
  George, 109
Greer, Theos., 2
Grew, Theophilus, 6
  Theos., 2
Griffee, Richard, 162, 220
Griffith, Richard, 196
  Timothy, 155, 165, 224
Grindley, Jeremiah, 161
Groom, ____, 74
Groome, Samuel, 120
Grub, Emmanuel, 6
Grubb, Ann, 33, 178
  Ann (Hitchcock), 33
  Emanual, Jr., 178
  Emanuel, 33, 178, 210
  Emanuel, Sr., 178
  Peter, 178
Grunvin, Thomas, 7
Gudgeon, Step'n., 149
Gueycett, Law., 19
Guieren, Gasper, 15
Guilder, Hukel, 192

Guilder *cont'd*
  Hukill, 212, 214
Gullick, Ann, 12
  Daniel, 12
  John, 12, 171
  John, Jr., 12
Gullicks, John, 79
Gundry, Benjamin, 34
  Gideon, 34
  Mary, 34
  Spry Godfrey, 34
Gutheries, Hugh, 79
Hack, Peter, 121
  ____, 205
Hackett, Mich'l., 146
Hagley, John, 71
Haines, Elizabeth, 130
  Joseph, 108, 130
Hall, Andrew, 71, 167
  Elihu, 75, 110, 128, 134–
    135
  Elisha, 128, 134–135
  Elliason, 167
  George, 50, 72, 116
  Gervas, 94
  James, 37
  John, 7, 27, 50, 116, 175,
    183
  Richard, 167
  Sam'l., 221
Haltham, *see also* Holtham,
  Altham
  Ann (Latham), 156
  Jno., 156
  John, 75, 83, 92, 206
  Spencer, 206
Ham, *see also* Hams, Hamm
  Abraham, 124
  Ephearm, 185
  Esther, 124
  Isaac, 133, 184
  Jacob, 124
  John, 185
  John, Jr., 139
Hambleton. *see* Hamilton
Hamilton, George, 157
  I., 169
  J., 149
  John, 180
  John, Rev., 146
  Margaret, 70

Hamilton *cont'd*
  Margarett, 176
  Patrick, 220–221
  William, 37
Hamm, *see also* Ham, Hams
  Ephraim, 185
  Isaac, 98, 133
  John, 98, 185
  John, Jr., 5–6
  Mary, 6
  Thomas, 6
Hammond, Charles, 28, 49, 89, 116, 122
  John, 180–181
Hammondorsey, Jo., 126
Hampton, David, 101–102, 125–126, 156
Hams, *see also* Ham, Hamm
  Isaac, 187
Hance, Elonar, 205
  John, 205
  Peter, 193
Hands, B., 172
  Bed, 172
  Beddingfield, 147
Harbuson, James, 73
Hardman, George, 171
Hargrave, Abraham, 94
  Charles, 124
  Isaac, 54, 94
  Thomas, 94
Harker, Catharine, 151
  Cathrine, 151
  Samuel, Jr., 151
  Samuel, Sr., 151
Harman, *see also* Herman
  Col., 37
  Ephraim Augustine, Col., 181
Harper, Jacob, 61–62, 95, 148, 181
  James, 95, 181
  John, 53, 61, 95, 102, 110, 126, 142, 148, 181
  Nicholas, 73, 77
  Sarah, 181
  Susanah, 73
  Thomas, 46, 61–62, 95, 148, 181
  William, 61, 95, 151, 181

Harris, Ariana Margaretta, 160
  Augustina, 38
  James, 4, 7, 38, 72, 89, 116, 179
  Mary, 172
  Mas., 38
  Matthias, 171–172
  Patrick, 217
  William, 4, 7, 72, 123, 139–141, 145, 160, 179, 185, 202, 211
Harrison, Hen., 133–134
  Henry, 190
  _____, 199
Hart, Robert, 147, 222
Hatcher, Ann, 23
  Ann (Vansandt), 23
  William, 23
Hatham, John, 60
Hattery, James, 160
Hawkins, Deborah (Carnall), 58
  John, 58
  John Stone, 201
  Mr., 78
Hayes, John, 89
Haynes, Hezekiah, 109
Hays, John, 89, 213
Hazlehurst, Benjamin, 85–86
  John, 85–86
  Mary, 86
Heath, Cha., 144
  Charles, 144, 173
  Chas., 141
  Daniel Charles, 142
  J. P., 144
  Ja. Paul, 84–90
  James, 2, 33, 90, 105, 107, 133–134, 152, 173, 179
  James Paul, 2, 7, 19, 33, 42–43, 46, 48–49, 63–64, 74, 78, 86, 91–92, 94, 99–100, 105–107, 109, 115–116, 121, 127–128, 131, 134–135, 140–144, 152, 162
  Jas. Paul, 1–4, 8–9, 11,

Heath, Jas. Paul *cont'd*
  13–21, 23–27, 31–45, 49–54, 56, 58–64, 66–68, 71–75, 79, 82–83, 85, 87
  Rebecca, 33, 92, 99–100, 106–107, 141, 152, 173
Hedges, Rebecca, 186
  William, 186, 190, 220
  Wm., 186
Hedrick, John, 177
Hendrickson, Catharine, 107
  Christopher, 26, 52–54, 58
  Elizabeth, 103
  Hendrick, 86, 140
  Henry, 5, 9, 52, 58, 88, 102–103
  Henry, Jr., 103
  Mary (Kilton), 53, 58
  Matthias, 88, 173
  Peter, 107, 126
  Samuel, 107
Henrexon, *see also* Hendrickson
  Henry, 18
Henry, William, 149
Herman, *see also* Harman
  Anna Margaretta, 192
  Araminta, 16, 20, 24–25
  Augustine, 68, 158, 165, 192, 195, 206
  Casparus, 186
  Catharine, 192
  Col., 10
  Eph'm. Aug., 139
  Eph'm. Aug't., Col., 156, 176
  Eph'm. Augt'n., Col., 139
  Ephr. Aug., Col., 7
  Ephr. Augt., 76
  Ephr. Augt'n., Col., 98
  Ephraim, 16–17, 25
  Ephraim Aug't., 11, 203
  Ephraim Augustine, 5–6, 41, 46, 49, 56–57, 60–61, 64, 66, 69, 84, 88, 105, 107, 125, 132, 151, 164, 169, 177,

Herman, Ephraim *cont'd*
    187, 191, 199–200
  Ephraim Augustine,
    Col., 16, 19, 29, 53–
    54, 61, 70, 75, 78,
    113, 120, 124, 126,
    192
  Franciana, 158
  Francina, 165
  Francine, 206
  Francinea, 195
  Godfrey, 46
  Mary, 192
Hiland, *see also* Hyland
  Nicholas, 178
Hill, Aron, 151
  Elizabeth, 182
  L., 162
  Mary, 83, 134
  Mary (Reynolds), 83
  Richard, 142
  Richard, Dr., 142
  Rich'd., Dr., 45
  Samuel, 45, 182
  William, 83, 132, 134,
    182
Hinchman, James, 94
Hind, Elizabeth
    (Richardson), 73, 91
  Richard, 73, 91
Hinton, Rees, 107
Hitchcock, Ann, 33
  Thomas, 33, 51
  Thomas The Younger,
    138
  Thos., 175
Hitchman, William, 182,
    198–199
Hobson, George, 98
Hodgson, Jonathan, 187
  Robert, 59, 127
Hoe, Jane, 1
  Richard, 1
Hog, *see also* Hogg, Hugg
  William, 96
Hogg, *see also* Hog, Hugg
  William, 17, 114
Holland, George, 115
  Jno., 73, 92, 105, 171
  John, 56, 189
  Mary, 189

Hollands, Christopher, 201
Hollet, John, 132
Holliday, *see also* Hollyday,
    Holyday
  Jam., Jr., 83
  James, 89
  Jas., 206
  Jas., Jr., 109
Hollingsworth, Abra., 71
  Abraham, 8, 11, 111,
    117, 120, 123, 167
  Abram, 155
  Ann, 71
  Grace, 7–8
  Henry, 28, 157, 165, 198
  Jacob, 8
  Jesse, 165
  John, 190
  Joseph, 71, 167
  Mary, 198, 221
  Mr., 171
  Stephen, 8, 17, 65, 114–
    115
  Thomas, 7–8
  Zeb., 165, 210
  Zebulon, 26, 28, 32, 55,
    65, 71, 95, 106, 109,
    167, 198, 221–222,
    224
  Zebulon, Capt., 71, 197,
    224
  Zebulon, Captain, 221
  ———, 48
Holloway, James, 36
Hollyday, *see also* Holliday,
    Holyday
  Ja., 222
  James, 116, 122, 192
  James, Jr., 126
  John, Jr., 115
Holt, Obadiah, 54
Holtham, *see also* Haltham,
    Altham
  Ann, 92
  John, 92, 114, 185, 200,
    206, 222
Holton, Jesse, 74
  Sarah, 74
Holy, Ann, 12, 45, 78, 114
  Anne, 209–210
  Robert, 12, 17, 45, 54,

Holy, Robert *cont'd*
    78, 93, 111, 114–115,
    123, 148, 163, 168,
    172, 209–210
  Robt., 24
  Thomas, 12
Holyday, *see also* Holliday,
    Hollyday
  James, 49
Hood, Alee, 176
  Alice, 29, 70
  William, 29, 70, 86, 120,
    176
  Wm., 29, 75, 176
  Wm., Mr., 30
Hooper, Henry, 114
Hope, Jno., 215
  John, 215
Hopkins, William, 134–135
  Wm., 134–135
Horah, Henry, 222
Hoser, *see also* Ozier
  Jacob, 187
Hosier, Jacob, 132
Houghton, Richard, 31
Houston, Joseph, 127
  Lydia, 191
  Samuel, 21
  William, 67, 69
Howard, John, 183
  Michael, 7, 28, 31, 49
Hugg, *see also* Hog, Hogg
  Mary, 40
  William, 40
Hughes, *see also* Hughs,
    Huse
  Alice, 65
  Ann, 195
  Elisha, 193
  James, 55–56, 65, 89,
    109, 135
  Thomas, 109
Hughs, *see also* Hughes,
    Huse
  Samuel, 10
Hukill, Daniel, 10
  Richard, 10
Hunt, John, 215
Hunter, John, 118
Hurd, Francs., 21
Husband, James, 5

238

Husband *cont'd*
John, 117
Will., Jr., 193
William, 140, 167
Husbands, Alice, 48, 64
James, 48–49, 64
John, 195
Mary, 48
Thomas, 48
W., Jr., 192
William, 32, 48, 193
Wm., Jr., 218
Huse, *see also* Hughes, Hughs
Joseph, 89
Robert, 72
Hussey, John, 21
Hutches, Thomas, 134
Hutcheson, Alexander, 79
Gavin, 2, 160
William, 178
Hutchinson, Gavin, 95
Martha, 95
William, 41, 50, 63, 75, 77
Hutchison, William, 63
Wm., 37, 44
Hutchman, William, 161
Hyland, *see also* Hiland
Jno., Jr., 199
John, 84, 90, 95, 106, 109, 137, 146, 157, 205, 208, 221, 224
John, Jr., 220
Martha, 95
Nic., 110, 112–113
Nich., 88, 91, 101, 107, 117, 120, 147, 149, 151
Nich'ls., 104
Nich'o., 164–165, 168, 171, 175, 183, 190–191, 193, 196–198, 205–207, 210–212, 218, 220–221, 224
Nicho., 154, 157, 159, 162
Nicholas, 6, 50, 84, 89, 96–97, 116, 119, 122, 126, 132, 137–138, 143, 172, 180, 208,

Hyland, Nicholas *cont'd*
218
Nicholas, Capt., 172, 197, 208
Nich's., 95–96, 106–107, 109–110, 118, 122, 147, 153
Nichs., 93, 97–98
Hynson, Charles, 38, 43, 120, 139–140
William, 150, 160
Ingram, Sam'l., 126
Irwin, William, 96
Ivary, Theophilus, 14
Jackson, Edward, 3–4, 6–7, 10, 14–17, 19, 25, 28, 32, 35–36, 39–40, 45, 47–49, 54, 56, 69, 73, 75, 78, 93, 98, 189
Edw'd., 3, 12–13
Edwd., 6
Eliz., 3
Elizabeth, 93
Henry, 93
Jane, 2
John, 1–2, 115, 205
Rob't., 42
Samuel, 15–16
William, 2
Jacob, Bartholomew, 215
Tho., 41
Jacobs, Ann, 95
Bartholomew, 24
Bartholomew, Sr., 110, 149
Henry, 149
Jacob, 110
Joseph, 210–211
Martha, 197
Thomas, 32, 65, 95, 129, 197, 210, 221
Jaffray, Thomas, 128
James, Evan, 79
Howel, 158
Howell, 41, 76, 143, 183, 200
Isaac, 79
Philip, Rev., 137
Thomas, 98
William, 137
January, Francis, 58

Jawert, *see also* Jewert
John, 4, 7, 186
Jempson, Wm., 91
Jenings, *see also* Jennings
Edmund, 49
Jenkin, John, 137
Jenkins, Enoch, 41, 45–46, 61, 69, 78, 113, 169
Enoch, Sr., 113
John, 61
Jennings, *see also* Jenings
Ariana, 214–215
Edmond, 7, 116, 160, 215
Edmund, 28, 89, 122
Edward, 147
Jewart, *see also* Jawart
John, 72
Jobson, Ann, 51
Esther, 58
Esther (Kilton), 53, 59
John, 23, 51, 53–54, 58–60, 122
John, Dr., 86, 122
Michael, 60
Philip, 51
John, Henry, 155
Rebecca, 39
Thomas, 39
Johns, Aquilla, 208
Johnson, Andrew, 101–102, 126
Bartholomew, 14–15, 74, 123
Catharine, 165
Catherine, 138
Catren, 165
Daniel, 203
Edward, 33, 40, 147, 153, 159, 193, 220
Escoll, 71
Ezekiel, 71
Garret, 139
George, 97, 191, 193
Hannah, 115, 170
Henry, 11, 71, 98, 138
John, 52, 182
Mary, 97
Matthias, 28, 162, 177
Michael, 98, 138
Morris, 101–102

Johnson *cont'd*
  Rebecca, 78, 84, 147
  Robert, 97
  Sarah, 15
  Simon, 15, 101, 110, 115, 125, 165, 221, 224
  Simon, Jr., 90, 138, 165
  Symon, 224
  Thomas, 7, 28, 34, 39, 49–50, 66–68, 84, 147, 153, 159
  Thomas, Jr., 6, 44, 108, 130–131, 178
  Thos., 65
  Thos., Jr., 2–9, 12–13, 17, 20–21, 24–25, 33, 36–37, 41, 48, 62, 64
Jones, Anne, 45
  Edward, 86, 103, 123, 140
  Elizabeth, 177, 211
  Griffith, 79, 104
  Hugh, Rev., 183
  Isaac, 184
  Jacob, 176, 211
  John, 6, 9, 14, 39, 45, 177, 223
  Margaret, 167
  Mary, 9, 78
  Moses, 167, 208
  Peter, 89, 136, 176
  Robert, 118, 171, 177, 218
  Samuel, 39, 45, 95
  Sarah, 167
  Th., 184
  Thomas, 23, 89, 211
  William, 177, 183, 211
  William, Jr., 78
  Wm., 155
Julian, Mary, 99, 184, 187
  Rene', 99, 184, 187
Julien, Peter, 200
  Rene, 56–57
  Rene', 84, 151, 200–201
  Stephen, 200
Jump, Bennet, 29, 196
  Bennett, 86
Justice, Susanah (Penington), 24
Kaighin, John, 94

Kankey, Ann, 147, 168, 221
  John, 14, 109, 121, 221–222
Kanky, Jno., 16
  John, 12–13
Kay, John, 94
Keene, Richard, 115
Kees, Thomas, 200
Keith, James, 166
Kelley, Rachel, 25
Kelly, Rachel, 28, 71
  Rachell, 12, 20, 39, 45, 47–48, 59–61, 68, 71
Keltham, Will'm., 215
Kemp, Mary, 11, 20
Kempston, John, 157
  Richard, Jr., 157
  Richard The Elder, 157
Kennard, Richard, 202–203
Kennedy, Alexander, 205
  Elizabeth, 112, 174, 224
  Hugh, 112, 174, 224
  Margaret, 112, 174, 224
Kenward. *see* Kennard
Kenword. *see* Kennard
Ker, *see also* Carr, Kerr
  Walter, 148, 210
Keran, Patt., 38
Kerr, *see also* Carr, Ker
  David, 182
  Walter, 24
Key, Francis, 91
  Fran's., 168, 207, 217
  John, 117
Kilton, Esther, 53, 59
  Mary, 53, 58–59
  Thomas, 53–54, 58–59
Kimbar. *see* Kimber
Kimber, Catharine, 152, 173
  Catherine, 131
  James, 27
  John, 5, 131, 152, 173
  Thomas, 26–27, 103
  Thomas The Elder, 27
  Thomas The Younger, 27, 103
Kimlar. *see* Kimber
King, Peter, 116
Kinkey, Harman, 23
  John, 48
Kinsey, Joseph, 222

Kinword, Richard, 203
Kirkpatrick, J., 15
  James, 185
  John, 184
  John, Jr., 185
  Mary, 185
  Tho., 222
Knaresborough
  Mary, 177
  Wm., 37
Knight, Cordelia, 93
  John, 82–83
  Mary, 106
  Rachel, 142
  S., 31, 60–61, 89, 124
  Stephen, 25, 60, 76–77, 87, 92–93, 121, 177
  William, 40–41, 60, 72, 75–77, 92, 101, 105, 107, 122, 124, 133–134, 142
  Wm., 1–144
Knox, James, 151, 167
  Jas., 167
Lackey, John, 204
Lacky, John, 192
Lancaster, Benjamin, 24, 139
  William, 86
Land, Christian, 11, 98, 104
  Francis, 11, 98, 148
  John, 148
  Samuel, 98, 104, 148
Lander, *see also* Landers, Sander, Sanders, Saunders
  Isaac, 32
Landers, *see also* Lander, Sander, Sanders, Saunders
  Isaac, 47
Lane, Samuel, 94
Lang, Alexander, 17
Langwall, *see also* Langwill, Longwill, Longwell, Longwool
  Hugh, 179
Langwill, *see also* Langwall, Longwill, Longwell, Longwool
  William, 178–179

Laper, James, 207
Largent, *see also* Sargent
 Eviess, 4
 John, 4, 33, 39
Larkin, Jer'h., 176
 John, 34
Larkins, Jere., 70, 75
 Thomas, 93
Larramore, *see also*
  Lattemore
 Augusteen, 66
 Augustina, 117
 Augustine, 20
 Margaret, 77, 84, 117, 127
 Rodger, 117
 Roger, 26–27, 77, 84, 103, 127, 140, 170
Larrence, *see also* Lawrence
 Andrew, 210
Larrimore, *see also*
  Larramore
 Roger, 179
Latham, Aaron, 70
 Ann, 156
 Aron, 156
 John, 98, 180, 203
 Joshua, 86
 Sarah, 203
 Susannah, 203
Lattemore, *see also*
  Larramore
 Diana, 50
 James, 50
 Roger, 86
Lattomus, *see also*
  Larramore
 James, 115
Lauranson, Laurance, 88
Lawrence, Thomas, 23
Lawrenson, Lawrence, 107
Lawson, Aug'n., 205
 David, 73, 77, 114, 116
 G., 9, 14, 129
 Geo., 90, 114, 120, 150, 163, 172, 188, 198
 George, 16, 69, 95, 117, 158, 189, 198, 215
 Hugh, 35, 97, 157–158, 165, 198
 J., 29

Lawson *cont'd*
 John, 15, 114, 116, 186, 203
 John Aug., 203
 John Aug'n., 210
 John Aug't., 190, 192, 195–196, 203–204
 Margaret, 158
 Mary, 190, 204–205, 210
 Mary (Herman), 192
 Peter, 73, 76–78, 93, 98, 133, 143, 183, 189–190, 195, 200, 203
 Rodger, 157, 165
 Roger, 148, 189, 198
Leak, Richard, 36, 51, 94
Leake, Richard, 91
Leatham, Moses, 78
Lee, Fra., 148–155
 Fran., 149–150, 153–154, 156
 Francis, 145–149, 155
 Fra's., 157
 Philip, 7, 28, 49, 81–82, 89, 116, 122
 Thos., 115
Leslie, Robert, 173
Lesly, John, 73
Lewis, Alexander, 147
 David, 137
 Esther (Penington), 24
 George, 186
 Heaster (Penington), 24
 John, 50–51, 61, 175, 198
 Mary, 198
 Richard, 50–51, 59, 61, 102
 Richard, Jr., 50
 Richard, Sr., 50
Lightfoot, Thomas, 180
Lilly, Joseph, 170
Lindsay, *see also* Lindsey, Linsey
 Margaret, 98
Lindsey, *see also* Lindsay, Linsey
 Margaret, 138
 Thomas, 9–10, 103, 220
Linsey, *see also* Lindsay, Lindsey
 Thomas, 52

Little, Margarett, 7
Lloyd, Ann (Carnall), 58
 Edward, 122, 171–172, 176
 Henrietta, 147, 160
 James, 58
 John, 24
 Philemon, 147, 160
Loage, Manasseh, 113
Lockerman, J., 90
 John, 50
Lodge, Adam, 95
Loftain, Eleanor, 32
 Thomas, 32
Loftus, John, 21, 37
 Susanah, 21
Logan, Alex., 37
 Alexander, 25, 38, 212
Loggan, Alex'r., 163
Longwall. *see* Longwill
Longwell, *see also* Langwall, Langwill, Longwill, Longwool
 William, 163
Longwill, *see also* Langwall, Langwill, Longwell, Longwool
 William, 154, 179, 211–212
Longwool, *see also*
  Langwall, Langwill, Longwell, Longwill
 Hugh, 163
Lord Baltimore, 17, 32, 43, 49, 93, 96, 104, 115, 135–137, 141, 145–146, 150, 162, 166–167, 182, 184, 189–191, 207, 216, 220, 224
 Cecilius, 23
 Charles, 7, 12, 14–15, 17, 20, 25–28, 31, 44–45, 49, 59, 63, 71, 89, 96, 107, 109, 111, 116, 118, 122, 167, 175, 197, 213
Love, Thomas, 218
Lovering, Jno., 186
 John, 64
Low, Robert, 146

Lowe, Henry, 118
  Henry, Col., 121
  Vincent, 79
Lowman, Elizabeth, 121, 170
  Joseph, 55, 119, 121, 170, 207, 219
  Samuel, 55, 121
Loyd, R'd., 139-141
  Richard, 140-141
  Rich'd., 140
Lucas, Mary, 65
  Robert, 65, 95
Lum, Mary, 175
  Michael, 138, 175, 198
  Mich'l., 153, 155
  Mich'll., 147
Lunan, Alexander, 174, 187, 193, 214
  Alex'r., 192-193
Luntley, Thomas, 215
  Thos., 215
Lusby, John, 56, 70, 73, 84-85, 88, 90-104, 106, 108-113, 117, 127
  Margaret, 84, 88, 104, 117
  Margaret (Larramore), 84, 117, 127
Lusk, Sarah, 195
Lynch, Anthony, 181
Maccay, see also McCay
  James, 53
Maccoy, see also McCoy
  _____, 29
Maccubbin, Zachariah, 180
Macdowell. see McDowell
MacGregory, Hugh, 83
Macgregory, Hugh, 181
MacGregory, Joseph, 83
Macintosh
  Alexander, 220
MackDowell. see McDowell
Mackenna, Rebecca, 201
Mackey, James, 114, 172
  John, 127
  Robert, 114-115
  William, 111
Macknet, John, 7
Maddocks, Thomas, 3
Maddox, Joshua, 125

Maffit, William, 154, 166-167
Maffitt, William, 71, 154
Maghar, Catherine, 131
Mainley, see also Mainly, Manly
  John, 1, 212
Mainly, see also Mainley, Manly
  William, 207, 219
Makey, Henry, 6
  James, 7
Manadore, Peter, 159
Manadow, Elizabeth, 172
  Paternella, 172
  Paternella (Carr), 172
  Peter, 172
Manley, see also Mainley, Mainly
  James, 212
Mannering, Hannah, 129
  John, 129
  Thomas, 129
Mansfield, James, 196
  John, 196
  Robert, 196
Manwaring. see Mannering
Manycosens, Michael, 92, 100
Manycousens, Michael, 105
Manycousins, Michael, 92
Manycozens, Michael, 92, 100
Manyer, Jane, 3
Marcer, see also Mercer
  Elizabeth, 115
  John, 115
  Robert, 5, 141
Marr, Thomas, 211
Marsh, Mary (Thompson), 82, 89
  Richard, 59
  Thomas, 82, 89, 100
Martin, Dorothy, 3, 6
  George, 3, 6, 106, 178
Mason, William, 3
  _____, 57
Massey, Aga., 34
  Peter, 24, 81, 198, 209
  Sarah, 24, 198
  Sarah (Toes), 81, 209

Matthews, Hugh, 33, 42, 55, 57, 76-77, 142
  Hugh, Dr., 76-77, 105
  Hugh, Jr., 115
  Hugh, Jr., Dr., 151, 201
  Patrick, 142
Matthiason, Ann, 186
  Hendrick, 197
Matthias, 62, 186, 196-197
Mauldin, Francis, 146, 190, 218, 222
Maver, Alexander, 52, 58
  Esther, 52, 58
Maybury, Francis, 168
  Rosanna, 199
Maynard, La., 54
McCallmont, John, 14
McCarris, _____, 38
McCaskey, Neal, 224
McCay, see also Maccay
  Henry, 27, 56-57, 201
  James, 57
  John, 211
  Robert, 17
  Rosannah, 57
McClannan, John, 222
McClean, John, 189
McClen, John, 189
McClure, James, 23
  Rich'd., 2, 23
McComb, Grace, 211
McCombes, James, 148
McCool, John, 69
McCoy, see also Maccoy
  Henry, 84, 195
  James, 161
  John, 83, 154
  _____, 196
McCreary, John, 184, 187
McCreery, John, 100, 129, 133
  Robert, 100
McCuistion, Thomas, 224
McCullach, John, 146
McCulloch, John, 117-118
McCullock, John, 69, 190
McCullough, John, 56, 66, 73
  Tole, 56, 73
McDaniel, Michael, 221

McDermont, John, 178
McDermot, John, 38
   Thady, 89
McDermott, John, 178, 187
   Thaddy, 83
   Thady, 109
McDonald, John, 173
McDowal. *see* McDowell
McDowel, Alex. 157–158
McDowell, Alexander, 172–173, 188, 209–210
   Elioner, 177
   John, 177
   Samuel, 74, 122
   William, 3, 47
McDuel. *see* McDowell
McElroy, Sarah, 54
McFarland, Ann, 119
   John, 12, 21–22, 66, 118–119, 166
McFarlin. *see* McFarland
McGlaughlin, Philip, 177
McGregory, Elizabeth, 22, 83
   Hugh, 22, 83
   Joseph, 82
   Rebecca, 82
McIheney, John, 65
McKedy, William, 126
McKenne. *see* McKenney
McKenney, Alexander, 11
   Garrat, 11
   Garret, 20
   Gerard, 11
   Gerratt, 20
   John, 189
   Margaret, 189
McKenny, Garrett, 189
McKey, James, 16
McKinna. *see* McKenney
McKinne, *see also* McKenney
   Garret, 71
McKnight, Will, 39
McKnitt, John, 143
McLachlan, James, 187, 211
McLacklan, James, 186, 190
Mcmanus. *see* McManus
McManus, _____ (Campbell), 35

McManus *cont'd*
   Elizabeth, 42, 52
   J., 31
   John, 7, 10, 27, 31, 35, 42–43, 52, 82, 89
McNabb, James, 174, 187
Means, Edward, 169, 203
Meek, Thomas, 201
Meekins, Elizabeth, 77
   Joshua, 76–77
   Peter, 70
Mekine, Alexander, 168
Melmouth, William The Younger, 133
Mercer, *see also* Marcer
   Elizabeth, 8–9, 13, 145
   Jane, 9, 102
   John, 13, 145
   Robert, 9, 13, 90, 99–100, 102, 108, 145
   Thomas, 5, 9, 13, 145
   Thomas, Jr., 8–9, 102
   Thomas, Sr., 8, 13
Meredith, Charles, 125
   Reese, 176
Merrick, *see also* Myrick
   David, 79, 98, 104
   Roger, 79, 98, 104–105
Milbourn, John, 69
Miles, Edward, 137
   Thomas, 102, 223
Mill, Wm., 74
Miller, Abraham, 157
   Abram, 157
   Anne, 158
   Arthr., 31
   David, 74, 153, 156
   Isaac, 9, 117
   Jane, 117
   John, 74, 158
   Oliver, 201, 222–223
   Robert, 117
Milles. *see* Mills
Milligan, Catharine (Baldwin), 181
   George, 181, 185
Mills, Anna, 73
   John, 73
   Mary, 206
   Robert, 182
   Thomas, 145, 185, 206

Milward, John, 3, 16
Miner, Margaret, 9
Mitchell, Ed, 174
   Edward, 193, 223–224
   Mary, 98, 163
   Robert, 129, 159, 163
   William, 32, 43–44, 49, 97–98, 129, 151
Moll, John, 55
Money, Elizabeth, 150
   John, 77, 150, 170, 179
   Margaret, 77
   Marg't., 170
   Robert, 77, 104, 150, 170, 179
   Robert, Sr., 77
   Thomas, 150
   _____, 199
Moody, Benjamin, 46
   James, 196
   James, Capt., 29, 45–46
   Sarah, 45–46
Moor, *see also* Moore
   Andrew, 178–179
   Nathaniel, 153–154
   Rachel, 153
   Robert, 39
   Thomas, 153, 203
Moore, *see also* Moor
   James, 109
   Richard, 215
   Thomas, 75
   William, 98
Moran, Mar'n., 209
Morgan, *see also* Morgin
   Edward, 103, 116–117, 121, 123
   Elinor, 121
   Gartis, 31
   Hugh, 222
   James, 222
   James, Sr., 103
   Jarvis, 36
   Jervis, 109
   M., 98
   Morgan, Capt., 98
   Rachel, 222
   Robert, 3
   William, 3, 104
Morgin, Gartis, 8
Morton, John, 27, 43

Mory, Enoch, 199
Mary, 199
Robert, 199
Thomas, 199
Mount, William, 45
Willm., 45
Mounts, Christopher, 51
Moxon, Thos., 12
Mullins, Charles, 200
Murdock, Add'n., 180
Murgatroyd, William, 124
Musgang, John, Dr., 217
Myrick, see also Merrick
David, 80
Roger, 79–80
Nash, Elizabeth, 60
Richard, 17, 59–60, 83, 135
Negroes, Bess, 127
Bobb, 221
Bohemia, 202
Bristow, 221
Cate, 180
Cesar, 221
Cuff, 221
Davi, 218
Davy, 66
Gabriel, 221
George, 202
Hannah, 201
Harry, 221
Isaac, 220–221
Jack, 186, 190
Jam, 221
Jane, 216
Jenny, 221
Jeny, 66
Jo, 199
Lincoln, 221
Little Harry, 66
Luck, 66
Mingo, 127
Moll, 222
Nan, 217
Nead, 211
Nell, 221
Parraway, 222
Patience, 202
Patt, 200
Pender, 216
Peter, 202

Negroes cont'd
Philis, 216
Pompey, 221
Ragoo, 199
Sall, 202
Sam, 66
Sarah, 223
Suckey, 221
Sudy, 222
Toby, 222
Tom, 202
Toney, 202
Will, 220–221
Neide, see also Neidy
Anne, 187
Daniel, 196
Joseph, 187
Michael, 187
Neidy, see also Neide
Michael, 190
Nellson, see also Nelson, Nilson
Jared, 212
Nelson, see also Nellson, Nilson
John, 14–15, 142
Nevill, William, 220
Newman, Jonathan, 41, 46, 69
Richard, 46, 69
Samuel, 41, 46, 69
Walter, 41, 46, 69, 113, 169, 203
Walter, Jr., 69
Walter, Sr., 69
William, 46, 69
Wm., 113
Nicholas, Abel, 137
Griffith, 9, 24–25, 137, 142
Griffith The Elder, 142
Griffith The Younger, 142
Margaret, 24
Martin, 203
Mary, 24, 142
Nichols, Ann E., 65
Nicholson, Martin, 75
Nilson, see also Nellson, Nelson
Jared, 180–181

Noeland, see also Nowland
Mary, 17
Nooland. see Nowland
Noones, Antony, 165
Norton, Richard, 127, 154, 159
Richard, Jr., 126
Rich'd., Jr., 155–156
Unity, 154
Nowland, see also Noeland
Dennis, 27, 61, 122, 143, 170
Dinis, 160
James, 170
Mary, 45
Nox, James, 151
Noxon, Peter, 173, 177, 220
Thomas, 63
Thos., 63
Numbers, John, 23–24
Numberson, John, 24
O'Bryan, James, 194
Sarah, 42–43
Sarah (Avelman), 43
Terrance, 42–43
O'Dweyer, Edmond, 209
Edward, 209
Odwyer, Edmond, 81
Ofment, John, 24
Ogg, John, 220
Ogle, Mary, 203
Saml., 7
Sam'l., Gov., 71
Samuel, 50
Samuel, Gov., 28, 146, 150, 162, 166–167, 184, 189–191, 207
Samuel, Lt. Gov., 89
Thomas, 183, 200, 203–204
Thomas, Sr., 203
Oldham, Edward, 97, 112, 174
Olment, John, 24
Onion, Deborah, 128
Stephen, 124, 128
Osment, John, 24
Othoson, Garret, 74, 102
Otho, 179
———, 115
Otterson, Garret, 27

Overstock, Mary, 38
Ozier, *see also* Hoser
   Elizabeth, 210
   Francis, 195
   Jacob, 41, 187, 210
   Mary, 195
   Sarah, 210
   Stephen, 210
Paca, Aquila, 34
   Jno., 180–181
   John, 181
Painter, Nicholas, 143, 202
Pannel. *see* Pennal
Panthom, Mary, 119
Parker, Elizabeth, 106
   John, 106, 110
   Sarah, 110
Parks, John, 208
Parson, William, 206
Parsons, William, 69, 107, 186
Passmore, Augustine, 93
   John, 8, 96, 155, 165, 168, 224
   William, 8
Patten, *see also* Patton
   Amelia, 150
   Hance, 7
   Hans, 12
   James, 150
   Rebecca, 150
   Richard, 150
   Rich'd., 174
   William, 150
Patterson, Charles, 119
   David, 97
   James, 118
   Robert, 43–44, 49, 119
Patton, *see also* Patten
   Dorithy, 135
   Dorothy, 131
   Francis, 79
   Hance, 171
   Hanse, 79
   Morgan, 148, 157, 164–165, 168, 198
   Phebe, 79
   Rebecca, 191
   Richard, 191
   Robert, 7, 9, 17, 59, 83, 90, 113

Paul, William, 161
Peacock, Richard, 34, 36, 83
Pearce, *see also* Pierce
   Andrew, 192
   B., 1–2
   Ben, 88, 91–92, 170, 177
   Ben., 64
   Benj., 117
   Benja., 13
   Benja., Col., 5
   Benja., Jr., 1
   Benjamin, 12, 21, 63, 76, 102, 118, 171, 192, 221
   Benjamin, Mr., 79
   Henry, 1
   Henry Ward, 192
   Margaret, 171
   Margaret (Ward), 192
   Margarett, 76
   Marg't., 221
   Mr., 70
   Thomas, 18
   William, 149, 192, 216
   William, Jr., 216
   Wm., 13, 33, 78, 103, 132, 164, 200, 203, 216–217
Pecow, *see also* Picoe
   Daniel, 149
Penal, Caleb, 108, 130–131
   Sarah, 108, 130–131
Penington, Abraham, 3, 9, 210, 220
   Abram, 2, 10
   Ann, 36, 67
   Anne, 24
   B., 200
   Benedict, 200
   Ebenezer, 183
   Elizabeth, 24, 60, 70, 72, 142, 179
   Esther, 24
   Heaster, 24
   Henry, 31, 36–37, 44, 60, 62–63, 65, 94, 201
   Henry, Jr., 65, 67, 78
   Henry, Sr., 62, 67
   James, 142, 159
   John, 8, 24, 34, 36, 70,

Penington, John *cont'd*
   72, 79, 221
   John, Jr., 67
   John, Sr., 117
   Jos., 120
   Mary, 36, 42, 47, 52, 65, 78, 94
   Mary (Atkey), 43
   Otho, 149, 173
   Rachel, 27, 37, 40, 44, 63, 67, 82, 101, 200
   Rebecca, 62, 200
   Rich'd., 43
   Robert, 31, 36–37, 40–41, 44, 47, 63, 68, 77, 101
   Robert, Jr., 27, 40
   Robert, Sr., 13
   Rosamond, 37
   Sarah, 216
   Stephen, 40–41, 63, 67–68, 77
   Susanah, 24
   Thavanta, 183
   Thomas, 37, 205
   William, 42, 71, 132, 179, 183
Penn, William, 28, 67
Pennal, Caleb, 95
Pennall. *see* Pennal
Pennell, *see also* Pennal
   Caleb, 34
Penniel. *see* Pennal
Pennington, Abraham, 33, 49
   Henry, 8, 11
   Henry, Jr., 18
   J., 29
   Rachel, 13, 16–17, 30, 33
   Robert, 15, 17, 30
   Robert, Jr., 13, 16, 30, 32–33
   Robert, Sr., 13
Pennock, William, 208
   Wm., 165, 176, 212
Pepper, Robert, 32
Perkins, Isaac, 45
Peters, Christian, 64, 73, 154, 159
   Unity, 154
Peterson, Adam, 95

Peterson *cont'd*
　Andrew, 83, 92, 99, 177
Philip, Rodey, 172
Philips, Edward, 214
　Elizabeth (Manadow), 172
　John, 164
　Manadow, 172
　Mannado, 150
　Nathan, 150, 197
　Samuel, 172
Phillips, Edward, 199
　Eliner, 21
　Manadaw, 147
　Manadow, 168
　Matthew, 128
　Rebecca, 106
　Rebecca (Clements), 106
　Thomas, 21, 151
　Thomas, Jr., 106
　William, 150
Pickering, John, 27
Picoe, *see also* Picow
　Daniel, 172
　Peter, 172
Pierce, *see also* Pearce
　Henry, 50
　Sarah (Smith), 1, 50
Pilose, Benj., 95
Plater, Geo., 114
　George, 7, 28, 49, 89, 116, 122
Poilloun, John, 44
Poillown, Hannah, 72
　John, 72
Pollock, Margaret, 29
　William, 29, 129, 163
Polson, *see also* Polston, Poulson
　Peter, 54
Polston, *see also* Poulson, Polson
　Paul, 75
　Williamincher, 75
Poole, John, 36
Port, Dutton, 125
Porter, Elinor, 218
　James, 129–131, 162, 167, 169, 172–173, 218
　R., 90

Porter *cont'd*
　Robert, 84, 117, 176, 183–184
Poughfer, George, 189
Poulson, *see also* Polson, Polston
　Ann, 97
　Elizabeth, 213
　Ellneer, 184
　Jacob, 115
　Paul, 39, 90, 97, 100, 138, 162, 165, 196, 213
　Peter, 138
　Powell, 127
Pratt, Henry, 125
Presey, Caleb, 119
Price, Andrew, 137–138, 181
　Bosen, Jr., 179
　Elinor, 90
　Elizabeth, 137, 153
　Ephraim, 19
　Hugh, 152
　Jane, 219
　Jno., 186
　John, 18, 62–63, 86, 140, 189
　Joseph, 219
　Margaret, 152
　Mary, 4, 7, 62–63, 86
　Nicholas, 137, 152–153
　Richard, 10, 15
　Rich'd., 218
　Sarah, 15, 19, 148
　Thomas, 3–4, 7, 59, 72, 90, 120, 123, 138, 145, 171
　Thomas, Jr., 59–60, 90, 96
　Thomas, Sr., 3, 70
　William, 19, 26, 30, 79, 120, 148, 171, 175, 179
　William (Bosen,) Jr., 179
　Wm., 148
Prichcot, John, 15
Prichot, ____, 197
Pryer, Thos., 212
Pullen, Richard, 203
Pusey, Caleb, 119

Rainey, M., 19
Ramsey, Hannah, 209
　William, 81, 209
Rankin, Samuel, 214
　Wm., 109
Rannals, *see also* Reynolds
　William, 19
Rawson, ____, 6
Rea, Hugh, 220
Read, *see also* Reed
　James, 53
　John, 17, 104, 109, 205
Real, Hercules, 141
　Rebecca, 141
Reddus. *see* Redus
Redford, Thos., 15
Redgrave, Joseph, 176
Redus, Catharine, 185
　James, 90, 185, 211
Reed, *see also* Read
　John, 103, 109, 123
Rees, Elias, 165
　Tho's., 179
　William, 165
Reese, Thomas, 176, 179
　Tho's., 178
Reiduih. *see* Redus
Reiley, *see also* Reyley, Riley
　Michael, 29
Renalds, *see also* Rannals, Rennalds, Rennals, Reynolds, Runnalds
　William, 36
Rendell, Jno., 133–134
Rennalds. *see also* Rannals, Renalds, Rennals, Reynolds, Runnalds
　Edward, 61
　John, 83
　William, 61
Rennals, *see also* Rannals, Renalds, Rennalds, Reynolds, Runnalds
　John, 134
Rew, *see also* Rue
　Elizabeth, 213
　Elizabeth (Poulson), 213
　Isaac, 213–214
Reyley, *see also* Reiley, Riley
　Briant, 160
　Bryan, 170

Reyley cont'd
  Mary, 170
Reynolds, see also Rannals,
  Renalds, Rennalds,
  Rennals, Runnalds
  Edward, 19
  Eleanor, 34
  Elizabeth, 15
  Francis, 166
  Henry, 14–15
  Johanna, 166
  Johanna (Alcock), 166
  John, 34, 36, 64, 83
  John, Sr., 19
  Margaret, 149
  Mary, 19, 83
  Nicholas, 34, 64
  Richard, 149
  Thomas, 119
  William, 19, 34, 36, 64
Rice, Jno., 107, 123, 138
  John, 106
Richards, Mary, 108
Richardson, Elizabeth, 73, 91
  Elizabeth (Eldersly), 91
  Samuel, 73, 91
  Sarah, 73, 91
  William, 17, 59
Rickets, Mary, 59
  Thomas, 59, 61
Ricketts, David, 123, 142, 184, 200
  Edward, 162, 203
  John, 98, 104, 121, 137, 197
  Mary (Atkey), 184
  Thomas, 95, 137, 177, 196
  Tho's., 197
  Thos., 121–122, 165
Rider, John, 7, 28, 49
Ridgeley, Nicholas, 217
Ridgway, Rid., 223
Rigbie, Nathan, 164
  Nathan, Colonel, 164
  Sabina, 164
  Vg., Jr., 162
Riley, see also Reiley, Reyley
  Bryan, 160, 170
  Mary, 170

Ringgold, Anna Maria, 160
  Th., 160
  Tho's., 222
Ringold, Thomas, 192–193
Rippen, Henry, 7
Rippon, Henry, 87, 89
Risteau, Talbot, 180
Ritchy, James, 155
  John, 81, 155–156
  Joseph, 75
  Margaret, 155–156
  Robert, 155–156
Rob. see Robb
Robb, James, 15, 69, 154
  Jane, 154
Robert, James, 218
Roberts, John, 20, 86, 140
  John, Jr., 104
  Mary, 155
  Robert, 14, 84, 90, 104, 154, 179, 212
  Tim., 224
  Tim'o., 159, 163, 165, 177
  Timo., 165
  Timothy, 155, 165
  Wm., 150
Robinet, Mary, 129
  Samuel, 96, 129
Robins, Samuel, 199
Robinson, Esbiarl, 174
  George, 21, 93, 96, 111
  Isabella, 224
  Joseph, 96
  Martha, 174
  Valentine, 96
  William, 174, 224
Rock, Geo., 149, 154–156, 165–167, 172–175, 178–180, 197–199, 204, 206–208, 210, 212, 216, 219, 221–224
  George, 149, 171, 176, 187, 190, 199, 216–217
  Mary, 176
Rogers, Jacob, 109, 114, 118, 123
  Mary, 74, 109, 118
  Mary (Copson), 109, 114,

Rogers, Mary (C.) cont'd
  118, 123
  Thomas, 74
Roose, see also Rose
  Thomas, 70, 176
Rose, see also Roose
  Jane, 190
  Peregrine, 190
  Thomas, 70, 75, 86, 147, 176, 190
  William, 147
Rosentwist, Ann Elizabeth, 90
Ross, Elizabeth, 114
  G., 115
  Hugh, 56, 114
  J., 135
  Jane, 117
  Jno., 114–115, 124, 136–137, 166, 185
  Mary, 201
Rousby, John, 7, 49, 89, 116, 122
Rowland, David, 104
  Isabella, 212–213
  James, 162
  Robert, 111, 162, 188, 198, 212–213
  William, 162
Roycraft, John, 58
Rucketts, Thomas, 156
Ruddell, John, 96
Rudolph, Ann, 221–222
  Hance, 221–222
Rudulph, Hance, 198–199
  Tobias, 210
Rue, see also Rew
  Joseph, 141
  Matthew, 141
Ruley, Ann, 97
  Anthony, 120
  Michael, 120
  Michell, 184
  Seth, 97, 119–120, 217
  Sieth, 97
Rumsey, Charles, 107
  Edward, 12, 21–22, 65, 118
  John, 106, 132, 136
  Margaret, 65
  Richard, 71, 153

Rumsey *cont'd*
Robert, 30
Sabina, 11–12, 22, 26,
   99–100, 102, 132,
   134, 136, 164
Susanna, 216
Thomas, 71
William, 1, 7, 11–12, 18,
   20–22, 26–28, 30–32,
   34–37, 41, 44, 49–50,
   52–54, 58–59, 63,
   65–68, 77, 81, 83, 85–
   87, 89, 94, 99–102,
   105–107, 112, 118,
   132, 134, 136, 156,
   164, 177, 216
William, Capt., 5, 102
William, Mr., 1
Will'm., Mr., 97
Wm., 1–3, 7–9, 11–12,
   14, 19–23, 26–27, 29,
   31–34, 36–38, 42–44,
   46, 48–49, 52–53,
   55–57, 61–65, 68–70,
   76–78, 84–85, 87,
   89–91, 93, 95, 98–
   104, 107, 164, 216
Wm., Jr, 107
Wm., Jr., 84
Runnalds, *see also* Rannals,
   Renalds, Rennalds,
   Rennals, Reynolds,
William, 35
Rus, David, 151
Rusby, *see also* Rousby
John, 28
Russell, Thomas, 189
Rusteau, Talbot, 181
Ruth, Moses, 9–10
Rutter, Mary, 145
Moses, 145
Richard, 145
Rye, William, 52
Ryland, John, 48, 70, 88, 91,
   104, 173
John, Jr., 47–48, 70, 76,
   86, 92, 104
John, Sr., 128
Mary, 128
Rebecca, 48, 104
Thomas, 128

Ryon, Daniel, 190
Saftlawe, William, 178
Saintwell, Peter, 186
Salkeld, Robert, 133–134
Sample, Esther, 103
William, 14, 103–104
Samson, Mary, 36
Sander, *see also* Lander,
   Landers, Sanders,
   Saunders
Isaac, 32
Sanders, *see also* Lander,
   Landers, Sander,
   Saunders
Isaac, 31, 34, 47, 169,
   173, 220
James, 63
Sappington, Hartley, 195,
   201
Sargent, *see also* Largent
John, 4, 33
Saunders, *see also* Lander,
   Landers, Sander,
   Sanders,
Isaac, 97
Savin, Elizabeth, 22
Esther, 182
John, 181–182
Sarah, 181–182
Thomas, 71, 211, 217
Tho's., 218, 221
Thos., 82, 84, 207
William, 22, 82, 181–182
William, Jr., 82
Schee, James, 191
Jas., 186
Scott, Baptist, 186
Cha., 172
Charles, 1, 18, 101, 172
George, 26, 60
Grace, 1
Jas., 73
Jno., 154
John, 111, 195
Robert, 45–46
Sam'l., 215
Samuel, 158
Walter, 45–46, 60, 76,
   81, 93
Walter, Jr., 1, 124
Walter, Sr., 1, 124

Seagar, *see also* Segar,
   Seegar
John, 56–57, 73, 88, 188,
   209–210
John, Jr., 88
John The Elder, 88
John The Younger, 88
Samuel, 88
Seal, Elizabeth, 136
Mary, 136
Mathias, 208
Matts., 93
Samuel, 136, 214
Sealey, Joseph, 11
Mary, 11
Seegar, *see also* Seagar,
   Segar
John, 172
John, Jr., 75
John, Sr., 75–76
Seelye. *see* Sealey
Segar, *see also* Seagar,
   Seegar
John, 56
Seidell, *see also* Sliddell,
   Slidell
John, 102
Sequence, John, 72
Sequences, _____, 24
Severson, John, 63, 102–
   103
Sarah, 63, 103
Thomas, 67, 87, 102,
   104, 174, 187
Sewall, Charles, 81
Nicholas, 142
Nicholas, Maj., 81
Susannah, 81
Sharp, Elizabeth, 163
Isaac, 151
Isabella, 25, 163
Thomas, 12, 25, 159,
   163–164, 188, 219
Thomas, Jr., 25, 163
Thomas, Sr., 163
Tho's., 188
Sharpe, Thomas, 163, 209,
   212–213
Thomas, Jr., 163
Sheirvine, John, 45
Shepard, Ann, 216

248

Sheperd, Thomas, 91
Shepherd, C., 162
   Thomas, 58, 119, 222
Shepperd, Thos., 58
Sherrill, Adam, 31
   Elizabeth, 31
Sherwell. *see* Sherwill
Sherwill, Adam, 31–32
   Elizabeth, 31
   Margaret, 129
   William, 32
   William, Jr., 129
   William, Sr., 129
Shewall, Walter, 103
Shewell, Walter, 26–27
Shoemaker, Benjamin, Mayor, 125
Short, Adam, 67, 70
Sidler, John, 200
Sillcock, Valentine, 52
   Vall'tin, 38
Simco, George, 49, 146, 169
Simcoe, Elizabeth, 157
   George, 157
Simmons, John, 124
Simpass, John, 191
Sinclar, William, 54
Sinklar, William, 203
Skelton, Thomas, 3
Sliddell, *see also* Seidell, Slidell
   John, 77
Slidell, *see also* Seidell, Sliddell
   John, 76
Sliter, *see also* Sluyter
   Henry, 194
Sluyter, *see also* Sliter
   Benja., 68
   Benjamin, 183, 194
   Henry, 55, 194
   Peter, 55, 114
   Petrus, 68, 116
Smallwood, Stephen, 168
Smith, Anthony, 161, 174, 182–184, 222
   Bartlet, 84
   Bartlett, 82
   Elizabeth, 82
   Fargus, 26
   Forgus, 26

Smith *cont'd*
   Francis, 1, 50
   Grace, 175, 192, 203, 208
   Grace (Baxter), 216
   Hannah, 175, 213
   James, 38, 43, 66, 120, 140–141, 147, 150, 160, 166, 171–172, 180–181, 216
   Jane, 183
   Jean, 161
   Jno., 168
   John, 25, 47, 53, 74, 114, 121, 150, 153–154, 161–162, 169, 171, 174–175, 178, 182, 184, 192, 203, 208–209, 214, 216–218, 223–224
   John Harper, 53
   Margaret, 224
   Mary, 166
   Matthew, 63
   Richard, 82, 84
   Robert, 82, 114, 215
   Ruth, 214
   Sam'l., 209
   Samuel, 91, 119, 146, 182
   Sarah, 1, 50, 114, 218
   Thomas, 27
   William, 113–114, 118, 166, 175, 213, 218
   Wm., 15, 205
Smithson, John, 43
   Thomas, 43
Smyley, William, 150
Snell, James, 107
Snicker, Catherine, 34
   Henry, 34
Snow, Prince, 141
Sockerman, John, 50
Spencer, Jerves, 150
   Thomas, 16, 41, 72
   Thos., 37, 184
Stanly, Luke, 24
Starat. *see* Starrat, Starratt
Starrat, John, 111–112
   Leah, 111
Starratt, Benj., 150
Stasy, Mathew, 12

Steadham, Suloff, 98
Steawart, *see also* Stewart
   James, 24
Stedham, Ann, 138
   Suleff, 138
   Suluph, 71
Stedman, Anne, 157
   Richard, 157
Steel, *see also* Steele, Steil, Stile, Still
   Archibald, 88
   James, Jr., 63
   John, 88, 126–128, 180
   Joseph, 12, 111, 188, 209, 212
   Matthew, 37
   Sam'l., 159
   Walter, 180
Steele, *see also* Steel, Steil, Stile, Still
   George, 78
Steelman, John Hance, 127–128, 134–135
Steil, *see also* Steel, Steele, Stile, Still
   George, 61
Stephenson, *see also* Stevenson
   Thomas, 212, 215
Stevens, Jno., 23
Stevenson, *see also* Stephenson
   John, 104
   Thomas, 14, 23, 32, 83–84, 90, 154, 158, 179
Stewart, *see also* Steawart
   Alexander, 177
   Ann, 195
   Geo., 54, 171, 188, 190, 198
   James, 26, 33
   Margaret, 169
   Thomas, 64–65, 169, 195
   Thos., 43, 67, 133
   William, 195
Stidham, Henry, 205
Stile, *see also* Steel, Steele, Steil, Still
   George, 61
Still, *see also* Steel, Steele, Steil, Stile,

Still *cont'd*
  Exill, 48
Stilley, Jonathan, 11, 20
Stockton, John, 150
Stokes, J. Wells, 34
Stooby, *see also* Stubey
  Ann, 138
  William, 138
Stoope, Philip, 85–86
Stoopes, Philip, 51, 85
Stoops, Margaret, 122
  Philip, 38, 51, 60, 73,
    119, 122, 159–160,
    211, 217
  Phillip, 23
  Sippry, 73
  William, 73
Storey, Brooks Range, 176
  Enoch, 115
  Mary, 115, 176
  Robert, 118
  Thomas, 115
Story, Mary, 96
  Robert, 28, 33, 35, 37,
    40, 43–44, 47, 49, 53–
    55, 61, 71, 74, 84, 88–
    89, 91, 93, 95–96
  Rob't., 74
Strand, Abraham, 36
Stratlett, Rob't., 193
Stratton, Hannah, 7, 17
  Thomas, 7, 17, 59, 135
Street, Joseph, 94
Stuart, Thomas, 169
Stubey, *see also* Stooby
  William, 98
Stump, Henry, 200
  John, 189
  Mary, 200
Sumorfield, Francis, 6
Sutton, John, 38, 41, 86–87
  Josias, 38, 41
  Mary, 38, 87
Swift, John, 63
  Samuel, 63
Tailor. *see* Taylor
Talbot, George, 33, 131
  Sarah, 33
Tasker, Benja., 28
  Benjamin, 7, 44, 49, 89,
    113, 115–116, 122,

Tasker, Benjamin *cont'd*
    124–125, 135–137,
    141, 145–146, 149–
    150, 162, 166–167,
    182, 184, 189–191,
    207, 216, 218, 220
  Frances, 221
Tatcher. *see* Thatcher
Taylor, Ann, 168
  Edward, 20, 22, 66, 155,
    166, 168
  Edw'd., 15
  Elenor, 185
  Ellen, 185
  James, 16–17, 69
  John, 203
  Mary, 20, 66, 191
  Richard, 203
  Silas, 124
  William, 66, 69
Teage, Edward, 3
  William, 3
Teague, Edward, 44, 97–98
  Isabella, 31
  Izabla, 31
  William, 10, 31, 43–44,
    49, 220
  Wm., 9
Terry, Ann, 185
  Augustine, 101, 191
  Benjamin, 101
  Hugh, 13, 47, 85–86,
    125, 206
  James, 215
  John, 18, 101, 185
  Sarah, 125
  Thomas, 185
  Thomas The Elder, 101
Testas, Matthew, 133–134
Thatcher, Abigail, 81, 126,
    209
  Amos, 81
  Jacob, 81, 126, 209
  Richard, 81, 126, 209
  Thos., 209
Thomas, Benjamin, 98, 104
  Elinor, 104
  Jno., 26
  John, 14, 121, 137
  Joseph, 98, 104
  Philip, 116, 122

Thomas *cont'd*
  Rees, 157
  Thomas, 104
  William, 156, 203
Thompson, Andrew, 9
  Aug., 10, 50, 85
  Augustin, 82, 89
  Augustine, 30–31, 42–43
  Ephraim, 187
  George, 166
  Ianat, 152
  Iennett, 152
  Inat, 152
  James, 164
  Jane, 191
  John, 22, 36, 65, 82–83,
    85, 87–88, 101, 106,
    116, 121, 125, 129,
    136, 199
  Joseph, 45, 66, 129, 146
  Martha, 164
  Mary, 62, 82, 87, 89, 99,
    106, 184, 187
  Mary (Julian), 99, 184,
    187
  R'd., 2, 4–7, 9–10, 12, 17,
    19, 29, 33–34, 37–39,
    41–42, 44, 48–49,
    52–53, 57–58, 62–65,
    67–69, 72–76, 78–80,
    82–84, 86, 90, 93, 95–
    96, 98, 100, 102, 104–
    105, 113–114, 123–
    124, 126, 135, 139,
    141, 149, 151, 155,
    157–160, 164, 169–
    170, 177–181, 183,
    186–187, 189, 193–
    194, 196–197, 199–
    203, 205, 215, 219,
    224
  R'd., Jr., 99–100, 102,
    169
  Richard, 7, 12, 21, 28, 40,
    43, 49, 84, 85, 89,
    100, 113, 116, 118,
    122, 131, 133, 143,
    206
  Richard, Jr., 98–99, 184,
    187, 211
  Richard, Sr., 98–99, 184,

Thompson, Richard *cont'd*
 187
 Rich'd., 11, 30, 43, 69, 93, 135
 Robert, 22, 62, 164, 184, 191, 199, 204
 Rob't., 67
 Sam'l., 66
 Samuel, 139
Thomson, Ianat, 152
 Iennett, 152
 Inat, 151–152
 Joseph, 45
 Martha, 151
Tilghman, James, 148, 152
 Matthew, 118
 R'd., 152
 R'd., Jr., 50
 Richard, 7–8, 25, 27, 49, 59, 148
Tilton, Elizabeth, 132
 John, 132
Toas, *see also* Toes
 John, 24
Tobit, Cornelius, 41
Tobitt, Cornelius, 41
Toes, *see also* Toas
 Daniel, 81, 209
 Daniel, Sr., 81, 209
 John, 81, 209
 Sarah, 81, 209
Tomson, Thomas, 11
Touite, Christian, 10
Town, Benjamin, 144
Tracts Of Land
 Abraham's Promise, 141, 179
 Addition, 13, 54, 75, 125, 153, 191, 206
 Addition To Campbell's Devident, 119
 Addition To Heath's Third Parcel, 142
 Addition To The Forest, 180
 Addition To Ward Oake, 30
 Alexandria, 170
 Allman's Privilege, 177
 Amorous Choice, 97
 Anchor And Hope, 4, 58

Tracts of Land *cont'd*
 Anna Catharina Neck, 169
 Ant Castle, 164
 Antego, 132, 136
 Arrundell, 24, 70, 72
 Arsmore, 60
 Ashmore, 1, 19
 Askmore, 35
 Back Creek Mill, 76, 183
 Bailey, 1
 Baldwin's Dispatch, 110
 Baldwin's Lot, 66, 68
 Ballyconnell, 39
 Banks, 70, 88, 91–92, 101, 185
 Barbados, 99
 Bare Point, 93
 Barrons, The, 6
 Barry's Meadow, 172
 Batchellor's Content, 28
 Batchellor's Fund, 21–22
 Batchelor's Fun, 111–112
 Batchelor's Fund, 12, 66, 118, 166
 Batchelor's Hope, 137
 Bateman's Tryal, 87
 Bayley, 53–54, 214
 Beatle's Folley, 3
 Beetle's Folly, 3
 Benjamin's Levell, 69–70
 Bennett Jump's Old Field, 86
 Black Marsh, 15, 149
 Blancestine's Park, 215
 Blanford, 185
 Blankensteen's Park, 175
 Boarn's Forest, 127
 Bohemia Manor, 6, 11, 16, 19, 24–25, 29, 37, 45–46, 49, 55–57, 61, 64, 69–70, 75–77, 88, 98, 105, 107, 116, 120, 139, 186, 192–196, 200, 203–205, 210
 Bolding's Rest, 174
 Bonnington, 23
 Booker's Uppermost, 33, 42, 99, 105

Tracts of Land *cont'd*
 Boren's Forest, 180
 Bottle, 121, 137
 Boulding's Rest, 113, 131
 Bouldin's Rest, 125, 175
 Bourn's Forest, 134–135, 180
 Bourn's Walnut Thicket, 193
 Bown's Forest, 128
 Brereton, 119
 Bretton, 121
 Brewerton, 153
 Bristol, 125, 173, 175
 Bristoll, 131
 Brownly, 171
 Buck Head, 177
 Bulin's Range, 7
 Bullen's Range, 59
 Bullin's Range, 17, 83
 Buntington, 16, 36–37, 40, 44, 68, 77, 94, 101
 Burley's Journey, 148, 152
 Caffanrwry, 149
 Capt. John's Manor, 24
 Carr's Manor, 172
 Cartmell's Addition, 190
 Castle Fin, 219
 Castle Finn, 218
 Cavan, 131
 Cefen Kure, 15
 Chance, 48, 110, 118, 127
 Charles' Camp, 72, 145
 Charlosis Camp, 202
 Chesterfield, 44
 Chick's Choice, 147, 160
 Chick's Enlargement, 147
 Civility, 60, 132, 205
 Clay Fall, 146
 Clayfall, 219
 Clemenson, 74
 Clements' Venture, 14, 106
 Clementson, 63, 74
 Clifton, 60, 76–77, 93, 124
 Coasters Harbour, 171

Tracts of Land *cont'd*
Cockatrice, 173
Collecton, 183
Collet, 3
Colleton, 57, 92, 161, 221
Collet's Land, 185
Colletton, 1–2
Comwell Addition, 210
Concord, 102
Confusion, 12, 111, 163–164, 172, 209–210, 212
Connecticut, 10
Consent, 96, 111
Contention, 142
Copson's Intent, 113, 118, 218
Copson's Park, 113, 118, 205, 218
Copson's Pasture, 125, 180
Copson's Whim, 124
Corengem, 85–86, 122
Cornealson, 186
Corneliason, 197
Corneluison, 62
Cox Forest, 29
Coxes Fancy, 47, 129
Coxes Forest, 2, 44, 72, 143, 149
Coxes Park, 12, 17, 21–22, 66, 118, 166
Coxes Prevention, 151
Cox's Park, 112
Cox's Purchase, 50
Crow's Delight, 7
Dailey's Desire, 84
Daniel's Denn, 71, 153, 164, 205
Dayley's Desire, 27, 61, 82
Derry, 102
Devidend, 142
Devidings, The, 119
Dividend, The, 19, 33, 35–36, 78, 81
Divident, The, 81
Dividing, The, 15, 217
Dividings, The, 123, 137, 181

Tracts of Land *cont'd*
Doe Hill, 21, 93, 111
Dogwood Field, 139
Dolevan, 9
Dougherty's Desert, 10
Dougherty's Desire, 49
Dougherty's Endeavor, 9, 220
Dowdall's Fancy, 30
Duck Neck, 175, 213
Dutton Port, 176
Elk River Manor, 189
Elsecks Lodge, 38
Emery's Choice, 97
Emery's Endeavor, 110
Emmitt's Mill, 90
Enlargement, 111
Essex Lodge, 38, 41, 87, 89
Fair Hill, 190
Fatigue, 95
Fedard, 11, 20
Feddart, 71, 98, 138
Forlorn Hope, 91
Francina, 165, 206
Francinea, 195
Freeman's Land, 186
Freeman's Park, 85
Friendship, 65, 95, 221, 224
Frisby's Addition, 148, 152
Frisby's Farm, 180, 215
Frisby's Meadows, 58
Frisby's Neglect, 211
Frisby's Prime Choice, 215
Frisby's Wild Chase, 99
Fryer's Hills, 84, 117
Gardner's Gift, 218–219
Glascow, 143
Glass House, 39, 75, 97, 100, 162, 196, 213–214
Glasshouse, 220
Good Luck, 100
Good Will, 145, 190
Goodwill, 66, 69
Gorry, 139
Gotham Bush, 189
Grange, 124

Tracts of Land *cont'd*
Green Spring, 182
Greenfield, 37, 85, 119, 161
Green's Delight, 4
Griffin, 79, 104
Grove, The, 133, 148, 152
Guiel Glass, 25
Guilder's Forest, 214
Guill Glass, 163, 188
Hackley, 205
Hackly, 121
Hack's Town, 121
Hail Hill, 39, 67–68
Haile Hill, 28
Hamilton's Lott, 180
Hamm's Necessity, 6
Happy Harbor, 16, 23, 36–37, 40, 44, 51, 60, 68, 77, 86, 94, 101, 122, 132
Hart's Delight, 93
Hassell Branch, 84
Hazel Branch, 117, 127
Hazelmore, 133–134, 148, 152
Hazelwood, 148
Heaths, 91
Heath's Adventure, 119, 174, 182, 184, 208
Heath's Fifth Parcel, 60
Heath's Fourth Parcel, 2, 92, 99
Heath's Middle Parcel, 2, 92
Heath's Range, 2
Heath's Second Parcel, 2, 92, 99
Heath's Third Parcel, 33, 105, 107, 142
Heath's Third Parcel Addition, 33
Helena, 131
Henderson's Choice, 86
Hendrick's Choice, 140
Hendrickson, 63
Hendrickson's Choice, 26–27, 103
Hendrickson's Oversight, 217

Tracts of Land *cont'd*
Herman's Mount, 46
High Park, 97–98, 171
Highspaniola, 143
Hill' Adventure, 205
Hispaniola, 7, 59
Hispaniole, 17
Hogpen Neck, 64
Holland, 146, 161, 174, 183–184, 208, 216
Holland's Point, 189
Hollingsworth's Fourth Parcel, 28
Hollingsworth's Second Parcel, 71, 167
Homely, 67, 102
Hope, 110
Hopewell, 11, 16–17, 31, 43, 45, 54, 114, 189, 218
Horn Hill, 7
Horns, 70
Husband's Choice, 195
Huse's Lot, 72
Indian Range, 71, 92, 105, 145, 148, 177, 215
Inspection, 53
Jacob's Adventure, 8
Jacob's Chance, 197
Jamaica, 52, 58–59, 116, 120
Jamaico, 4
Jawert's Delight, 186
Joan's Green Spring, 185
John Crow's Delight, 6
John's Delight, 50–51
Jones' Addition, 211
Jones' Green Spring, 3–4, 7, 72, 96, 145
Jones' Land, 155
Jones' Spring Green, 202
Jones' Venture, 177
Judith's Neck, 98–99
Kemton's Delight, 157
Kennedy's Adventure, 112, 174, 224
Kenny's Meadow, 189
King's Aim, 30, 35, 38, 87, 215
King's Delight, 52, 131

Tracts of Land *cont'd*
Kinly, 139
Kinsby, 20
Kinsley, 109, 123, 142
Kinsly, 24
Kittavilly, 186, 196
Knowledge, 2
Knowlswood, 113
Knowlwood, 1, 50, 135
Landive, 24–25
Landue, 150
Landuel, 142
Largent's Neck, 33, 158
Larkin's Desire, 91, 115, 119
Larramore, 140
Larramore's Addition, 127
Larramore's Neck, 77, 87, 150, 170, 174, 187
Larramore's Neck Enlarged, 104, 127, 140, 170
Larymore's Neck Enlarged, 179
Lattemore's Neck Enlarged, 86
Lawson's Mill, 113
Leake's Addition, 91
Level, The, 103, 215
Levell, The, 18, 52, 131, 167, 173
Levell's Addition, The, 167, 218
Lidia's Joynture, 66, 145
Little Bohemia Manor, 60
Locust Neck, 171
Lone Tree, 185
Lydia's Joynture, 190
MacGregory's Delight, 83
Macgregory's Delight, 181
Manchester, 119
Manor Of Baltimore, 115
Manor Of New Connach, 146
Manor Of New Connah, 162, 191, 207, 220
Manor Of New

Tracts of Land *cont'd*
Connaught, 97, 141
Manor Of New Connough, 205
Manor Of North East, 135–137, 150, 214, 218
Manor Of Susquehanna, 97, 141, 146, 162, 182, 184, 191, 207, 216, 220
Manwaring Hall, 33, 42, 105, 107, 142
Mapleton, 85
Marshfield, 116
Martin's Delight, 3, 6, 39, 106, 204
Martin's Enlargement, 6, 39, 106, 204
Mary's Joynture, 52
Mary's Park, 18
Matson's Range, 197
Matthiason's Point, 62, 196
Matthiason's Range, 62
Mattson's Range, 62
Meekin's Adventure, 70
Mesopotamia, 86, 140
Micham, 119
Middle Grounds, 69
Middle Neck, 36, 44, 60, 76–78, 109
Middle Parcel, 65, 87, 99–100, 105
Middle Plantation, 86, 100, 103, 140
Moneyworth, 164
Monon, 156
Montgomery, 140
Moulton's Marsh, 97
Mouncefield, 108
Mounsfield, 90, 99
Mount Harman, 102
Mount Herman, 145
Mount Hermon, 9
Mount Hope, 78
Mount Joy, 120, 123
Mount Pisga, 32
Mount Pleasant, 32
Mounts Field, 148
Mountsfield, 152

Tracts of Land *cont'd*
Moyn, 29, 129
Mulberry Dock, 128
Mulberry Mold, 70
Mulberry Mould, 88, 91, 128
Nevan, 159
New Connach, 216
New Connought Manor, 10
New Garden, 150, 154
New Hall, 34
New Intersection, 63
New Munster, 56, 88, 104, 111, 126, 154, 158–159, 165, 198, 201, 209, 212, 215
Newcastle Back Landing, 74, 123
Newconnaught Manor, 131
Newmunster, 14, 23, 26, 81, 83, 88, 90, 114, 129, 142, 163, 178–179, 224
Noble Town, 151
Nobles Town, 84
None So Good In Finland, 21, 30, 35, 82, 87, 89, 101, 136, 217
Norland, 34, 179
North East Manor, 190
Old Field Lot, 145, 189
Pain's Lot, 62, 142, 159
Pain's Lott, 161
Paradise, 33
Partner's Parcell, 8
Pasture Point, 171
Patten's Desire, 150
Penbroke, 97
Pennyworth, 11, 26, 31
Penyworth, 8
Peredice, 190
Philips' Neglect, 164
Phillips' Bottom, 21
Plain Dealing, 7
Pleasant Garden, 127
Poplar Neck, 146, 221
Poplar Valley, 3, 6, 34, 95, 108, 130, 162, 178

Tracts of Land *cont'd*
Price's Intelligence, 87
Price's Venture, 15, 26, 47, 197
Prosperity, 140
Providence, 96, 111, 114, 116, 129, 199
Pullen's Refuse, 202–203
Purchase, 153
Raccoon Point, 152
Raccoon Range, 164
Rambles, The, 148, 152
Rattlesnake Neck, 131, 152, 173
Repensation, 178
Reponsation, 6
Rich Hill, 93
Rich Neck, 68
Richard's Chance, 126
Rook And Pill, 119
Rose's Choice, 190
Round Stone, 11, 32, 150
Roycraft's Choice, 4, 58
Ruke And Pill, 73
Rumsey's Discovery, 132
Rumsey's Double Parcel, 132, 136
Rumsey's Ramble, 12, 21–22, 66, 112, 118, 166
Rumsey's Range, 132, 136
Salem, 139, 154
Sarah's Jointure, 99
Sarah's Joynture, 2, 19, 34–36, 61, 64, 83, 92, 134
Sargent's Neck, 33
Saven's Rest, 22
Savin's Rest, 62
Scott's Tanyard, 60, 124
Scraps, The, 99–100
Second Neck, 193–194
Severson's Delight, 63, 102
Sewall's Pasture, 89
Sheffield, 31, 42–43
Shepherd's Fortune, 174
Shrewsbury, 92, 103, 120–121, 123
Simmes Forest, 157

Tracts of Land *cont'd*
Siniqua Point, 97
Sinklair's Purchase, 40
Sivility, 184
Skelton, 2, 92, 99–100, 110
Slate Hill, 6, 34, 108, 130–131, 162, 169, 173, 178
Sligo, 9, 155–156
Small Hope, 113
Smith's Addition, 207
Smith's Discovery, 121
Smith's Hill, 84
Smoking Point, 67
Smoaky Point, 102
Snow Hill, 28
Snow Hill Addition, 28
Snowhill, 38–39, 67–68
Snowhill Addition, 67–68
Snowhill's Addition, 38–39
Society, The, 12, 93, 111, 117, 157–158, 163–164, 172, 188–189, 198, 209–210, 213
Sparnal's Delight, 3
Sparnon's Delight, 29
Sperman's Delight, 3
Spermon's Delight, 70
Springs Head, 26
Spry's Hill, 121
St. Augustine Manor, 102
St. Augustine's Manor, 147, 160
St. John's Manor, 14, 50–51, 61, 150, 159, 197–198, 208
St. John's Town, 153
Stillington, 48
Stockton, 24, 148–149, 215
Stockton Addition, 90
Stockton's Addition, 92, 99, 105
Stoney Chase, 21
Stony Chase, 112
Strange, 114, 154
Succesor, 115

Tracts of Land *cont'd*
  Success, 110, 180
  Successor, 47–48, 59, 90, 101, 125, 138, 165, 171
  Suffolk, 185
  Susquehanna Manor, 131
  Swaile, 166
  Swamp, The, 33
  Swan Harbor, 36, 38, 41, 85–87
  Sylvania's Folly, 132
  Talbott's Manor, 141
  Teague's Chance, 31, 49
  Teague's Delight, 44, 97–98
  Teague's Endeavors, 31, 43
  Teague's Forest, 31
  Terson's Neck, 50
  Terson's Neglect, 50
  Thompson's Town, 117
  Three Bohemia Sisters, 12, 19, 30, 98, 165, 171, 184, 187, 192, 195, 206
  Three Partners, 31–32, 129, 210
  Three Sisters, 100, 158
  Tilly Broom, 166
  Town Point, 69, 185
  Triangle, 92, 107
  Triumph, 78, 84, 147
  True Gaim, 154
  True Game, 53, 119
  Tryall, 59, 102
  Two Necks, 3
  Uppermost, 59–60, 90
  Vanbebber's Forest, 64
  VanBebber's Forest, 73, 154, 159
  Venture, 207
  Vulcan's Delight, 113, 168
  Vulcan's Rest, 122, 160, 170, 195, 207
  Vulcan's Tryal, 124
  Wademous Neck, 147
  Wadmore's Neck, 1
  Wales, 3

Tracts of Land *cont'd*
  Wallace's Scrawl, 105
  Ward Oake, 30
  Ward's Addition, 161
  Ward's Knowledge, 161
  Warmast, 171–172
  Warwick, 92
  Welsh Tract, 137
  Wheeler's Point, 3, 16
  Wheeler's Warren, 171
  White Point, 167
  White's Folly, 117
  Whitton's Forest, 33
  Withers, 53–54, 94
  Woodbury, 86, 100, 140
  Worsell Manor, 2
  Zebulon's Fancy, 222
Trather, Thos., 209
Tree, John, 83
Tuite, James, 13
Tulien, *see also* Julien
  Rene', 151
Turnbull, Margaret, 14
  Robert, 14, 106
Tute, Christian, 10
Tweedy, Robert, 129
Twiddy, Mary, 115
Tyler, Lydia, 151
Tyliard, Ephesus, 22
  Hester, 22
  John, 22
Uringson, Cornelius, 46
  Eleanor, 46
Van Ekelin, Johannes, 119
Vanbebber, *see also* VBebber
  Adam, 122–123, 127, 132–135, 142
  Ann, 68
  Elizabeth, 122–123
  Jacob, 122–123
  James, 55, 68
  Matthias, 45, 77, 114
VanBebber, Adam, 148–151, 153, 158–161, 164, 166, 169–170, 173, 175, 181–183, 185–186, 190–194, 196–197, 201–202, 204–206, 215–216, 222, 224

VanBebber *cont'd*
  Henry, 95, 206
  Jacob, 165, 224
  James, 95
  Matthias, 76, 147, 154, 160–161
Vandegriff, Nicholas, 196
Vandegrift, Nicholas, 29
Vanderheyden, Ann Margarett, 12
  Ann Margretta, 12
  Anna Margaretta, 19, 79
  Anna Margreta, 30
  Jane, 172
  Matthias, 51, 60, 172
Vandike, *see* Vandyke
Vandyke, Nicholas, 145
  Sarah, 145
Vanel, John, 88
Vangezle, John, 116
Vanhorn, Barnet, 215
Vanhorne, Barnett, 210
  John, 210
Vansandt, Ann, 23
  Elizabeth, 23
  Jacobus, 23
  Johannas, 23
  John, 23, 88, 215
  Rachel, 23
Vansant, John, 56, 114, 158
  Widow, 115
Vbebber, Ja., 160
  James, 66, 124, 155
  Jas., 124
Veazey, Edward, 110, 190, 220
  George, 20, 69, 79
  James, 25, 155
  John, 7–8, 10, 12–13, 15–16, 18–19, 22, 24, 26–30, 32–33, 35–38, 41, 43, 46, 48–52, 54, 56–60, 62–63, 65–66, 70–74, 77–79, 82–83, 85–92, 95, 99–106, 108–111, 115–118, 120, 122, 125, 128, 131, 134–136, 138–139, 141, 143–146, 148, 152–154, 159, 168–171, 173–176,

Veazey, John cont'd
  178–181, 183, 186,
  189, 192, 195, 197,
  202–203, 206, 210–
  211, 215, 218, 220–
  222
 John, Capt., 73
 John, Major, 149
 John, Mr., 79
 Rebecca, 62
 Robert, 3, 17, 24, 41,
  143, 203, 206
 Robert, Jr., 185
 Robert, Sr., 206
 William, 29, 53
Vestal, William, 167
Vickers, George, 208
Vincent, Charles, 3
Vorsman, Peter, 55, 114
 Petrus, 68, 116
Waddall, Alexander, 65
Waddle, Alexander, 64
 David, 19
 Jane, 64
Wagg, James, 176
Wakely, Robert, 125
Walker, Hugh, 11, 56, 111
 John, 100, 131, 186, 191,
  204
 Margaret, 111
 Susanah, 69
Wallace, see also Wallis
 Adam, 9, 40, 170
 Andrew, 40, 175, 215,
  218–219
 Barbara, 28, 67
 Barbra, 67
 Cath., 202
 Catharine, 218–219
 David, 28, 39, 67–68
 Elennor, 218
 Elinor, 219
 James, 9, 52, 72, 170
 Jane, 121–122
 Jo., 65
 Johanna, 105
 John, 141, 158, 160, 187,
  215
 Joseph, 75, 105, 126,
  155–156, 218–219,
  221–222

Wallace cont'd
 Ketrine, 202
 Margaret, 9
 Mary, 219
 Matthew, 105
 Michael, 48, 79, 145,
  155–156
 Mich'l., 111
 Robert, 170
 William, 72, 185, 202,
  218–219
 Wm., 219
Waller, John, 130
Wallis, see also Wallace
 James, 40
Walmsley, Catharine, 170
 Catherine, 77, 179
 Elizabeth, 170
 Robert, 138–139, 150,
  170, 179
 Sarah, 120
 Thomas, 77, 170
 William, 92, 108, 120–
  121
 Wm., 220
Ward, Ann, 46
 Col., 115
 Hannah, 161
 Henry, 4, 7, 50, 72, 110,
  145, 161, 185, 192,
  202
 James Chattam, 161
 Jno., 1
 Jno., Jr., 102
 John, 5, 37, 46, 91, 144,
  149, 161
 John, Col., 29, 37, 57, 62,
  91, 110, 114
 John, Colonel, 73, 91,
  143
 John, Jr., 1, 29, 46, 48,
  52–53, 65, 86, 114,
  120, 128, 134–135
 Josias, 58
 Margaret, 192
 Mary, 37, 57, 91, 161
 Mathew Tilghman, 7
 Matthew Tilghman, 27–
  28, 49, 89
 Per., 62
 Pereg., 91–94, 99–103,

Ward, Pereg. cont'd
  107, 109–110, 117,
  119–123, 153, 186
 Pereg'n., 46, 48, 50–56,
  58–63, 65, 70–75, 77,
  79, 82–83, 85–86,
  125, 128
 Pereg'r., 131–132, 134–
  135, 142–144, 146,
  149, 152, 159, 164,
  166, 169–171, 177,
  180, 183, 195, 202–
  203, 217
 Peregrine, 37, 50, 57, 69,
  89, 116, 122, 161, 184
 Peregrine, Capt., 149
 Pere'r., 125
 Susanna, 29
 Thomas, 3, 16, 57
 William, 46, 49, 71, 131
 Wm., 18
Warner, Edward, 133–134
 Mary, 133–134
Watkins, John, 183
 Joseph, 219
Watson, Abraham, 40
 Abram, 40
 Hugh, 70, 91, 185, 191
 John, 27, 65, 73
 John, Capt., 73
 Joseph, 123
 Susanah, 40
 William, 40
Watts, Thomas, Jr., 208
 William, 208
Wayt, Andrew, 143–144
Weare, Jno., 215
Weatherspoon, David, 177
Weaver, John, 109, 118,
  123
Webb, Thomas, 94
Webby, Wm., 186
Webster, Ann, 146
Weir, Edward, 212
 Thomas, 154, 212
Welch, John, 69
Weldon, Robert, 38
Welsh, George, 121–122
 Hannah, 121–122
 John, 200
 William, 200

Weylie, John, 171
Whan, William, 164–165, 198
Wheeland, Wm., 196
Wheeler, Ignatias, 206
　John, 11, 31–32, 35, 54, 110, 179
　Sarah, 11
Wheland, Wm., 195, 215
Whichcote, Paul, 160
Whit, *see also* White
　Alexander, 151–152
　David, 151–152
　Easter, 151–152
　Ester, 152
Whitacres, *see also* Whitaker, Whitker
　Robert, 166
Whitaker, *see also* Whitacres, Whitker
　Robert, 17–18, 21–22, 66, 112
　William, 133–134
White, *see also* Whit
　Alexander, 93, 117, 139
　David, 152
　Easter, 152
　Elizabeth, 139
　Ester, 152
　Hannah, 182
　Jane, 117, 139
　Jean, 139
　Jno., 129, 139
　Nicholas, 166
　Samuel, 10, 182
　Samuel, Jr., 182
　Thomas, 26
　William, 182
　———, 199
Whithorne, Conway, 134
Whitker, *see also* Whitacres, Whitaker
　Robert, 25
Whittington, John, 166
Whitton, Rich., 6
　Richard, 54
　Ruth, 53
　Thomas, 53–54
Wickham, Nath., 201
　Nathaniel, 201
Wield, John, 153

Wight, Edward Jno., 99–100, 102, 120
Wilcocks, John, 74
Wild, *see also* Wilds
　Mary, 26
　Samuel, 24–26
Wilde, *see* Wilds
Wilds, John, 15
　Joshua, 9, 15
　Joshuah, 15
　Josiah, 15
　Nathaniel, 15
　Samuel, 9, 137
　Thomas, 9
Wiles, Thomas, 223
Wiley, John, 74
　Mary, 74
Wilkins, Wm., 81–82
Williams, Abel, 142
　Abraham, 201
　Ann, 165
　John, 4, 18, 54, 58
　Joseph, 97
　Lidia, 97
　Mary, 54, 58, 142
　Mary (Nicholas), 142
　Nathaniel, 165
　Providence, 97–98
　Robert, 66
　Rowland, 22
　Sarah, 97
　Thomas, 43, 116, 215
Willimott, Robert, Lord Mayor, 124
Willis, Samuel, 105
Willmore, Simon, 157, 164
Wills, Dane, 197
　Daniel, 197
　Edward, 133–134
Wilmer, S., 82, 84, 211
　Simon, 84
Wilmore, Mary, 147
　Simon, 147
Wilson, Adam, 90
　Christopher, 8
　G., 1
　Garrate, 96
　John, 125
　Josiah, 189–190
　Mary, 10
　Robert, 96

Wilson *cont'd*
　William, 65
Wimsley, Ben., 56
　Benjamin, 56
Winsley, Benj., 88
　Mary, 88
Winslow, Benjamin, 88
　Mary, 88
Winterbeary, John, 53
Winterberry, John, 29, 53
Winterbery, John, 13
Winterbury, John, 26–27, 53, 103
　Mary, 53
　Rachel, 103
Withers, Robert, 45, 53, 57, 61, 68, 76, 78
Witherspoon, David, 116, 215
　D'd., 187
　Esther, 215
　Hester, 215
Wolaston, *see also* Wolliston
　Thomas, 79
Wolbough, Christopher, 151
　Frederick, 151
Wood, Catherine, 36, 138
　John, 184
　Jos., Jr., 9
　Joseph, 76, 158, 165–166, 195, 200, 206
　Nicholas, 169, 204
　Robert, 138–139
Woodberry, Hugh, 139
Woodbury, Andrew, 86, 103, 140
Woodhead, George, 23
Woods, John, 202
　Joseph, 139
　Rebecca, 202
　Robert, 139
Woodward, H., 171
Wooliston, *see also* Wolaston
　Cornelius, 151, 161, 200–201
Worley, Anne (Penington), 24
　Nathan, 192

Worth, Elez, 189
   James, 189
Wright, F. H., 50
Wroth, James, 18, 69, 86,
   103, 139–140
Wyat, Andrew, 144
Wye, Rebecca, 147
   Will'm., 95
Wyle, Luke, 127
Yorkson, Jno., 11
   Tho., 35
   Thos., 19, 56
Young, Araminta, 66
   Jacob, 99, 146, 158, 165,
     187, 195, 206
   James, 93
   John, 146
   Joseph, 219
   Minian, 78
   Sam'l., 51
   Saml., 3, 19
   Samuel, 12–13
   W., 180–181
   William, 128, 180–181
   Wm., 127–128
   ____, 196
Zelafroe, Andrew, 143
____, Samuel, 99, 184, 187

www.ingramcontent.com/pod-product-compliance
Lightning Source LLC
Chambersburg PA
CBHW071329190426
43193CB00041B/1036